HOW THE WORLD SEES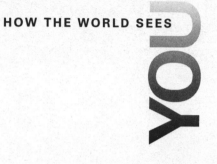

ALSO BY SALLY HOGSHEAD

*Fascinate: Your 7 Triggers to
Persuasion and Captivation*

CREATED BY SALLY HOGSHEAD
DISCOVER MORE AT HOWTO**FASCINATE**.COM
EMAIL: HELLO@HOWTO**FASCINATE**.COM
©2014 SALLY HOGSHEAD

PRESTIGE You earn respect with higher standards	**TRUST** You build loyalty with consistency	**MYSTIQUE** You communicate with substance	**ALERT** You prevent problems with care
THE TRENDSETTER Cutting-Edge • Elite Progressive	**THE ARTISAN** Deliberate • Thoughtful Flexible	**THE PROVOCATEUR** Clever • Adept Contemporary	**THE QUICK-START** Prolific • Thorough Diligent
THE TALENT Expressive • Stylish Emotionally-Intelligent	**THE BELOVED** Nurturing • Loyal Sincere	**THE INTRIGUE** Discerning • Perceptive Considerate	**THE ORCHESTRATOR** Attentive • Dedicated Efficient
THE MAESTRO Ambitious • Focused Confident	**THE GUARDIAN** Prominent • Genuine Sure-Footed	**THE MASTERMIND** Methodical • Intense Self-Reliant	**THE DEFENDER** Proactive • Cautionary Strong-Willed
THE IMPERIAL Arrogant • Cold Superior	**THE BLUE CHIP** Classic • Established Best-In-Class	**THE ARCHITECT** Skillful • Restrained Polished	**THE SCHOLAR** Intellectual • Disciplined Systematic
THE DIPLOMAT Levelheaded • Subtle Capable	**THE OLD GUARD** Predictable • Safe Unmovable	**THE ANCHOR** Protective • Purposeful Analytical	**THE GOOD CITIZEN** Principled • Prepared Conscientious
THE ROYAL GUARD Elegant • Astute Discreet	**THE WISE OWL** Observant • Assured Unruffled	**THE DEADBOLT** Unemotional • Introverted Concentrated	**THE ARCHER** On-Target • Reasoned Pragmatic
THE EDITOR-IN-CHIEF Productive • Skilled Detailed	**THE MEDIATOR** Steadfast • Composed Structured	**THE DETECTIVE** Clear-Cut • Accurate Meticulous	**THE CONTROL FREAK** Compulsive • Driven Exacting

HOW THE WORLD SEES YOU

DISCOVER YOUR HIGHEST VALUE THROUGH THE SCIENCE OF FASCINATION

SALLY HOGSHEAD

HARPER
BUSINESS

An Imprint of HarperCollins*Publishers*
www.harpercollins.com

HarperCollins books may be purchased for educational, business, or sales promotional use. For information, please e-mail the Special Markets Department at SPsales@harpercollins .com.

FIRST EDITION

Designed by Renato Stanisic

Interior graphics created by Emily Johnson

Library of Congress Cataloging-in-Publication Data has been applied for.

ISBN: 978-0-06-223069-0

14 15 16 17 18   OV/RRD   10 9 8 7 6 5 4 3 2 1

To my mother and father,
who taught me how to become
more of who I already am.

CONTENTS

WHERE IT BEGINS: UNLEARN BORING

I stood alone onstage, paralyzed. Seconds ticked by, each more excruciating than the last. The spotlight had seemed so luminous a moment before, but now it burned me with its bitter circle. I'd let everyone down.

It was in this moment that I learned how to be boring.

FRANKLY, I HADN'T really expected to perform in that dance recital. The year before, my older sister Nancy was anointed fastest swimmer in her event by the *Guinness Book of World Records*, and my older brother Andy was accepted into Harvard. I couldn't outswim my sister or outthink my brother. How could I stand out, and make my parents proud?

Dance, I decided, would allow me to define myself away from the over-crowded family trophy mantel of sports and Ivy League schools. So I took dance lessons and learned pirouettes and jazz hands, grapevines and old classic tap maneuvers like the "Shuffle Off to Buffalo."

I wasn't a great technical dancer, by any means. The other girls in my class were more skilled, more talented, and more classically beautiful. That said, I doubt any of them had as much fun as I did in class. My dance teacher, Miss Mervyn, apparently agreed. "Sally, you're not a great dancer," she once commented, "but you do have a certain spark."

I beamed. A spark? I can work with that. Hand me the kerosene.

That year, she gave me a solo in the dance recital. This was in part an honor, and, I suspect, also a way to fund the performance since it required dozens of individual lessons and a hand-sewn costume. I was ecstatic. Finally, I'd get to be good at *something*.

We rehearsed for several hours a week, my mom driving me to the studio after Brownies and before dinner. At the dinner table, I would look around and just glow. Nancy had swim practice, Andy had school, and now at last I too had my place among them. I would make the family proud. I pointed my toes and practiced my steps under the dinner table.

I spent every moment mentally rehearsing in order to get the steps just right. The steps, however, felt painstakingly intricate. Secretly, I would have preferred a simpler routine so I could enjoy the dancing instead of counting out the choreography. But since none of the other girls struggled with their dances, I didn't want to disappoint Miss Mervyn.

At last came opening night. My costume was finished: a confection of itchy and highly flammable nylon bedazzled with sequins, held up by too-tight elastic straps.

It was the most beautiful thing I'd ever seen.

I stood backstage, watching my teacher intently, awaiting my cue. My music began. I was ready. As I was about to prance onstage, Miss Mervyn whispered into my ear.

"Just don't forget the steps."

Well, you can probably guess what happened next. My mind went blank. Those carefully engineered steps fled from my brain like rats abandoning a sinking ship. I froze with panic. The music stopped awkwardly mid-note. The audience was silent. The spotlight turned off with a loud clank, echoing through the auditorium.

I glanced backstage to find Miss Mervyn. She looked horrified. It was the first time I'd ever worn mascara, and a black teardrop cascade began.

I never took another dance lesson.

Ever.

YOU ARE ALREADY FASCINATING

On the day you were born, you already knew how to fascinate. Like breathing and swallowing and smiling, the ability to fascinate is a hardwired survival mechanism. Fascination is an instinctive form of connection. We all have this ability in some form.

But over time, people can lose their innate ability to fascinate. They acquire layers of boring. Like an oyster protecting itself against the grain of sand, people build shells that they believe can shield them from a negative outcome. You've seen this before, or perhaps experienced it. It's the student who learns how to camouflage himself to blend into the popular high school crowd. The employee who waters down his ideas in order to shield himself from criticism. The new entrepreneur who tries to run her business just like everyone else, and ends up with a "me-too" product. In any pressured environment, it can be easier to stay in the background. Unnoticed seems easier than unworthy.

Hiding works for a while. But it always backfires. You will never be your most successful when evaluated according to criteria that do not allow you to stand out.

There's a certain puritanical goodness to avoiding attention. It's almost a moral cleanliness, like organized closets and modest hemlines. It's beyond reproach, in a "nobody gets fired for buying IBM" sort of way. Across geographic borders and cultural boundaries, attention attracts danger while anonymity can be seen as a virtue.

When the stakes rise, so does perceived danger. Just as chameleons rush to hide by changing colors to match their surroundings, people tend to want to hide.

In a sense, most of us were schooled to avoid being too fascinating. As kindergartners we're taught to stand in line for class. Color within the lines. Raise a hand. Wait your turn. Standing out is labeled as misbehaving.

The problem is, the real world isn't like that. At least, not anymore. In today's world—the one with distracted clients, bigger competitors, and people who are willing to work for less than you—the old model is deeply flawed. You will not win by being invisible. Today, you win by being seen and remembered.

I've never met anyone who doesn't have a few insecurities about how they're perceived by others. Why do we care so much about what others think of us? An easy answer would be to say it's fear of looking bad in front of others, or making a fool of ourselves. Yet, I believe the real answer goes deeper than that.

Most people are afraid they have nothing special to give. They think there's nothing distinctly valuable that they can offer. Most people don't want to ask for attention, because they're afraid nobody cares. Even when people do want to rise above the fray, they are terrified by the prospect of what to do with attention once they've successfully earned it.

Your most fascinating traits are your most valuable traits. Too often, these traits are the first to go in favor of blending in or avoiding criticism. Yet when you dull your edges, on some level you're giving up.

I gave up dance. What did you give up?

DID YOU GIVE UP YOUR ABILITY TO FASCINATE?

The Study of Fascination is the first in-depth national marketing study about why we become fascinated by certain types of communication, how fascination drives the workplace, and how much fascination is actually worth. It was developed and executed specifically for my company, How To Fascinate. It was conducted by Kelton Global, one of the world's top global marketing research firms. This initial research includes more than one thousand people around the United States, in a wide range of ages, industries, and professional levels. Our survey measured what types of communication are most likely to fascinate people, and which types of marketing, news, conversations, and media are most likely to engage others. We measured their level of engagement in the workplace (only 8% of employees think their boss is extremely fascinating) and in their lives (96% of parents think their children are fascinating).

For instance, most people would rather be compelling on a job interview than on a first date.

With the results, we analyzed the ROI ("return on investment") of improving the quality of communication within a company, and with customers. For instance, we measured how much it is actually worth to a company, in dollar amounts, to make its products more fascinating to customers (they will pay up to four times as much for a fascinating version of the same product).

We found that on average, a woman will pay more to be fascinating than she pays for food and clothes combined—an average of $338 per month, or roughly 15% of her net income. (The lesson: If you can help someone feel that they are more fascinating, they will pay you a premium. This is especially true with women. When selling to women, highlight how your product can help her feel more fascinating—in other words, can your product help her have more interesting conversations, or more emotional moments with kids? Will it help her be more powerful at work, or more attractive on a big night out?)

In our study, we measured whether people already consider themselves fascinating. Sadly, we found that only 40% have found their lives fascinating in the previous year. You'll see more insights on this research and application in this book's Appendix B, "Inside the Research," but there's one piece I want to show you right now.

These results were perhaps most surprising of all. Let's see how *you* compare to our study.

Ask yourself a question: *Am I a better driver than the average person?* Just answer with a yes or no. Got your answer? Overwhelmingly, the odds are that you said "yes." Over and over, studies show that people overestimate their driving ability. When asked if they're a better driver than the average person, 93% will report that they are. (That's impossible, of course. On a bell curve, 50% of people are above average and 50% are below.)

Now ask yourself a different question: *Am I more fascinating than the average person?* If you don't think that you are more fascinating than the average person, you are not alone. Only 39% of people do.

Huh? Only 39% consider themselves more fascinating? But yet 93% consider themselves better drivers? Why do we so grossly overestimate our ability to drive, but we underestimate our ability to fascinate? My first thought was . . . How sad is *that*?

Yet now, having interviewed several thousand people, it's clear to me why people are reluctant to think of themselves as fascinating. On some level, most people have a fear of being fascinating.

Stop and think about it. At some point in your life, did you have a defining moment like I did at my dance recital? Was there an incident that undermined your confidence because you put yourself out there, and lost? Was it a harsh comment from a teacher? Humiliation in front of friends? A missed pass in a basketball game, a failed contest, a rejection from a friend? Were you the very last kid picked for the softball team? The very first student to sit down in the spelling bee? Most people can remember their moment. It shattered their confidence at the time and (although they might not realize it) still holds them back today.

The greatest value you can add is to become more of yourself.

AFTER COLLEGE, I discovered the field of advertising and instantly fell head over heels. My personality felt custom-built for this profession: the creativity, the hallway brainstorming, the opportunity to create pop culture and invent taglines from a handful of ordinary words.

Right from the start, in my second year in the business, I was the most award-winning copywriter in the country. I opened my first advertising agency at age twenty-seven and went on to become a global creative director for major brands. Over the course of my advertising career, my clients broadcasted billions of messages through advertising campaigns for brands such as MINI Cooper, Nike, Godiva, Coca-Cola, and BMW. I studied every great agency, devoured books and magazines, and honed my craft so that I could develop new ideas for my clients. Advertising and I had a torrid affair for more than a decade.

Along the way, I learned how communication is received and interpreted, and which types of messages stand out in a crowded marketplace. Yet, that's not the most important thing I learned. My experience in advertising taught me how to look at words and ideas through the eyes of others, and identify what others value.

I learned *how the world sees you.*

Great advertising isn't about what a company wants to *say.* It's about what the market wants to *hear* about, *talk* about, and *buy.* When companies don't listen to what consumers need and want and value, they can damage their own brand.

Imagine a car manufacturer creates a massive national advertising campaign around a new feature in its cars ("extra uncomfortable seats to keep you from falling asleep at the wheel!"). The car manufacturer thinks this is a great new safety feature, but didn't bother to see how customers perceive the feature. The campaign would probably flop. As a result, the company wasted its energy and money on messages that didn't work. Worse, consumers now have a negative impression.

It matters less how a company sees the world and more how the world sees that company. Increasingly, the same is true for you. Just because *you* perceive yourself a certain way doesn't mean that your team or customers necessarily see you the same way (both positively and negatively). In a connected workplace, your success relies on understanding the impressions you create.

It matters less how you see the world. It matters more how the world sees you. If you fail to understand what your audience truly values, then you can't communicate yourself in a way that makes people want to build connection and loyalty.

THE SCIENCE AND ART OF FASCINATION

In 2006, I began studying why certain messages earn attention but others are ignored. I spent three years learning about a broad range of disciplines, including neurology, linguistics, and biological anthropology, looking for patterns behind different approaches to communication, and why certain types of messages earn attention. I looked to economics to find correlations between attention and purchase decisions. I searched hundreds of years' worth of historical source material to find out what types of messages have the most consistent and lasting effect.

One day, while reading a dusty journal, I happened to notice that *fascination* is one of the oldest and most feared words in written language. Tracing back the Latin roots, it means "to bewitch." For thousands of years, fascination has been feared as an evil power that could grip anyone's attention, holding them captive, powerless to resist. I stopped reading, transfixed by this piece of information. Fascination used to be more powerful than witchcraft? What happened?

In researching, I found that fascination has been a powerful influence in cultures around the world, since the beginning of recorded time. Since the dawn of written history, ancient and modern civilizations have precisely described the same force of influence. From Renaissance scholars to Sigmund Freud, scholars have used the word *fascination* to describe the same hypnotic power of persuasion. The literature on the topic is incredibly rich and descriptive. But then, abruptly, in the twentieth century, the exploration of fascination just stopped. Fascination was toppled from its mighty throne by a new force of persuasion . . . modern marketing.

I wanted to understand the difference between fascination and marketing. Why do we become fascinated by certain messages, but not others? What are the patterns behind this force of attraction?

That's when I realized the difference. Fascination is not the same as interest. It's a neurological state of intense focus, one that creates an irresistible feeling of engagement. It's almost the same as falling in love.

By 2009, I'd isolated seven different types of communication that each trigger a specific type of fascination response in a listener's brain. These were my original seven Triggers of fascination: Power, Lust, Mystique, Prestige, Alarm, Vice, and Trust.

Think of these seven Triggers as a set of tools, or a set of golf clubs. Each one has a different purpose, and each creates a different result. When you're mesmerized by an advertisement or political speech, your brain is responding to one of these seven forms of fascination.*

The results of my research were published in my book *Fascinate: Your 7 Triggers to Persuasion and Captivation.* That book centers on how our brains respond to different types of marketing and brands, and how a company can captivate its customers. For instance, Brooks Brothers triggers Trust, because the classic designs feel timeless. The Harry Winston brand triggers Prestige with flawless craftsmanship and detail.

That book led to this one, in an unexpected way.

As most authors can attest, publishing a book is a fairly nerve-racking process. Personally, I find the months of editing the manuscript to be grueling. I'm more of a big-picture communicator, so painstakingly proofing a hundred thousand words is an OCD hell that makes me want to poke out my eyes with a mechanical pencil.

Suddenly, after all the deadlines and detail-obsessed agony, there's a bizarre stage when the manuscript has to be turned into an object called a book. The words have to become molecules. It has to be printed, shipped off to bookstores, put on shelves. The book is finished, but it hasn't been born

---

* The word *trigger* originally described how brands "trigger" a response in consumers with different types of cues such as marketing, product design, or customer experience. However when I refocused my research on personalities, I renamed these Trigger categories "Advantages," since they point to the ways in which your personality can help you can gain an advantage in communication.

yet. I find this stage disarmingly silent. It's the eye of the hurricane before the book's publication date.

During this stage of silence, while *Fascinate* was being printed, my husband said something that would change the course of my life. He said, "What if you did a personality test for people, based on the seven different ways to fascinate?"

The assessment went live in 2010 as a side project, just an experiment. It worked. We realized that people want to know what makes them interesting to others. The test grew faster than I could have imagined, and pivoted the course of my company.

And here we are today: me writing this book, and you reading it.

HOW YOU ADD VALUE

There are seven different ways to successfully communicate. Seven ways to add value. Seven different ways to break through and win.

Of these seven, each has a different way of standing out. Each fascinates for a different reason. Each follows its own set of patterns.

Your personality has a specific Advantage. When you communicate according to this Advantage, you will be more likely to add distinct value.

In certain situations, your Advantages make you intensely valuable. In other situations, you're far less likely to succeed, because you're unable to apply your Advantages.

My team and I have measured hundreds of thousands of participants and worked with teams inside AT&T, Unilever, General Electric, and Cisco. Based on this research, we developed a training curriculum to teach how to add more distinct value. Every day I study communication in our real-world laboratory, measuring how people are applying this system within teams and organizations. This book is your gateway to the system.

You might be asking yourself: What makes the Fascination Advantage system different from other assessments?

Most assessments measure how you see the world. This is different. This system looks at the cues and signals that you're intentionally or unintentionally sending to the world, and the pros and cons of each. If you've already done a test such as Myers-Briggs® or DISC or StrengthsFinder®, you already know *how you see the world.* This used to be the most important metric to know. It's still an important one today. But it's no longer the *only* metric.

POWER	Leading through authority
PASSION	Creating warm emotional connections
MYSTIQUE	Thinking before speaking
PRESTIGE	Achieving success with higher standards
ALERT	Careful precision
INNOVATION	New ideas and solutions
TRUST	Building loyalty over time

As conversations become more compressed, and the marketplace more crowded, you need to know how others see you and respond to you. Rather than just knowing your strengths, you need to know your *differences.*

That's where this book comes in. Until now, if you wanted to measure how others perceive your communication, you had to make a choice: You could either take a test like Myers-Briggs, and try to figure out how to apply your results to your personal brand and marketing. Or, you could learn about marketing, and try to figure out how to plug in your own personality traits. The Fascination Advantage combines both personality *and* marketing into one system.

Together, you and I will use the modern lens of branding to study your personality. You'll learn how to see yourself through the eyes of your clients and co-workers so that you can build rapport more quickly. By the end, you'll find out what makes you distinctly valuable to others, so that you can become the most valuable you.

LOUD VOICES, QUIET VOICES

Within a team, loud voices can drown out the quieter voices. Outgoing personalities can overshadow more subtle ones. That's why it's so important for organizations to understand how individuals contribute to the whole. There are many, many ways to communicate and become more valuable. Understanding the full spectrum helps to make sure that each person makes a real difference.

You'll fascinate differently than I. You might be more detailed, more reserved, more analytical. These differences between us are good. They give us diversity, and make us stronger as a whole. If we partnered on a team, our differences would improve our results more than our similarities.

Diversity strengthens a team and makes it more multifaceted, as long as each person understands and develops his strong suit. Leaders need to know how to tap into their team's variety of Advantages so that they can help each person develop signature areas of performance.

You already have built-in differentiators, and they don't have to be brash and flamboyant. In fact, subtle personalities can have the most distinguishing features. Yet no matter what your natural approach, you must learn how it's being perceived by others. In order *to* communicate, you must learn how *you* communicate.

Whether you are soft-spoken or outspoken, you speak a certain "language" of fascination.

WHAT LANGUAGE DO YOU SPEAK?

When I say "language," I'm not asking whether you speak English or Portuguese. I'm referring to all of your verbal and nonverbal signals that shape how the world sees you.

If you have the Passion Advantage, you speak the language of *relationship*. You make a lot of eye contact; you choose highly descriptive words and phrases with expressive inflection. If you have the Mystique Advantage, on the other hand, you speak a different language. You speak the language of *listening*. Unlike a Passion personality, who can sometimes "overcommunicate," you are seen as someone who carefully thinks before speaking so that you can get the facts right the first time.

POWER	is the language of confidence
PASSION	is the language of relationship
MYSTIQUE	is the language of listening
PRESTIGE	is the language of excellence
ALERT	is the language of details
INNOVATION	is the language of creativity
TRUST	is the language of stability

When you understand which of these languages comes most naturally to you, you can see how your communication is being heard by others. If you're taking a road trip to Italy, you don't need to be fluent in Italian, but you'll want to know a few key phrases so that you can reach your destination and maybe even make a few friends along the way. Similarly, if you have a meeting with a new client, you might want to know what "language" they speak so that you can communicate in a way that builds rapport. And while you might never be fluent in every language, you can learn how to recognize the most essential points.

If you believe that you have a message worth listening to, then you have a responsibility to get your message out into the world. That's true whether you are delivering a newsletter or a church sermon. You are the guardian of your message. Even if you are shy or reluctant, it's your duty to help your important message be heard.

Having an important message means nothing if nobody notices or cares.

UNLEARN BORING

My daughter Azalea is nine years old, and she expresses herself with the fearlessness of a young girl who has not yet acquired the self-doubt of public failure. She hasn't learned *boring*, yet. I know she'll probably learn it soon. Or more accurately, the world will teach her. One day she will forget the steps, or miss the ball, or flunk the test. Someone will tell her she's not good enough or smart enough or cool enough, too *this* or not enough *that*.

And no matter how untrue it is, no matter how much evidence there is to the contrary, she'll take a little piece of her personality and hide it away in a box. Here's what I want to tell my daughter, and yours, and you:

You don't need to find the light. You *are* the light. When you let your personality shine, you can light up the world.

In this book, you and I are going to discover the most extraordinary parts of yourself. You will see the *best* of how the world sees you. By the time we're finished, you will have the words to communicate your highest distinct value . . . why people hire you and promote you and befriend you and champion for you and fall in love with you.

This book will not change who you are. Quite the opposite. This book will help you become more of who you are.

HOW TO READ THIS BOOK

On our journey together, you'll discover the best parts of yourself: your hidden talents and highest worth, your untapped opportunities and unrealized potential. You'll find out how your personality naturally captivates others, and how to build your career and your team around your signature style of communication.

You'll also learn how you could be turning people off without even realizing it. You might not know it yet, but you have certain blind spots when it comes to how the world sees you. Those are not necessarily negatives, and the key is not to "fix" those, but instead to see yourself from a new perspective so the blind spots are no longer blind.

In the coming pages of Part I, we'll explore why you must learn how the world sees you, and how that shapes your perceived value. I'll take you inside three crucial emerging trends so you can see why you can't rely on the same habits that you could even five years ago.

Next, in Chapter 2, we'll explore the science and art of fascination. We'll dig more deeply into the seven different ways to communicate (the seven Advantages). Then it will be time to take the Fascination Advantage assessment. Your online report is your first step toward seeing the best of how the world sees you.

In Part II, you'll meet the entire kingdom of Archetypes in your life: from the silver-tongued communicators such as The Diplomat to social butterflies like The Rockstar. You'll meet intellectual communicators such as The Royal Guard, and goal-oriented achievers such as The Victor. You'll see the spectrum of ways that different personalities can find a niche to specialize their value.

Finally, in Part III, you'll create your Anthem: a tagline for your personality.

This part of the book includes tools and exercises to help you build stronger teams and better relationships, and attract more customers. You'll have the opportunity to apply a quick-start version of my training program for immediately capturing and sustaining attention with your own brand of conversation starters and deal closers.

With the strategies in this book, you'll learn how to gauge what's working when you communicate (and what's not), and adjust accordingly to get your desired result. You'll learn how to find your "zone of genius," so you can use these traits to become your most valuable self every single time you communicate: whether writing a business email or chitchatting with your neighbor, whether you're on a big stage or in a small meeting room, whether you're giving an employee review or persuading a prospect. You'll know how you're naturally suited to win.

You'll see how to differentiate yourself by leveraging the specific *language* of your distinct Advantages. You'll learn how to connect with your audience by being more of who you already are.

Ultimately, it's not enough to know what makes you persuasive and fascinating. You must also understand how to consciously communicate and apply your core specialty. That's where your Anthem comes in.

The Tagline for Your Personality

An Anthem is a short phrase, only two or three words long, explaining who you are, at your best. Yet while this phrase is quite short, it epitomizes your highest value. Your Anthem is like a tagline for your personality.

In a distracted, competitive, and commoditized world, a personality tagline is crucial. People need to immediately grasp what you bring to the table. If you make it easy for people to understand why they should work with you, they're far more likely to hire you.

Your Anthem helps others understand what you do best, so that you can do more of what you do best.

This relieves you of the anxiety of trying to figure out how to market yourself, or introduce yourself, or even be yourself when the pressure's on. You can just go straight to your strong suit, every time. You'll see how team performance rises, and conflict falls, when everyone understands how each person adds value.

As you learn to see yourself in a new way, make a conscious effort to see your team in a new way. You might realize that the personalities you most need on your side are not necessarily the ones you want to hang out with after work.

Along the way, don't be afraid to experiment with new ways to describe yourself. Test out new words to explain how you add value. Take a look at the suggested words in your "Top 5 Adjectives" (found in your online report, and in this book). Think how you can be applying these in every interaction. Finally, keep an open mind about yourself, and how others see you. This is an opportunity to honestly assess yourself with new information and a new perspective. Give yourself time to start to see yourself through the eyes of others.

This process is not about *changing* who you are. It's about seeing what you're already doing right, so you can do it on purpose.

You're about to see yourself in a new way . . . the best of how the world sees you.

PART I

HOW DOES THE WORLD SEE YOU?

CHAPTER 1

WHY DISCOVER YOUR HIGHEST DISTINCT VALUE

Let's say you think you're funny. As far as you're concerned, a sense of humor is one of your best traits. There's just one problem: Nobody else thinks you're funny.

This is indeed a problem. Humor is a two-sided exchange. It's a feedback loop between you as the joke teller, and your audience. Humor doesn't happen in a vacuum. It's not enough to only consider *how you see yourself.* You must also consider *how the world sees you.* If nobody else thinks you're funny . . . well, you're probably not funny.

Humor is in the eye of the beholder. So are likability, leadership, and a range of other subjective qualities that are rooted in the perception of others. You get a vote, but your listener has veto power.

For example, you might see yourself as *lovable,* but if the world sees you as a coldhearted curmudgeon, there's a disconnect. You might think that you're *respected* or *independent* or *practical,* but if nobody agrees, you're out of luck. You might see yourself as *good with kids,* but if small children cry and run to the other side of the street at the very sight of you, there's a disconnect (as well as a serious impediment to any career aspirations you might have of becoming a birthday party clown).

By looking at yourself from the outside in, and systematically measuring the effect you have on your listener, you can improve results. Whether you're a comedian or a kindergarten teacher or a crisis negotiator, you can become more successful by understanding how the world *sees* you and *hears* you and *responds* to you.

HOW DOES THE WORLD SEE YOU?

You might never have considered this question before. It might feel unfamiliar. It might make you feel awkward or self-conscious or vain, like you're staring at your reflection for too long in the mirror.

Yet if you ignore this perspective, you're putting yourself at a disadvantage. If you want your messages to be heard and remembered, if you want to share big ideas and important opinions, you need a full and accurate picture about how you're actually communicating—and how others perceive your communication.

In the modern work world (unless you find yourself alone and shipwrecked on a desert island, where physical survival is your chief and only concern) you *do* need to know how to communicate and connect. If nobody hears or remembers your message, it failed.

Forbes magazine reported research findings that indicate that 85% of your financial success is due to skills in "human engineering," your personality and ability to communicate, negotiate, and lead. Shockingly, only 15% is due to technical knowledge.

We live in a social environment, one that's about as far as you can get from an isolated desert island. Our survival depends upon our ability to build bridges between ourselves and others. Most of us interact all day long with others, whether in person or online. We have to convince and cajole. For the 99% of life that is not a desert island, you'll want to find out how the world sees you.

HOW YOU SEE YOURSELF

You already have a good sense of how you see yourself. Yet if you only measure your personality from this perspective, you're missing a crucial piece of information about yourself. And that missing piece is this:

How does the world see you?

How do others respond to you? Do they pay attention to what you say, or do they ignore you? Do they seek your opinion, or do they consider your ideas irrelevant? Do your words prompt clear action?

To understand what's at stake here, let's turn to the world of marketing.

Imagine you're writing a blog post intended to get donations for a nonprofit. You spend weeks researching and polishing this blog post on fund-raising. Your post is articulate. It's insightful. It has the potential to change the model of nonprofit fund-raising. You want people to read it, share it, comment on it, apply your insights, and feature your post on other blogs or even major media. Above all, you want donors.

In a perfect world, this post *deserves* to be read. But if nobody reads the post because they're distracted by YouTube videos about cute kittens and the inexplicable trend of bacon products,* then your post will never fulfill its purpose. It doesn't matter how brilliant your post is if it just gets lost. Writing a world-changing blog post means nothing if nobody reads it.

Even the most worthy messages are often forgotten and ignored. If you fail to fascinate your audience, your message withers. This can be disheartening. If you write a children's book that nobody reads, or send a proposal that gathers dust in an email inbox, your message dies cold and alone without ever having achieved its purpose.

No matter how you're communicating, whether you're writing for your website or marketing for a politician, you face the same challenge. Blog posts have "readers" and politicians have "voters," but ultimately they are both an *audience* that needs to be convinced of the value of your message. (When I say "audience," I'm using it as a catchall term to include readers and voters, as well as employees and consumers and clients and boards of directors and shareholders and family and the media and everyone else with whom you must communicate in order to succeed in a goal.)

THE BATTLE FOR ATTENTION

Say you're running for political office, and spend several sweaty days posting signs all over town. You want people to notice and remember your signs, hoping it will sway their vote your way on election day. But it's not enough to just create the message and put it out there. That's wasted energy if you don't generate a result from others. You don't live in a vacuum.

---

* Examples include bacon vodka, bacon mints, bacon lip balm, bacon-flavored toothpicks and toothpaste, bacon gumballs, bacon baby formula, and bacon perfume and air freshener. My dog's name is Bacon (last name Hogshead).

A political campaign doesn't live in a vacuum, and neither do you. You'll succeed by communicating, connecting, and convincing.

You aren't funny if nobody else thinks you're funny. And you aren't *communicating* if nobody is *listening*.

Who do you need to fascinate? Over the course of a day, you might want shoppers to buy, your local community to get involved, your students to learn, your start-up to grow, your forgetful spouse to put the cap back on the toothpaste. You want your messages to connect, or to educate, or to inform, or to inspire.

No matter what your message is *about*, each one of your messages has an intended purpose. Each time you communicate, you want people to listen and remember that message, and to positively anticipate your future messages. You want them to take action, change a behavior, or be inspired.

WHAT THE VIOLIN PLAYER LEARNED

In certain situations, your personality is more likely to earn attention. In these situations, you are more likely to be noticed, heard, and respected. Yet if you don't realize which situations play to your Advantages, you will be underestimated or even ignored.

In a recent experiment, one the most famously exquisite violinists of our time, Joshua Bell, played in Washington, D.C. Yet unlike his standard concert hall performance with a thousand-dollar-per-minute fee, for this performance he was rewarded with pennies.

Joshua Bell played down in the subway, anonymously and without fanfare, drawing attention to his music only with his skill and priceless violin. "No one knew it," says *Washington Post* journalist Gene Weingarten, "but the fiddler standing against a bare wall outside the Metro in an indoor arcade at the top of the escalators was one of the finest classical musicians in the world, playing some of the most elegant music ever written on one of the most valuable violins ever made." Yet a thousand people moved right past him through rush hour, oblivious. In addition to not earning a standing ovation, Bell also did not earn his $45,000 fee for this performance. Instead he earned $32.12, or roughly .07% as much.

If one of the most celebrated musicians of all time cannot compete to earn attention in a distracted, competitive environment, how can you?

Today it's not enough to be the world's best if no one realizes you're there. Unnoticed communication cannot make a difference. In the battle against competition, our talents and skills are hopelessly lost unless we find a way to fascinate our listener. The world doesn't need another violinist. Or another job applicant. Or another lawyer advertising on TV. It's your job to show us why we should care.

Luckily, you already have the defining traits you need to stand out and be heard. Which is good, because you'll need to call upon every one of them.

You're doing battle in a distracted and competitive world.

Get ready to encounter the three deadly threats.

MEET YOUR ARCHENEMIES

Distraction threatens your connection with others.

Competition threatens your ability to stand out and win.

Commoditization threatens your relationships and loyalty.

Dark forces lurk in your environment, waiting to defeat your communication. They poison your results. They suck your marketing dollars right out of your company. They kill your best ideas before those ideas have even had a chance to breathe. Each threat is a formidable adversary. The first one stands in the way of you even beginning the conversation: distraction.

THE THREAT OF DISTRACTION

Distraction is a jealous seductress. It refuses to share your listener's attention. It whispers, "Pay attention to this shiny object." Distraction lures people away from you and your message by tempting them with a Facebook notification or a text from a friend. Distraction prevents you from earning the attention of your prospective clients.

It's true. Your listeners are distracted. Your customer goes from vendor to vendor. Your co-worker goes from email to email. Your employees go from putting out one fire to the next. People are so distracted by voicemails and emails and tweets and retweets that each one of your messages has a lower likelihood of actually breaking through and connecting.

How do our brains respond to all this distraction? We may think more quickly in this age of media assault, but we also become distracted more easily. One of my favorite quotes on the subject is from BBC News: "The addictive nature of Web browsing can leave you with an attention span of nine seconds—the same as a goldfish."

Nine seconds? Like a goldfish? Yikes. That's all we might get before people's brains make a decision to either stay focused or relocate to a new topic.

Every time you introduce yourself, you have about nine seconds to engage your listener. This is your window of opportunity for connection. If you earn their interest during those nine seconds, people will be more likely to engage further. If you fail to add some sort of value in that golden window, they're less likely to listen to what you say, let alone remember it or take action on it.

This can be frustrating, especially if you are trying to lead a meeting or make a point or have a real conversation. In such a crowded and noisy world, you have ridiculously little time to introduce yourself, let alone make a strong first impression.*

Now you need to "front-load" your value. Cut to the chase. Get to the point. Make it short and sweet. The pressure is on.

It's almost as if people have developed collective ADD, swimming like a goldfish from one message to another, jumping from one email to the next. And what does this constant distraction really look like? Let's take a look inside your brain, and see what goes on when you feel stressed by distraction.

HOW DISTRACTION RUINS FLOW

Imagine you and your team have been working hard on a great project for a client. The deadline is getting close, but you've got it under control. Your brain doesn't have to work as hard to concentrate. You feel focused and energized, primed to operate at peak performance.

But then, distraction enters the picture.

---

* Since I first described the nine-second attention span in 2010, the body of research on this topic is becoming far bigger (although, one might think, the articles themselves will become *shorter*). Some sources say the attention span is now only eight seconds. Others say it's only six seconds. Stick with me long enough to complete this footnote, okay?

Suddenly you get an email from your client. The deadline changed. Now your work is due tomorrow. Bam! Instantly, your brain goes from cruising along in fifth gear to careening all over the place. Emails and calls start flooding in from your team, with everyone going into panic mode. Including you. Your brain was cruising along in fifth gear, and now it slams into a grinding crisis mode.

On an MRI scan, a fascinated brain is in a state of relaxed focus. On the other hand, a distracted brain lights up in an unpleasant state of crisis and confusion. As you kick into high gear, you burn more glucose and oxygen. Your brain is only about 2% of your weight, but even under normal conditions, it consumes about 20% of your energy. When stress kicks in, your brain consumes even more oxygen to cope. Blood flow can increase up to 400% as your entire body heightens its response to increased demands.

If your listener becomes distracted while you communicate, they are more likely to feel confusion or doubt about your message. If you're not communicating clearly, you're less likely to add value.

You might even damage their perception of you, thereby disincentivizing them from connecting with you in the future.

On the other hand, if you communicate clearly and purposefully, your listener is less likely to feel overloaded or confused. They feel more confident in you, and more confident in your message. Your communication is more likely to influence your listener's actions, because they will fully absorb what you're saying. They can receive the full value of your message. Best of all, they can appreciate why you are the person who is best suited to help them reach their desired result.

It's a value cycle: When you add value to your audience, you fascinate them. When you fascinate them, they become intensely focused and you can build a valuable connection.

This value cycle leads to loyalty. That's key in long-term relationships. After all, you probably don't just want people to listen to you once. You want to build up a long-term relationship, with repeat business that continues week in and week out, year in and year out. Once people become loyal to you, communicating becomes so much easier. Once you've established that you deliver value with every interaction, customers will call you back, colleagues will open your emails, and your boss will free up space in her busy schedule to meet.

Yet the road to loyalty is not an easy one. Distraction stands smack-dab in your way, and it sabotages your ability to deliver value at the start of an interaction. Your challenge is to engage someone right from the start, whether in person, online, or over the phone. You need to stop people from fidgeting, glancing at their watch, and checking their emails while you speak in order for them to derive the full value of your message. How will you keep them focused?

The fact is you must do more than "get noticed." (Getting noticed is easy: Just jump up and down, yelling and screaming. That's what toddlers do at the checkout line in a crowded grocery store to demonstrate their unhinged desire for a pack of Skittles. That's what marketers do when they put a blinking banner ad on the website you're visiting. It says "notice me," but it also smacks of desperation and typically fails long before even the goldfish has swum away.)

Instead, to defeat distraction you need to truly *earn* the attention of your prospective customers, and you do this by spotlighting your individual Advantages—and fascinating your audience.

Once you know how to orient all your communication around your signature qualities, you'll eliminate the threat of distraction. You can confidently explain how you are most likely to deliver a solution—thereby reducing stress for you, and eliminating confusion in your listener.

It all begins with a first impression, and continues to loyalty and lasting value.

> **If people are distracted when you communicate, they are less likely to listen to what you say. Worse, they are less likely to find value in what you say. A positive first impression gets an introduction on the path to a loyal relationship. You are most likely to combat distraction and make a memorable first impression by tapping into your personality's natural way of fascinating others—your Advantages. If your listeners' brains are not distracted, they can hear your message more clearly. They're more likely to want to engage with you. Then you can move on and focus on building a lasting and prosperous relationship.**

NINE-SECOND SUMMARY OF DISTRACTION
- Distraction threatens your ability to connect with your audience.
- Triumph over distraction by using your personality's natural Advantages.
- A compelling first impression paves the way to long-term relationships and loyalty.
- It's better to avoid communicating with people than to waste their time with messages that don't add value.

Just when you've overcome the threat of distraction and have succeeded in fascinating your prospects, the next threat awaits to thwart your chances of closing the deal. Prepare yourself for the threat of competition.

THE THREAT OF COMPETITION

Competition is a public executioner. Competition might motivate you at first, urging you to expend more dollars and energy to win. But if competition leads you down the wrong path, you'll be stuck playing someone else's game.

We grew up with a myth. The myth says: Try hard to be "better." Be better than everyone else. Better than the other students in the classroom, better than the other players on the team, better than the other applicants. Have better skills or a better résumé. We've been taught to compete by copying and then surpassing the top performers at school, at work, and in the gym.

The reality, however, is that "better" is not better. Better is a mirage. It keeps you chained to the same way of working as your competition. Better is temporary. Better is a flimsy edge that can be toppled in a millisecond by someone with a bigger following, a lower price, a more convenient location, a fancier degree, a shinier award, a newer technology, a more skillful skill. Better is not always better. Sometimes, it's worse.

While businesses have been focusing on being "better," customers have gone in a different direction. They've become more fickle, flirting without long-term commitment. They switch back and forth to get the best deal, upgrading and downgrading. This is the expensive and exhausting situation facing many businesses that typically compete on price, such as banks and cellular carriers. As soon as they get a new customer, others leave, because the artificially low price that tempted the customer to sign up has passed and now they're off to the next deal. And companies aren't the only ones facing the threat of competition.

While competition can push people to be their best, it can also force them to run on a hamster wheel, going faster in the same direction as everyone else, instead of going in a different direction entirely.

When you successfully differentiate yourself, however, you become the go-to person in your category for one particular reason. This is when you can start to charge higher prices and have a lot more control in your market. You not only establish the playing field, now you control it.

BETTER VERSUS DIFFERENT

Different is better than better. Different doesn't try to turn you into something else. Different allows you to highlight the singular traits you already have within you. You aren't necessarily better than your competition. But you are already different.

As a marketplace becomes ever more crowded, *strengths* matter less than *differences*. Strengths become the standard. Competing on the basis of strengths forces you into an endless cycle of incremental improvements in which it's hard to outdo the competition. Good used to matter more, when competition focused on price, quality, or service features.

But today, it's not enough to compete just on those merits. Even B2B (business-to-business) markets, which tend to focus more on rational benefits than B2C (business-to-consumer) companies in their sales approach, are seeing how the driving force behind decisions today is compelling communication. In fact, in a *Harvard Business Review* article in 2012, a poll of one hundred thousand decision-makers found that "39% of B2B buyers select a vendor according to the skills of the salesperson rather than price, quality, or service features." Even in the relatively conservative B2B markets, it's no longer enough to be good without adding value in some other way.

If you want to influence decision-makers, invest in understanding your personality Advantages and how best to apply them. Learn what makes you fascinating so those traits become your competitive edge. Remember, when competition increases, *strengths* matter less. *Differences* matter far more. When everyone offers more or less the same product or service, fascinate customers by leading with your Advantages.

It might seem risky to stand out, but risk is the safer of your options. The greater danger lies on the other side of the coin: being ignored. Feeling a little discouraged by the threat of competition? Most people are struggling with the same problem of standing out. Our research shows that two-thirds of people think they are less fascinating than the average person. That means your competition is probably not successfully fascinating the marketplace. The bar is low. You can raise the bar, if you focus on your Advantages.

How does the world see you, at your best?

Knowing what others want and expect from you, and how you deliver it like nobody else, requires you to look at yourself from the perspective of how the world sees you. And this means combatting the competition by focusing not only on how your offering is different, but also on how you, the person, are essential to that solution.

"WHAT YOU DO" VERSUS "WHO YOU ARE"

Your job title provides a handy frame of reference for explaining what you do. ("Hi, I'm Jim. I'm in sales.") That's a mistake. If you want to increase perceived value for you and your work, you need to focus on *who you are*, rather than *what you do*.

Otherwise, you can be seen as a commodity, which will make it very difficult to reach your top earning potential. This becomes increasingly important over the course of your career, so you don't get stuck in a dead-end role.

> "The higher the income, the more the person is paid for *who they are*, rather than *what they do*."—Dan Kennedy, author and marketing entrepreneur

No matter what your profession, you need a specialty of some kind—a signature way of adding value. Your personality Advantages are the easiest and fastest way to create a specialty.

In her book *Lean In* Sheryl Sandberg describes her intense hiring negotiation process with Facebook founder Mark Zuckerberg. She turned down his first offer to become the company's chief operating officer—a move that was both surprising and strategic. She told Zuckerberg, "Of course, you realize that you're hiring me to run your deal teams, so you want me to be a good negotiator. This is the only time you and I will be on opposite sides of the table." Sandberg reinforced not only *what she does*, but also *who she is*. She didn't just show *how she would do* her job; she also reiterated *who she would be* in her job.

When someone negotiates brilliantly in her own hiring process, she will likely negotiate just as brilliantly on behalf of her company.

The lesson: When you hire an employee, you are hiring an outcome—and while we usually think of that outcome as being linked to tangible attributes such as skills and knowledge and experience, it is also directly linked to personality Advantages. Sheryl Sandberg did an expert job of communicating *who she is* in the hiring process, highlighting her differences and how they could benefit Facebook.

Recently my company conducted a training program with Unilever. (They're the global consumer goods company behind brands such as Dove, Q-tips, Lipton, Ben & Jerry's, and many others.) We asked Unilever employees to describe how they introduce themselves in a professional context. We found, almost without exception, that people introduce themselves according to *what they do*. This is normal. Employees almost always define themselves by *what they do*.

Over the course of a few hours, we helped them understand their own personality Archetype—the combination of their top Advantages, which in essence is what makes them fascinating. Based on their Fascination Advantage report, each employee wrote a quick summary of how they're most likely to contribute to their team. (You'll do this as well, in Part III.) Then we compared their levels of confidence before the exercise.

Confidence levels increased by 34% when employees communicated *who they are* rather than *what they do*. They now know how they are most likely to engage others, and how they can compete effectively for attention, so that their emails are opened and their messages are acted upon. When you clearly understand your differences, you can escape the gloomy, gray world of the lowest common denominator and start to shine. And outshine the competition.

Overcome the threat of competition by resisting the urge to try to be "better," and instead highlight how you are different. Your personality already has effective differences (your Advantages), which provide an individualized platform on which you can earn the business you are competing for. When you build your career or business around these built-in differences, you escape having to be "better" than the competition. Instead, you can develop your own compelling way of attracting business, and getting results.

NINE-SECOND SUMMARY OF COMPETITION

- Rather than putting all your energy into being "better," focus on the ways in which you are different, how you are uniquely suited to tackle certain types of problems.
- If you are not the biggest player in your market, it's dangerous to compete on the basis of price.
- Rather than focus on what you do, instead, focus on who you are.
- To succeed in a competitive environment, don't *change* who you are. Become *more* of who you are.

THE THREAT OF COMMODITIZATION

If distraction is a jealous seductress and competition is a public executioner, then commoditization is a silent assassin. It oozes into the cracks and breeds quietly in the darkness. It permeates your relationships with complacency, shaving off your points of difference, sapping your defining qualities, and eventually transforming you and your vibrant one-of-a-kind edge into a generic replica.

If you become a commodity in the eyes of your customers, it means you're vulnerable. You can be easily replaced. As business gets busier, it's no longer sufficient to keep existing customers happy and loyal by maintaining the status quo. Maintenance is for tires, a big-time commodity. You have to fight commoditization by infusing every ongoing communication and interaction with your unique Advantages.

You become a commodity once you cease to remember why the customer chose you in the first place. You can't just put your energy into winning the deal and then allow your customer base to gather dust in the closet. Your client base deserves—no, demands—that you continue to fascinate them on an ongoing basis.

Does it really matter if your existing customers stick around? Only if you want to stay in business. According to a 2012 Geoffrey James article in *Inc.* magazine, "regardless of what you're selling, your long-term profitability is largely dependent upon your ability to keep current customers, rather than your ability to acquire new ones." In other words, you simply can't afford to become a commodity. And consistent with the logic that once you become a commodity you are replaceable, James offers that "when it comes to keeping your existing customers, customer service is three times more important than price—and *five* times more important than functionality." In other words, how you interact with the customer is way more important than what you charge or even how well your product works. And the salesperson ultimately is the one driving the relationship and managing the service the customer gets, ensuring that the customer is cared for and not just satisfied, but "happy."

Forbes describes how Daniel Kahneman, a Nobel Prize-winning psychologist, discovered that "people would rather do business with a person they like and trust rather than someone they don't, even if the likeable person is offering a lower quality product or service at a higher price."

Your personality is your natural weapon against distraction, competition, and commoditization. The more value you add, the less you have to compete on price, and the less likely you are to become a commodity.

THE BATTLEGROUND OF COMMODITY

For some professionals, "adding value" means literally adding dollars to a customer's bottom line, or to a client's account. There is an ever-growing number of industries in which the battle to maintain customers is hard fought because these industries have become largely commoditized. Let's talk about financial services first. This is a field where the temptation for customers to go elsewhere—to get in on the next better-performing fund with a lower commission—is ever present. Many financial advisors are selling the same products and services as everyone else; financial products and services on the surface are pretty much the same, and to the untrained eye, advisors are, too.

As a result, financial advisors face the daunting challenge of setting themselves apart in order to build loyalty among current clients, despite the fact that they are selling largely the same product as their competitor. So how can a financial services advisor keep his customers loyal? By emphasizing his personality Advantages with every interaction.

A financial advisor who can lead with his ability to instill Trust (one of the seven Advantages) each time he communicates by providing accurate and essential details will never become a commodity in the eyes of his clients. A financial advisor who can demonstrate his Innovation Advantage by consistently presenting unique and well-researched options that coincide with his client's individual interests will never be perceived as replaceable. The fact is that the financial advisor must find ways to distinguish himself not just during the initial sales process, but equally importantly on an ongoing basis to keep his clients from going elsewhere.

Let's take a look at dentistry, also one of the most rapidly commoditized businesses out there (and it is, if you still have a mouth full of teeth, likely an industry you've already had a lifetime of interaction with). Over the last twenty years or so, patients have become decidedly less loyal, particularly as the market is flooded with more dentists and more "products and services" (teeth whitening and other cosmetic options, improved implements to prevent grinding) for them to leverage while competing. In this commoditized environment, many patients are starting to believe that one dentist might be just as good as another. So in this climate, how can a dentist avoid commoditization, and grow a business around his own signature way of adding value?

A couple of years ago, I began going to a dentist named Dr. Glass. Admittedly, I chose Dr. Glass because he's right around the corner from my home, and hey, there appeared to be plentiful parking. In other words, it was a commodity decision. If he'd been booked, I would have just picked someone else.

But it turns out Dr. Glass was not at all a commodity. In fact, in the days between when I scheduled my appointment and arrived at the office, Dr. Glass had taken the initiative to look me up online, learn that I had created an assessment, and made the effort to take it himself. Wow.

Turns out, Dr. Glass has a primary Passion Advantage, which means that he communicates through the language of relationship. As with most Passion personalities, he differentiates himself by creating a warm emotional connection. I'd never had a dentist ask about my emotional state rather than just the state of my teeth.

Does Dr. Glass have the most sophisticated X-ray technology in his office? I have no idea. Do his hygienists use the latest and greatest technology for cleaning my teeth? Probably, but I'm not sure and I don't really care. Dr. Glass is a good dentist not just because he can fill a cavity, but because he understands that his personality is a key differentiator in standing out among his peers. He is a great dentist not only for his skill, but because he adds a small but significant effort to demonstrate that his patients are each personally important to him, and to his practice. His personality is the anti-commodity. The same is true of you.

I've since learned that this is how Dr. Glass connects with everyone in his practice. He doesn't have patients; he has fanatics. I'm one of them.*

NINE-SECOND SUMMARY OF COMMODITIZATION

- Companies must either have the biggest marketing budget, or be the most fascinating.
- If others perceive you as a commodity, you are replaceable, and vulnerable.
- Avoid commoditization by focusing on the ways in which your personality is ideally suited to solve certain types of problems and create certain types of opportunities.

---

* Dr. Glass didn't realize it at the time, but the few minutes he spent with me was a very wise investment. My husband and I have eight children between us. Now we schedule dental appointments by the bulk.

TRIUMPH OVER ALL THREE THREATS BY ADDING DISTINCT VALUE

Those nasty threats of distraction, competition, and commoditization will continue to thwart your efforts to attract, establish, and keep customers—in other words, as long as you are trying to do business in today's nine-second world. And we've talked about what you can do to combat each one. However, even beyond earning attention, leading with your specialized personality traits and fighting the good fight even after you have earned the business, there is something you can be doing—should be doing—that will allow you to fascinate and succeed at every phase of the business cycle: *Add distinct value.*

But what does it mean to "add value," exactly? And more importantly, what does it mean to add *distinct* value?

These days, most people recognize the importance of adding value in a somewhat generic sense. Problem is, despite the popularity of the buzz phrase "adding value," few people actually know precisely what kind of value to add. This confusion is understandable, since adding value can be relative, depending on a variety of factors. But there are some standard principles to apply, no matter where you work, what you do, or to whom you are selling if you want to add value.

After working with organizations ranging from sporting goods retailers to rural telecommunications companies, I've distilled a few guidelines.

HOW TO KNOW IF YOU (OR ANYONE ELSE) ARE ADDING VALUE

- **You become admired for a noteworthy ability to contribute a specific benefit.** Your specific benefit might be deep knowledge, a highly prized skill, special service, or elite network. For example, if you're a mortgage broker, you find better rates and niche financing.
- **You're worth more than you're being paid.** If you are only worth what you are paid, that's not adding value. That's called doing your job. And the more you're paid, the more difficult it becomes to add value. The bar is lower for an entry-level assistant than for a CEO.
- **You deliver more than would normally be expected.** You go above and beyond the norm. For instance, as a dentist, your fillings are longer lasting, more cosmetically attractive, or less painful than the norm. If you are an agriculture equipment manufacturer, you might listen to help

your customers customize their equipment to help get the best result for their crops. If you sell medical supplies, you don't have to try to win in a crowded market by selling the cheapest supplies.

- **You are the preferred option, even if you are more expensive or less convenient.** Your clients want to work with you, even if you have a long waiting list, even if they have to travel far to see you, and even if they pay twice as much compared to your competitor.

HOW CAN YOU TELL IF YOU ARE ADDING VALUE?

- Co-workers go out of their way for your opinion and participation.
- Clients actively choose to work with you even when other options are more convenient or less expensive.
- Your boss seeks your input and invests energy into your future relationship.
- Partners consider the relationship you share to be healthy and thriving.

If you're not adding value, you're taking up space. The more space you take up, the more difficult it becomes to continuously earn your spot, and the more likely you are to become ignored and irrelevant.

"HIGHEST AND BEST"

Earlier I described how many people say they want to add value, but few know exactly what type of value they want to add. When you magnify and leverage your Advantages, you don't just add value, you add your *highest distinct value.*

Real estate uses the concept of "highest and best use." When evaluating a property's value, an appraiser must base his valuation on what he assumes is the highest and best use of a property. For instance, imagine a scenic two-mile plot of waterfront property ("Location, location, location!"). The highest and best use is more likely to be a luxury high-rise than a storage warehouse. This highest and best use is hypothetical, based on maximally productive use, regardless of its actual current use.

Similarly, your personality has a highest and best use. It's the way in which you are most likely to add the value that, for the most part, only *you* can add. It's when you deliver your highest distinct value.

YOUR HIGHEST DISTINCT VALUE

You're already quite familiar with these three words, but they take on special meaning when combined. Let's break it down:

Highest: The pinnacle of who you already are; what makes you already exceptional.

Distinct: How you are different.

Value: Your specialized ability to deliver above and beyond what's expected.

When you live according to your highest distinct value, you become your most fascinating—and most valuable self.

Later in this book, you'll take your Fascination Advantage assessment. You'll find out which two personality Advantages are most likely to help you add value.

INCREASING YOUR VALUE

The great majority of communication is un-fascinating. It loses the battle against distraction, competition, and commoditization. As you become more fascinating, however, you rise above the din.

Think of this as a pyramid. At the bottom of the pyramid, you're not standing out. You're not fascinating, or valuable, because you are like everyone else.

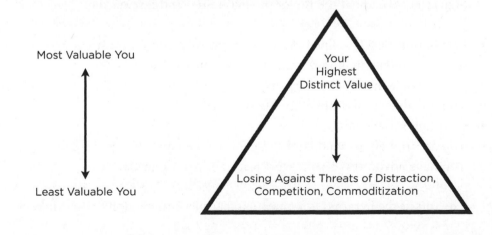

When your communication looks and sounds like everyone else's, you are at the bottom of the pyramid. You're forced to do hand-to-hand combat with the three threats (and at serious risk of losing). Here, you're stuck in the world of the "lowest common denominator."

Signs that you are at the bottom of the pyramid—and un-fascinating:

- Your communication is not breaking through. Emails are not read, calls are not returned. It's difficult to convince others to take action on your words.
- Your prospects don't understand why they need to buy from you rather than from your competitors, which means that you are interchangeable with others.
- You are not able to raise prices or fees, and must compete on the basis of lowest price because you don't offer something distinctly different.
- You are defined by *what you do* rather than *who you are*.
- You advertise more, but lead quality declines.

The cream always rises to the top, right? To rise in your career, you must increasingly add more of your highest distinct value. This is the top of the pyramid, where you become rare and irreplaceable. Here's where your highest value lives. This is your personal zone of genius, with your most specialized, distinct personality Advantages.

Signs that you are at the top of the pyramid—and fascinating:

- You have a clearly defined presence and way of communicating. You are highly differentiated, and unlikely to be confused with others.
- Once people meet you, they remember you.
- You are able to raise prices and fees.
- Customers are loyal.
- You are in high demand, and can choose *when* and *how* you work.
- You have advocates in your workplace and your market.

The top of the pyramid is a much happier place to be, don't you think? So here's our goal together: Find your highest distinct value, so you can *add* your highest distinct value.

CUSTOM VERSUS ONE-SIZE-FITS-ALL

Your personality is custom built for certain situations. In these situations, you have the highest likelihood of significantly contributing to your employer, client, or friend. These are the moments when you're most likely to excel. And these are the moments when you are exercising your Advantages.

When you fascinate someone by leading with your Advantages, they open themselves up to your message. Then, and only then, do you have the opportunity to persuade. And the more that you can understand and identify your own one-of-a-kind approach, the more you can *replicate* your success in persuading other people. The goal here is to make your success an intentional and controllable act, rather than a series of lucky (random) breaks.

Think back to those times in your life and career when you achieved a breakthrough. When your Advantages stood out and allowed you to add distinct value and succeed. Now consider the future: What are those moments when you are most likely to be at your best? How can you create more of those moments?

When you look back upon your career successes, see them not as isolated and arbitrary events but as markers pointing to your greatest gifts. By looking at these moments, you can begin to find patterns and understand how you add value.

If you don't know your own value, don't expect anyone else to know it, either.

YOUR DIMENSIONAL PERSONALITY

Ever watch a 3-D movie without the 3-D glasses? It's a distorted jumble of information. You're more likely to feel confused than impressed. But then, when you put on those plastic 3-D glasses, your vision whips into focus. Suddenly, the confusing jumble becomes clear. The scene has depth and meaning. You can grasp the information in front of you, and understand everything that's happening.

In a way, this book functions as your personal 3-D glasses for clearly understanding the patterns happening around you. Situations that once seemed puzzling will now become clear. You'll see how the people around you are communicating according to different Advantages.

Here's an example: Until now, you might have been confused about certain people in your life. Why does that office manager keep coming by your cubicle to ask for an update? Why does that friend of yours brag about her latest professional conquest?

When you have an initial understanding of the seven Advantages, you can already better interpret behavior. You can use the "lens" of the seven Advantages to see what's really happening around you. Once you realize the underlying code of how people communicate, your interactions will become more productive. You will realize why one employee obsesses over details, while another resists sticking to even a basic schedule. It'll begin to make sense why one client begins every meeting with a chat, while another can't ever seem to let his guard down. When you understand the "languages" that people speak, you can more quickly and authentically build a connection.

Know exactly how others see you at your best, so that you can confidently deliver more of your best. See what you're already doing right, and do more of it. Find your wellsprings and multiply them.

I'll point out your patterns in Part II, and give you examples of how to apply them in Part III. In the meantime, let's take a look at how you see other people.

You probably already know that you are attracted to certain personalities, and put off by others. However, as we'll see, the people who attract you are not necessarily the ones you need on your team. You can't recognize who you need around you until you understand the patterns. In fact, the people that you are *least* likely to hang out with might be the ones you *most* need, to balance your traits so that you don't have to focus on those areas.

As we dive deeper into the patterns that go back and forth during every interaction, you'll begin to see why that co-worker who rubs you the wrong way might actually be the perfect fit on certain projects. And you'll see how there's a consistent thread between all the different ways in which you fascinate all the different people in your life.

Sometimes it's easier to see the patterns when you apply them to someone other than yourself. Let's pause for a minute, and put on that pair of "Fascination Advantage" 3-D glasses. Look at the people you already know, and you may get a new perspective of how they're seeing you.

Mentally scroll through your list of key contacts. Think of your clients and customers, your employers and co-workers. Think about how you see them. Consider *why* you see them in a certain way, and *how* that shapes your overall impression of their value.

Think of your co-workers. There's probably someone who bursts into the room with an energetic smile, or someone else who's erudite and restrained. Of these two personalities, one might be your favorite buddy for a quick lunch, while the other is your go-to resource in a pinch. You value them differently, for different reasons, and more or less depending on different circumstances. In the same way, *you* have an effect on your co-workers every time you speak.

You might impress some but annoy others—for exactly the same reason. A trait that acts as an Advantage in one scenario can quickly become a pitfall in others.

If you're an entrepreneur, think about your ideal clients. When you evaluate them, the ones who are your biggest fans, who truly understand and appreciate what you bring to the table, and willingly reward you to do more of your best . . . how would you describe that genre of client? For instance, are they likely to be big-picture thinkers who enthusiastically invest themselves in the brainstorming process? Or are they more likely to be intensely analytical, requiring multiple detailed reports?

If you're a manager, think of your employees. There's the employee who begins each day with a meticulous checklist, but often gets flustered if things change. And then there's the one who can't seem to get in gear until the deadline looms, but then magically delivers the Big Idea. How can you structure your workflow and environment to help each employee deliver to her potential?

While reading about the Archetypes in Part II, think of this as a catalogue filled with the different Advantages to add to your team, or bring out in your existing team. Retain your best employees by helping them amplify their Advantages. As you're interviewing prospects, don't just go by the chemistry in the first meeting, or how they look on paper. Great leaders know that each person on their team will be most likely to "win" when the circumstances are optimal for putting their Advantages to best use. Great leaders provide those conditions as often as possible.

If you are a leader (and really, at some level, who isn't), you'll succeed if you support everyone on your team to focus on their Advantages rather than force-fitting a culture of "better." The more you can help your employees focus on work that allows them to use their natural areas of performance, the more productive and fulfilled they become.

PEOPLE FASCINATE WHEN THEY ARE FASCINATED

In my market research on fascination, we polled 1,059 Americans about the role of fascination in their jobs. We learned that when employees are fascinated in their work, they're more engaged and focused. They are more productive, more purposeful, and more satisfied. They are more loyal. Yet employee engagement is not a one-size-fits-all proposition.

If you know your employees, you can see patterns in how they'll respond to both criticism and praise. You can anticipate what type of first impression they'll make with customers. Everyone has a range of behaviors and a "personality" is not a rigid blueprint; for the most part, people tend to exercise certain traits somewhat consistently and these traits become behavioral patterns. These hidden patterns determine an individual's reputation, relationships, and results.

Hidden patterns determine how you see others. Similarly, patterns determine how others see *you*.

As you're reading through Part II, start to match Archetypes to people you adore or admire (and people who tick you off, but you don't exactly know why). The goal here is not to staple a scorecard to someone's forehead. Rather, the goal is to illustrate that you see others in a certain way—just as the world sees you in a certain way. Perception isn't necessarily reality, but it is connected to perceived value. Your value is directly tied to *how the world sees you*.

You're about to understand which innate Advantages can skyrocket the trajectory of your career. By harnessing the power of that knowledge, you'll become the leader who earns respect, the salesperson who wins the deal, the new hire who gains attention from management.

In a crowded, competitive environment, the most fascinating option always wins.

Unrecognized greatness achieves nothing. Greatness can win only by being noticed and remembered. And in a competitive and overcrowded world, the same is true for you.

You are already fascinating. Our research proves it. Now it's only a matter of applying your Advantages to become *most worthy* of attention.

CHAPTER 2

HOW TO DISCOVER YOUR HIGHEST DISTINCT VALUE

THE SCIENCE AND ART OF FASCINATION

Fascination is an intense focus. When you fascinate your listener, they're more likely to connect with you and remember you.

In certain types of situations, you will fascinate your listener. People will pay close attention to what you say. They'll ask your opinion and value your input. In these moments, you'll feel energized and purposeful, because it's clear you're adding value. In these moments, you're applying your most natural mode of communication.

On the other hand, other situations put you at a real disadvantage. When you communicate in these situations, you'll struggle to get your point across. You won't be confident or feel at ease. You are unlikely to fascinate.

Which types of interactions set you up for success?

Which types of interactions impair your odds of success?

"QUICKSAND" AND "WELLSPRINGS"

Around 1995, there was an iconic Nike commercial in which Michael Jordan soared through the air toward the basket, gliding weightlessly, effortlessly, perfectly, until he released the ball with a swoop through the net. That's fascination. Your mind and body glide effortlessly toward your goal.

Elite athletes talk about being "in the zone." They're not inside their head, worrying or feeling confused. They're not distracted. They don't have to think about what they are doing. (As Nike suggests, they just do it.) When you're in the zone, you're more likely to have an epiphany or reach a solution. As you become less self-conscious, you're more confident, which feels emotionally gratifying.

Fascination Is a Wellspring

You know what fascination feels like. Fascination happens when you're reading a book, and you're so mesmerized by the story that the world outside those pages ceases to exist. Fascination happens when you're engrossed in a cool project at work, and feel so purposeful and focused that you completely lose track of time. It's when you're at a family party and your toddler takes her first steps and for a time, everything else disappears. It's when you're watching a favorite TV show on Netflix, and you become so involved that you lose track of time and run through the entire series in one sitting. When you're leading a meeting, and the words fall perfectly into place. It's when you meet someone new, and you don't have to *pretend* to be interested in what they're saying—you actually are. This is the mental, emotional, and physical state of focus, of being completely engaged. When you're fascinated, you're not pretending or posing. You can drop the mask, and just *be yourself.*

Quicksand

These types of situations feel difficult, even exhausting. You are not in the flow, because you're prevented from communicating in your natural, effortless style.

At first you might be confused why people aren't listening, and eventually you become discouraged and exhausted. If you allow doubts or anxiety to take over, you're less likely to perform at your best.

THE FASCINATION FLOW

The concept of flow was beautifully defined by psychologist Mihaly Csikszentmihalyi: "Being completely involved in an activity for its own sake. The ego falls away. Time flies. Every action, movement, and thought follows inevitably from the previous one. Your whole being is involved, and you're using your skills to the utmost." *

During a highly engaging activity or conversation, your brain surges ahead at peak performance.

Start to become more aware of when you're entering the state of fascination, so that you can create more of these moments in your life. Identify those moments when you become fully focused. Close your eyes, and capture the experience in your mind (unless you are listening to this on an audiobook and driving, in which case you should not close your eyes).

Soon, we will dig into how your personality is most likely to fascinate. But first, I want to bring you inside the surprising science and art of fascination.

THE SCIENCE OF FASCINATION

Turns out there's a reason why fascination gets you in that state of flow. And one of the prime examples of fascination is falling in love.

Falling in love soothes fear and doubt. It heightens your sense of presence in the moment. It increases your focus. And the same thing happens when you fall into a state of fascination. (If you've ever had a crush on somebody, you know what it's like to be fascinated.)

What exactly is going on inside your brain when you enter this euphoric state of intense concentration? To understand how our brain operates in a state of fascination, I did a series of interviews over the course of three years with a number of scientists, including respected neuroradiologist Dr. Mark Herbst. He describes neuroimaging studies in which volunteers who were deeply in love viewed pictures of their loved one. Just the sight of the photograph would deactivate the amygdala, which is the brain's fear center.

Emotionally, you experience fascination as a feeling of confidence and clarity. It's a wellspring. You are calm and focused, your brain enters a semi-euphoric state. Dr. Herbst describes this as "relaxed happiness," and the opposite of fear.

In a study published in the *American Journal of Neuroradiology*,

---

* Do you have a hobby? In my national study, we found that among people who do have a hobby, 92% find it fascinating, while only 68% of employees find their work fascinating.

researchers took a group of golfers and separated them into two sets: One set was expert golfers, the other, novices. They asked both sets of golfers to mentally imagine swinging a golf club on the tee, over and over again. The two groups of golfers imagined their own swing while they were inside an MRI machine so the researchers could map their brain activity.

And the result? As skill level increases, less brainpower is used.

The better the golfer—in other words, the lower the handicap—the less of the brain was used in mentally preparing for each swing. These golfers were in a state of flow. When you can achieve this fascination state in your job, you become the most valuable to your customers, your manager, and your company, because you're able to deliver at the very top of your game.

Inexperienced golfers, on the other hand, used far more of their brain; their sense of uncertainty and unfamiliarity required strenuous focus. Their brains were in a state of disruption. If you're leading a conference call with your colleagues, and anxiety is flooding your brain with doubts, you're less likely to enthrall your listeners. You can't get on a roll if you're distracted by fears, such as "What's the next slide? Am I too loud? Are they still on the call . . . or are they just scrolling through Facebook?".

In your wellspring, you can use your natural personality. You aren't distracted by fear and anxiety. You can relax and get into your groove. Your brain happily hums along. In this state, you can achieve your greatest breakthroughs. This state is one of the most powerful experiences in all of humanity, leading to world-changing discoveries, unfathomable feats of athleticism, and the greatest examples of artistic achievement.

In this state of "superfocus," not only do you get more done—you might also earn more. When you feel connected to your work, you are more effective and potentially more lucrative. Our market research found a surprising link between fascination and income.

The higher a person's income, the more likely they are to find their job fascinating.

Why is this? For many people, higher-level work is inherently more fascinating than entry-level work. But more to the point, when you love what you do, you reap far more personal satisfaction from your career and invest more of yourself. It's probably a chicken-and-egg cycle. If you find your work fascinating, you're more likely to rack up a series of successes. And, simultaneously, higher-paying jobs often provide juicier and satisfying challenges than their lower-paying counterparts. As Dr. Herbst might say, you "fall in love" with what you do for a living when it brings you joy and meaning.

When you feel fascinated by your work, you become more excited about what you're doing, which feeds your achievements. When you're fully immersed in a task, you're more able to reject distraction. You might not even hear your phone beeping, or notice people walking by your office. Your brain can more effectively battle disruption by suppressing outside stimulation.

When your listener's brain is relaxed and focused, they are more likely to get in that same flow with you. They are less likely to be distracted when you communicate.

Dr. Herbst describes fascination as a "single concentration on one point," as in meditation. In a recent study, researchers found that experienced meditators were able to use their intense concentration to protect themselves from distraction. The researchers were surprised. (After all, during meditation, aren't people supposed to be turning their brains off?) Participants meditated in the MRI machine, and the scientists played random beeps to see how well they ignored the distractions. It turned out that experienced meditators activated the parts of the brain that suppress interruptions and they were able to completely block out the beeps. They protected their own state of fascination.

When *you* are experiencing this state of flow, you are also more likely to fascinate *others*. You are less likely to get distracted and confused. This builds your listener's confidence in your message (whether they consciously realize it or not).

Whether you're trying to sell widgets or trying to "sell" environmental issues, you're more likely to achieve success if you can bring your listener's brain into this state of intense focus. When you fascinate someone, you become most worthy of his attention.

If you fascinate a client, he's more likely to want to connect with you. His barriers drop. He ceases to be skeptical or cynical. He is more likely to believe what you say and trust your opinion. It's almost as if you've pushed a button in his brain.

How can you tell if you're successfully engaging someone? Just look.

As you are reading this, are both of your feet planted flat on the floor? If so, body language indicates you'll be more fascinated by this next round of insights, more open to my opinions and ideas, and more likely to make a decision in my favor. (Go ahead. Take a moment to get those feet on the ground, and I'll explain more in a minute.)

So how can you tell if you're fascinating someone?

Let's say you're going through a routine sales presentation for a client. Are you able to tell from your client's body language if you're successfully engaging her (or if she's actually stabbing her palm with a sharp object under the table while praying for you to finish)?

Body language expert Dr. Jack Brown says that when a client is fascinated, he becomes less self-conscious. His face slackens, eyes widen, pupils dilate, palms relax.

You might already know these basics of body language, and already realize that a scowl is not a good sign. But if you really want to get serious about fascinating your client—if you want to sell an idea or a product—get his feet on the floor, uncrossed.

People tend to make a decision more in your favor if their feet are solidly on the floor. They are more likely to make a positive decision and to act on it. This holds true whether you are asking them to clean their room, or go out for dinner, or cast a certain vote.

If your client's arms are crossed, watch out. People rarely cross arms in their own home, unless having an argument or seeing a politician on TV who ticks them off. However, if you can get someone to uncross their arms, their brain will be figuratively "uncrossed" and more open to your ideas as well. The body leads the brain, says Brown. Not only are crossed arms a signal of disengagement, but they can actually cause it: People who cross their arms even retain less information.

You can "uncross" your own arms by making sure that as you communicate, your hands and arms are not visually blocked. Your client will trust you more. If you're giving a speech, that means you should not use a handheld mike, because it creates a barrier between you and your audience. And if you're a trial attorney, it means your jury should have armrests.

Armrests? Yes, says Brown. If jurors cross their arms, they retain less. Again, the body leads the brain. Open body, open mind. You're more likely to fascinate someone if both of their feet are planted on the floor, and their arms are on either side.*

When you fascinate customers, they become totally, completely focused on you and your message. They stop fidgeting. They stop texting. They stop thinking about to-do lists and what to feed their kids for dinner. They stop focusing on all the shiny objects competing for attention, and focus completely on you. They emotionally connect with you.

HOW EMOTION LEADS TO ENGAGEMENT

When the brain experiences an emotional connection, that emotion is almost impossible to ignore. Your brain can forget data, but you're less likely to forget an emotion. Researchers have long known that emotion stimulates learning and memory. In his book *Brain Rules*, John Medina tells us that the brain remembers the emotional component of an experience better than any other aspect.

Dr. Medina also reveals why traditional learning formats are so ineffective: "If you wanted to create an education environment that was directly opposed to what the brain was good at doing, you probably would design something like a classroom. If you wanted to create a business environment that was directly opposed to what the brain was good at doing, you probably would design something like a cubicle. And if you wanted to change things, you might have to tear down both and start over." Traditional meetings are more like classrooms and cubicles, which inhibits the brain's connection to the material. Want your listener to engage and remember your presentation or ideas? Consider an alternate seating configuration or even alternate location for your big presentation, creating an ideal environment for your client to become fascinated by your messages.

---

*What about eye contact, that dictionary of body language? Dr. Brown dropped this bomb: People who don't enjoy eye contact won't be as satisfied "in the bedroom." They won't be as open, they'll have less enjoyment, and they will not engage as often and in as much depth. Eye contact, he says, is predictive of sexual activity. If a couple who is having trouble stares into each other's eyes for three minutes daily, it will bring forth romance, affection, and fascination.

A tip for applying this learning: To get people to "fall in love" with your ideas, don't solely rely on numbers and data. People can tune out this type of input relatively easily. But if you communicate with a story or experience, you create an emotion. Start your next meeting with a story instead of a spreadsheet. Make your audience *feel* as well as *think*. Connect emotionally with them by telling a personal anecdote that reinforces the point of your presentation. Or draw upon a nostalgic shared memory. Once you inspire emotion, your listener will be less likely to disengage, and more likely to remember and respond to your message.

Hard science gives us some of the answers. We can study how your customer's brain will activate when engaged by conversation, and we can record how co-workers respond to your presentation by watching their body language. But science only gives us part of the story.

Our journey of fascination now continues outside the ivory tower, beyond the safe confines of academia. Science can only take us so far when it comes to fascination, just as Myers-Briggs can only take us so far when it comes to understanding how others perceive you.

Science has many of the answers, but not all. To get the full picture, we need to see how the world sees you. For that, we turn to branding and marketing. So it's time to leave the fluorescent lights of the research lab behind and wave good-bye to the scientists who guided us up to this point.

Say hello to the art of fascination.

THE ART OF FASCINATION

Think of your own favorite brands, maybe Apple or Pinkberry, Southwest or Zappos. When consumers are fascinated by a brand, it no longer has to compete on price. All great brands triumph over the three threats of distraction, competition, and commoditization in the same way: by *adding distinct value*.

Together we'll overcome those three threats by emphasizing how *you* are most likely to add distinct value. We've glimpsed the science of fascination, and now we'll explore the art of fascination.

When I first started as a junior copywriter in the 1990s, the branding process baffled me. How could anyone possibly distill the intricacies of market research, honing the numbers into an idea sharp enough to cut through people's natural resistance, into their hearts and brains, ultimately connecting with the magical decision-making hot button that decides which toothpaste or hotel room or politician to choose? How does a boring product become a fascinating one, so that it doesn't have to compete on price? Why do people become intensely devoted to a certain brand of coffee (Starbucks) or running shoe (Nike) or vodka (Ketel One), when the actual product itself has very little appreciable difference?

At this point in my career, I couldn't see the patterns in the art of fascination. To my inexperienced eyes, branding looked like alchemy, transforming commodities into gold.

Today, after two decades of developing campaigns for many of the most successful brands in the world, I recognize the patterns. The most successful brands fascinate their customers.

Fascination really *is* alchemy. It transforms ordinary companies into exceptionally desirable brands. And, as we'll see, it makes otherwise ordinary people extraordinarily valuable to their company and customers. Your personality's most fascinating qualities are worth more than gold.

WHEN A $100 PAIR OF SUNGLASSES IS WORTH $400

In my Study of Fascination market research, I found that people will pay up to four times more for a product that fascinates them in some way. For instance, sunglasses! Here's a common example of how fascination increases perceived value for a commodity product. Morton salt costs about 187% more than a generic equivalent. Yet it's exactly the same salt. The salt itself is a commodity. You're paying a premium for your emotional connection to the brand.*

---

*Want something a little more spicy than Morton salt? Chew on this: People will pay only $33 for a "satisfactory" tattoo, but will pay $88 for one that's "intensely captivating."

THREE COMMUNICATION LESSONS FROM THE MOST FASCINATING BRANDS

1. **Don't focus on how you are *similar* to others, but how you are *different*.** Leading brands stand out by sharpening their points of difference. The more clearly and distinctly a brand can pinpoint its differences, the more valuable it becomes. If a brand can carve out a very clear spot in people's minds, the product or service ceases to be a commodity. As we'll see in Part II, *different personality* Advantages can be more valuable than *similar* ones.

2. **Your differences can be very small and simple.** The reality is, most products are virtually indistinguishable from their competitors. Yet a leading brand can build a strong competitive edge around very minor differences. Similarly, you don't need to be dramatically different than everyone else—your difference can be minute, as long as it is clearly defined. The more competitive the market, the more crucial this becomes.

3. **Once you "own" a difference, you can charge more money.** People pay more for products and people who add distinct value in some way. And just as customers pay more for fascinating brands, employers pay higher salaries for employees who stand out with a specific benefit. If you are an entrepreneur or small business owner, your clients and customers will have a higher perceived value of your time and services if they can clearly understand why you are different than your competitors.

The more crowded the environment, the more crucial these lessons become.

When a product is successful it fascinates its customers; it is treated very differently than the generic version. People are willing to not only spend more, but spend more time with it. They make a greater effort to find it, they take better care of it, and they derive more enjoyment from it. The same is true for you.

When you make it easy for others to understand *how you are different*, and *what you do best*, you're more likely to be rewarded for it. In a distracted and competitive world, people need shortcuts. Give them a shortcut to understand your most valuable qualities.

The key here is to fully recognize your *differences*, rather than just your *strengths*. The reality is, strengths can be copied. It's true for your company, and also for you. Products can be replicated. Benefits can be improved upon, secret formulas uncovered, winning systems beaten. People can outdo your strengths. But nobody can outdo who you are. Your personality is the only aspect of your work that nobody can copy. People can copy your product, your pricing, your actions, your recipe or program or formula. But they can never replicate who you are. Who you are is the greatest differentiator you've ever had.

Eventually I left the world of television commercials and global print campaigns to become an entrepreneur. Yet my role today is essentially the same as it was when I worked in advertising. The difference is, I used to help brands communicate their most valuable qualities. Now I do it for people. I show you the best of how the world sees you.

I want to help you identify your highest value, and then give you a tagline to easily convey it, and live it. Instead of building your brand around your superficial benefits or a commoditized value proposition, I'm going to give you the words to build your communication around your most extraordinary natural abilities. By the end of this book, you'll have the words to do this, with your Anthem.

When I was a copywriter, one of my early clients was BMW. Their long-standing tagline, as you probably recall, is "The Ultimate Driving Machine." A few years later, I was a copywriter on MINI Cooper. As you probably know, that's a different car and different brand, with a different tagline: "Let's Motor."

Those two taglines convey the distinct personalities of the cars: BMW is victorious, a bit intimidating, and unapologetically built around engineering. "The Ultimate Driving Machine" describes BMW cars, the BMW company culture, and the values of BMW owners. On the other hand, MINI Cooper is fun, inclusive, and inspiring. (You can imagine a sporty little MINI inviting you to jump in the car for a road trip: "Let's Motor!")

You should have your own tagline, too. It should encapsulate what you offer at your best, in just a handful of words, to attract exactly the right person to you.

Your Anthem: The Tagline for Your Personality

In Part III, we'll select the exact words to describe your personality's core specialty. This is your Anthem.

Your Anthem is a very short phrase, only a few words long, identifying your personality's most valuable difference. It's a quick snapshot of your defining quality.

The Anthem exercise itself is fairly simple, because most of the "heavy lifting" is being done by the Fascination Advantage system. Your report will even include a customized list of words and phrases you can use to describe yourself. It's easy to do. More importantly, it will allow you to make it easy for your listener to become more fascinated by you. You can make it easy for your co-workers and customers to understand *how you are different*, and *what you do best*.

Your Anthem is your own personal tagline. It's almost a mantra. A rallying cry. You can orient your whole career around this short phrase, because it points to your personality's strongest area of performance.

If BMW is "the ultimate driving machine," your Anthem is the ultimate differentiator.

It's a compelling future, right? Now think of your listener. Think of how you can create this experience for them, and how valuable this is for *them*.

Fascination is a force of attraction, one that we can channel. Instead of just waiting for happy accidents to happen, we can predict and control them. We can harness it and apply it to enrich and deepen almost every aspect of our lives.

TO BEWITCH OR HOLD CAPTIVE

The word *fascination* is one of the oldest in written language, coming from Latin:

Fascinare: *to bewitch, or hold captive; be impossible to ignore.*

Fascination is a force that can rule our thinking and our emotions, like falling in love. Your personality has certain captivating qualities. As we explore the art of fascination, you'll begin to understand what makes you fascinating to other people. You'll see why people are most likely to want to hire you, promote you, connect with you, buy from you, follow you, respect you, and just plain *like* you. Or perhaps even fall in love with you.

It's a virtuous cycle: When you *feel* more fascinated, you *become* more fascinating. And it has little to do with the traditional idea of being charming or charismatic. Which is good. Charisma isn't exactly an equal-opportunity trait.

Sometimes the ability to fascinate is confused with *charisma*. Yet charisma is only one flavor of fascination. (Soon, we will explore different "Archetypes," such as Ringleaders and Talents, who are often quite charismatic, and other Archetypes, such as Wise Owls and Royal Guards, who are more observant and reflective. Yet each of these personalities can be equally fascinating.) To understand why, let's give a moment to the attention-getting quality of charisma.

Charisma is easy to identify, yet hard to describe. It's personal magnetism. The X-factor. In one person it might be an air of confidence, while in someone else it might be a sense of mystery. While it's relatively simple to define a person's skills, experience, and achievements on a résumé, charisma is more elusive on paper. In Hollywood cattle call auditions, when hundreds of beautiful aspiring starlets walk through the door, one or two will get the audition because they have an indefinable allure that mesmerizes the director and the camera. In business, charisma can help a job applicant rise to the top of the pile, even if the interviewer has a hard time putting his finger on exactly why he chose that particular candidate.

Yet charisma plays favorites. You either have charisma, or you don't. You were either born with it, or you weren't.

There are even classes that *teach* charisma. And for a short time, you can *pretend* to have an instantly magnetic personality. But that takes a huge amount of effort, and it doesn't last. Fake tans, fake gold, and fake laughter quickly lose their charm, and so does fake charm.

Frequently, people mistakenly think that they should fascinate in a certain way. Not so. There is room for many options, and in fact when it comes to teams, there's a need for many options. Some Archetypes are more rare. In situations or teams that can benefit from their unusual advantages, these Archetypes become more precious.

THE RINGLEADER AND THE ARCHITECT

Ad agency life includes a lot of stress, personality, and caffeine. Ferociously competitive new pitches for new clients drive the machine. A single pitch for a marquee client such as Porsche or Bacardi or Harley-Davidson might cost more money than an agency makes in its entire first year. For account executives, the process might include weeks of late nights and cold pizza.

In this zero-sum game, careers can be made and broken, fortunes won and lost. Even trivial casual communications could mean the addition or subtraction of jobs. To add to the maddening competition, politics skew the game. A particularly good dinner conversation with the client the night before the actual morning meeting could have a bigger impact on the results than the actual presentation. (Don Draper is still alive and well and he just ordered another scotch at lunch.)

In more traditional midwestern agencies, promoting oneself was often viewed as pretentious or flashy. That was the location of my first job as a junior copywriter, at an agency headquartered in Minnesota. The culture was dominated by an old-fashioned work ethic and humility.

This conscientious approach was embodied in an account executive with whom I worked. He was quiet and unassuming, yet exceptionally brilliant. His mind was as precise as a Swiss timepiece. Had he taken the Fascination Advantage assessment, he would likely have been the Architect (a combination of Prestige + Mystique, with the advantages of being *skillful*, *restrained*, and *polished*).

One day, the new, charismatic agency president showed up, wearing daring red glasses and a bold attitude to match. He was known as a rainmaker, a creative force who could woo new clients. When he arrived, the account executive made a quiet aside that the president and his glasses were too "hey-look-at-me." He was The Ringleader (Power + Passion, with the advantages of being *motivating*, *spirited*, and *compelling*).

To the account executive's modest taste, he was the distasteful equivalent of a dog-and-pony show. But at the same time, from the quiet account executive's point of view, it likely called into question whether he should adjust his own approach in order to fascinate in a more conspicuous way.

The president and account executive offered different competitive advantages. Both of these men were exceptional in their jobs. Both were respected by peers and co-workers. One competed by leveraging his personal magnetism, the other by quietly and systematically solving problems. They shared the same goal, which was to captivate clients. And even while they were on the same team, they had completely different ways of pitching new business. Which Archetype triumphed?

Does a pair of trendy spectacles win the day, with the Advantages of being *motivating*, *spirited*, and *compelling*? Or is practical diligence a more compelling choice, with the Advantages of being *skillful*, *restrained*, and *polished*?

The answer is . . . both. But in totally different ways.

Individually, they each maximized their own Advantages to fascinate the client. Together, their differences complemented the team's ability to win. There is no one right way of fascinating people. Sometimes the president would dramatically read a TV commercial script, to wow the client with a big idea. Yet when high-level thinking was in order, the account executive captured everyone's attention with his strategic approach.

Together they were a one-two punch for the agency, yin and yang counterparts that supplemented and optimized each other. Had these two men tried to mirror each other, their differences would not have increased the agency's odds of winning. As a result, the agency was world class.

The most successful teams allow everyone to focus on how they are different, rather than how they are similar. Ringleaders and Architects communicate differently, and add value differently. Although these two personalities may not always see eye to eye, the team wins in the end with the addition of multiple Advantages.

100% YOURSELF TRUMPS 100% PERFECT

Your Archetype might be extroverted or introspective; it might be bubbly or intense. What's certain is that you are already captivating, whether you are "charismatic" (read this word with air quotes) or not. You don't have to change yourself, only to become more of yourself.

The more you can amplify your innate Advantages, the less likely you are to be a commodity, and the more likely you are to be heard and remembered. This is the key to differentiating yourself. It's how you are most likely to rise above the crowd and excel—to effortlessly glide toward the basket, like Michael Jordan. It doesn't take effort to be yourself.

Being yourself is not a struggle. In fact, it makes you more relaxed and at ease. You don't learn how to be fascinating; you unlearn how to be boring.

THE LANGUAGE OF FASCINATION

In his book *Men Are from Mars, Women Are from Venus*, John Gray writes that relationship problems between men and women can be summarized with a metaphor: Men are from one planet, women from another. Each gender understands the language and customs of its own planet, but the other planet often seems foreign. This leads to frequent misunderstandings and conflicting expectations.

Similarly, Gary Chapman describes five ways to express and experience love in his book *The 5 Love Languages: How to Express Heartfelt Commitment to Your Mate*. He describes the five love languages: quality time, acts of service, physical touch, gifts, and words of affirmation. (I'm a "words of affirmation" person, myself.)

Just as men and women might be from different planets, or speak different love languages, you speak different "fascination languages" than people around you at work. This can, at times, lead to discomfort and misinterpretations. For example, Innovation personalities speak the language of *creativity*. They have an edge in situations that call for big, exciting, untraditional ideas. They tend to be focused on the big picture rather than details. However, imagine if the Innovation personality has a co-worker with primary Alert. As you might recall, Alert speaks the language of *details*. They are organized and to the point.

Uh-oh. This is a very common problem in the workplace. To an Alert personality, someone with primary Innovation Advantage can seem unpredictable, disorganized, or even reckless. (Alert is quietly thinking, "Enough already. Let's just make a decision and move on.") To the Innovation personality, Alert can seem rigid or micromanaging. (Innovation says, "Stop pressuring me with deadlines. Let's explore options before we lock ourselves in!")

Though they may not always see eye to eye, this seemingly incompatible pair can actually be a match made in heaven. Their opposing Advantages can compensate for each other's pitfalls. Once they have a basic understanding of each other's native language and recognize that their differences are actually producing a more balanced outcome, together they'll make the organization stronger as a whole.

Once we decipher your own native language of fascination, you can use it to stand out from the crowd. Like this book you're reading, it's part science, part art.

It's your personality's own secret sauce. A sauce made with *umami*, the fifth flavor.

THE NEW FIFTH FLAVOR

Quick, name the four different types of flavors that your tongue can taste . . .

sweet
sour
bitter
salty

Right?

For thousands of years, people believed that these four comprised the full extent of your tongue's taste repertoire. However, recently a fifth flavor has been discovered. Or more accurately—it was *identified* and *named*, since the flavor itself has existed as long as humans have had taste buds.

This new flavor is umami: a savory taste that coats the taste buds with a lingering impression that dallies on the tongue. Your mouth perceives umami as sublimely gratifying in a rich, round, brothy sort of way.

Umami is a distinct experience, one that's more of a sensation than just a taste. You know it when you taste it, but it's not easy to describe or categorize. Not exactly a flavor in itself, but it makes other flavors more meaty and luscious. A flavorsome nonflavor. Your mouth's savory Shangri-la.

Comparatively speaking, regular flavors are simplistic, and one-dimensional. While your tongue can relatively quickly and easily identify the flavors of bitter and sour, umami is a flavor bomb all its own. Our mouths contain taste receptors specifically to appreciate the proteinish flavors of finely aged steak, slow-cooked veal stock, a cheeseburger with ketchup, anchovies, and . . . lest we forget, Smoky Bacon Pringles.

Umami has a long and delectable history, dating back to ancient foods including Parmesan cheese with sun-dried tomatoes in Rome, and seaweed dashi in Japan. Just about every human who has ever walked the planet has experienced umami, yet only very recently did we name it.

Giving umami its name legitimized it and gave it a well-deserved place in the world of taste vocabulary. The point is that once you have a word to frame a phenomenon, you tend to perceive that phenomenon differently. When you assign a word to a concept, it becomes more tangible. The word itself helps define what would be an otherwise abstract concept, giving people a common platform on which to agree that they are familiar with the experience.

Umami was simultaneously and independently identified by two different experts: a chemistry professor at the Imperial University of Tokyo, and a chef in France. They looked at flavor in a new way, reconceiving it, distilling it down, identifying the building blocks, and showing how it systematically fits in with the rest. Before that, umami was only a vague impression.

Similarly, your personality has underlying qualities that are yet to be named. As you become more refined and skilled at understanding how the world sees you, you can begin to name and understand the Advantages that make up the highest and best use of your personality. Whether you draw people in with stories or influence them with opinions, your communication will stand out, because you're deliberately applying your Advantages into your communication in an umami-ish way. Once you can "name" your Advantages and identify your Archetype, you can put a strategic framework in place to intentionally fascinate in a way that leverages your natural differentiators. (And later, when you write your Anthem in Part III, you will be able to describe yourself in two or three words.)

Once you know which two Advantages you're already using to the highest degree, you can synchronize the various aspects of your interactions with others so that you have a defined niche, and so that you don't have to keep reinventing the wheel. When you can clearly see your own most specific and valuable traits, they become familiar and easily identifiable qualities.

Your secret sauce is your own flavor, your umami of personality. This is your own flavor bomb. Consciously or not, people perceive it from the moment they meet you. Your own umami can be a subtle force of attraction that pulls your listener in your direction. It enriches your words, it adds flavor to your messages, it brings depth and nuance to your presentations, your conversations, your writing. Your umami has always been there, yet until someone points it out, you don't realize how it's shaping people's perception of you. When you consciously channel this force of attraction, your communication is more likely to be savored by your audience. They'll eat up what you say, what you write, what you sell.

Do you know which signals you're sending to attract others, or push them away? The more accurately you understand how others are reading *your* cues, and the more accurately you read *their* cues, the more successful your communication will be. Consider what type of first impression you're making. (Personally, I'd say you make an outstanding first impression. On me, at least—based solely on your taste in books.)

Think of the thousands of cues you unintentionally exude, all day long. Every time you hold eye contact a millisecond too long when angered . . . every sentence that trails as you lose confidence in a meeting . . . every audible exhale that broadcasts your frustration . . . every stammer you leave on an awkward voicemail to a client. They shape how the world sees you.

You send signals about your value, too, and these enhance people's perception of you. Your eyes might light up and excite others when you get an idea, or your voice might confidently emphasize strong points. The people around you read these signals, whether they consciously realize it or not.

When these seemingly unrelated fragments come together, they form a telling picture of what we really think, how we feel, what we desire, and how we are most likely to succeed. This is your "halo effect."

YOUR FASCINATION HALO EFFECT

Have you heard of the halo effect? It describes the brain's tendency to quickly form overall opinions, often based on one trait. For example, if we determine that a person is intelligent, we might also imagine that they are successful or hardworking. The halo effect explains how people quickly form positive first impressions, from Steve Jobs and the iPhone to love at first sight.

You also create your own halo effect. It radiates all around you, encircling you. Your halo is based on those signals you (intentionally or unintentionally) emit every time you walk into a room. These simple first impressions become the basis for people's whole perception of you, and your value. Once you understand your halo, you can shine more brightly in a crowded field or marketplace.

How does the world see your halo? Which of your personality traits defines how the world sees you? When you are using your personality Advantages, you create your fascination halo effect.

The more information you can have about your fascination halo, and how you're perceived by others, the more you can predict how others will respond to your communication. Yet another reason why first impressions, and knowing and leveraging your Advantages, are so critical.

Over the long run, quiet or shy or low-key personalities can be just as fascinating as the most vibrant ones. If you're soft-spoken or introverted, you can stand out through reliability or discretion or any number of traits that are more introspective. (For examples of personalities that can superbly succeed in these ways, see The Veiled Strength or The Anchor.)

Throughout your career, you will compete against people who are more established, more famous, more connected, more specialized. But they can't be you. They can't capture your highest distinct value. Only you have you.

The more you can you-ify your career, to infuse it with double helpings of you-ness, the more distinct value you will add. It's your quintessence: the purest and most concentrated essence of yourself. Over time, job titles change. Companies change. Clients change. But who you are is everlasting.

So how do you find your you-ness? Let's review how the pieces fit together.

STAND OUT, OR DON'T BOTHER

Once you understand how the world sees you, you also gain insight into what makes you different. This is critical, because once you understand what makes you *different*, you can leverage those differences to avoid commoditization.

You are perfect for certain things. You are wrong for others. You do not have to be perfect for everything.

Find the challenges that you're truly perfect for, rather than merely adequate for. Find the situations in which you distinguish yourself, situations where you can exercise the Advantages of your Archetype that allow you to fascinate effortlessly.

If you look back over the course of your life, and pinpoint those occasions when you had so-called failures, you'll likely find that you failed because somebody asked you to do something that you simply weren't built for. This is not your fault, any more than it's your fault if you're allergic to pollen or hamsters.

Me, I'm allergic to pre-algebra.

In the seventh grade, my math teacher described how my creative thinking should be less erratic, and more consistent. Take a look at the report card I include here. (No value judgment there, right?) She debated between a C and a D for my pre-algebra. But if you read what she says, you'll see I got an A for creativity.

Maybe, if I'd worked with a tutor or studied through every weekend, I could have marginally pulled up my pre-algebra grade. But would it have been worth it, at the cost of developing my love of words? (Mrs. Stevenson might disagree, but I say no.) We will never be our most successful when evaluated according to criteria that are a natural disadvantage.

Here's what I now understand: Mrs. Stevenson's report card perfectly summarizes my personality strong suit, and pitfall. I don't naturally organize information into a highly systematized order of black or white rules. When I read Mrs. Stevenson's words that day, on the way home from school, I remember feeling really down on myself. Why did I have to be so *creative*?

EPISCOPAL HIGH SCHOOL
TEACHER'S REPORT

Student _Sally Hogshead_   Form _I_ Date _March 1, 1982_

Subject _Pre-Algebra_   Advisor _Dr. Dyer_

	Excellent	Good	Satisfactory	Poor	Unsatisfactory
Progress	—	—	✓	—	—
Effort	—	—	✓	—	—
Class Participation	—	—	✓	—	—
Homework Preparation	—	—	✓	—	—
Conduct	—	✓	—	—	—

There is a fine line in math between being creative and being lunatic. I will continue to support Sally in using her creativity but becoming more consistent in her work.

	Exam	Grade
First Trimester	C+	C
Second Trimester	D+	C
Third Trimester	—	—
Year		—

Estimated Grade ____

Teacher _Barbara Stephenson_

What about you? Those times in your life when you supposedly didn't measure up, when you didn't get the job or make the grade . . . is it possible that you were being expected to excel in a way that simply didn't play to your Advantages? In Part II, I'll take you inside your *dormant* Advantage—your natural *disadvantage*. This is the mode of communication that is most exhausting and stressful for you. Once you know your personality's dormant

Advantage, you'll understand why certain tasks feel like struggling through quicksand, and how to avoid spending your energy on those traps.*

Here's an example: You might be right-handed. If someone put a pencil in your left hand and asked you to write with that left hand, you could, theoretically. However, it would feel awkward, you probably wouldn't get optimal results, and it sure would take a lot more effort. Similarly, if you have an employee with primary Mystique Advantage, and you expect her to sparkle with gregarious banter while schmoozing clients, you might be disappointed. But does the problem lie with her characteristics, or with your expectations?

My personality's Archetype communicates with creativity, because my Archetype is The Catalyst.

....

The Catalyst = Passion + Innovation: out-of-the-box, social, energizing

....

I'll be most successful in situations that allow me to communicate and differentiate myself through being *out-of-the-box*, *energizing*, and *social*.

Your so-called failures also have another side. You can look at them as backbreaking, often painful defeats, or see them as defining moments. I prefer the latter: They are the rallying cry to the way in which you are most likely to add distinct value.

Mrs. Stevenson called my work *erratic*. (And yes, my work probably *was* erratic, as pre-algebra goes.) Yet, just for a minute, think about that word. *Erratic* means unpredictable. Not following predictable patterns. Once might say that "erratic" is the flip side of "creative."

You have a pitfall, too. You'll find it inside your Fascination Advantage report. You can go off track when you do a job that doesn't suit you, or you work in the wrong environment, or you try using skills that aren't natural to

---

*Think about our educational system. Are we identifying each child's natural mode of communication, so they can flourish in their greatest Advantages? In my future research, I want to develop a version of the Fascination Advantage for kids. Imagine being able to understand how every child in the classroom naturally communicates, so that each one can learn and express themselves in their own unique way.

you. For example, The Maestro's pitfall is being *overly independent*. The Mediator's pitfall is *overanalysis*. And The Catalyst's pitfall is . . . being *erratic*.

I've measured over twenty thousand Catalysts, as I write this in 2014. Overwhelmingly they are creative types who dislike rigid structure. Catalysts like to multitask and explore a wide range of options. They can be perceived as *erratic* when doing tasks such as preparing long Excel docs, or doing pre-algebra.

The same is true for you, in your job, your relationships, and your life. If you're trying to force yourself into a one-size-fits-all profile, you can do it for a while, but it will exhaust you. If you're role-playing in your job, you're probably pretty tired and demoralized.

Who are you *not*? Understanding who you are *not* is a cornerstone to becoming more of who you *are*. To explain what I mean, let's return to the world of flavors. Specifically, the flavors of vanilla and pistachio.

ARE YOU VANILLA? OR PISTACHIO?

My refrigerator is always stocked up with vanilla ice cream. We intentionally buy plain vanilla, because even though nobody *loves* vanilla ice cream, nobody *hates* it. It appeals to the maximum number of people with the minimum whining. You can put almost anything on top of vanilla ice cream and suddenly it becomes a sundae. Vanilla is a crowd pleaser.

Far fewer people, on the other hand, like pistachio ice cream. It's a distinct and polarizing choice. Yet while fewer people buy pistachio, it has a competitive edge: The people who like pistachio usually love it. Re-e-e-a-lly love it. Crazy-love it. Pistachio focuses on serving a tightly defined core with a distinct point of difference. People will drive across town for it, they'll pay more for it, they'll talk about it and remember it.

Pistachio doesn't try to please everyone. It successfully engages a minority of the population really, really well. Vanilla, on the other hand, is a commodity. A flavor for the masses, appealing to the broadest range of situations and people.

You *can* be the vanilla ice cream of your category, if you're already the most famous, or if you have the biggest budget to market yourself. (More on that later.) In this case, you can afford to be a little bit boring. You already have high awareness and sales, so you don't need people to love you and champion for you. Yet while vanilla might be an easy choice for the majority, it's not necessarily the right choice for *you*.

The smaller base of pistachio-loving customers has the potential to become intensely dedicated. Even fanatical. Pistachio defeats commoditization. In our Study of Fascination, we found when people experience a brand that they perceive as fascinating, the majority of them will talk about it with friends and in social media.

By embracing the pistachio within your personality, you create a base of devoted fans. When you stop trying to be all things to all people, you can stop worrying about being *liked* and start building relationships that allow you to be *loved*.

If you are not creating a negative response from somebody, you're probably not very fascinating to anybody.

Odds are high that your competition is not very fascinating to anybody. As with any bell curve, most people will cluster smack-dab in the middle, where vanilla and chocolate and strawberry live: in the comfort zone. That's fine. Let your competitors continue down their blissfully ignorant path toward dangerously unremarkable vanilladom. You have a more fascinating flavor to serve.*

If you don't have the biggest marketing budget, or if you're not the most famous, you can compete only by being more fascinating.

This has always been one of my hard-core beliefs for my advertising clients. When I was twenty-seven, I opened my first ad agency, built on a premise: *Have the biggest marketing budget, or be the most fascinating.* This rule still holds true today. If you have the biggest marketing budget in your category, you can be "safe" and easy. You can afford to buy more ads than your competitors. You can hammer in a message, over and over, wham-wham-wham, until people are forced to remember.

Dell is vanilla, and Apple is pistachio. Ford Taurus is vanilla, and Fiat 500 is pistachio. Starbucks used to be pistachio, but now it has become more vanilla (albeit a vanilla macchiato). It's expensive to be vanilla, because you're not fascinating. You have to either lower your price or increase your marketing budget.

---

*Pistachio not quite fascinating enough for you? Head to Venezuela for a double scoop of Viagra ice cream. Or on a hot summer day, you can stroll with your sweetie in Tokyo and share a cone of Raw Horse Flesh ice cream.

When a brand becomes a commodity, customers switch back and forth to get the best deal, upgrading and downgrading, flirting without long-term commitment. People don't commit if there is nothing rare or memorable offered!

Many category leaders keep their position by simply spending more on marketing than anyone else. The product itself is a commodity, and not different or better than the competition, yet people still buy it because they're aware of it. The company's enormous marketing budget has ensured that even if people don't recognize their product or service, they will have a sufficient familiarity with it to buy it anyway.

But once you're perceived as the vanilla in your company or industry (because you are just peddling the same services as everyone else, or doing the same tasks), you're in a vulnerable position. Your market value will not increase as quickly as it otherwise might, or it could even decline. You may lose your job to someone who's cheaper, younger, and willing to be the pistachio.

How to Beat Commoditization with Pistachio

- **Identify ways in which you are distinctly unique.**
- **Rather than spreading yourself thin by trying to be good at everything, insanely overdeliver in these specific areas.**
- **Don't just have customers. Have fanatics.**
- **Don't be afraid to "strategically polarize" your audience. If you are right for everyone, you're probably not fascinating anyone. The goal is not to be liked by everyone, but to be loved by a core audience.**

To build any multifaceted robust system or organization or team, you'll probably want a diverse range of Advantages. When a group has an extremely high concentration of one Advantage, but lacks others, it usually creates an unhealthy balance. (Ever seen a bodybuilder who only works out his upper body, but has chicken legs? Like that.)

If your group faces specific challenges from within, could there be patterns you're not seeing? Could you get better results if you start to look at things a little differently, and think about how the members of your team are most naturally suited to adding distinct value?

In the past, when I'd hire team members, I gravitated toward people with whom I felt "connected" during the interview. Over time, I realized that I was not optimizing myself—I was just *replicating* myself. If you only replicate yourself, you are not supplementing your Advantages. In fact, you might be canceling them out. Now I give people the assessment so I can read their report and see who they are—even before I interview them. During an interview, I spend less time looking at the résumé than the Fascination Advantage report.

Business owners tend to hire people they like—thereby, as I said, *replicating* themselves, rather than *optimizing* themselves. In the HR hiring process, the sheer crushing volume of résumés favors people who know how to look good on paper—yet often, the best hire will be the quietly methodical communicator who doesn't radiate charisma in an interview, or the pragmatic detail manager whose Advantages don't always shine on a job application. It's understandable that a business owner will unintentionally hire to replicate themselves, or that a gatekeeper will evaluate on the basis of résumés submitted yet not necessarily effective. It leads to imbalanced teams and conflicted cultures. It's difficult for members of a team to each add their highest value if nobody knows each other's highest value in the first place. I'll give you tools to do this in Part III.

You probably already recognize *strengths*. If you want more value from your team, start to recognize *differences*.

Your Fascination Advantage results will identify your *primary* and *secondary* Advantages. These are your wellsprings. You'll also learn your *dormant* Advantage—the area that feels like quicksand, forcing you to struggle and deplete your energy.

MAXIMIZE VALUE, SUBTRACT EVERYTHING ELSE

One of my *least* favorite tasks is expense reports. Some people don't mind them, but I find them exhausting because they require rigidly systematic accounting, which is a form of the Trust Advantage. Trust is about doing the same thing over and over: being stable, reliable, and even predictable.

Creative people often have a dormant Trust Advantage, because they succeed through *change* rather than *consistency*. This is true for me. (To Mrs. Stephenson, my pre-algebra teacher, you were right, even in seventh grade!) For me, it's exhausting to follow a rigid schedule or pattern, or complete long and intricate lists.

Last year, I made a decision that my company would not continue doing expense reports. This wasn't an administrative decision about the paperwork. Rather, it's a *marketing* decision. And it's the type of decision that you must make, too, if you want to overdeliver in your specialized area of value. Here's why.

Every single time you communicate with someone, you are either *adding value* (and reinforcing why they should prioritize you) or *taking up space* (and reinforcing that your messages are irrelevant spam). You have dozens or hundreds of occasions to interact with those around you, and in each instance you'll add value or take up space. In marketing, these interactions are sometimes called "touchpoints." They are points of contact. In your own life, a touchpoint will include any interaction with another person: in person, over the phone, through email, or other point of communication. Every single interaction is a touchpoint. You will probably have hundreds or thousands of touchpoints throughout the day.

Every touchpoint should highlight what makes you different, and better. Every business email, every business lunch, every direct mail piece, every social media update, and every expense report should reinforce your value proposition. If you can't improve people's perception of you, or at the very least maintain it, then reconsider whether you should be engaging in the first place.

My company, How To Fascinate, specializes in fascinating communication. That's our highest distinct value. Every single time a customer or client interacts with us, we want to fascinate them, to reinforce our position in their minds, over and over, every time, very clearly. For any touchpoint that does *not* support our distinct value (and in fact could even damage someone's perception of us), it's in our best interest to get it off the table. When it comes to expense reports, since we are not in the business of tax preparation or financial services, we are a commodity.

Let's say I've just delivered a flawless presentation, one that required weeks of work from my team and my client. I gave people a new way to see themselves. At that point, I want my client to do nothing more than bask in the afterglow of an amazing decision to hire me, and think of how we'll work together next. Expense reports aren't going to put a shine to their afterglow, and in fact, they could just burst the magic bubble. Sure, my team can be fast, accurate, and friendly, but it's practically impossible to *exceed* expectations when it comes to expense reports in my world.

Worse, a missing six-dollar receipt can lead to back-and-forth emails, and while this might not hurt the relationship, it's not helping, either. As a bonus, nobody has to deal with receipts (and nobody knows that I sometimes eat Cinnabon for dinner). Since I can't add value when it comes to accounting, I want to eliminate this. (Do I get reimbursed for my expenses? Of course. Just not through expense reports. I simply have a standard flat travel fee.)

Which types of interactions allow you to impress others? Which could potentially damage their perception of you? I'll show you how to showcase your highlights in Part III, when we create and apply your Anthem. You will learn how to stop exhausting yourself by trying to be all things to all people.

You will never rise to your greatest potential by being all things to all people.

Maximize value. Subtract everything else. Remove it from the equation, so that you're not being evaluated according to your dormant Advantage. Then you're far more likely to exceed expectations at every turn.

Now let's look at a different scenario. Let's imagine you're an accountant who is really, really good at balance sheets and income statements. Anyone who knows you can vouch that you're brilliant with numbers, and have been ever since you started winning math awards in elementary school. Among clients, you're revered for your ability to turn a messy folder of receipts into an IRS-approved report.

This is your pistachio. Debits and credits give you the opportunity to highlight your highest and best use.

Your Archetype could well be The Detective (Alert + Mystique). It's easy for a Detective to spot errors or missing information. Under your scrutiny, an Excel column of numbers obediently lines up in perfect formation. As all areas of your life, your personality adds distinct value to clients by being *clear-cut*, *accurate*, and *meticulous*. Methodical reports actually improve how the world sees you.

In your case, you should not *avoid* detail work—in fact, you should do as many expense reports as possible, and as intricately detailed reports as possible, because every time you do, you're reinforcing what makes you different and better than other accountants. Meticulous reports are your forte, and when you turn them in, it's a moment in the sun.

On the other hand, if because of your innate desire for privacy (for yourself and your clients), you dislike sharing details on social media such as Facebook and Twitter, then think twice about doing it. It's an inefficient use of your personality resources.

It's pretty simple, really:

....

Identify how you are MOST likely to add distinct value. Do more of this.
Identify how you are LEAST likely to add distinct value. Do less of this.

....

YOU ARE THE CUSTODIAN OF YOUR PERSONALITY

Few people recognize the full worth of their personality, let alone protect it. Yet your personality is an asset to be protected and watched over, just as you would carefully watch over your stock portfolio. You are the custodian of your personality. You have a duty to derive the most value from it, as well as preserve it, or else you won't be able to contribute your value to employees, family, or anyone else. And you won't get the most value out of your best natural asset.

If you are giving a presentation, for instance, the information in that presentation is only part of the value that you're delivering. Otherwise people could just read the PowerPoint deck and call it a day. If you are not 100%

focused and confident, the audience won't be as focused on and confident in you. Take steps to preserve and protect your highest distinct value.

I have a finite amount of personality to give while traveling. To proactively protect my highest value, I follow a few ninja rules. For instance, I don't make major decisions while traveling, because decisions create stress, and stress ruins confidence. I never confuse business travel with tourism. I go to bed at 10 p.m. eastern time before the speech, no matter what time zone I'm in, even if it's sunny outside. On a ten-city tour, I try to remind myself that my personality is a gas tank filled with my distinct value. It's my responsibility to conserve it for the highest and best use.

Whether you are reading this from thirty thousand feet or while wearing bunny slippers in your home office, protect your value for all its worth. Know how to be in top form, like an athlete preparing for an event.

What is your personality's emblem? What brings that out? *Who* brings it out?

When you work with a client or manager who appreciates you for the differences that your personality provides, you can leverage this to your advantage. You can win a promotion, gain a bigger budget, do work that you enjoy. And you can also avoid battling in the wrong job, with the wrong clients, the people who drain your energy and get in the way of your potential.

At this point, you might not be able to put your finger on which qualities are most valuable to others. Not to worry. As our journey together continues, you'll discover and articulate your points of difference so that others can see and appreciate the best of you. That's where your Fascination Advantage assessment comes in. Your assessment is the key to unlocking your Archetype, and the patterns of what makes you valuable to your customers, manager, and everyone else around you.

In a moment, you'll discover how the world sees you, with your custom assessment code at the end of this book.

Next, in Part II, we'll explore your primary and secondary Advantage, and how they combine to form your Archetype. You can also find out the Archetype of your team members, so you can improve the performance and results of the entire organization by leveraging what you already have.

There has never been a time when it's more important to understand how your personality is seen by others, and how to apply that insight to add distinct value. There has never been a greater opportunity to stand out and win based on who you already are.

The greatest value you can add is to become more of yourself.

PART II

THE
FASCINATION
ADVANTAGE
SYSTEM

CHAPTER 3

THE SEVEN FASCINATION ADVANTAGES

There are seven different ways to successfully communicate. Seven different ways to break through and win.

These are the seven Fascination Advantages.

Each of these has a distinct way of adding value. Each follows a particular
formula. Each has a different approach to building relationships, and fascinates for different reasons. Which of the seven Advantages best describe how
the world sees you, at your best?

In certain situations, when you can fully apply your Advantages, you'll
have the upper hand. You're more likely to break through and be heard. In
other situations, you're at a disadvantage. You will not be seen in your best
light. You'll become frustrated and demoralized. If you're evaluated according
to these criteria, you will be more likely to fail.

There isn't one Advantage that's better than the others. However, there are
one or two that will be most effective and authentic for you. Tap into your
particular Advantages, and you'll become the most valuable you.

Your goal is to focus on your Advantages, while avoiding your pitfalls, in
order to build communication that fascinates others.

What's the best of how the world sees you? Let's find out. You're about to
learn how to recognize and apply the seven Fascination Advantages. You'll
find out which two Advantages are your most attractive professional traits.
Once you know your Advantages, you can see why you thrive in certain roles,
but not in others; you can understand why you find yourself at ease in certain

group situations, while struggling to add value in others. You will also learn the value of recruiting people with specific Advantages in order to complement your existing team.

Don't worry if the Advantages sound a little abstract or vague to you at this stage. We're going to take it step by step. You don't need to memorize the Archetype Matrix—you just need to remember your core differences.

We're about to dig into more hands-on application. Take a break now to connect with me on Facebook at Facebook.com/HowToFascinate or on Twitter at @SallyHogshead and tell me your Archetype. Ask your questions by sending me and my team an email at hello@howtofascinate.com. We're here to help you become the most valuable you.

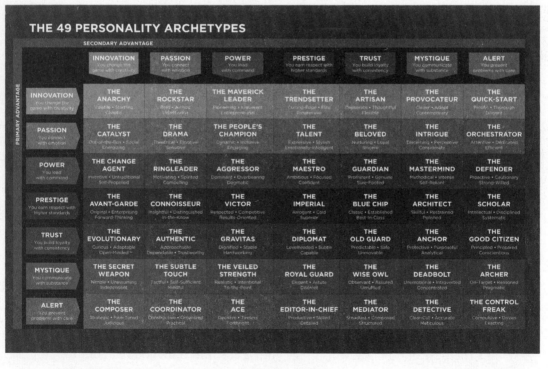

Find the full-size version of the Archetypes Matrix on the inside covers of this book.

A LOOK AT ADVANTAGES INSIDE A HIGH-PERFORMANCE COMPANY

The room hummed, filled to capacity with director-level executives, buzzing with a combination of caffeine and curiosity. I was leading a Fascination Laboratory workshop at the global headquarters of Intuit in California. I separated the participants into seven different teams, according to their primary Advantage. For instance, Team Alert included all the participants with a primary Alert Advantage. The same for each other Advantage: Team Innovation, Team Trust, Team Mystique, and so on. Each team was defined by one primary personality Advantage.

I gave the teams fifteen minutes to work together to develop solutions to a problem. When time was called, a representative from each team presented their team's ideas to the larger group. With that, the Team Advantage exercise began.

My certified coaches and I have done this exercise with corporations and small business groups ranging from gigantic corporations to tiny retail shops, from hundred-year-old global brands to ferociously aggressive start-ups. Yet while the *groups* are different shapes and sizes, the *principles* are simple and universal. Adding value begins with understanding what others value from you.

All seven teams were given the same task: develop one potential solution to a common challenge. Every director in the room was equipped with different skills and knowledge and areas of expertise. While job function and title were relevant, they were not the most essential piece. When teams work together, the highest level of performance is not merely a function of *what each individual does*. It's a result of *who each personality is*.

After we divided the group into teams based on their primary Advantage, we observed how they interacted. True to form, each team acted in accordance with the patterns of their strongest qualities. For example, Team Power pulled their chairs into a perfect square formation, facing each other directly, missing only the boardroom table. They each confidently put their opinions before the group, then debated their merits.

Team Trust kept their chairs in two orderly, straight lines, never moving them from where they'd been set up at the start of the day. They were consistent and prepared in their idea development, never interrupting each other, staying close to the framework of the assignment.

Team Mystique spoke little, working solo alongside each other, writing notes on their own pads of paper before going around the circle. One by one, they quietly outlined their thoughts to each other. Each of them had carefully considered their ideas before putting them forward to the team.

Innovation speaks the language of creativity. As expected, Team Innovation was very, very creative. They moved their chairs into an amoebic circle, a free-form gathering of unlaced shoes and crumpled paper. Immediately they began launching a water cannon of ideas, one after another, each leaping higher than the last.

A representative from Team Alert raised her hand, politely asking how much time remained before the deadline. These directors were diligent in their assignment, highly attuned to the pros and cons of each option discussed. Alert personalities speak the language of details, and I felt safe just standing next to them.

Next I walked over to Team Prestige. They had many excellent ways to improve results and raise the bar. (And I'm not entirely certain, but I think I overheard the Prestige members debating which of them should be selected to present their idea—before they'd even begun discussing ideas.)

Of all the groups, Team Passion was hands down the most rambunctious. Awash in high-fives, backslaps, and woo-hoos, they furiously scribbled their concepts with a fat marker on an oversized Post-it note that quickly became filled with half thoughts and word associations. *"Yes! Great job. Love that!"* Working on Team Passion seemed more a game of charades than a corporate ideation session.

All of the Advantage Teams solved the marketing challenge in a way that matched their shared Advantage. Although they all worked on the same task, each Advantage team worked together very differently, according to their shared primary Advantage. They all solved the task, but they used very different approaches and tools.

I intentionally gave each team just fifteen minutes to develop a marketing solution. Short time frames intensify team interaction, and accentuate personality styles.

After those fifteen minutes were up, each group picked one person to share the team's solution. When it was time to present ideas to the overall group, each of the seven teams sent one person to the front (except Team Prestige, which sent two, almost like co-chairmen).

Team Innovation went first. Innovation personalities are born to brainstorm, and independently choose their agenda. They presented a whole range of ideas and then dropped them, moving on to brainstorm on a completely unrelated issue. (A fire hose streams fiercely, yet not always with precision.)

Team Alert shared a solution that was practical, straightforward, and imminently doable. Team Mystique shared an idea that was subtle at first, almost unremarkable, yet after further explanation, proved brilliant. And then there was Team Passion. Still on a sugar-buzz high of camaraderie, they cheered on their teammate who went to the front of the room. While the oversized Post-its had been filled with ideas, they loved all the ideas so much that they couldn't pick just one. That's the Passion personality: expressive, social, optimistic. They wear their heart on their sleeve (and sometimes it covers their whole outfit).

This exercise was a metaphor for the everyday workplace. It reveals how each Advantage is most likely to add distinct value to her team, company, and customers. I was giving them a live demonstration—using *themselves* as the example—of how different Advantages communicate in predictable and identifiable ways.

The exercise also illustrates that each Advantage speaks a different "language." We each communicate in a certain way, and it determines how the world sees us. Passion personalities speak the language of relationship, for example. Trust speaks the language of stability, and Mystique speaks the language of listening. Everyone on your team speaks a certain language. You do, too. It's the way you're most likely to communicate in meetings, in memos, and every other step of your job.

But we're getting ahead of ourselves. Let's explore the seven Advantages.

THE SEVEN FASCINATION ADVANTAGES

I developed this system and calibrated it over the past several years, based on data and feedback from companies and teams.

For example, which type of professional scores highest on Power Advantage? CEOs of small- to medium-sized businesses. That makes sense, because

Power is the language of *confidence*. Contrast that with high-end financial advisors who guide conservative, wealthy clients. Those advisors usually score very high on Trust Advantage. Their clients want to speak the language of *stability*. In fact, when we measured participants from four different groups of successful Wells Fargo financial advisors, they scored 2.5 times higher than the average population on Trust.

If Trust is the language of *stability*, who is most likely to apply Innovation, the language of *creativity*? The answer might surprise you: Female entrepreneurs. The four thousand female "solopreneurs" in our research score 66% higher than the average population on Innovation.

Every personality can be better understood with the seven Advantages of Fascination. Each person you work with uses the Advantages. You use them. Your partners use them. Your employees use them. So do your customers and your prospects. The seven Advantages explain how we persuade and influence each other throughout the day. Yet we each use the seven Advantages differently, applying unique combinations, in varying amounts. Look at how the seven Advantages drive all interaction, and you'll begin to realize why people around you interact with you in very specific ways, to both positive and negative effect. Through this understanding, you can more effectively interact with others. As we explore this together, you'll be comparing your own personality with that of two hundred thousand research participants, representing groups that range from Fortune 500 corporations to elite entrepreneurial shops.

Let's be clear: *There is not one Advantage that's better than another.* Certain Advantages are suited to certain tasks or goals.

For instance, salespeople typically score high on Power and Passion. They tend to be proactive about taking the initiative, jumping into the conversation. They often score very low on Mystique. Overwhelmingly, Mystique is their *dormant* Advantage, the one they are *least* likely to use. However, this pattern does not mean that all salespeople should fit into a stereotype. It may depend on what they're selling, or, to whom they're selling.

A salesperson with primary Mystique can have an upper hand in closing the deal in complex sales such as technology or mortgages. While their competitors might come across as pushy or saccharine sweet, the Mystique salespeople take time to listen first. They ask questions to get information before offering opinions. If they don't already know the facts and answers, they know where to find them, rather than rattling off a half-baked response. Mystique gives these personalities an edge with customers who want extra information or a no-pressure pitch.

MYSTIQUE: THE LANGUAGE OF LISTENING

People with primary Mystique Advantage tend not to seek the limelight. But let's bring this Advantage into the spotlight.

In certain situations, personalities with Mystique have a certain advantage. They think before speaking. They observe. They watch. Mystique is the language of *listening*.

These communicators edit what they say, removing the fluff and excess. They say just enough, then pause to listen before going on. When they do call attention to a situation, take notice. They won't ask for attention unless it's merited.

With Mystique, substance wins over style. They're never gimmicky. Never tacky or flashy or brassy. They don't pitch fits or throw tantrums. Mystique personalities worry less about how they look on the outside, and more about what's going on inside someone's head.

If you have a complex problem that requires high-level thinking, find someone with Mystique. They'll dig deeply into a problem or situation, sorting through the variables and nuances, take the time they need to figure out a solution. When they do present that solution, it will be carefully considered.

Their first impression is only the tip of the iceberg. But look under the surface. You might have to take more time to get to know them, because their greatest value can lie hidden under the surface. Take the time you need. They're worth it.

YOUR PRIMARY ADVANTAGE

Your primary Advantage describes your main style of communication. It feels easy and natural for you to express yourself in this way. Your words come more easily, and you don't feel self-conscious. In this mode, your brain is less likely to become stressed or anxious.

There are seven different Advantages, and you have all seven in your personality. You can think of them as your set of golf clubs.

You *could* use any of the seven Advantages, theoretically, but there's going to be one that's most effective for you. This Advantage is the way in which you most effortlessly and effectively communicate. This is your most persuasive means of communication, when you have the greatest likelihood of influencing others.

A Quick Overview of the Seven Advantages

- If your primary Advantage is **Power**, you communicate with authority and confidence.
- If your primary Advantage is **Passion**, you build connections with your warmth and enthusiasm.
- If your primary Advantage is **Mystique**, you impress with your analytical skills and thoughtful communication.
- If your primary Advantage is **Prestige**, you earn respect by setting high standards.
- If your primary Advantage is **Alert**, you keep people and projects on track by managing the details.
- If your primary Advantage is **Innovation**, you push a company to innovate with your creative ideas.
- If your primary Advantage is **Trust**, you earn loyalty as a consistent and familiar presence.

Your primary and secondary Advantages can light the path to communicating your points. Using them will make you more confident, more persuasive, and more you.

INNOVATION	PASSION	POWER	PRESTIGE	TRUST	MYSTIQUE	ALERT
Creative	Expressive	Confident	Ambitious	Stable	Independent	Proactive
Visionary	Intuitive	Goal-Oriented	Results-Oriented	Dependable	Logical	Organized
Entrepreneurial	Engaging	Decisive	Respected	Familiar	Observant	Detailed

WHAT ADVANTAGES DOES *YOUR* TEAM USE?

The actions and communication of a team reflect the composition of its individuals' Advantages. For instance, teams with a high proportion of Passion are engaged and energetic. They succeed by connecting with each other, as well as with customers, clients, and co-workers.

Teams with a high proportion of Mystique are less overtly social, and more focused on the tangible result. They're purposeful and logical in their communication.

With a high percentage of Prestige, a team will seek to win through competition (with other teams and each other).

The point of evaluating your team in this way is to demonstrate how leaders can assemble a specific "team recipe" to better predict and improve outcomes.

A TEAM'S COMBINATION OF ADVANTAGES DRIVES THE OUTCOME

Me, I'm an embarrassingly bad golfer, though I can hold my own on a mini golf course, at least when my opponents are under ten years old. Yet I'll bravely offer this golf metaphor.

Imagine that you and I are just beginning a round of golf. I turn to you and ask: "Should I begin the game with a driver, or a putter?" (Even if you don't play golf, you probably know the answer: a driver. Right?) Now a few hours have gone by, and we're at the end of the eighteenth hole. I want to sink the ball into the hole with just a tap. Again I ask the same question as before: Should I use a driver, or a putter? (This time, as you probably know, the answer is different: a putter.) Drivers and putters are two different tools. They achieve different types of results.

Advantages are like golf clubs. Each one gets a different sort of result. The result is somewhat predictable, so you choose your Advantage to get your desired response. In certain scenarios, one club will be more effective than another. You wouldn't start your round of golf with a putter. You wouldn't finish with a driver. (You *could*, I suppose, but then even I might have a shot at winning this game.) An organization can look to the Advantages of its employees like a golfer might look to a set of golf clubs, to fit specific needs.

When two people with the same primary Advantage join forces, the result is often a more pronounced use of that Advantage. When a dozen or more people of the same primary get together, as shown in my workshop exercise, the communication becomes an even more obvious, even exaggerated, use of the Advantage. A team will succeed in predictable areas, and lag in others, based on the composition of Advantages within that team.

Having a team composed entirely of the same primary Advantage is rare. Yet it's not unusual for a team to have an unusually high concentration of one particular Advantage. This shapes how the team will be seen by outside parties (including customers and clients). Perhaps more importantly, individual members of the team will see each other in certain ways. To learn more about this, refer to "Inside the Research: Our Fascinating Findings" in the Appendix.

HR managers can handpick certain Advantages, hiring specifically to balance and complement existing team members, or hone specific specialty personality traits for the overall group.

The more accurately you've assessed how a team is seen by the outside world, the more precisely you can guide that team's interaction with customers and clients. Corporations can better understand and optimize their employees for anything that requires communication, from sales and customer service to hiring and nurturing high-performing talent.

It's even more important for each team member to understand which of her Advantages are most valuable to the team.

DIVERSITY IN THE WORKPLACE (WITH ADVANTAGES, THAT IS)

Diversity isn't just about hiring a balance in terms of ethnicity, gender, and age. It's also about hiring a balance of personalities.

If your company has become stale and you struggle to innovate, you probably want to recruit people with a primary Innovation Advantage, because they're creative and tend to challenge the status quo.

If your start-up is full of enthusiastic, larger-than-life characters, you will do well to recruit people with a primary Trust or Mystique Advantage to balance the team. Each Advantage contributes a different form of value. Each speaks a different "language," based on their approach to communication.

Often you'll find raw gems of potential hidden underneath layers of one-size-fits-all expectations. Your team might already have everything it needs to improve results—without spending more on new hires or marketing—if you get each person communicating in sync with their natural strong suit. For instance, if you are a doctor, and it turns out that your office manager has a primary Mystique Advantage, don't expect her to be conversationally touchy-feely with new patients. Instead, expect her to carefully learn about each patient, shadowing you with skilled professionalism.

HOW A TEAM'S ADVANTAGES REFLECT AND BUILD A COMPANY'S BRAND

A company is composed of individual personalities, and those personalities are shaped by Advantages. By understanding your employees' Advantages, you can better understand your company—and how it is perceived by others. Your employees are a living, breathing extension of your brand.

Often when we study the people behind a brand, we find that the collection of personality Advantages within the group correlates to the brand. Here's an example of how strongly an organization's members can reflect the brand promise (and how the brand promise influences which members the organization attracts).

The American Society of Association Executives (ASAE) is the mack daddy of associations. It is literally the association *for* associations. When we looked at ASAE membership, we found a very strong use of three Advantages: Prestige, Passion, and Power. Then, when we looked at the ASAE brand, we found a direct correlation with those same three Advantages.

Here is ASAE's promise: *"ASAE provides exceptional experiences, a vibrant community, and essential tools that make you and your organization more successful."*

Let's look at that promise in terms of Advantages: *"ASAE provides exceptional experiences* [that's Prestige] *. . . a vibrant community* [that's Passion] *. . . and essential tools* [that's Power] *that make you and your organization more successful."* The organization's promise matches the people it recruits, retains, and promotes. Does your organization? In other words, does the communication style of your people match the promise you're making to your customer?

Advantages are the basic building blocks of every personality. They provide a simple way to categorize different communication styles for people and brands. Let's have a look at each of the Advantages in more detail now. I'll take you through each of the seven Advantages, one by one.

Your personality has seven different ways of communicating. You may not realize it, but you're probably using all seven different Advantages throughout the day, from hurrying your kids out the door for school in the morning to kissing your spouse good night.

Look at each member of your team through this lens: What is the highest and best use of her personality? What Advantages does she use to communicate, and how can you leverage that innate specialty to support the success of the overall team?

THE SEVEN FASCINATION ADVANTAGES

THE POWER ADVANTAGE
Leading through authority

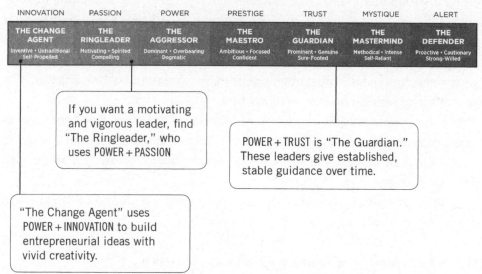

POWER

INNOVATION	PASSION	POWER	PRESTIGE	TRUST	MYSTIQUE	ALERT
THE CHANGE AGENT	**THE RINGLEADER**	**THE AGGRESSOR**	**THE MAESTRO**	**THE GUARDIAN**	**THE MASTERMIND**	**THE DEFENDER**
Inventive • Untraditional Self-Propelled	Motivating • Spirited Compelling	Dominant • Overbearing Dogmatic	Ambitious • Focused Confident	Prominent • Genuine Sure-Footed	Methodical • Intense Self-Reliant	Proactive • Cautionary Strong-Willed

If you want a motivating and vigorous leader, find "The Ringleader," who uses POWER + PASSION

POWER + TRUST is "The Guardian." These leaders give established, stable guidance over time.

"The Change Agent" uses POWER + INNOVATION to build entrepreneurial ideas with vivid creativity.

Power personalities speak the language of confidence.

They inspire others through bigger goals and stronger opinions. Since they usually know what they want, they often lead the discussion. You'll find they ask direct questions, taking charge of a conversation, leaning in, and stepping forward.

In the heat of an argument, these formidable debaters know how to put their own case forth. They strongly emphasize their key points. They don't shy away from head-to-head sparring, or back down from counterarguments. This gives them an edge when challengers step up.

They're comfortable in leadership positions, and motivate others to rise to their best. Decisive and self-assured, they don't mind being the ones who make difficult decisions. They know they need to take considered risks to achieve ambitious company targets. (Sometimes they use a carrot, other times, a stick.)

In their personal lives, as with business, they get things moving forward. They might sit on the school board, or spearhead a community fund-raising campaign. Others look to them to take the lead.

At networking events, they know who they want to connect with to further their career.

Many respected CEOs and opinion leaders apply the Power Advantage. They develop their authority by understanding their field of expertise, developing a strong opinion.

You'll recognize Power in the high school football coach who pushes each player to do more—faster, better, harder—and motivates them to keep them going if spirits start to drop along with the score.

It's the bystander who immediately steps forward in an emergency, not hesitating or waiting for others to act first.

It's the controversial blogger who is unafraid to give love-it-or-hate-it opinions (and gets tons of comments and social media shares as a result).

It's the Realtor who sells houses with her confident recommendations and proactive advice.

It's the mentor who encourages you to stop sitting back and to start taking charge of your career.

Strategically Increasing Your Use of the Power Advantage

How comfortable are you with using the Power Advantage? When do you speak in absolute terms to stamp your authority on a situation? When do you step forward to take control?

Now think about your co-workers. Who is using Power least? For those with a dormant Power Advantage, playing "bad cop" is extremely uncomfortable. Hire more Power personalities if your company needs stronger, more decisive leadership. As managers, for instance, they'll push the team to meet the quota.

Who is using Power most? Too much use of Power can be seen as aggressive and adversarial. If your team has a disproportionate number of Power personalities, you might notice too many egos or "cooks in the kitchen." Hire more primary Trust or Mystique (who tend to take a more supporting role) to balance the mix of the team.

THE PASSION ADVANTAGE
Creating warm emotional connections

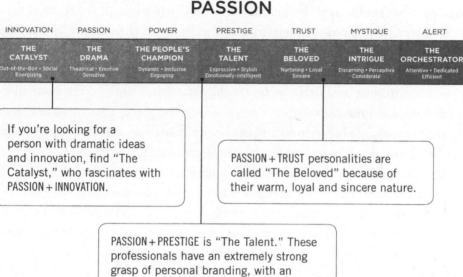

PASSION

INNOVATION	PASSION	POWER	PRESTIGE	TRUST	MYSTIQUE	ALERT
THE CATALYST	**THE DRAMA**	**THE PEOPLE'S CHAMPION**	**THE TALENT**	**THE BELOVED**	**THE INTRIGUE**	**THE ORCHESTRATOR**
Out-of-the-Box • Social Energizing	Theatrical • Emotive Sensitive	Dynamic • Inclusive Engaging	Expressive • Stylish Emotionally-Intelligent	Nurturing • Loyal Sincere	Discerning • Perceptive Considerate	Attentive • Dedicated Efficient

If you're looking for a person with dramatic ideas and innovation, find "The Catalyst," who fascinates with PASSION + INNOVATION.

PASSION + TRUST personalities are called "The Beloved" because of their warm, loyal and sincere nature.

PASSION + PRESTIGE is "The Talent." These professionals have an extremely strong grasp of personal branding, with an expressive and stylish approach.

Passion personalities speak the language of relationship.

Their ability to forge relationships builds wide networks, both socially and professionally. At a cocktail party, standing in line for the cheese puffs and crab wontons, they effortlessly strike up conversations with whoever happens to be next in line. Do you see one nearby? Just look for the life of the party.

Approachable and gregarious, they usually build rapport with prospects, customers, and colleagues, which allows them to excel in positions that require strong interpersonal skills.

These social butterflies express themselves with animated facial expressions, body language, and vocal intonation. In pitches and presentations, this helps them add emphasis to the points they are making. Their expressive style keeps people focused and engaged.

You'll usually know what they're thinking. In fact, some might call them an open book. Passion makes their emotional state transparent to others. Their expressions are easy to read, immediately revealing their thoughts and feelings. Every event, both good and bad, is immediately broadcasted to the world . . . a characteristic that's advantageous for presenting and storytelling (less so for poker playing). They have difficulty masking their emotions; situations that require negotiation and "bluffing" are difficult for them. This is quite different than Mystique personalities, who tend to carefully vet their ideas and shield their personal opinions.

And just as you can read their feelings, the Passion personality is attuned to yours. Intuitive and socially savvy, they modulate and mirror your interactions, looking for cues about your own internal state. This intuition stems from their natural ability to form bonds with a wide spectrum of people, and adjust their message to resonate with their audience.

During meetings, you'll see them watching for cues from others, taking "temperature checks" of the group while moving forward.

In positions of leadership, you'll see them making decisions with a visceral approach rather than purely hard data. They go with their gut. As managers, they're usually known for watching after their people, taking into account the emotional state of their team.

As part of a team, they're often cheerleaders, who keep everyone involved along the way. Once they become buoyant supporters of a cause, they can be hard to resist. Their enthusiasm can build energetic participation.

You can identify them creating experiences that give them the opportunity to interact and participate with others. They seek out colors, textures, music, scents, and flavors. When they really want to turn it up, they know how to get people on their side by flirting and coaxing, inspiring and cajoling.

This is the college buddy who never met a stranger.

It's the co-worker who walks over to your office to talk in person, rather than emailing from the cubicle down the hall.

It's the presenter who lights up the room with dramatic gestures.

It's the Girl Scout who shows up at your door selling cookies, with a big smile and irresistible sales pitch.

It's the receptionist who gives warm eye contact. The customer service rep who empathizes with your plight.

It's the seeker of Technicolor experiences, living life to the fullest. More is more. Why have either ice cream *or* whipped cream on your pecan pie if you can have both?

Hire more Passion personalities if you want to build stronger personal connections with customers. For example, in customer service, they bring the human touch: empathetic listening, sincere compliments, a handwritten thank-you note, or warm cup of coffee.

If your group has a disproportionate number of Passion personalities, balance the group by hiring more Trust (for consistency) and more Mystique (for objectivity). The Trust and Mystique folks add value through building connection within your organization as well as by connecting your group to other groups.

Strategically Increasing Your Use of Passion

What are you like? Are you someone who's quick to chat with people you don't know? Or do you tend to keep a certain distance?

Even if you don't have a strong Passion Advantage, you can benefit from using it from time to time—start a conversation with a warm smile, stress the key points in your presentation with strong body language, or change that Skype call to a face-to-face meeting at your local cafe.

Who in your environment is a Passion personality? Can you learn from them to add a human touch to your interactions, and connect more quickly?

THE MYSTIQUE ADVANTAGE
Thinking before speaking

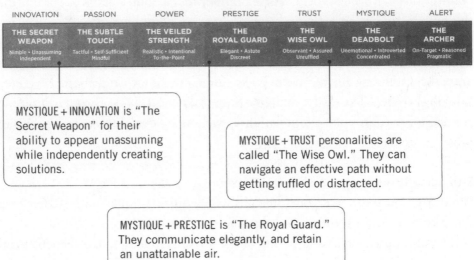

MYSTIQUE

INNOVATION	PASSION	POWER	PRESTIGE	TRUST	MYSTIQUE	ALERT
THE SECRET WEAPON	**THE SUBTLE TOUCH**	**THE VEILED STRENGTH**	**THE ROYAL GUARD**	**THE WISE OWL**	**THE DEADBOLT**	**THE ARCHER**
Nimble • Unassuming Independent	Tactful • Self-Sufficient Mindful	Realistic • Intentional To-the-Point	Elegant • Astute Discreet	Observant • Assured Unruffled	Unemotional • Introverted Concentrated	On-Target • Reasoned Pragmatic

MYSTIQUE + INNOVATION is "The Secret Weapon" for their ability to appear unassuming while independently creating solutions.

MYSTIQUE + TRUST personalities are called "The Wise Owl." They can navigate an effective path without getting ruffled or distracted.

MYSTIQUE + PRESTIGE is "The Royal Guard." They communicate elegantly, and retain an unattainable air.

Mystique personalities speak the language of listening.

While others draw attention to themselves with loud greetings or fraternal backslapping, Mystique personalities tend to be solo intellects behind the scenes. Their ability to see the nuances of a situation, and think things through, gives them an edge over more outgoing personalities. These pragmatic thinkers communicate with facts, not fancy.

While Passion and Power personalities sometimes "overcommunicate," people with primary Mystique are more likely to "undercommunicate." Independent and analytical, they systematically gather evidence before reaching a conclusion and analyze statistics before making up their mind. They are good at managing their own work. They excel at decoding nuances. They skillfully outline strategies, but only after careful reflection.

These introverts naturally restrain their emotions, and are unlikely to succumb to the "mood du jour." You might find it difficult to gauge what they really think, but this makes their conclusions more credible, because they've probably vetted their thinking before sharing it.

Even at an office party you'll find that Mystique personalities are relatively quiet. You're unlikely to find them leading the discussion or out on the dance floor. (Limbo line? No.) They enjoy observing people rather than being in the spotlight themselves. They'd be able to tell you exactly what's going on, but they generally keep their observations to themselves.

Need a negotiator on your team? Look for a Mystique personality. Poker-faced, they keep their cards close to their chest. They won't be distracted by bullying or tricks. They remain unruffled under pressure. Their interaction style can occasionally be perceived as intimidating and aloof, which can sometimes give them a favorable position. Others might get hotheaded or make snappish comments, but with Mystique, they remain cool.

You might not be certain what a Mystique personality is thinking, which means it can be difficult to predict their next move.

Measured, deliberate, and carefully prepared, they objectively weigh options rather than foolishly following advice. They carefully research before offering you their opinions.

As advisors, they present facts, statistics, and relevant details. They won't overwhelm you with too much information. Instead, they summarize key points and carefully communicate these. They are nonaggressive, nonflashy professionals who impress clients with their objective views.

As part of a team, they provide an independent voice. They're not likely to suffer from groupthink. You notice them slowing the group down when others spontaneously follow exciting ideas and risk going down the wrong track. They argue their case carefully. They are a great balance to more expressive personalities like Passion or Innovation.

Mystique personalities avoid distractions and don't spend much time around the water cooler. They prefer to get on with their job rather than spend time in lighthearted social chats. Their time management skills are excellent.

Mystique personalities are respected because everything they say is carefully considered. They rarely improvise. You can follow their recommendations and allow them to carry on with their work independently.

This is the respected co-worker you've worked with for a long time, but still feel you don't know very well.

This is the quiet personal assistant who expertly manages your diary.

It's the account manager who sells based on rational facts.

It's the poker player who doesn't show his emotions as the pot grows larger.

It's the eighty-one-year-old who tells her grandchildren stories about her past, but never reveals the whole picture.

It's the doctor whose facial expression doesn't reveal whether an examination is good or bad.

It's the celebrity who carefully guards her privacy.

It's the business owner who's able to negotiate the best deals; and you never quite understand how he does it.

Hire more Mystique personalities if you want to implement a more analytical approach or need to boost your team's negotiation power. As part of the purchasing team, for instance, they'll save you costs by negotiating better deals. As part of the manufacturing team, they'll improve productivity and enhance quality standards. As part of the finance team, they'll analyze the figures and tell you how to increase revenue without lowering profitability.

Mystique might not dominate the conversation, but they can dominate the winner's circle. If your group has a high number of Mystique personalities, balance the group by hiring more Passion (to build strong, emotional connections) and Power (to lead the team).

Mystique adds value through a careful, analytical approach. They help you to save costs and boost profitability by discreetly monitoring the most important details.

Strategically Increasing Your Use of the Mystique Advantage

Let's step back for a minute and consider Mystique. Are you someone who's quick to offer an opinion, or do you carefully consider your suggestions?

Everyone can benefit from a dose of Mystique. Step back to observe the reaction of others before jumping ahead. Make your passionate plea more compelling by supporting it with rational arguments and facts. Carefully research your next career move rather than jumping at the next opportunity.

Mystique personalities don't dominate the conversation, but you're wise to pay attention to their views. Think about the people on your team: Who is quiet but always makes valid points? Who could you listen to more often?

THE PRESTIGE ADVANTAGE
Achieving success with higher standards

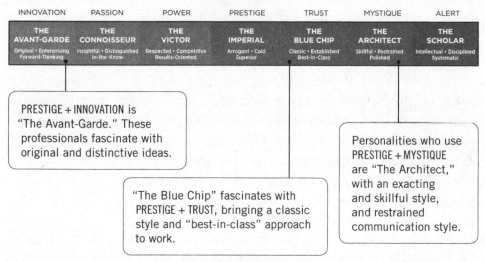

PRESTIGE

INNOVATION	PASSION	POWER	PRESTIGE	TRUST	MYSTIQUE	ALERT
THE AVANT-GARDE	**THE CONNOISSEUR**	**THE VICTOR**	**THE IMPERIAL**	**THE BLUE CHIP**	**THE ARCHITECT**	**THE SCHOLAR**
Original • Enterprising Forward-Thinking	Insightful • Distinguished In-the-Know	Respected • Competitive Results-Oriented	Arrogant • Cold Superior	Classic • Established Best-in-Class	Skillful • Restrained Polished	Intellectual • Disciplined Systematic

PRESTIGE + INNOVATION is "The Avant-Garde." These professionals fascinate with original and distinctive ideas.

"The Blue Chip" fascinates with PRESTIGE + TRUST, bringing a classic style and "best-in-class" approach to work.

Personalities who use PRESTIGE + MYSTIQUE are "The Architect," with an exacting and skillful style, and restrained communication style.

Prestige personalities speak the language of excellence.

Their personal and professional aim is to always get better to exceed expectations. When excellence matters, they know how to push for success. Ambitious and determined, they don't want to disappoint. They help and encourage co-workers to achieve in everything they do.

When organizing a thirtieth birthday party for a partner, they arrange each detail in advance. They'll have the invitation list ready. They ask the printer about the thickness of the paper for the invitations. They'll go to the restaurant to discuss the menu in advance, and they've decided to wear a classic Paul Smith suit long before the party. They call you to be sure you'll arrive on time.

These overachievers are admired for their assertiveness, expertise, and high-quality results. They don't do *just good enough*. They don't rely on luck. Instead, they ensure each detail is taken care of. They strive to improve their performance, and continuously achieve their goals.

They prepare their sales pitches meticulously. They do several practice runs in front of a mirror. They study Steve Jobs's product launch videos to emulate his presentational skills. Their PowerPoint slides reveal their ambitious process.

They study their personal and business heroes to enhance their own communication skills. In turn, they're admired by their peers. Co-workers, friends, and sometimes even their boss will look to Prestige personalities to guide them in what to do, how to do it, and where to go. They set the standard for others to follow.

They are proud of their achievements. And rightly so. They may display diplomas, prizes, and awards in their home study or on their office wall. Among the various academic achievements you may find a high school football trophy, too.

Prestige personalities know their own strengths and weaknesses. They avoid failure by focusing on what they know they do well. They don't do *average*—not even for a hobby. They practice playing the piano daily. And they play impressively well. It makes you think that if they had become a professional pianist, they would have played with the New York Philharmonic.

In positions of leadership, they're intensely focused on achieving results. Their uncompromising attitude drives their team to achieve what some team members might not have thought was possible. You can expect them to develop resolute plans and implement them relentlessly. They expect top-notch results from everyone working with them.

When negotiating with Prestige personalities, you'll find they don't bend easily. They have their agenda and work toward it with conviction. Uncompromisingly. They'll scrutinize each detailed point in a contract. Nothing escapes their attention.

These are the people you turn to when you need to get results, and when you can't compromise on quality.

This is the star performer on your swimming team. The girl who practices her freestyle flip turns to perfection.

This is the university graduate who has his career already planned out.

This is the boy who doesn't try out his Spanish skills while on vacation in Mexico because he's afraid he'll make a fool of himself.

This is the editor who takes out a comma, and then puts it back.

This is the sommelier who prepares her wine list with each detail planned and executed to dizzying perfection.

Hire more Prestige personalities if you want to raise standards, improve team performance, or iron out quality issues. As a customer service manager, they'll train the team and improve scripts. As product manager, they'll improve an existing range.

If your group has a high number of Prestige personalities, balance the group by hiring more Innovation (they'll successfully generate and implement big ideas together) and Passion (for team spirit).

Prestige adds value by meeting and exceeding your goals.

Strategically Increasing Your Use of the Prestige Advantage

Since you're reading this book, you're probably at least a little interested in improving yourself. You want to get better at what you do—and that's the Prestige Advantage at work.

The Prestige Advantage helps you to achieve more by aiming higher and by planning how to reach (or exceed) your goals. Prestige also reminds you to evaluate your work and analyze how you could push yourself to be even better.

Can you think of someone in your environment who already uses Prestige?

THE ALERT ADVANTAGE
Careful precision

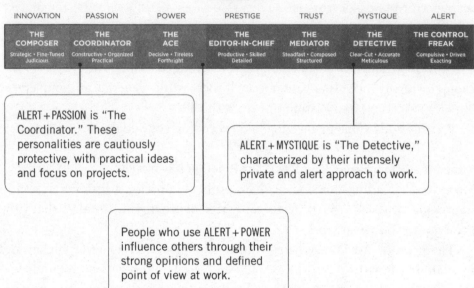

ALERT

INNOVATION	PASSION	POWER	PRESTIGE	TRUST	MYSTIQUE	ALERT
THE COMPOSER	**THE COORDINATOR**	**THE ACE**	**THE EDITOR-IN-CHIEF**	**THE MEDIATOR**	**THE DETECTIVE**	**THE CONTROL FREAK**
Strategic • Fine-Tuned Judicious	Constructive • Organized Practical	Decisive • Tireless Forthright	Productive • Skilled Detailed	Steadfast • Composed Structured	Clear-Cut • Accurate Meticulous	Compulsive • Driven Exacting

ALERT+PASSION is "The Coordinator." These personalities are cautiously protective, with practical ideas and focus on projects.

ALERT+MYSTIQUE is "The Detective," characterized by their intensely private and alert approach to work.

People who use ALERT+POWER influence others through their strong opinions and defined point of view at work.

Alert personalities speak the language of details.

When details matter, Alert has an upper hand over less structured personalities. They are watchful, aware, with an ability to manage complex projects.

Their risk-adverse attitude helps them to avoid mistakes. They know the critical path of their projects by heart. They understand that minor issues can cause major delays. They never lose track of deadlines. They're able to juggle conflicting requirements, such as meeting tight deadlines without compromising product specifications.

By keeping their eye on the ball, they don't lose sight of the process or lose track of details. Practical and pragmatic, they take a step-by-step approach to reaching team goals.

While Innovation personalities dislike the rules, and Passion personalities sometimes prioritize gut feeling over the facts, the Alert personality stays on track. When others get distracted, they maintain concrete deliverables to move forward with the team. They focus on the task at hand, whether it's improving quality standards, raising productivity, or lowering call waiting times.

As project managers they'll focus on delivering results on time and within budget. As senior managers they'll watch the bottom line. No matter what the role, they organize projects to keep everyone lined up for success. They keep an eye on what could go wrong, and they spot potential pitfalls ahead of time.

By day, they make sure everyone has what they need in order to deliver, so that even creative types stay on task. If hosting an after-work party, they have clear directions to the location, remind everyone to bring an umbrella in case of rain, and then once on site they make sure that problems don't arise (and that crumpled napkins aren't left lying around).

You'll find them pointing out the negative consequences if someone doesn't deliver. They aren't afraid to deliver a reality check, if that's what's needed to keep the project on track. Their sense of clarity and structure helps them find practical compromises.

Alert personalities are natural project managers. They work out solid project plans, and make them as intricate as required. You'll also find them regularly checking in with the team to make sure everyone is happy and on track. You'll see them anticipating potential tension among team members in order to prevent it.

In leadership positions, you'll find that Alert personalities are always in control. They know what needs to happen when. They keep a detailed to-do list. They're able to get people to take immediate action when required. They create urgency, and don't accept complacency.

They are sensitive to other people's wishes and expectations. You'll find they do their utmost to accommodate requests to make the office a comfortable, productive environment.

You'll also find that Alert personalities keep health and safety in mind. Whether it's their responsibility or not, they're quick to notice risks and get them corrected immediately.

When they're chairing a meeting, you can be sure it'll be finished by 10 a.m. as agreed. They prepare a detailed agenda and email it out two days in advance. They work through the agenda in an orderly manner and ensure everyone gets a chance to contribute their thoughts. They keep the discussion focused. Small talk can wait until business is done.

It's the manager who meticulously plans product improvements for the next three years.

It's the dentist whose appointment schedule always runs on time.

It's the friend who'll text you if she's only five minutes late.

It's the credit controller who gets invoices paid. It's the local charity's fund-raising manager who accounts for every penny coming in.

It's the perfectly punctual assistant.

It's the mother who plans ahead for the child's birthday party with sanitary wipes and disposable cups (and stain-resistant fabric on the sofa).

Hire more Alert personalities if you want to get things done. They eradicate procrastination and keep your team intensely focused on meeting objectives. No detail escapes their attention. As HR managers, for instance, they keep up-to-date with the latest regulations and ensure all contracts comply. As finance directors they watch the bottom line. As product managers they implement practical solutions to get products to the market as specified.

If your group has a high number of Alert personalities, balance them by hiring more Prestige (for higher goals) or Power (for strong-willed confidence).

Alert personalities add value by organizing the team. Always firmly in control, they get projects delivered, and make things happen.

Strategically Increasing Your Use of the Alert Advantage

Are you an eternal optimist, flinging yourself out into the world? Or are you a more cautious character, looking before you leap?

The Alert Advantage can help you manage your career (and your life!) by staying focused on concrete goals and considering the consequences of changing direction. Alert reminds you to check in with co-workers, friends, and family to ensure everyone is fine.

Teams need a balanced approach. Alert personalities will keep the team on track, nip problems in the bud, and avoid excessive risk-taking.

In contrast, *dormant* Alert personalities have a can-do attitude. They worry less about risks—and can embark on projects without thinking through all the potential consequences.

How's the balance in your team? Do you need more or less Alert?

THE INNOVATION ADVANTAGE
New ideas and solutions

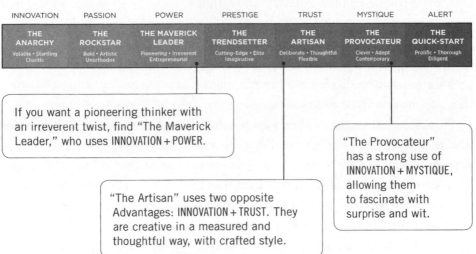

INNOVATION

INNOVATION	PASSION	POWER	PRESTIGE	TRUST	MYSTIQUE	ALERT
THE ANARCHY Volatile • Startling Chaotic	**THE ROCKSTAR** Bold • Artistic Unorthodox	**THE MAVERICK LEADER** Pioneering • Irreverent Entrepreneurial	**THE TRENDSETTER** Cutting-Edge • Elite Imaginative	**THE ARTISAN** Deliberate • Thoughtful Flexible	**THE PROVOCATEUR** Clever • Adept Contemporary	**THE QUICK-START** Prolific • Thorough Diligent

If you want a pioneering thinker with an irreverent twist, find "The Maverick Leader," who uses INNOVATION + POWER.

"The Provocateur" has a strong use of INNOVATION + MYSTIQUE, allowing them to fascinate with surprise and wit.

"The Artisan" uses two opposite Advantages: INNOVATION + TRUST. They are creative in a measured and thoughtful way, with crafted style.

Innovation personalities speak the language of creativity.

Their creativity gives them an edge when old solutions don't work anymore. These are the seekers of adventure. The experimenters. The proponents of the new. Life is too short to follow conventions. How about we try something different instead?

Their talent for new thinking helps them to propose unexpected solutions. They are able to develop a profusion of ideas, often quickly. Irreverent and entrepreneurial, they encourage others to break habits and to try new products and fresh ideas. They prefer reimagining something from the ground up rather than tweaking existing ideas.

At a product development meeting, when everyone is discussing how to improve an existing product, they'll suggest developing a completely new product, something totally different from anything in the current catalogue.

These entrepreneurial personalities prevent companies from going stale. Notice how they get a little impatient when they have to follow routines. Hear how they make the mundane look like an adventure. See how they encourage others to try new techniques.

You'll find they get energy from brainstorming sessions. Procedures may wear them down. They love experimenting with anything new, both in their business and personal life. Whether it's a gadget or new marketing tool, they're comfortable with change. This is quite different from Trust personalities, who tend to prefer the predictable routine to the unknown or unusual.

You can count on Innovation personalities to shake things up when required. Sometimes, they go off script. Weary of following the norm, they can make impulsive, ad lib remarks in the middle of a big presentation. At times, they can be perceived as sarcastic.

You might struggle to keep up with Innovation personalities. It may feel like they keep jumping ahead. That's because they don't think in a linear way. Their minds make unusual associations. They're able to look at things in unconventional ways, and worry little about how you're "supposed" to do it.

They embrace and promote new music or ideas (and may drop their support after something goes mainstream).

In positions of leadership, they'll focus on the big picture and rely on their team to fill in the details. They tend to be visionaries forging ahead to implement change. They're happy to take risks, because it's part of the adventure. They tend to make snap decisions based on a gut feeling rather than analyze options in detail.

This is the entrepreneur who redefines an industry. The early adopter of new technology. The tastemaker in fashion.

It's the chiropractor who's not afraid to integrate a revolutionary new treatment.

It's the chef who dreams up a different menu each week with fanciful ingredients.

It's the Web designer exploring new software and platforms.

It's the friend who refuses to stand in line—and gets in through the back door.

Hire more Innovation personalities if you need to challenge the status quo or if you need more creative thinking. In research and development, for instance, they bring new product ideas. In marketing, they create breakthrough campaigns. In design they reimagine products.

If your group has a high number of Innovation personalities, hire more

Trust for stability and consistency. Hire Passion to build engagement within the team and with clients. Hire Alert to follow the plan.

Strategically Increasing Your Organization's Use of the Innovation Advantage

To make a quantum leap forward, your group may need a dash of Innovation. If you're uncomfortable with change (and many of us are), move the team forward in small steps. Tweak a procedure slightly. Experiment in small doses. Try a new approach occasionally, or consider switching up your website design.

Let's have a look at your use of the Innovation Advantage. Does a set schedule put you at ease? Or do you resist routine?

Let's look inside your organization again. Who's always coming up with new ideas? Who's always bending (or breaking) the rules? Can you see how these Innovation personalities provide a healthy balance for those with a strong Alert or Trust Advantage?

With an Innovation personality in the mix, things will never get stale.

THE TRUST ADVANTAGE
Building loyalty over time

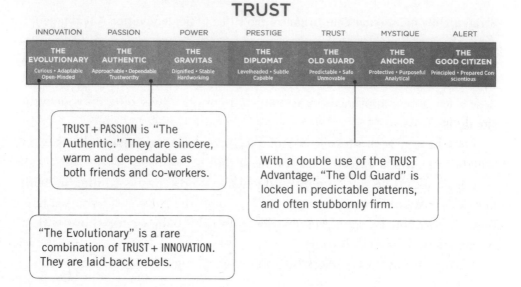

TRUST

INNOVATION	PASSION	POWER	PRESTIGE	TRUST	MYSTIQUE	ALERT
THE EVOLUTIONARY	**THE AUTHENTIC**	**THE GRAVITAS**	**THE DIPLOMAT**	**THE OLD GUARD**	**THE ANCHOR**	**THE GOOD CITIZEN**
Curious · Adaptable Open-Minded	Approachable · Dependable Trustworthy	Dignified · Stable Hardworking	Levelheaded · Subtle Capable	Predictable · Safe Unmovable	Protective · Purposeful Analytical	Principled · Prepared Conscientious

TRUST + PASSION is "The Authentic." They are sincere, warm and dependable as both friends and co-workers.

With a double use of the TRUST Advantage, "The Old Guard" is locked in predictable patterns, and often stubbornly firm.

"The Evolutionary" is a rare combination of TRUST + INNOVATION. They are laid-back rebels.

Trust personalities speak the language of stability.

Their consistency defines their reputation. They follow through on what they promise and deliver on time. They are dependable, committed, and trust-worthy—of course.

Going out for a drink with colleagues? A Trust personality prefers to go to a comfortable bar rather than try a newly opened, trendy café. They probably have their favorite table and the owner knows what they like to drink.

Steady and focused, they get things done. They like to follow a proven method. They're less keen on experimenting—unlike Innovation personalities. Trust personalities create order in chaos. They develop a solid plan of action. They act and respond in predictable ways.

Trust personalities make decisions that benefit the team even if that means extra work or complications for themselves. They prefer to work with familiar faces. Once they know you (and your way of working), you'll get along extremely well. You know exactly what to expect from them. Trust personalities are usually hard workers. They're committed to getting a job done.

During team meetings, you'll see them waiting for their turn to speak.

They'll point out what worked in the past. They'll explain how things are usually done. When they meet resistance from other team members, they're likely to give in to stronger personalities. They tend to go with the flow, and don't upset the applecart.

You know what to expect from Trust personalities. They follow certain routines. For example: They come to the office exactly at 8 a.m. each day, they switch on their computer, have their coffee, and get on with the schedule they prepared the evening before. They like to know ahead of time what needs to get done. You'll see them having lunch at the same time every day.

In sales presentations and client meetings, they're keen to point out how a product has been proven to work over the years. They explain the unfamiliar using familiar points. They launch new products by pointing out what has remained the same.

These are not flashy, pushy salespeople. They sell by building long-term relationships. Their messages are consistent. They stress long-standing relations and remind you that you've always been able to trust them.

Trust personalities are dependable clients to have. They won't switch to other suppliers easily, because they prefer to deal with people they know. They expect a consistent standard from you. Don't change the recipe of their favorite snack!

In managerial positions, they keep the ship steady. They're calm leaders who don't take big risks. They tend to favor organic growth over a risky takeover strategy. They prefer gradual innovation to breakthrough ideas. They like to be organized. They deliver quality work consistently.

They enjoy working with longtime colleagues, but they do believe in fairness and treat newcomers the same as old stalwarts. They don't easily lose their temper. Their behavior is even. Their demeanor is steady. They are respected for their hard work, quality, and reliability.

Trust personalities won't rock the boat. They follow tried-and-tested methods. Rather than being busybodies you'll see them intensely focused on the tasks ahead.

It's the business owner who has steadily grown the company over the past ten years.

It's the childhood friend who continues to send you birthday cards every year.

It's the customer who comes back to buy the same pair of jeans year in and year out.

It's the politician who doesn't flip-flop.

It's the neighbor who never runs out of milk or eggs—so you can always borrow some.

It's the co-worker quietly getting her job done, always delivering on schedule.

Hire more Trust personalities if you want to create stability. As a manufacturing manager, for instance, they'll consistently maintain quality standards. As a factory manager you can count on them to deliver. As a personal assistant they bring order to your chaotic schedule.

If your group has a lot of Trust personalities, balance the group by hiring more Innovation (to come up with big ideas) or more Passion (to create a warmer atmosphere).

Trust personalities add value by delivering on what they promise. They do as they say.

Strategically Increasing Your Use of the Trust Advantage

What are you like? Does routine make you feel comfortable or restless? People with a high use of Trust tend to prefer the familiar to the unproven.

Think about two people trying to sell enterprise software to you. One is bouncing up and down, excited to show you the latest, newest product. His excitement is contagious, and that's how he persuades you to buy. The other plans regular, scheduled visits. You gradually come to rely on her steady, reassuring, objective advice. The latter salesperson, of course, has a stronger Trust Advantage. There's no right or wrong here; everyone closes a deal using the Advantages that come most naturally.

Who in your environment has a strong Trust Advantage? Who is reliable and dependable? Are they ever at risk of being seen as traditionalists who might resist change?

WHAT ARE *YOUR* ADVANTAGES?

Do you have an idea of your primary Advantage? Have you started to see which Advantages you use *most* frequently in your work? And which ones you call on the *least*?

In just a few pages, we'll begin exploring the full spectrum of Archetypes. But first, let's find out what *yours is.*

In your Fascination Advantage report, you'll identify your top Advantages in about five minutes. (***Turn to the back of the book to get your access code and take the assessment.***) You go ahead. I'll wait for you here.

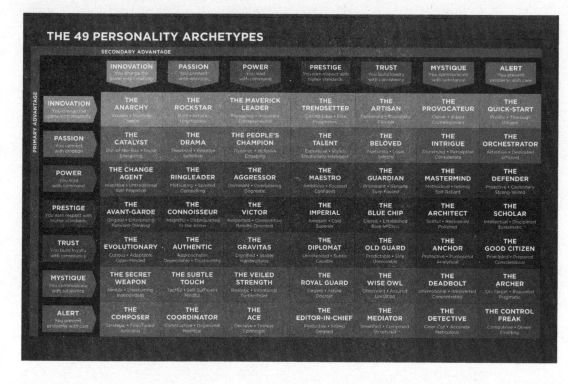

THE 49 PERSONALITY ARCHETYPES

	INNOVATION You change the game with creativity	PASSION You connect with emotion	POWER You lead with command	PRESTIGE You earn respect with higher standards	TRUST You build loyalty with consistency	MYSTIQUE You communicate with substance	ALERT You prevent problems with care
INNOVATION You change the game with creativity	THE ANARCHY Volatile • Startling Chaotic	THE ROCKSTAR Bold • Artistic Unorthodox	THE MAVERICK LEADER Pioneering • Irreverent Entrepreneurial	THE TRENDSETTER Cutting-Edge • Elite Progressive	THE ARTISAN Deliberate • Thoughtful Flexible	THE PROVOCATEUR Clever • Adept Contemporary	THE QUICK-START Prolific • Thorough Diligent
PASSION You connect with emotion	THE CATALYST Out-of-the-Box • Social Energizing	THE DRAMA Theatrical • Emotive Sensitive	THE PEOPLE'S CHAMPION Dynamic • Inclusive Engaging	THE TALENT Expressive • Stylish Emotionally-Intelligent	THE BELOVED Nurturing • Loyal Sincere	THE INTRIGUE Discerning • Perceptive Considerate	THE ORCHESTRATOR Attentive • Dedicated Efficient
POWER You lead with command	THE CHANGE AGENT Inventive • Untraditional Self-Propelled	THE RINGLEADER Motivating • Spirited Compelling	THE AGGRESSOR Dominant • Overbearing Dogmatic	THE MAESTRO Ambitious • Focused Confident	THE GUARDIAN Prominent • Genuine Sure-Footed	THE MASTERMIND Methodical • Intense Self-Reliant	THE DEFENDER Proactive • Cautionary Strong-Willed
PRESTIGE You earn respect with higher standards	THE AVANT-GARDE Original • Enterprising Forward-Thinking	THE CONNOISSEUR Insightful • Distinguished In-the-Know	THE VICTOR Respected • Competitive Results-Oriented	THE IMPERIAL Arrogant • Cold Superior	THE BLUE CHIP Classic • Established Best-In-Class	THE ARCHITECT Skillful • Restrained Polished	THE SCHOLAR Intellectual • Disciplined Systematic
TRUST You build loyalty with consistency	THE EVOLUTIONARY Curious • Adaptable Open-Minded	THE AUTHENTIC Approachable Dependable • Trustworthy	THE GRAVITAS Dignified • Stable Hardworking	THE DIPLOMAT Levelheaded • Subtle Capable	THE OLD GUARD Predictable • Safe Unmovable	THE ANCHOR Protective • Purposeful Analytical	THE GOOD CITIZEN Principled • Prepared Conscientious
MYSTIQUE You communicate with substance	THE SECRET WEAPON Nimble • Unassuming Independent	THE SUBTLE TOUCH Tactful • Self-Sufficient Mindful	THE VEILED STRENGTH Realistic • Intentional To-the-Point	THE ROYAL GUARD Elegant • Astute Discreet	THE WISE OWL Observant • Assured Unruffled	THE DEADBOLT Unemotional • Introverted Concentrated	THE ARCHER On-Target • Reasoned Pragmatic
ALERT You prevent problems with care	THE COMPOSER Strategic • Fine-Tuned Judicious	THE COORDINATOR Constructive • Organized Practical	THE ACE Decisive • Tireless Forthright	THE EDITOR-IN-CHIEF Productive • Skilled Detailed	THE MEDIATOR Steadfast • Composed Structured	THE DETECTIVE Clear-Cut • Accurate Meticulous	THE CONTROL FREAK Compulsive • Driven Exacting

You just discovered how the world sees you, at your best. (What was your biggest a-ha? Tweet me at @SallyHogshead to let me know.)

You already have everything you need to stand out in a distracted, competitive, and commoditized world.

The first step in becoming an effective communicator is to understand how others see you. Then, once you know how the world sees you, you can concentrate on the best of those qualities, and intentionally apply them.

It all begins with knowing your top two Advantages.

Your **primary Advantage** is the mode of communication you most naturally use. It's the most effortless way for you to speak, write, and share ideas. It most closely describes how others are likely to see you. You know those times in your career when things just seem to flow effortlessly? When you're being your most productive and effective? In those occasions, you're applying your primary Advantage. It feels good to use your primary Advantage. It gives you energy and momentum.

Your **secondary Advantage** is the second most likely way for you to communicate. Each Archetype is based on a different combination of a primary and secondary Advantage.

Your **dormant Advantage** is the one you're *least* likely to use. More on that in a minute.

Your primary and secondary Advantages combine to form your **Archetype.**

Archetype = Primary Advantage + Secondary Advantage

Your personality Archetype is composed of the top two Advantages that you are most likely to use in your communication to persuade and influence. For example, if you are The Wise Owl, your primary Advantage is Mystique and your secondary is Trust. If you are The Avant-Garde, you are most likely to communicate with the Prestige Advantage, followed closely by Innovation.

Together, your primary and secondary Advantages illustrate how you're optimally perceived. When you speak either of these two modes, you are confident and effective. These represent your built-in wellspring, energizing and propelling you.

Your personality also has a *dormant* Advantage.

Your dormant Advantage is the way in which you are *least* likely to persuade and captivate others. It feels exhausting to use your dormant Advantage. Imagine drawing with your left hand, if you are actually right-handed. Sure, you can do it if you have to but it's difficult and awkward. And it doesn't get the best possible result. Minimize these types of tasks or scenarios, or else you could be seriously setting yourself up for failure.

For instance, if you have a *dormant* Alert Advantage, you do *not* speak the language of details. You probably don't care for highly structured projects and meetings about minutiae. Detail-oriented meetings? No thanks. You can do it when you absolutely must, but it's not exactly setting you up for success.

If you have a *dormant* Passion Advantage, you do *not* speak the language of relationships. You dislike drama or emotional upheaval. You're a logical and intellectual communicator. Hugging a stranger? Yikes. You probably want to avoid jobs that require a lot of hand-holding for needy co-workers.

When forced to use your dormant Advantage, it exhausts your energy and focus. Because this is your *least* natural mode of communication, it requires tremendous additional energy in order to relate to others in this way. It feels awkward and unnatural. It leaves you drained.

So here's your goal: Find *more* opportunities to apply your top Advantages. Start looking for people and projects that really need these qualities. Intentionally look for challenges and clients who most need these qualities in order to succeed. They are a perfect fit for who you are.

A Quick Review of the Seven Advantages

POWER: You lead with authority.

PASSION: You connect with emotion.

MYSTIQUE: You communicate with care.

PRESTIGE: You set the standard.

ALERT: You protect the details.

INNOVATION: You bring creativity.

TRUST: You build loyalty.

After a short time, these seven categories will become second nature. You'll find yourself applying them every time you meet someone. With a little practice, you can master these Advantages, and apply them throughout your entire life to transform how you see yourself—and how others see you, too.

As you consciously apply your Advantages throughout your work, you'll see a difference immediately. The real win here is to build your entire career—and your life—around your signature way of adding value. If you are an entrepreneur, grow your company around your personality Advantages. If you are an employee, spot the ways in which you are most likely to stand out and earn recognition.

The same goes for scenarios outside of work. Are you looking for love, and wondering how to make a more attractive first impression on a date? Are you hoping to snag that prime internship or club membership? You definitely need to know how the world sees you.

Which Advantage do you use most to persuade people? How about your team members? How about your clients? In Part III, you'll start to understand how to identify a person's primary Advantages so that your business can recruit and retain the Advantages that best solve its particular needs.

Now, ONWARD TO the Archetypes. In the following pages, you'll meet understated thinkers such as The Royal Guard and The Architect, energetic guides in The Ringleader and The People's Champion, skillfully detailed communicators such as The Detective and The Diplomat, and forward-thinking visionaries like The Avant-Garde and The Trendsetter. And you . . . which Archetype are you?

CHAPTER 4

THE ARCHETYPES

YOUR ARCHETYPE

Your Archetype has certain naturally appealing qualities. For instance:

- The BELOVED (Passion + Trust) is nurturing, supportive, and comforting. Like warm chocolate chip cookies.
- The CHANGE AGENT (Power + Innovation) is entrepreneurial and creative with strong goals. Imagine Steve Jobs.
- The CONNOISSEUR (Prestige + Passion) is insightful and in the know. He has high standards and a discerning approach.

Your Archetype is almost like your personality's own built-in superpower. It's already there. Remember: Each Archetype adds value in a different way, making it uniquely persuasive.

Your Archetype defines how you intentionally or unintentionally express yourself and your ideas. You might be rationally inclined and use facts and figures to make your arguments. You might be a more expressive personality, painting vibrant pictures when you talk about your ideas.

There's no right or wrong here. Everyone has a highest distinct value. You can help your team members discover their own.

YOUR FASCINATION ADVANTAGE

When you understand how the world sees you at your best, you can concentrate on what you do best. When you can predict how you are *most* likely to win, and how you are *least* likely to win, you can focus on the areas that give you the highest likelihood for success.

Your Fascination Advantage is the way in which you are most likely to add distinct value. This is your highest and best value as an employee, an entrepreneur, or leader. It's your strong suit.

You've probably heard of a "killer app"—a piece of software that's so desirable, so important, it drives up the value of a whole system. With a killer app, regular things are transformed into "must-have" investments. When email became available in the 1980s, for instance, it drove up computer sales. People loved the idea of email, so everyone wanted to buy computers. Email made computers more valuable and more desirable; it made computers a must-have investment.

Your personality has a killer app. It's your Fascination Advantage.

When you align your goals, actions, and words around these aspects of your personality, you get into perfect alignment with how others see you, so that you can continually operate at your best, with less effort. This is how to become the most authentic you. The you-est you. This is you, just being yourself. (And 100% yourself trumps 100% perfect any day.)

It's not a coincidence that you tend to succeed in certain situations, and tend to become discouraged in others. Your success is not a random occurrence. Once you see the patterns, success will becomes a measurable and controllable outcome.

Today this matters more than ever. In a distracted, competitive, and commoditized world, people don't have time to read a long résumé, or sit through a lengthy pitch. They want you to cut to the chase. Give them the bottom line. Tell them how you are going to add value, right from the start. Make it easy for them to understand. Make it fast. (Remember, you're battling a nine-second attention span.)

It's not your manager's responsibility to figure out how you can help solve a problem. It's not your client's responsibility to see what makes

you different. Same goes for your co-workers, your customers, and your audience. It's not their responsibility. It's yours.

If this news makes you feel stressed or confused, that's understandable. Now the pressure is on *you*, rather than on your *listener*.

YOUR ARCHETYPE'S "TWIN"

Every Archetype has a Twin. The Twin is the Archetype that most closely resembles your score. Under different circumstances, or in a different mood, you could be your Twin. It's the Archetype that most closely resembles your natural communication style.

Here's how to find your Twin.

1. Find your **Archetype**.
2. Now find your **Twin**. Your Twin is your same primary and secondary Advantages, but, in opposite order. For instance:

   If your **Archetype** is The Maestro (Power + Prestige),
   your **Twin** is The Victor (Prestige + Power).

   If your **Archetype** is The Diplomat (Trust + Prestige),
   your **Twin** is The Architect (Prestige + Trust).

See how that works? Same two Advantages, just in reverse order.

Your "Twin" is the Archetype that is closest to yours, with subtle differences. The purpose of pointing out your Twin is to supplement your understanding of how the world sees you by giving a slightly different, yet very similar, facet of yourself.

People do not live in pigeonholes. You communicate differently, in different scenarios. By understanding multiple data points about your personality, you'll have a multifaceted look inside how the world sees you.

On the color Archetype Matrix (on the inside front and back covers), take a look at the three adjectives associated with your Archetype. These adjectives will be important later, as we develop your Anthem, giving you a very tangible and practical application for everything you are learning here.

For now, look at those three adjectives. How does each one describe your way of interacting with others? Think back to the past. . . . How do these adjectives describe how you've created a better solution than your co-workers? Have you exceeded a customer's expectations, because you approached the problem from a slightly different angle? These adjectives illustrate *how you are different*.

If you don't know your own value, don't expect anyone else to.

Fortunately, there's a simple exercise to overcome this challenge. It's your Anthem.

What is an Anthem? It's a very short phrase, only a few words long. It gives a quick snapshot of what makes you most valuable to others. Your Anthem is who you are, at your best.

Your Anthem helps others understand what you do best, so that you can do more of what you do best.

I look forward to helping you and your team create your own Anthem, in Part III. In the meantime, you'll find an example at the end of each Archetype description in Part II.

A PREVIEW TO BUILDING YOUR ANTHEM

In Part III, we'll build your own Anthem. We'll identify the two most important parts of adding value. First, we'll see *how you are different*. Next, we'll pinpoint *what you do best*.

You'll pair an adjective with a noun, giving you a short description of yourself. Here's a preview of how that will work:

1. THE ADJECTIVE: How you are different
2. THE NOUN: What you do best

You don't have to invent any words for this. I'll show you.

Your Fascination Advantage report will automatically include the top adjectives that tell us *what makes you different*. Then I'll give you a list of nouns, and you'll select one that identifies *what you do best*.

Once you pair your adjective with your noun, you'll have an Anthem to confidently convey your highest value.

You'll learn how to build and apply your Anthem in Part III of this book. You'll learn how to apply it to all your communication, from sales and marketing to team building and leadership. You'll finish with a clear road map for how you are most likely to solve problems, and how others are suited to contribute to your group.

WHY YOU MUST HAVE AN ANTHEM

Ever struggle to find the right words to describe yourself?

For instance, have you sat down to write a bio, or apply for a job or school, or fill out a social media profile . . . and then felt uncertain about exactly what to say?

You might start to go around and around in circles (typing, deleting, typing, deleting). You might start to question the whole thing.

Once you create your Anthem, you'll have a strong and persuasive phrase to confidently describe how you are most likely to add value. This short phrase goes a long way toward a positive impression.

When you know exactly how your personality is most likely to add value, you can make it extremely easy for other people to grasp what you bring to the table. People will "get" you more quickly.

As we saw earlier, every time you introduce yourself, you have about nine seconds to engage your listener. This is your window of opportunity for connection. If you earn their interest during those nine seconds, people will be more likely to trust you, respect you, and like you. But if you fumble—if you fail to fascinate—they'll become distracted from you and your message. Or worse, they'll ignore you entirely. Your Anthem is nine seconds long (no longer!), to fit within the nine-second attention span of your listener.

In career-defining situations, when you have to hold someone's full attention (making a presentation or interviewing for a job), those first nine seconds are a golden window of opportunity to make a connection. And it's not just about *first* impressions. This is about tailoring all your communication to deliver *lasting* value.

Now we're going to continue our journey by going inside the Archetypes themselves. Here you will meet everyone you know: Your most treasured friends and college buddies, your work allies and competitive rivals. You'll understand why you see people in certain ways, and how those traits are correlated to their success.

THE PATTERNS BEHIND YOUR SUCCESS

As you read about your Archetype, you'll be applying the research behind it to your own career. You can assess the commonalities that link all of your career's shining moments. And you can more clearly assess the types of negative interactions that seem to consistently get in the way.

Once you learn how to objectively assess a particular role, conversation, or project, you can determine how to proactively achieve your best result. You'll find yourself evaluating your words and behaviors differently, to achieve a different outcome. When you operate in alignment with how the world sees you, things get a lot easier.

This is when you'll really start to stand out. You can stop shouting to be heard. You can stop forcing artificial techniques, like a memorized sales script. You'll just be doing more of what you naturally do, better.

As you read, be thinking of various people you know. You'll probably start to see the patterns that define how they present themselves.

Once you get the hang of the system, you'll probably find yourself beginning to apply it intuitively every time you meet someone new. You'll be able to think of old friends in a new way. Who knows, you might even start looking at people in line at the coffee shop in terms of whether they placed their order with Prestige or Passion.

Which types of projects give you energy and a sense of direction? Which deplete your energy? When you feel productive, you are more likely to add value, because these areas are your wellsprings.

WELLSPRINGS VS. QUICKSAND

For some people, the creative process feels effortless and fun. I can do a creative task all day long and never feel tired or bored. It gives me energy, rather than costing energy. Creativity is a wellspring of productivity that never runs dry. Proofreading, on the other hand, is exhausting for me. It requires tremendous energy and optimism and requires self-discipline. And I'm not likely to add distinct value in this way.

Creativity is my *wellspring*, but proofreading is my *quicksand*. What about you? What areas of work are your wellsprings? What's your quicksand?

No doubt you've already noticed that certain projects help you feel focused and "in the flow." For you, these projects are less effortful and less stressful than other projects. Your wellsprings and your quicksand are linked to your personality Advantages. Tasks and activities that encourage you to apply your *primary* and *secondary* Advantages are likely to be your wellsprings. Those that require you to apply your *dormant* Advantages will feel more like quicksand.

Start to notice: Which areas of work tend to invigorate you, without taking a toll? Which areas allow you to add more value, without *costing* more? These are your wellsprings. These tasks or endeavors fill you with a sense of vitality and focus, and even happiness. Why do these areas feel so productive compared to others? Because they encourage you to concentrate on the ways in which your personality is already custom-built to add value.

All right. Let's begin.

THE PERSONALITY ARCHETYPES

THE POWER ADVANTAGE
THE POWER ADVANTAGE IS LEADING THROUGH AUTHORITY.
POWER PERSONALITIES SPEAK THE LANGUAGE OF CONFIDENCE.

THE CHANGE AGENT: POWER + INNOVATION

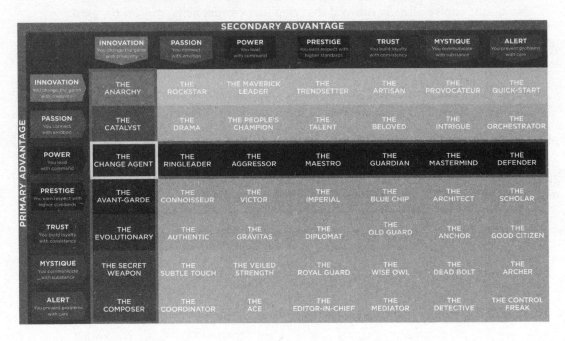

		SECONDARY ADVANTAGE						
		INNOVATION You change the game with creativity	PASSION You connect with emotion	POWER You lead with command	PRESTIGE You earn respect with higher standards	TRUST You build loyalty with consistency	MYSTIQUE You communicate with substance	ALERT You prevent problems with care
PRIMARY ADVANTAGE	**INNOVATION** You change the game with creativity	THE ANARCHY	THE ROCKSTAR	THE MAVERICK LEADER	THE TRENDSETTER	THE ARTISAN	THE PROVOCATEUR	THE QUICK-START
	PASSION You connect with emotion	THE CATALYST	THE DRAMA	THE PEOPLE'S CHAMPION	THE TALENT	THE BELOVED	THE INTRIGUE	THE ORCHESTRATOR
	POWER You lead with command	THE CHANGE AGENT	THE RINGLEADER	THE AGGRESSOR	THE MAESTRO	THE GUARDIAN	THE MASTERMIND	THE DEFENDER
	PRESTIGE You earn respect with higher standards	THE AVANT-GARDE	THE CONNOISSEUR	THE VICTOR	THE IMPERIAL	THE BLUE CHIP	THE ARCHITECT	THE SCHOLAR
	TRUST You build loyalty with consistency	THE EVOLUTIONARY	THE AUTHENTIC	THE GRAVITAS	THE DIPLOMAT	THE OLD GUARD	THE ANCHOR	THE GOOD CITIZEN
	MYSTIQUE You communicate with substance	THE SECRET WEAPON	THE SUBTLE TOUCH	THE VEILED STRENGTH	THE ROYAL GUARD	THE WISE OWL	THE DEAD BOLT	THE ARCHER
	ALERT You prevent problems with care	THE COMPOSER	THE COORDINATOR	THE ACE	THE EDITOR-IN-CHIEF	THE MEDIATOR	THE DETECTIVE	THE CONTROL FREAK

HOW THE WORLD SEES THE CHANGE AGENT

Change Agents are creative thinkers who thrive on reinventing.

Change Agents are different from the pack. They are independent, witty, and sharp. They see a future no one else sees. They have a strong drive to come up with a different approach. They bring alternative opinions to dull meetings. They bring fresh ideas to stale companies. They overturn the status quo in business, in politics, and charitable organizations.

Archetype Twin

The Maverick Leader (page 248)

The Change Agent's Top 5 Adjectives

1. **Inventive**—Change Agents are resourceful and artistic. As marketers, they come up with creative campaign ideas. As CEOs, they reinvent business models from the ground up. They find new solutions to depart from traditional methods.

2. **Untraditional**—They are unafraid to go against the grain. They can look at the *same old* from a fresh perspective. When people suggest, *That's how things are done over here*, they ask, *Have you tried it another way?* They thrive when encouraged to experiment.

3. **Self-propelled**—They are highly motivated to keep developing new ideas. Each time they write their monthly report, they add a new section or change their colorful graphs. Their aversion to routine means they test alternative approaches.

4. **Vivid**—Their communication style is rarely shy. When presenting their ideas they may use a surprising story or challenging opinion. They captivate their audience by avoiding a predictable format.

5. **Quick-witted**—They think quickly, and perform well on their feet. In both professional and social situations, they enjoy witty conversation and spontaneous discussion.

"Highest and Best Value" of The Change Agent

Their energy and direction give them the power to inspire other people to be innovative, too. They have a naturally curious personality. They tend to be pretty fearless in their approach, and this is clear in how they communicate. When they get on a roll, they can bring people in with a flurry of untraditional approaches. When everyone else has staid PowerPoint slides crammed with text, you'll see a Change Agent use bright slides with graphics and few words; they experiment with video and music; and when they talk they sketch their ideas with colorful metaphors.

They are not afraid to be different. In fact, they enjoy being unlike anyone else. They encourage others to step out of the box, too. That's how they help companies to improve.

What Is Not the "Highest and Best Value" of The Change Agent?

Not a fan of deadlines and step-by-step processes, Change Agents are more excited about instigating new plans than finishing them.

To help your Change Agents implement their bounty of ideas, consider teaming them up with methodical communicators (such as Alert and Mystique), to turn ideas into reality.

How to Work with a Change Agent

Is your company stuck in a declining market? Do you struggle to come up with new opportunities and business ideas? Look for a Change Agent to reinvigorate your business.

They tackle problems with a sense of adventure. They invent new methods to work around obstacles. They love to brainstorm. They improvise. They formulate new business models, new products, and new processes.

Their creative spirit might be squelched at a traditional, hierarchical organization. They don't respond well to being micromanaged. You get most out of your Change Agents if they are in a position to bring new ideas to the table.

Archetypes That Can Optimize The Change Agent

Steadfast and methodical, The Diplomat (page 280) delivers quality results. They can map an efficient plan to implement ideas from The Change Agent. While The Change Agent focuses on new opportunities, The Editor-in-Chief (page 232) tends to avoid negative consequences. Together they are a balanced team to implement innovation.

A Lesson That Everyone Can Learn from The Change Agent

Breakthrough innovation requires going against the grain.

One-Minute Coaching to My Change Agents

You get a rush from change. Sometimes your constant flow of ideas can come across as impulsive. (That's the downside of creativity—it's not locked into a simplistic formula.) Try to step back occasionally. See how others react to your ideas. Ensure that changes are embedded into the organization before you push for the next innovation.

Not everyone enjoys change as much as you do. Lean on your Power Advantage to direct the team and use the stability of Trust to earn their loyalty.

Famous Change Agents
Steve Jobs and Arianna Huffington

Example of an Anthem for The Change Agent
INVENTIVE ANSWERS

How The Change Agent Might Apply This Anthem
Other employees in Kevin's consulting company operate on autopilot. They simply follow established procedures and proven methods to meet expectations. Kevin, on the other hand, has a pioneering and entrepreneurial mindset. He's quickly risen to a leadership role because he doesn't just rehash the same clichéd approach. He finds untraditional solutions, solving old problems in new ways. He adds value by applying a "what if" mentality, so that his project managers avoid getting in a rut with their teams. He takes initiative to uncover inventive solutions. His team feels challenged and inspired to push the boundaries.

THE RINGLEADER: POWER + PASSION

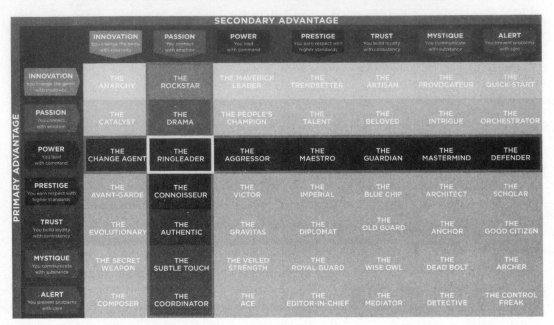

HOW THE WORLD SEES THE RINGLEADER

Ringleaders have the ability to energize their team. While some personalities might make you feel shut down or emotionally flatlined, a Ringleader is more likely to get you charged up.

Their secondary Passion Advantage means that they know how to make you feel valued. Their personal dedication motivates you to contribute more as well.

When you're struggling to explain a problem you're facing, a Ringleader intuitively understands and responds. He addresses your problem and validates your concerns. It feels like you're in it together, and he makes you feel confident that you'll succeed.

Ringleaders are driven personalities but not in a cutthroat, competitive way. They're inclusive; they know how to engage and inspire. They spark participation among teams; their enthusiasm is contagious.

(Anecdotally: We have noticed that many of our clients who are chief marketing officers are Ringleaders, because they have both the strength and energy to move a marketing team.)

As you'd expect from a Ringleader, they're enthusiastic supporters. They inspire and organize others to help reach objectives. They're passionate spokespeople for groups and ideas.

Archetype Twin
The People's Champion (page 152)

The Ringleader's Top 5 Adjectives
1. **Motivated**—Ringleaders are ambitious. Have a Ringleader in your sales team? Others in your sales team most likely look up to her. She inspires them all to work harder and smarter to achieve company targets.

2. **Spirited**—They are energized by working toward goals. Ringleaders in your call center always sound happy on the phone. At the end of the day, when others are tired and start shutting down their computers, they might make that one extra call. They're always full of life.

3. **Compelling**—They are quick to gain the buy-in of their audience. As senior managers they make a strong case for their ideas. Their presentations are charged and expressive.

4. **Strong-minded**—Determined to succeed and unfazed by setbacks, Ringleaders are extremely confident in their ability to generate solutions and reach goals. Has their most successful salesperson left their team? They'll work extra hard to train a junior member of the team to help hit targets.

5. **Empathetic**—They read others and understand "where they're coming from." At a cocktail party they easily mingle with people they don't know. As CEOs they have an open-door policy; even junior staff members are comfortable asking them for advice. They connect with others quickly.

"Highest and Best Value" of The Ringleader
Their attractive and expressive personality makes them influential.

They are cheerleaders for people and ideas. Their primary Power Advantage keeps them focused on achieving objectives, while their Passion Advantage draws others into their goals.

Ringleaders are clearly in command. They keep meetings on track. They energize discussions. Their natural optimism inspires others.

What Is Not the "Highest and Best Value" of The Ringleader?

Ringleaders aren't quiet observers. Don't expect them to passively sit back during a conversation. Ringleaders enjoy being at the front of a room, leading discussions. Being relegated to the back of the room is a waste. They thrive in cheering others.

How to Work with a Ringleader

Ringleaders believe that the sum of the parts is greater than the whole. They're strong team leaders. They fire up the team spirit, and keep everyone focused on the big picture.

Ringleaders certainly have leadership potential (as you'd expect with such a name). Allow them to step forward and take advantage of their expressive personality.

They're influencers who are at their best when fighting for ideas, people, or a good cause.

Archetypes That Can Optimize The Ringleader

The Subtle Touch (page 176) is a quiet observer who will stay calm in the most hectic circumstances.

The Architect (page 212) keeps an eye on the details and the quality of results.

A Lesson That Everyone Can Learn from The Ringleader

Lead by enthusiastic example.

One-Minute Coaching to My Ringleaders

You are an influential personality. Your team members enjoy working for you. Sometimes your innate enthusiasm can overwhelm others. Take more time to observe the reaction of others. Sometimes it's good to control your boundless energy to avoid dominating the conversation.

Famous Ringleaders

Richard Branson and Tim Tebow

Example of an Anthem for The Ringleader
MOTIVATING CONFIDENCE

How The Ringleader Might Apply This Anthem
As the chief marketing officer of a mid-sized company, Selena is responsible for developing marketing ideas that motivate consumers to purchase her company's products. In order to do this, she also needs to motivate her staff. In weekly meetings, she encourages her team with spirited energy and compelling ideas. Selena starts each meeting with a list of achievements for the past week. She rallies her team behind what they have accomplished and then motivates them to make this week even better.

THE MAESTRO: POWER + PRESTIGE

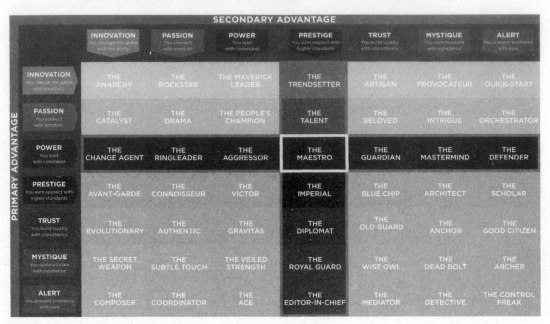

		SECONDARY ADVANTAGE					
	INNOVATION You change the game with creativity	PASSION You connect with emotion	POWER You lead with command	PRESTIGE You earn respect with higher standards	TRUST You build loyalty with consistency	MYSTIQUE You communicate with substance	ALERT You prevent problems with care
INNOVATION You change the game with creativity	THE ANARCHY	THE ROCKSTAR	THE MAVERICK LEADER	THE TRENDSETTER	THE ARTISAN	THE PROVOCATEUR	THE QUICK-START
PASSION You connect with emotion	THE CATALYST	THE DRAMA	THE PEOPLE'S CHAMPION	THE TALENT	THE BELOVED	THE INTRIGUE	THE ORCHESTRATOR
POWER You lead with command	THE CHANGE AGENT	THE RINGLEADER	THE AGGRESSOR	THE MAESTRO	THE GUARDIAN	THE MASTERMIND	THE DEFENDER
PRESTIGE You earn respect with higher standards	THE AVANT-GARDE	THE CONNOISSEUR	THE VICTOR	THE IMPERIAL	THE BLUE CHIP	THE ARCHITECT	THE SCHOLAR
TRUST You build loyalty with consistency	THE EVOLUTIONARY	THE AUTHENTIC	THE GRAVITAS	THE DIPLOMAT	THE OLD GUARD	THE ANCHOR	THE GOOD CITIZEN
MYSTIQUE You communicate with substance	THE SECRET WEAPON	THE SUBTLE TOUCH	THE VEILED STRENGTH	THE ROYAL GUARD	THE WISE OWL	THE DEAD BOLT	THE ARCHER
ALERT You prevent problems with care	THE COMPOSER	THE COORDINATOR	THE ACE	THE EDITOR-IN-CHIEF	THE MEDIATOR	THE DETECTIVE	THE CONTROL FREAK

PRIMARY ADVANTAGE

HOW THE WORLD SEES THE MAESTRO

Maestros are natural leaders.

The Maestro speaks the language of confidence (that's Power) and the language of excellence (that's Prestige). You'll see them making decisions easily, reaching conclusions quickly, then taking action. In meetings, they convey self-assurance of thinking and purpose. In conversation, they express concepts directly.

Whether energetically outgoing or quietly intense, all Maestros share a strong will and driving force. They have the "horsepower" to achieve big goals. This is a core advantage for professional interactions. By keeping their eye on the prize, they often excel in competitive business environments.

Archetype Twin
The Victor (page 204)

The Maestro's Top 5 Adjectives

1. Ambitious—Their constant drive to improve keeps the bar high for themselves (and others!). In a job interview you'll find they have their career planned out. They know exactly what they want to achieve in five years' time.

2. Focused—As soon as a Maestro zeroes in on a goal, he pursues it with vigor and is unlikely to just passively observe.

3. Confident—They have a game-loving competitive spirit and pursue life ambitiously. In sales and account management you'll find them doing their best to exceed their targets by a higher percentage than the rest of the group; when taking part in a company sports day, they like to be on the winning team.

4. Uncompromising—Maestros stay committed in the face of challenges or obstacles. They don't allow their team to back down or settle too easily when faced with problems. As sales managers, they ensure their team knows how to overcome customer objections to buying.

5. Formidable—While their drive can sometimes be perceived as intimidating, it can also be a stellar leadership advantage. They are the CEOs everyone respects. They are the leaders everyone follows naturally.

"Highest and Best Value" of The Maestro

Influential leadership improves performance and results.

Maestros have very high standards for themselves, and their co-workers. Employees, partners, and customers often comment on their superior dedication. With a primary Power Advantage, they have strong opinions. Their secondary Prestige Advantage means they have and set high expectations.

While other Archetypes may become complacent (or stuck) in a job, Maestros rarely get into a rut. They have the Type-A determination necessary to push through tough challenges.

What Is Not the "Highest and Best Value" of The Maestro?

Don't put your Maestro on a professional treadmill and expect them to get very far. Don't overmanage their agenda and expect them to remain motivated.

The key to this personality's value is their drive to succeed. Maestros want to be in charge of their own deliverables—though they're rarely loners.

They're energized by leading a team, and they'll do their utmost to make their team the winning one.

How to Work with a Maestro

How to get the most out of your Maestro employees? They need to feel that they are contributing significantly. They are incentivized by recognition, and respond well to a clearly defined system of rewards. Coach them with specific feedback on how to improve. Rather than rigidly managing these overachievers, support them in exceeding expectations.

Is your manager or client a Maestro? Get really clear about his specific expectations, so you're aligned on how to build momentum. Know what matters. Be mindful that they set the bar high for themselves and for you.

Archetypes That Can Optimize The Maestro

The Beloved (page 160) will help Maestros by providing nurturing loyalty. The Provocateur (page 260) will complement the Maestro with a zing of unexpected thinking.

A Lesson That Everyone Can Learn from The Maestro

Identify your primary goal, and then concentrate your thoughts and actions toward that purpose. Steer yourself and others in that direction.

One-Minute Coaching to My Maestros

You are naturally independent. You tend to believe (often rightly so) that you can simply do things better yourself. Sound familiar? If so, you might find yourself stepping in to take over.

Take note: This approach can slow your goals if others feel they can't contribute enough. Coach your team members to improve their own performance. Allow them to learn by making their own mistakes. You'll progress further if you can help your team to develop their skills.

Famous Maestros

Michael Bloomberg and Enzo Ferrari

Example of an Anthem for The Maestro
AMBITIOUS RESULTS

How The Maestro Might Apply This Anthem
Maestros are Type-A leaders who seek results. For example, Amy, a sales manager, applies her Anthem by making a point to begin every production meeting with the same step: outlining exactly what type of AMBITIOUS RESULTS she expects from her team for the coming month. She assigns clear targets and recommendations for each member of the team so that everyone is very clear about next steps, and will stay focused on their goals.

THE GUARDIAN: POWER + TRUST

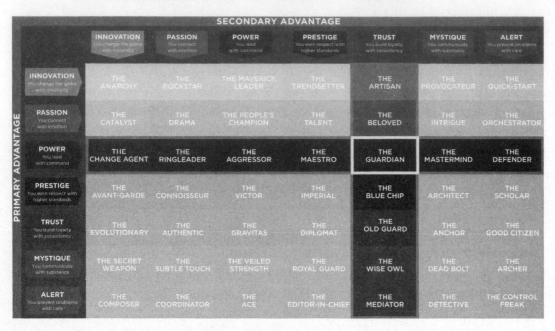

		SECONDARY ADVANTAGE					
	INNOVATION You change the game with creativity	**PASSION** You connect with emotion	**POWER** You lead with command	**PRESTIGE** You earn respect with higher standards	**TRUST** You build loyalty with consistency	**MYSTIQUE** You communicate with substance	**ALERT** You prevent problems with care
INNOVATION You change the game with creativity	THE ANARCHY	THE ROCKSTAR	THE MAVERICK LEADER	THE TRENDSETTER	THE ARTISAN	THE PROVOCATEUR	THE QUICK-START
PASSION You connect with emotion	THE CATALYST	THE DRAMA	THE PEOPLE'S CHAMPION	THE TALENT	THE BELOVED	THE INTRIGUE	THE ORCHESTRATOR
POWER You lead with command	THE CHANGE AGENT	THE RINGLEADER	THE AGGRESSOR	THE MAESTRO	THE GUARDIAN	THE MASTERMIND	THE DEFENDER
PRESTIGE You earn respect with higher standards	THE AVANT-GARDE	THE CONNOISSEUR	THE VICTOR	THE IMPERIAL	THE BLUE CHIP	THE ARCHITECT	THE SCHOLAR
TRUST You build loyalty with consistency	THE EVOLUTIONARY	THE AUTHENTIC	THE GRAVITAS	THE DIPLOMAT	THE OLD GUARD	THE ANCHOR	THE GOOD CITIZEN
MYSTIQUE You communicate with substance	THE SECRET WEAPON	THE SUBTLE TOUCH	THE VEILED STRENGTH	THE ROYAL GUARD	THE WISE OWL	THE DEAD BOLT	THE ARCHER
ALERT You prevent problems with care	THE COMPOSER	THE COORDINATOR	THE ACE	THE EDITOR-IN-CHIEF	THE MEDIATOR	THE DETECTIVE	THE CONTROL FREAK

PRIMARY ADVANTAGE

HOW THE WORLD SEES THE GUARDIAN

Guardians are sure-footed leaders.

They set big goals (that's their primary Power Advantage). As professional managers, they are role models for young talent. As literature fans, they strive to publish a bestseller. As senior managers, they have their eye on the top job. As CEOs they have ambitious plans for growth.

They exude a natural authority. They're composed. They express their opinions with a quiet, unwavering conviction. And they direct groups with gentle confidence.

Maybe considered gurus, but definitely experts, Guardians have strong reputations. They're Guardians because they are loyal leaders who protect their teams.

Archetype Twin

The Gravitas (page 276)

The Guardian's Top 5 Adjectives

1. Prominent—Guardians tend to be established and respected as leaders in their field. As search engine optimization specialists they get invited to speak at conferences. As copywriters they could be teaching a writing course. As CEOs they're interviewed to comment on the latest industry merger. They have earned a strong reputation for success.

2. Genuine—They are warm and authentic. You feel you can always ask them for help. They take their time to answer your questions. Their willingness to help feels sincere.

3. Sure-footed—They have an unwavering confidence in their own ability. When practicing their tennis shot, they do so with determination. They know how they'll get better. They see the right path to reach their goals. And in organizations they carefully lead others along with them.

4. Constant—Their stability is a significant advantage in competitive environments. In soccer, they might be the rock-solid defender who everyone expects to win a tackle. In business, they are the leaders who keep their cool— even when a long-awaited new product is delayed again. People know what to expect from Guardians and rely on them again, and again.

5. Resilient—They are unfazed by setbacks and tough challenges. When your stock price drops due to takeover rumors in the market, they calmly respond to press inquiries. You might occasionally find them working late at night to stay on top of their work. They are physically and mentally dedicated, and are slow to tire.

"Highest and Best Value" of The Guardian

Goal driven and strong, they bring certainty in dynamic environments.

They don't panic when a star achiever leaves. They don't lose their nerves when a new competitor quickly gains market share. They don't get distressed when a major customer goes into liquidation.

Guardians rarely show stress. They remain calm when an organization is under pressure; and others lean on them frequently.

What Is Not the "Highest and Best Value" of The Guardian?

They are unlikely to gush about their ideas or share early thoughts off the cuff. They don't wear their hearts on their sleeves. They don't lead in an impulsive, dramatic style. Guardians command with authority and build relationships over time.

How to Work with a Guardian

You can rely on their leadership. They have a sound long-term vision. They establish a certain stability and calmness to help them achieve their objectives. Their direct manner earns them respect, and influences others—even skeptics.

You can find them at universities as respected authorities. In business you can find them as experts in IT and world-class operations, in finance and statistics, in lean management and marketing strategy.

A Guardian thrives in a professional job where their expertise can develop over time. They're equally at ease in structured and chaotic environments.

Archetypes That Can Optimize The Guardian

An Editor-in-Chief (page 232) watches details while raising quality standards. A Quick-Start (page 264) has a quiet "can-do" attitude. Their creative abilities will add value to the team.

A Lesson That Everyone Can Learn from The Guardian

Overnight success doesn't exist. It takes time to build a solid reputation.

One-Minute Coaching to My Guardians

Our organization has come to depend on you a great deal. You are the rock everyone comes to rely on for advice. You've grown in your role and taken on a lot of responsibilities.

You can further develop your leadership skills by adding a jot of Innovation to your repertoire, and be a little more creative when the situation demands fresh ideas. Be a little more agile when quick action is necessary.

Famous Guardians

Warren Buffett and Superman

Example of an Anthem for The Guardian
SURE-FOOTED INFLUENCE

How The Guardian Might Apply This Anthem
Gina is a financial advisor. Most of her clients are older, retired, and risk-averse. They are not looking for an innovative approach; they want an established track record. Gina has gradually established a prominent reputation within her community. When meeting with prospective clients, she communicates SURE-FOOTED INFLUENCE by demonstrating how her investments have been stable and consistent over time. She provides clear examples of how her clients have increased their financial freedom by following her tested investment strategies.

THE MASTERMIND: POWER + MYSTIQUE

PRIMARY ADVANTAGE	SECONDARY ADVANTAGE						
	INNOVATION You change the game with creativity	PASSION You connect with emotion	POWER You lead with command	PRESTIGE You earn respect with higher standards	TRUST You build loyalty with consistency	MYSTIQUE You communicate with substance	ALERT You prevent problems with care
INNOVATION You change the game with creativity	THE ANARCHY	THE ROCKSTAR	THE MAVERICK LEADER	THE TRENDSETTER	THE ARTISAN	THE PROVOCATEUR	THE QUICK-START
PASSION You connect with emotion	THE CATALYST	THE DRAMA	THE PEOPLE'S CHAMPION	THE TALENT	THE BELOVED	THE INTRIGUE	THE ORCHESTRATOR
POWER You lead with command	THE CHANGE AGENT	THE RINGLEADER	THE AGGRESSOR	THE MAESTRO	THE GUARDIAN	THE MASTERMIND	THE DEFENDER
PRESTIGE You earn respect with higher standards	THE AVANT-GARDE	THE CONNOISSEUR	THE VICTOR	THE IMPERIAL	THE BLUE CHIP	THE ARCHITECT	THE SCHOLAR
TRUST You build loyalty with consistency	THE EVOLUTIONARY	THE AUTHENTIC	THE GRAVITAS	THE DIPLOMAT	THE OLD GUARD	THE ANCHOR	THE GOOD CITIZEN
MYSTIQUE You communicate with substance	THE SECRET WEAPON	THE SUBTLE TOUCH	THE VEILED STRENGTH	THE ROYAL GUARD	THE WISE OWL	THE DEAD BOLT	THE ARCHER
ALERT You prevent problems with care	THE COMPOSER	THE COORDINATOR	THE ACE	THE EDITOR-IN-CHIEF	THE MEDIATOR	THE DETECTIVE	THE CONTROL FREAK

HOW THE WORLD SEES THE MASTERMIND

Masterminds keep everyone focused on long-term goals without distractions. They radiate calm leadership. They are firmly in control. Intelligent and determined, they fascinate with their understated approach.

When you're interviewing a Mastermind for a podcast, you might feel he's too humble. He doesn't "sell" his achievements. During the interview he carefully considers each of your questions before providing a nuanced answer. He prefers to focus on his expertise and tends to avoid answering personal questions.

As you'd expect from Masterminds, they are comfortable to act on their own and to work out their own plan. Like chess players they always think two steps ahead, and they carefully observe people's reactions. They are respected for their impartiality and methodical approach.

Archetype Twin
The Veiled Strength (page 180)

The Mastermind's Top 5 Adjectives

1. Methodical—Masterminds present their ideas with clarity. Their responses are careful and rational. Has your Twitter account been hacked? They quietly take control of the situation, and implement a step-by-step plan to limit reputational damage. They inform their Twitter followers in a calm but decisive manner.

2. Intense—They are able to channel their energy to achieve their goals. When chairing a board meeting, they keep the discussion on track. Even in dynamic environments they're able to concentrate efforts on the company's priorities.

3. Self-reliant—Masterminds tend to define solutions on their own. They're comfortable setting out their own plan. They expect their team to work independently, too. They will set clear goals and then stand back to allow others to get on with the job.

4. Understated—They quietly execute their plans without shining the spotlight on themselves. They are ambitious, but not in a conspicuous way. They let their results speak for themselves.

5. Complex—Their personality is multilayered. They are calm leaders who are firmly in control, but who maintain a sense of privacy. They don't always reveal their opinions. They carefully choose which parts of their personality to bring out in the open.

"Highest and Best Value" of The Mastermind

They are comfortable with making decisions that have big implications.

They have a strong ability to absorb and analyze complex information. They base their decisions on data rather than emotion. They like to think things through. They take command of a situation. They act in a resolute way.

Masterminds are natural leaders who remain coolheaded even in chaotic situations.

What Is Not the "Highest and Best Value" of The Mastermind?

They're less likely to experiment, or to flood a frequent flow of communication, or to rally people with spirited get-togethers. They prefer to hold back until they're sure about which path to take. As a result, they set big goals and implement them in a systematic way.

How to Work with a Mastermind

Masterminds quietly execute their plans and deliver results. You get the most out of your Masterminds if you allow them a certain degree of independence. Is a Mastermind reporting to you? They don't respond well to micromanagement. Agree on clear objectives and let them plan the associated tasks themselves.

It can be difficult to get close to a Mastermind. They don't show their whole hand, and rarely give glimpses of their personal life. Probing too much into their personal life may make them uncomfortable. Sometimes they create an air of mystery; other times, they can come across as disinterested.

Archetypes That Can Optimize The Mastermind

A People's Champion (page 152) is an action-oriented go-getter who's comfortable with implementing group plans.

A Scholar (page 216) adds a sense of urgency and a focus on getting details right.

A Lesson That Everyone Can Learn from The Mastermind

People who quietly get on with their job can accomplish a lot.

One-Minute Coaching to My Masterminds

You are a strong leader. You keep the team focused on improving company objectives. You command with authority, but you may benefit from adding Passion to your leadership repertoire.

Show your excitement about great results. Share your enthusiasm about your products. Add a little more warmth and feeling to your presentations when you want to quickly build an emotional connection.

Famous Masterminds

Mark Zuckerberg and Prince Charles

Example of an Anthem for The Mastermind

METHODICAL SYSTEMS

How The Mastermind Might Apply This Anthem

Masterminds are seen as self-reliant implementers. These calm leaders are firmly in control. They excel in delivering a clearly defined, step-by-step process. One of our clients, a Mastermind named Greg, helps companies turn their chaotic sales funnels into an organized and replicable system. He consults with sales managers to turn disorganized and imprecise approaches into METHODICAL SYSTEMS. All of his communication is centered on this specific promise so that potential clients know exactly what to expect from him.

THE DEFENDER: POWER + ALERT

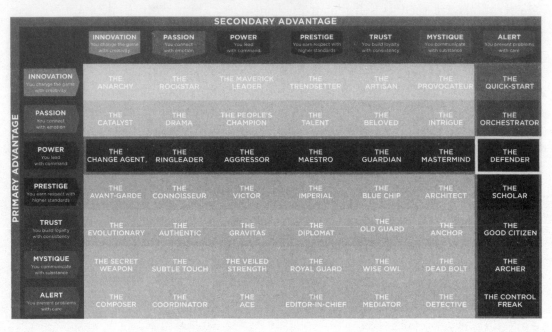

	SECONDARY ADVANTAGE						
	INNOVATION You change the game with creativity	**PASSION** You connect with emotion	**POWER** You lead with command	**PRESTIGE** You earn respect with higher standards	**TRUST** You build loyalty with consistency	**MYSTIQUE** You communicate with substance	**ALERT** You prevent problems with care
INNOVATION You change the game with creativity	THE ANARCHY	THE ROCKSTAR	THE MAVERICK LEADER	THE TRENDSETTER	THE ARTISAN	THE PROVOCATEUR	THE QUICK-START
PASSION You connect with emotion	THE CATALYST	THE DRAMA	THE PEOPLE'S CHAMPION	THE TALENT	THE BELOVED	THE INTRIGUE	THE ORCHESTRATOR
POWER You lead with command	THE CHANGE AGENT	THE RINGLEADER	THE AGGRESSOR	THE MAESTRO	THE GUARDIAN	THE MASTERMIND	THE DEFENDER
PRESTIGE You earn respect with higher standards	THE AVANT-GARDE	THE CONNOISSEUR	THE VICTOR	THE IMPERIAL	THE BLUE CHIP	THE ARCHITECT	THE SCHOLAR
TRUST You build loyalty with consistency	THE EVOLUTIONARY	THE AUTHENTIC	THE GRAVITAS	THE DIPLOMAT	THE OLD GUARD	THE ANCHOR	THE GOOD CITIZEN
MYSTIQUE You communicate with substance	THE SECRET WEAPON	THE SUBTLE TOUCH	THE VEILED STRENGTH	THE ROYAL GUARD	THE WISE OWL	THE DEAD BOLT	THE ARCHER
ALERT You prevent problems with care	THE COMPOSER	THE COORDINATOR	THE ACE	THE EDITOR-IN-CHIEF	THE MEDIATOR	THE DETECTIVE	THE CONTROL FREAK

(Left axis label: PRIMARY ADVANTAGE)

HOW THE WORLD SEES THE DEFENDER

They are strong, driven leaders who create momentum to get a project done.

You probably recognize a Defender as a traditional leader. They're not control freaks, but they're certainly aware of everything that's going on in an organization. They're quick to point out issues and avoid embarking on risky ventures.

Defenders are highly principled. They expect people to follow guidelines and instructions. If you have a Defender as vice president of human resources, then he's probably made sure someone has prepared an extensive employee handbook. He expects it to be followed. His approach to employee issues is strict but fair.

They are Defenders because they always look out for potential issues. They defend themselves and their team to prevent problems.

Archetype Twin
The Ace (page 228)

The Defender's Top 5 Adjectives

1. Proactive—Defenders consistently step forward to take charge, especially in situations where early action makes a difference. When an accident happens on their street, they're probably the first to call an ambulance. Quick to volunteer, they will help by diverting traffic or administering first aid.

2. Cautionary—They always think before they act. Looking to launch a new product range? As customer service managers, they will point out the need to get staff trained up well before the launch. Their thoughtfulness helps avoid errors and navigate obstacles.

3. Strong-willed—They have a competitive drive. They solve problems instantly and complete tasks promptly. Independent-minded and hardworking, they get the job done.

4. Regardful—They sense when issues arise that require a swift reaction. They change course before others realize something needs to be done. Has an employee turned up late a few times? They will issue a warning before latecoming becomes a habit. Are call waiting times increasing? They're swift to propose adding resources before the team gets overstretched. Determined and observant, they are cautious players.

5. Action-oriented—Despite carefully considering their reaction, Defenders are quick to take action and produce results. Are sales in the first week of the month lagging behind? They will consider potential actions before deciding on a specific price promotion to meet the budget. They keep their eye on long-term company goals.

"Highest and Best Value" of The Defender

Defenders can be tough taskmasters. They don't accept complacency. They're quick to notice underperformance and noncompliance to procedures. Where other managers may find an excuse to delay a disciplinary meeting, Defenders are unafraid to start difficult conversations. They quickly take control of a situation.

As salespeople, they can figure out what needs to be done to hit target by the end of the month. In client meetings, they don't easily accept *no* as an answer. They like to negotiate time-sensitive deals, like a 10% discount if you order before close of day tomorrow. And you can be sure they follow up the next day to ask for the order.

What Is Not the "Highest and Best Value" of The Defender?

Defenders are less likely to come up with radical ideas. Don't expect them to experiment with new procedures, if a *tried-and-tested* method is already in place.

Cautious and thoughtful, Defenders will choose a safe option for steady growth rather than a risky strategy that may bring either exponential growth or failure.

How to Work with a Defender

Defenders are careful decision-makers who have a rational approach to making choices. They're able to analyze situations in a methodical way. They weigh pros and cons. They clearly define expected outcomes.

Defenders are strong appointments in traditional hierarchies where their methodical approach is valued. However, don't overlook a Defender if you're at an innovative organization, since their cautiousness can form a useful balance in an Innovation-dominated team.

Archetypes That Can Optimize The Defender

Team a Defender up with an Artisan (page 256) to add creativity and an entrepreneurial spirit to the team.

When change is less important, you may want to consider the appointment of an Anchor (page 284) to build long-term relationships.

A Lesson That Everyone Can Learn from a Defender

It's best to detect issues before they become problems.

One-Minute Coaching to My Defenders

You can show leadership when you make decisive choices, especially when you consider the company's long-term goals. To rise to your highest level, you must also learn how to embrace the group and be open to possibilities. Your first instinct might be to say *no,* because your natural mind-set is to be cautionary and to avoid failure. When an opportunity arises, however, be sure to weigh the upsides as well as downsides. To further your career you need to take some calculated risks and stretch outside your comfort zone.

Famous Defenders

Al Gore and Suze Orman

Example of an Anthem for The Defender

PROACTIVE DETAILS

How The Defender Might Apply This Anthem

Holly is a Defender. She likes to direct the plan, and be aware of any potential problems in advance. When she's planning a vacation, for instance, she's on the lookout for every possible contingency. She makes backup arrangements just in case the unexpected strikes. She literally wants to steady the ship. Her cautionary PROACTIVE approach to the DETAILS makes others feel safe that things will be handled for them.

THE PASSION ADVANTAGE

THE PASSION ADVANTAGE IS THE ABILITY TO CREATE WARM EMOTIONAL CONNECTIONS.

PASSION PERSONALITIES SPEAK THE LANGUAGE OF RELATIONSHIP.

THE CATALYST: PASSION + INNOVATION

PRIMARY ADVANTAGE	SECONDARY ADVANTAGE						
	INNOVATION — You change the game with creativity	PASSION — You connect with emotion	POWER — You lead with command	PRESTIGE — You earn respect with higher standards	TRUST — You build loyalty with consistency	MYSTIQUE — You communicate with substance	ALERT — You prevent problems with care
INNOVATION — You change the game with creativity	THE ANARCHY	THE ROCKSTAR	THE MAVERICK LEADER	THE TRENDSETTER	THE ARTISAN	THE PROVOCATEUR	THE QUICK-START
PASSION — You connect with emotion	THE CATALYST	THE DRAMA	THE PEOPLE'S CHAMPION	THE TALENT	THE BELOVED	THE INTRIGUE	THE ORCHESTRATOR
POWER — You lead with command	THE CHANGE AGENT	THE RINGLEADER	THE AGGRESSOR	THE MAESTRO	THE GUARDIAN	THE MASTERMIND	THE DEFENDER
PRESTIGE — You earn respect with higher standards	THE AVANT-GARDE	THE CONNOISSEUR	THE VICTOR	THE IMPERIAL	THE BLUE CHIP	THE ARCHITECT	THE SCHOLAR
TRUST — You build loyalty with consistency	THE EVOLUTIONARY	THE AUTHENTIC	THE GRAVITAS	THE DIPLOMAT	THE OLD GUARD	THE ANCHOR	THE GOOD CITIZEN
MYSTIQUE — You communicate with substance	THE SECRET WEAPON	THE SUBTLE TOUCH	THE VEILED STRENGTH	THE ROYAL GUARD	THE WISE OWL	THE DEAD BOLT	THE ARCHER
ALERT — You prevent problems with care	THE COMPOSER	THE COORDINATOR	THE ACE	THE EDITOR-IN-CHIEF	THE MEDIATOR	THE DETECTIVE	THE CONTROL FREAK

HOW THE WORLD SEES THE CATALYST

Catalysts often make a vibrant first impression. They're valued for their enthusiastic approach and ability to generate ideas.

Buoyant and social, they embrace new situations and relationships with zeal. No matter what their actual job title, these personalities are most likely to add distinct value through dynamic interactions.

When presenting new products, you'll find their enthusiasm contagious. They speak with energy. They use expressive gestures and are keen to make eye contact with their listeners. They know how to captivate an audience—whether it's in an intimate boardroom, a hotel meeting room, or onstage.

These personalities are named Catalyst because they add value by starting action. (Remember high school chemistry class? A catalyst is an agent that provokes significant change or action.) Catalysts start ideas that provoke new thinking and action. Their passion is capable of igniting a team.

Archetype Twin
The Rockstar (page 244)

The Catalyst's Top 5 Adjectives

1. **Out-of-the-box**—When everyone else gets stuck, Catalysts can find unexpected ideas. For instance, when you need to shift an overstocked item and nobody seems able to find clients, they'll come up with a way to sell it through a totally new market channel. People often hire them for their ability to develop fresh solutions.

2. **Energizing**—They're at ease in unproven waters. If something becomes too routine or familiar, they like to challenge or reinvent it. As marketers they keep campaigns fresh, and you'll find they enjoy trialing new social media platforms.

3. **Social**—When they "turn on the juice," they can quickly build relationships and spread a message.

4. **Enthusiastic**—Catalysts vividly share their ideas and perspectives, adding energy to conversations. At the end of a long product development meeting, for instance, they ensure the meeting doesn't fizzle. They wrap up by reinvigorating the team toward success.

5. **Creative**—Catalysts naturally have colorful personalities, and make friends easily. Even in a rather formal interview setting you'll find that you quickly warm to them. They communicate with excitement, which encourages co-workers and customers to get involved in their projects.

"Highest and Best Value" of The Catalyst
Catalysts deliver value through creative change.

The more opportunities you give this Archetype to create change, the more you'll benefit from this Archetype's distinct value.

With a primary Passion Advantage, these personalities are most likely to contribute when emotionally involved. They feed off the energy in a room, and resist feeling shut off from the heart of the action.

Catalysts usually shine in the spotlight, so they frequently seek personality-oriented careers such as PR, marketing, and customer service.

What Is Not the "Highest and Best Value" of The Catalyst?

These are creative spirits. They often dislike repetitive, linear tasks. If forced to adhere to a rigid set of rules, they can become bored and distracted.

With a secondary Innovation Advantage, Catalysts excel when allowed to imagine.

These out-of-the-box thinkers often ignore "the box" entirely. When you need a fresh campaign you'll find a Catalyst will impress you with that Big Idea.

Free up your Catalyst for work that demands untraditional thinking.

How to Work with a Catalyst

When you encourage new thinking, your Catalyst will blossom.

Are you managing or teaming with a Catalyst? Recognize that they don't solve problems in a formulaic way. You'll get more distinct value from a Catalyst if you support their style of thinking and assign tasks accordingly.

Give them some freedom to experiment and do things in their own way. Rather than outlining an inflexible methodology, identify the ultimate outcome you seek to achieve, give them the tools, and tell them to knock it out of the park.

Archetypes That Can Optimize The Catalyst

The Good Citizen (page 288) will help Catalysts with clearheaded thinking. The Veiled Strength (page 180) will show Catalysts a linear, systematic path to replicate and automate certain aspects of their business efforts.

A Lesson That Everyone Can Learn from The Catalyst

There's rarely one "right" way to get things done. Try different options, so you can keep evolving your process.

One-Minute Coaching to My Catalysts

You feel passionately about things. Your enthusiasm livens up meetings and energizes your co-workers. Yet it's not enough to *feel* passionately—you must also learn how to turn that passion into tangible *results* for your client or team. Focus on the objectives you want your team to meet and agree on deadlines. Demonstrate how you contribute to the company's success.

Famous Catalyst

Leonardo da Vinci

Example of an Anthem for The Catalyst

ENERGIZING CONNECTION

How The Catalyst Might Apply This Anthem

Dirk sells cars. He has developed a welcoming method: When anyone enters the showroom, they receive a warm greeting. Nobody walks in through the door without being welcomed within five minutes. When the customer requests a test drive, they get to choose which car to drive, even if they aren't planning on buying that particular model. Dirk delivers a can-do attitude to all requests. He makes sure that every customer or prospect leaves with a positive impression of their experience with him, to create an ENERGIZING CONNECTION.

THE PEOPLE'S CHAMPION: PASSION + POWER

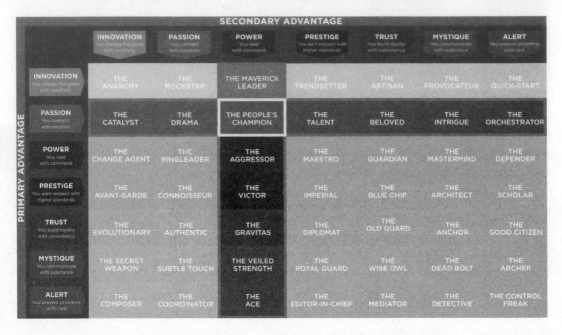

| | | SECONDARY ADVANTAGE | | | | | |
		INNOVATION You change the game with creativity	**PASSION** You connect with emotion	**POWER** You lead with command	**PRESTIGE** You earn respect with higher standards	**TRUST** You build loyalty with consistency	**MYSTIQUE** You communicate with substance	**ALERT** You prevent problems with care
P R I M A R Y **A D V A N T A G E**	**INNOVATION** You change the game with creativity	THE ANARCHY	THE ROCKSTAR	THE MAVERICK LEADER	THE TRENDSETTER	THE ARTISAN	THE PROVOCATEUR	THE QUICK-START
	PASSION You connect with emotion	THE CATALYST	THE DRAMA	THE PEOPLE'S CHAMPION	THE TALENT	THE BELOVED	THE INTRIGUE	THE ORCHESTRATOR
	POWER You lead with command	THE CHANGE AGENT	THE RINGLEADER	THE AGGRESSOR	THE MAESTRO	THE GUARDIAN	THE MASTERMIND	THE DEFENDER
	PRESTIGE You earn respect with higher standards	THE AVANT-GARDE	THE CONNOISSEUR	THE VICTOR	THE IMPERIAL	THE BLUE CHIP	THE ARCHITECT	THE SCHOLAR
	TRUST You build loyalty with consistency	THE EVOLUTIONARY	THE AUTHENTIC	THE GRAVITAS	THE DIPLOMAT	THE OLD GUARD	THE ANCHOR	THE GOOD CITIZEN
	MYSTIQUE You communicate with substance	THE SECRET WEAPON	THE SUBTLE TOUCH	THE VEILED STRENGTH	THE ROYAL GUARD	THE WISE OWL	THE DEAD BOLT	THE ARCHER
	ALERT You prevent problems with care	THE COMPOSER	THE COORDINATOR	THE ACE	THE EDITOR-IN-CHIEF	THE MEDIATOR	THE DETECTIVE	THE CONTROL FREAK

HOW THE WORLD SEES THE PEOPLE'S CHAMPION

Optimistic and gregarious, a People's Champion adds energy to any meeting.

They are optimistic communicators, and dislike negative perspectives. They advocate for others, stepping up to make sure everyone is heard.

When organizing a dinner party, you're never concerned about where they sit. They entertain whomever they're sitting next to and draw them into a conversation about movies, books, or the latest fashion trends. They are uplifting conversationalists.

They speak up for their team and the company. When the transport manager, for instance, criticizes their customer service department, they defend their team. Discussing the budget for next year and need to cut costs? You'll find a People's Champion passionately keeping everyone emotionally (and even spiritually) involved.

We call them People's Champions because they are advocates of people and ideas. Their energy makes them active voices for groups.

Archetype Twin
The Ringleader (page 128)

The People's Champion's Top 5 Adjectives

1. **Dynamic**—They are extroverted personalities who inspire those around them. Whether organizing a charity event or staff training day, they find it easy to get others involved. Their energy and excitement are contagious.

2. **Inclusive**—They understand group dynamics. In a team meeting, you'll find they solicit input from a quiet co-worker. They tell a dominant person to wait until others have had their say. They constantly work to keep everyone involved.

3. **Engaging**—Warm and colorful, they keep listeners engaged. When you interview a People's Champion for a podcast, they talk passionately about their latest book. They share colorful examples. They tell vivid stories to explain their points.

4. **Idealistic**—They are smart thinkers with a high emotional intelligence. When joining a new company, they quickly get the "vibe." They sense hidden agendas. They know who influences the boss. Even if they find themselves in a difficult position, they'll do their best to make the most of it. For them, the glass is half full.

5. **Intuitive**—They're able to read people and find common ground. They might have found their job when chatting with a fellow passenger on a flight. Whether they're lining up to buy concert tickets or waiting for a bus, they strike up a conversation easily.

"Highest and Best Value" of The People's Champion
Their natural optimism inspires others.

Personable and outgoing, they have an innate ability to connect with people. Their cheerful nature and engaging style make things happen.

Is your CEO a People's Champion? You'll find them going around at an office party to chat with each employee. They're good at helping everyone feel appreciated.

They enjoy "management by walking around" since it gives them the opportunity to get a good feel for what's going on. Even when facing stiff competition in difficult economic times, their monthly staff update remains positive and upbeat.

Well liked and respected, People's Champions can be highly influential, regardless of their position at the company.

What Is Not the "Highest and Best Value" of The People's Champion?

Don't expect a People's Champion to overplan a project, or know the financial figures by heart. They want to connect with their team before making a decision, so that everyone is empowered in the result.

As start-up entrepreneurs they win the backing of crucial investors based on their drive and passion—not necessarily on their exhaustive financial knowledge.

How to Work with a People's Champion

Need to "sell" a difficult project to your team? Maybe your team needs to finish a project a month earlier than planned, or the project budget has been reduced by 20%. Get a People's Champion on your side first. Once they understand the situation, they'll help you persuade the team. Their disarming manner draws even the most skeptical co-workers and employees to their side.

People's Champions thrive in environments where there's a lot of discussion. They enjoy working in an open organization where everyone digs in. Don't be surprised if, in the middle of a conversation about your latest project, they suggest calling a colleague to give them the feeling their opinion is appreciated.

Archetypes That Can Optimize The People's Champion

The Anchor (page 284) adds a pragmatic approach to solving problems.
The Subtle Touch (page 176) makes decisions based on carefully analyzed facts.

A Lesson That Everyone Can Learn from The People's Champion

It's the human touch that makes employees feel valued.

One-Minute Coaching to My People's Champions

You're an energetic presenter. You're able to quickly read people's reactions. When you're presenting to a big group of people, keep in mind that not everyone is driven by passion.

Mix your passionate message with logical arguments. Include a few statistics and independent reviews, so that you can also persuade more rational thinkers.

Famous People's Champions

U2's Bono and Ronald Reagan

Example of an Anthem for The People's Champion

ENGAGING TEAMWORK

How The People's Champion Might Apply This Anthem

The People's Champion engages and includes everyone in group activities. At his company's annual holiday party, Darren comes up with activities that help everyone share and feel valued. Because he is aware of his ability to build camaraderie, Darren makes a point to volunteer for activities that could provide opportunities to increase company spirit. He realizes that numbers are important, but he balances any crunch time with providing recognition to others. He sees the value of a confident, united team in reaching company numbers.

THE TALENT: PASSION + PRESTIGE

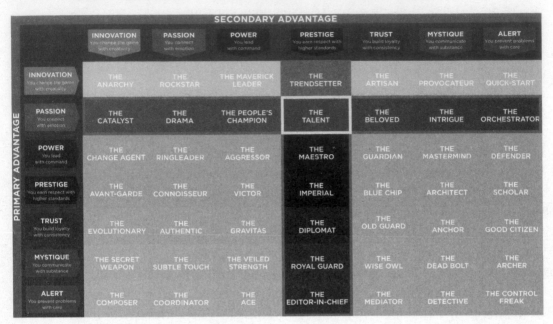

HOW THE WORLD SEES THE TALENT

Talents know how to make a great first impression.

They are naturally playful, and enjoy meeting people. They know how to get others to participate. They speak the language of relationship (Passion) and the language of excellence (Prestige).

You'll find that Talents enjoy getting to know new people, and new skills. Whether they're learning a new language, playing the piano, or taking dance lessons, every new experience they take on seems fun.

Talents project an ability to be successful at anything they do. But they're not born with more talents than others. They intensely focus on improving their skills. They dream big, and strive for excellence.

Archetype Twin
The Connoisseur (page 200)

The Talent's Top 5 Adjectives

1. Expressive—Confident and articulate, they communicate their ideas in a highly engaging style. Even when leaving a short voicemail, their tone is involved and connective. You can hear the warmth in their voice (and they know this gives you a good reason to call them back!).

2. Stylish—Their choices, purchases, and investments reflect their point of view. The pictures on their social media profiles are professionally made. They show a perfect, welcoming smile. From that first impression, you know they have good taste and you know they appreciate the best of yours.

3. Emotionally intelligent—They are excellent at reading situations and understanding the dynamics of relationships. Whether they're talking to the cleaner or the CEO, they make people feel important. People warm to them quickly.

4. Energetic—Working toward a goal invigorates them. Whether they're organizing a staff party or managing the development of a new product, they do so with gusto. Their enthusiasm, work ethic, and ambition inspire the team. They have a competitive spirit.

5. Academic—They set high standards for themselves and their team. They present themselves with finesse and expect the same from you. Don't turn up for a sales meeting unshaven or in jeans. They expect a professional attitude at all times.

"Highest and Best Value" of The Talent

Talents are respected team members. Their amiable personality means they're connected to clients and co-workers. Their enthusiasm and expressive style means they quickly gain buy-in on new ideas.

As marketers, for instance, they make sure all communication material reflects the brand values. When marketing a premium brand, they ensure that everything from the brochure paper to the product photography is of high quality. Whether writing the weekly e-newsletter to retailers or posting social media updates, they know how to capture the most effective tone.

What Is Not the "Highest and Best Value" of The Talent?

Don't expect them to use a lot of statistics to persuade a buyer, or memorize an endless brochure of facts and figures. They think on their feet, connecting in the moment.

Talents tend to be visually oriented. Colorful and articulate, they persuade by painting a vibrant mental image.

How to Work with a Talent

Have a Talent on your team? You'll get the most out of your Talents when they can use their people skills. When given the opportunity to make introductions, they can quickly win over prospects with charm.

Archetypes That Can Optimize The Talent

Good Citizens (page 288) are methodical workers who ensure deadlines are met.

The understated style of a Royal Guard (page 184) provides a balance to the more expressive Talent.

A Lesson That Everyone Can Learn from The Talent

Talent is nurtured through hard work and passion.

One-Minute Coaching to My Talents

You are engaging and enthusiastic, and you enjoy spending time with others. Sometimes, however, you might be eager for others to like you. Know when to be true to yourself, and to your values.

You also will want to make sure that you don't try to be perfect in everything you do. Review your responsibilities and decide which tasks require high-quality execution. Decide how much time to spend on each item on your to-do list. Be a little more pragmatic. Sometimes delivering on time is more important than achieving superb results.

Famous Talents

Wolfgang Puck and Audrey Hepburn

Example of an Anthem for The Talent

EXPRESSIVE SKILL SET

How The Talent Might Apply This Anthem

Josie is teaching online entrepreneurs how to infuse more of their personality into their digital marketing. She applies her keen emotional intelligence and brings a stylish approach to everything she does. Josie works with her clients to really get to know their unique style of communication. Once she has an idea of what makes their personality stand out, she helps them to craft messages that reflect it in their online presence.

THE BELOVED: PASSION + TRUST

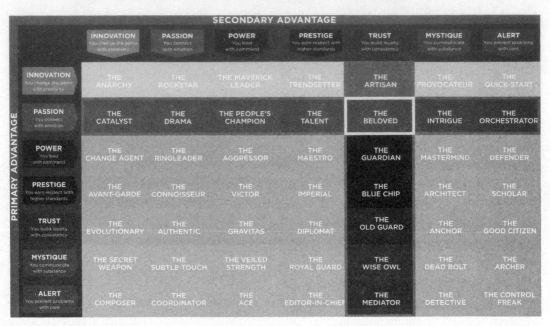

HOW THE WORLD SEES THE BELOVED

It's easy to like The Beloved. They build lasting relationships, and earn loyalty by communicating with comforting stability.

Beloveds are aware of relationships, and the effect of their actions on others. They help those who are falling behind. They encourage those who feel neglected. They make an effort to help others feel welcome and at ease during team meetings.

When a Beloved faces conflict, they won't scream or pound the table. They won't threaten. Instead, they'll gradually coax others to join their point of view. This ability to make people feel safe allows them to establish secure bonds over time.

Archetype Twin
The Authentic (page 272)

The Beloved's Top 5 Adjectives

1. **Nurturing**—People are attracted to the generosity The Beloved brings to all their relationships. As industry veterans, they will be quick to take newcomers under their wing. They share their knowledge and connect them to their business network.

2. **Loyal**—They display dedication to the people and ideas they believe in. They passionately present new products; and they strongly promote the good causes they support.

3. **Sincere**—The Beloved are completely authentic. They don't have a hidden agenda. Team members quickly pick up on their genuine commitment. New clients soon learn they can trust their recommendations.

4. **Tenderhearted**—Their empathy makes others feel safe in times of chaos and distress. You'll find that junior team members turn to them for advice, and even their boss may take them into their confidence when worried about the company's performance or future direction.

5. **Comforting**—They make others feel good. In a competitive situation, customers will turn to them because they enjoy their interaction. They appreciate the familiarity their warm personality brings.

"Highest and Best Value" of The Beloved

The Passion Advantage provides The Beloved with emotional depth.

They can be talented salespeople. They present your company and products with gusto. They quickly grasp the hesitation of a prospect. Their genuine enthusiasm converts doubters into buyers.

As senior managers, they're loved by their staff. They're likely to have a lower staff turnover than other departments. Their departmental meetings can be inspirational. They make everyone feel like they're part of the family.

The Beloved quickly builds relationships with new suppliers, staff members, and clients.

What Is Not the "Highest and Best Value" of The Beloved?

Don't put The Beloved in a position of taking a forceful approach, or impressing others with a dominant personality. Instead, they seek the affection of others. The Beloved incites action because others want to work for her.

How to Work with a Beloved

Is your team leader a Beloved? They're happy to introduce you to their contacts to help you with your work. They listen to your concerns and help you when required. They empower you to maintain a healthy work/life balance.

Is a Beloved working for you? You get the most out of them if you allow them to work in a team, interact with clients, or nurture new supplier relationships. They're also good coaches—especially for team members who are struggling to find their feet at work.

Archetypes That Can Optimize The Beloved

The Maestro (page 132) adds a competitive spirit and sets higher goals.
With their calm presence, Wise Owls (page 188) balance the team. They also keep an eye on all the details.

A Lesson That Everyone Can Learn From The Beloved

Stay connected to everyone on the team and you'll earn their trust.

One-Minute Coaching to My Beloveds

People enjoy being on your team. You make people feel comfortable, which can be helpful. But sometimes you need to direct people's focus to the objectives they need to achieve.

Occasionally you may want to point out the negative consequences of underperformance. Remind people that their contribution is required to finish projects and meet goals.

Famous Beloveds

Oprah Winfrey and Tom Hanks

Example of an Anthem for The Beloved

NURTURING RELATIONSHIPS

How The Beloved Might Apply This Anthem

In her medical equipment supply company, Barbara makes each employee feel welcome and appreciated. As an office manager, she is dedicated to building relationships. She makes it a point to stop by each employee's office at least once a week: to deliver their paycheck, follow up on a problem, or ask about their weekend or recent time off. She is generous with encouragement and frequently thanks employees for their contributions to the company's success. She maintains an open-door policy, and her employees know that they can come to her for guidance.

THE INTRIGUE: PASSION + MYSTIQUE

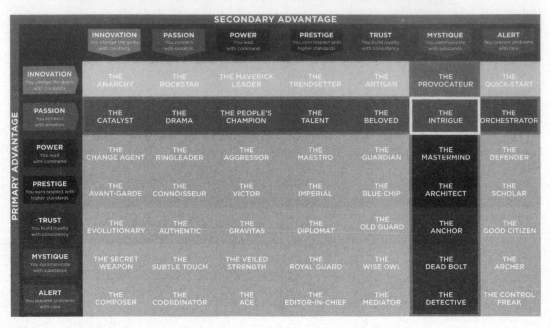

HOW THE WORLD SEES THE INTRIGUE

Intrigues have an uncommon combination of traits. They have a rare ability to switch between taking an analytical view (that's their Mystique Advantage) and emotionally connecting (that's Passion). They are hybrids. In fact, The Intrigue is the most complex of all the Archetypes.

They are named The Intrigue because of their inherent dichotomy. They don't always show what's on their mind. Their character is complex and rich. They're not superficial, and it takes time to get to know them well. It's not easy to predict how they will respond in different environments.

You can find them observing proceedings at a board meeting, watching as if from a distance. Yet at other times, they join in the meeting in a warm and affectionate manner, sharing a joke or story of their skiing adventures last weekend.

Their presentation style is multilayered. At times they are passionate advocates for a new project; they make eye contact and gauge the reaction of their listeners. But at other times they focus intensely on the rational points of their arguments. They quote statistics, they show tables and graphs, and they summarize research findings. They're capable of finding the most effective method to persuade an audience.

Archetype Twin
The Subtle Touch (page 176)

The Intrigue's Top 5 Adjectives

   1. Discerning—Sensitive and intuitive, they observe what's going on around them. You might think you're hiding well your disappointment about being passed over for a promotion. But your co-worker, an Intrigue, will notice subtle signs—like slightly sagging shoulders—even when you keep your happy smile on your face.

   2. Perceptive—They are discreet, but have their ear to the ground. As senior managers, they know the issues that concern their staff. As junior employees, they quickly grasp the politics at play.

   3. Considerate—They understand when to dial up the emotion, and when to pull back. Amid a heated discussion in the boardroom, you'll find they're able to take a step back. Coolheaded, they deal with uncomfortable situations by pointing out the facts in an objective manner. Even if they don't agree with someone, they won't let the situation get out of hand. When dealing with conflict or delivering bad news, they'll make sure that all parties involved feel like they've been heard.

   4. Selective—They are not automatically "sold" on new ideas. They won't act on impulse. They won't appoint a new vendor just because their price is lower. A new vendor needs to earn their interest. They carefully consider their decisions.

   5. Warm and cool—Their public persona tends to be warm. When first meeting an Intrigue you'll find it easy to make contact. You'll feel you know them already after your first meeting. They are approachable and share information freely. But at the next meeting you may discover that they guard their personal feelings closely. You don't really know what they think. Their ability to be both warm and objective is an advantage when the situation demands emotional complexity. They add value by turning on the right Advantage at the right time.

"Highest and Best Value" of The Intrigue

Their velvety, soft exterior hides a strong inner core.

Intrigues have the ability to relate to things both intellectually and emotionally. At an appraisal meeting, for instance, they know when to keep their feelings to themselves. They can open up and explain their keen desire to get promoted to a certain job. But they're also able to review their own performance in an objective, analytical way.

Intrigues can perform well in almost any role in both large and small companies. They can adapt to different situations because they access either their expressive or rational side when required.

What Is Not the "Highest and Best Value" of The Intrigue?

Don't expect them to make a split-second decision. They can be emotional, but they don't act without thought.

Intrigues are naturally curious. They can become utterly captivated by certain projects or ideas—but usually only after careful consideration.

How to Work with an Intrigue

You get most out of Intrigues in roles where they can use their analytical skills as well as engage clients or co-workers with their warm personality.

As call center managers, for instance, they'll be equally good at analyzing call statistics and at dealing with difficult customers. As marketers, they'll evaluate marketing effectiveness and understand how to build an aspirational brand. As HR managers, they'll understand the soft and the hard side of dealing with employees. As salespeople they'll know how to press the right buttons to get a buyer to close the deal.

Archetypes That Can Optimize The Intrigue

Team an Intrigue up with a Mediator (page 236) to keep projects on track and meet deadlines.

An Authentic (page 272) builds strong networks thanks to their loyalty and warmth.

A Lesson That Everyone Can Learn from The Intrigue

In some situations it's better to hide your feelings. At other times, allow emotion to win.

One-Minute Coaching to My Intrigues

You know how to persuade people using both rational arguments and your expressive personality. That can be a great asset. But sometimes people struggle to understand what's on your mind.

To progress further in your career, you want to become more consistent in your voice and attitude, so that co-workers and those reporting to you can learn what to expect from you. Observe how you change your style in different situations and take note of how others perceive you.

Famous Intrigues

Angelina Jolie, George Lucas, Denzel Washington

Example of an Anthem for The Intrigue

PERCEPTIVE INSIGHTS

How The Intrigue Might Apply This Anthem

When there's a problem with a particular client, Steve does a little research to discover what's really going on under the surface. Recently, when a client was overdue on a large payment, Steve found out that the company had just experienced a turnover in their accounting department. With the additional information, he extended the due date on the invoice, avoiding a potential conflict and preserving the client relationship.

THE ORCHESTRATOR: PASSION + ALERT

PRIMARY ADVANTAGE ↓ / SECONDARY ADVANTAGE →	INNOVATION You connect with creativity	PASSION You connect with emotion	POWER You lead with command	PRESTIGE You earn respect with higher standards	TRUST You build loyalty with consistency	MYSTIQUE You communicate with substance	ALERT You prevent problems with care
INNOVATION You change the game with creativity	THE ANARCHY	THE ROCKSTAR	THE MAVERICK LEADER	THE TRENDSETTER	THE ARTISAN	THE PROVOCATEUR	THE QUICK-START
PASSION You connect with emotion	THE CATALYST	THE DRAMA	THE PEOPLE'S CHAMPION	THE TALENT	THE BELOVED	THE INTRIGUE	THE ORCHESTRATOR
POWER You lead with command	THE CHANGE AGENT	THE RINGLEADER	THE AGGRESSOR	THE MAESTRO	THE GUARDIAN	THE MASTERMIND	THE DEFENDER
PRESTIGE You earn respect with higher standards	THE AVANT-GARDE	THE CONNOISSEUR	THE VICTOR	THE IMPERIAL	THE BLUE CHIP	THE ARCHITECT	THE SCHOLAR
TRUST You build loyalty with consistency	THE EVOLUTIONARY	THE AUTHENTIC	THE GRAVITAS	THE DIPLOMAT	THE OLD GUARD	THE ANCHOR	THE GOOD CITIZEN
MYSTIQUE You communicate with substance	THE SECRET WEAPON	THE SUBTLE TOUCH	THE VEILED STRENGTH	THE ROYAL GUARD	THE WISE OWL	THE DEAD BOLT	THE ARCHER
ALERT You prevent problems with care	THE COMPOSER	THE COORDINATOR	THE ACE	THE EDITOR-IN-CHIEF	THE MEDIATOR	THE DETECTIVE	THE CONTROL FREAK

HOW THE WORLD SEES THE ORCHESTRATOR

Orchestrators command attention and inspire others to reach goals.

Is your personal assistant an Orchestrator? Friendly and helpful on the phone, she quickly connects with people she doesn't know. But she's also cognizant of your busy calendar.

When she tells people over the phone you don't have time to speak to them this week, she has a smile in her voice.

Orchestrating means arranging something—for example, music, ballet, or a banquet—to achieve the best effect. That's what Orchestrators do. They have a keen understanding of people and inspire them to reach optimal results.

Archetype Twin
The Coordinator (page 224)

The Orchestrator's Top 5 Adjectives
 1. **Attentive**—They keep their team on track by paying close attention to

details. When in charge of organizing your annual supplier conference, for instance, they ensure that suppliers from abroad are met at the airport to be brought to the hotel. Gracious and considerate, they ensure everyone enjoys the conference.

2. **Dedicated**—They invigorate the team to work tirelessly to meet whatever goals they've set. When they join an organization as a new VP of marketing, for instance, the marketing team will soon realize they are in their corner. They help to solve struggles with other departments, so the team can get on with their work. Their positive attitude inspires the team.

3. **Efficient**—They deeply care about people, but also work to stay on track. When a team member's mother is taken to the hospital, they'll send him home to take care of her. They pair empathy with practicality.

4. **Open-eyed**—Their keen focus on meeting deadlines doesn't mean they skip details. When proofreading a new brochure, their eye will catch double spaces. When evaluating a new product, they notice tiny irregularities in the molded plastic. They review each task with a fine-toothed comb.

5. **Vigorous**—Working toward a goal energizes them. They take pleasure in getting projects finished. They enjoy getting ready for a big event. They love the buzz of new product launches. Unfazed by tight deadlines, they energetically work to get things done.

"Highest and Best Value" of The Orchestrator

Their attitude alternates between bright optimism and pragmatic execution.

Their positive approach inspires others. Their pragmatism keeps projects on track.

As managers, they understand both the emotional and the rational sides of running a company. When chairing a management meeting, they expect a detailed report before the meeting, outlining progress made with each project.

At the meeting they focus on the projects falling behind. They provide constructive criticism. They make sure everyone's workload is manageable. And they often close a meeting with a few upbeat words.

They can be tough taskmasters because they expect their team to do well. But they also create strong emotional bonds with co-workers and employees.

What Is Not the "Highest and Best Value" of The Orchestrator?

Don't expect them to challenge the status quo or spin off crazy ideas. They prefer *tried-and-tested* rather than *new and unknown*.

You get the most out of your Orchestrators if you allow them to encourage their team to follow the plan.

How to Work with an Orchestrator

They are natural problem-solvers. They can read a situation well and understand what's causing issues.

Is the team demotivated? They arouse them with an invigorating speech. Is there a problem with planning? They break the project down into doable chunks. They prompt the team to get on with each task.

Orchestrators are both inspirational managers and down-to-earth organizers. They get the plan right. And they get the team right.

You get the most out of them in people-focused roles. They thrive in structured environments where they can compel others to follow a plan. At a start-up they'll bring order into the chaos and ensure new hires are quickly embedded into the team.

Archetypes That Can Optimize The Orchestrator

Their focus on hitting deadlines means that Orchestrators are less likely to try out new methods. Team them with a Maverick Leader (page 248) to inject an experimental streak.

A Subtle Touch (page 176) will bring a calming force.

A Lesson That Everyone Can Learn from The Orchestrator

To get something done you need both a plan and a motivated team.

One-Minute Coaching to My Orchestrators

You influence your team through strong relationships. We can count on you to get a job done in the right way, and on time.

The company faces stiff competition from new entrants in the market. To maintain and grow market share, we need fresh ideas to challenge the status quo.

Look for the members in your team who have a more rebellious streak. Be open to their suggestions for experimentation. Not every idea will work, but after a few failed experiments, we'll find a winning idea.

Famous Orchestrators
Stephen Covey and Martha Stewart

Example of an Anthem for The Orchestrator
DEDICATED PLANNING

How The Orchestrator Might Apply This Anthem
Shelly is an event manager. Six months before an event, she's planned out every detail. She's friendly, yet firm. Because she works with creative types, she makes a point to give everyone the schedule far in advance, with clearly outlined expectations. She combines emotional savvy with nitty-gritty detail management to make sure that there are no surprises, and that everything stays on track.

THE MYSTIQUE ADVANTAGE

THE MYSTIQUE ADVANTAGE IS THINKING BEFORE SPEAKING.
MYSTIQUE PERSONALITIES SPEAK THE LANGUAGE OF LISTENING.

THE SECRET WEAPON: MYSTIQUE + INNOVATION

PRIMARY ADVANTAGE	SECONDARY ADVANTAGE						
	INNOVATION You change the game with creativity	PASSION You connect with emotion	POWER You lead with command	PRESTIGE You earn respect with higher standards	TRUST You build loyalty with consistency	MYSTIQUE You communicate with substance	ALERT You prevent problems with care
INNOVATION You change the game with creativity	THE ANARCHY	THE ROCKSTAR	THE MAVERICK LEADER	THE TRENDSETTER	THE ARTISAN	THE PROVOCATEUR	THE QUICK-START
PASSION You connect with emotion	THE CATALYST	THE DRAMA	THE PEOPLE'S CHAMPION	THE TALENT	THE BELOVED	THE INTRIGUE	THE ORCHESTRATOR
POWER You lead with command	THE CHANGE AGENT	THE RINGLEADER	THE AGGRESSOR	THE MAESTRO	THE GUARDIAN	THE MASTERMIND	THE DEFENDER
PRESTIGE You earn respect with higher standards	THE AVANT-GARDE	THE CONNOISSEUR	THE VICTOR	THE IMPERIAL	THE BLUE CHIP	THE ARCHITECT	THE SCHOLAR
TRUST You build loyalty with consistency	THE EVOLUTIONARY	THE AUTHENTIC	THE GRAVITAS	THE DIPLOMAT	THE OLD GUARD	THE ANCHOR	THE GOOD CITIZEN
MYSTIQUE You communicate with substance	THE SECRET WEAPON	THE SUBTLE TOUCH	THE VEILED STRENGTH	THE ROYAL GUARD	THE WISE OWL	THE DEAD BOLT	THE ARCHER
ALERT You prevent problems with care	THE COMPOSER	THE COORDINATOR	THE ACE	THE EDITOR-IN-CHIEF	THE MEDIATOR	THE DETECTIVE	THE CONTROL FREAK

HOW THE WORLD SEES THE SECRET WEAPON

They are creative minds who produce agile solutions even when under high pressure. They are creative in a nonflashy way, preferring to do their work quietly.

You'll recognize them as the member of your negotiation team who comes up with a clever idea to break through a stalemate. This is the quiet engineer working out an innovative solution to a complex problem. This is the designer who creates his best work late at night when he's on his own in the office.

Secret Weapons enjoy working independently. They don't boast about their achievements. But they can produce great inventions, creative ideas, and new product designs.

We've called them Secret Weapons because they are a company's secret weapon. They make great contributions to the company's performance, but they do so in an unassuming manner. They also may occasionally surprise you with an irreverent remark.

Archetype Twin

The Provocateur (page 260)

The Secret Weapon's Top 5 Adjectives

1. **Nimble**—They have the ability to generate many different solutions rather than being locked into one way of thinking. They solve problems by considering different viewpoints.

2. **Unassuming**—Their mild-mannered demeanor hides a free spirit. They have a minimalist communication style. They carefully and clearly explain their ideas, but prefer to do so to their inner circle.

3. **Independent**—They are comfortable with charting their own course. They aren't easily swayed by groupthink. That's why they come up with new ideas when everyone else is stuck. They're not confined to established methods.

4. **Reticent**—They restrain their emotions and contain their inner thoughts until they are ready to share them. During brainstorming sessions they may be quiet, but they may also come up with the best ideas.

5. **Autonomously creative**—They tend to keep their inventions to themselves before they've worked out a complete solution and are sure that it works. They are most creative when they can work out ideas with pencil and paper rather than in a big, loud meeting. Introspection rather than external stimulus guides their innovative thinking.

"Highest and Best Value" of The Secret Weapon

They combine analytical and creative skills.

They observe new situations and are able to assess quickly what needs to change. Unhindered by traditional ways of working, they come up with their own ideas of how things can be done differently.

They communicate without fuss. They provide rational arguments for their ideas. Their practical and logical mind helps them find new paths.

What Is Not the "Highest and Best Value" of The Secret Weapon?

While they rarely have a flashy personality, Secret Weapons have a sharp mind and insider observations. They do like to meet new people and encounter new situations, but often don't enjoy overtly drawing attention to themselves as Rockstars or Talents might. They are the quiet stars of your team who outshine most others with their creativity.

How to Work with a Secret Weapon

They are rich personalities below the surface. When you first meet a Secret Weapon you're not likely to get the full story. They tend to keep themselves at a distance. They won't immediately share their thoughts, their ideas, their way of working.

They may exude an air of mystery. But don't think they aren't watching. As employees, they are nimble problem-solvers.

You can get the most out of a Secret Weapon if you give them free rein to assess situations and come up with fresh ideas for change. They are more productive in a quiet office than in an open-plan environment.

Make sure you leverage their creativity and analytical abilities.

Archetypes That Can Optimize The Secret Weapon

The Coordinator (page 224) brings a methodical approach to implementing projects.

The Change Agent (page 124) and The Secret Weapon form a formidable team for innovation.

A Lesson That Everyone Can Learn from The Secret Weapon

Individual work can generate great innovations.

One-Minute Coaching to My Secret Weapons

You've contributed great ideas and are a quiet force for change at the company. You seem to enjoy working on your own. Be careful not to isolate yourself too much. Your creativity and analytical skills can help the team achieve even more.

Help people understand how you can contribute. Use Passion to connect and engage team members. It's absolutely fine to do most of your work in your office, but sometimes you need to get out to network. Even chance encounters at the water cooler can help you implement your ideas.

Famous Secret Weapons
Tina Fey and Oliver Stone

Example of an Anthem for The Secret Weapon
INDEPENDENT SOLUTIONS

How The Secret Weapon Might Apply This Anthem
Some people within a company need a lot of hand-holding and direction. Not Sanjay. As the social media manager for a health-care company, Sanjay developed the company's online communications platform by developing a creative strategy that helped the brand stand out in a cluttered marketplace. On the surface, Sanjay is unassuming. Yet he's known for his nimble flexibility, allowing his company to stay ahead of rapidly evolving curves in both social media and health care.

THE SUBTLE TOUCH: MYSTIQUE + PASSION

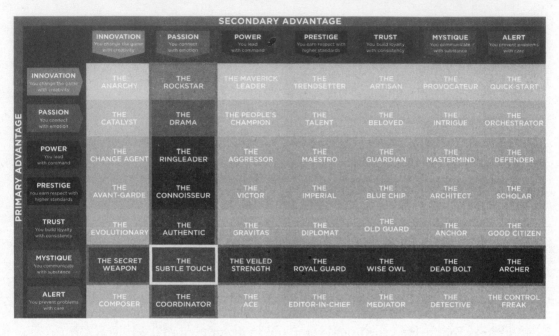

		SECONDARY ADVANTAGE					
		INNOVATION You change the game with creativity	PASSION You connect with emotion	POWER You lead with command	PRESTIGE You earn respect with higher standards	TRUST You build loyalty with consistency	MYSTIQUE You communicate with substance	ALERT You prevent problems with care
PRIMARY ADVANTAGE	INNOVATION You change the game with creativity	THE ANARCHY	THE ROCKSTAR	THE MAVERICK LEADER	THE TRENDSETTER	THE ARTISAN	THE PROVOCATEUR	THE QUICK-START
	PASSION You connect with emotion	THE CATALYST	THE DRAMA	THE PEOPLE'S CHAMPION	THE TALENT	THE BELOVED	THE INTRIGUE	THE ORCHESTRATOR
	POWER You lead with command	THE CHANGE AGENT	THE RINGLEADER	THE AGGRESSOR	THE MAESTRO	THE GUARDIAN	THE MASTERMIND	THE DEFENDER
	PRESTIGE You earn respect with higher standards	THE AVANT-GARDE	THE CONNOISSEUR	THE VICTOR	THE IMPERIAL	THE BLUE CHIP	THE ARCHITECT	THE SCHOLAR
	TRUST You build loyalty with consistency	THE EVOLUTIONARY	THE AUTHENTIC	THE GRAVITAS	THE DIPLOMAT	THE OLD GUARD	THE ANCHOR	THE GOOD CITIZEN
	MYSTIQUE You communicate with substance	THE SECRET WEAPON	THE SUBTLE TOUCH	THE VEILED STRENGTH	THE ROYAL GUARD	THE WISE OWL	THE DEAD BOLT	THE ARCHER
	ALERT You prevent problems with care	THE COMPOSER	THE COORDINATOR	THE ACE	THE EDITOR-IN-CHIEF	THE MEDIATOR	THE DETECTIVE	THE CONTROL FREAK

How the World Sees The Subtle Touch

Subtle Touches intrigue others with understated communication.

They possess a unique combination of talents: rational thinking and a warm personal style. At times they easily connect with people with their affectionate, friendly approach. Yet at other times they won't show their inner emotions.

Their character is multilayered. They know when to pull back and stay at a distance. And they understand when they need to use a more emotional approach.

At work, you'll find they avoid the spotlight. They're discreet—you won't find them gossiping in the hallway. They tend to be quiet workers who get on with their jobs. They know how to carry on a conversation about superficial pleasantries, but prefer to dig into the meat of a topic.

They are Subtle Touches because they touch you with their warmth, but in a refined, delicate way.

Archetype Twin
The Intrigue (page 164)

The Subtle Touch's Top 5 Adjectives

1. **Tactful**—They enjoy gaining an in-depth understanding of a situation or topic before making a choice. When faced with a difficult decision, such as should they appoint John or Matt, they systematically analyze the achievements, skills, and experience of the two candidates before making a choice. They tend to make decisions based on rational facts, but they can let their emotions play a role, too.

2. **Self-sufficient**—They're independent and self-directed. You may find them sneaking out of a conference to have some quiet time on their own and to process the day's impressions. They may feel smothered by too much contact, but you can rely on them to take their responsibilities seriously.

3. **Mindful**—They captivate audiences because they don't explain all the details. In negotiations, for instance, you won't be able to read their mind. But then during lunchtime, you'll be feeling close and connected as you're discussing the latest movies you've watched. Everything they say is carefully considered. They're attentive and aware of their surroundings.

4. **Profound**—They see beyond the obvious. They rarely draw conclusions at a superficial level. For instance, they're able to analyze a competitor's behavior and predict next steps. When they read press releases and blog posts, they notice between the lines subtle signs of a direction change—something many readers miss. They understand things at a deeper level than most.

5. **Unexpected**—They hold their cards close, so others may have no idea what they're thinking. Even when you think you might know a Subtle Touch, you can be surprised by their quiet and deliberate decision-making, because they don't belabor their choices. Their ability to hide their feelings is a distinct advantage in maintaining their cool, even under pressure.

"Highest and Best Value" of The Subtle Touch
The Subtle Touch blends rational thinking and emotional feeling.

Their Mystique Advantage keeps them grounded, and focused on facts.

Their secondary Passion Advantage provides them with an understanding of human nature.

On Twitter, for instance, they mainly share useful articles about the topics that interest them. But you also find them occasionally sharing their excitement about an upcoming holiday or a new customer they've signed up.

Subtle Touches select their words carefully. They won't waste your time when they speak or write. They only convey relevant information. Everything they say has a purpose.

What Is Not the "Highest and Best Value" of The Subtle Touch?

If you want theatrical expression or an over-the-top presentation, think twice before hiring a Subtle Touch. They prefer not to draw attention to themselves, and instead focus on the task at hand and on others around them.

They keep their own opinions under wraps and take their time to allow others to get to know them.

How to Work with a Subtle Touch

Independent and intelligent, Subtle Touches won't crack under pressure. They focus their attention on what matters. Without getting distracted.

Subtle Touches are attractive appointments for dynamic start-ups. They are a beacon of calmness in chaotic times. Their analytical skills and systematic approach to projects are distinct advantages in almost any situation.

Archetypes That Can Optimize The Subtle Touch

Victors (page 204) pursue excellence in everything they do. They will raise the standard of work done by the team.

The Provocateur (page 260) adds creativity to the team.

A Lesson That Everyone Can Learn from The Subtle Touch

The best decisions are based both on rational arguments and on feelings.

One-Minute Coaching for My Subtle Touches

You don't share a lot about yourself, but you've become a valued member of our team. You have a coolheaded exterior, which sometimes can be interpreted as standoffishness or disinterest to those who don't know you, such as new customers or new colleagues.

Try tapping into your Passion Advantage to build immediate rapport. Show your enthusiasm about making new connections. You have a subtle ability to engage, but sometimes you need to up the ante to draw attention to yourself and captivate your listeners in a more expressive way.

Famous Subtle Touches
Harry Potter and Johnny Depp

Example of an Anthem for The Subtle Touch
TACTFUL METHOD

How The Subtle Touch Might Apply This Anthem
As a business litigator, Kathy frequently has to deal with difficult people and defuse awkward situations. She's mindful of how others around her are feeling, and how she can negotiate for her clients. Because she's self-sufficient, she likes to have all the facts close at hand, so she does her legwork ahead of time. When working on a chaotic or volatile case, Kathy helps everyone in the situation stay cool and focused.

THE VEILED STRENGTH: MYSTIQUE + POWER

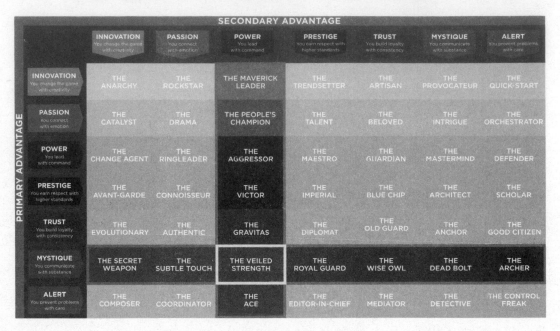

HOW THE WORLD SEES THE VEILED STRENGTH

They command respect with their rational approach to problem-solving.

Independent and self-reliant, they have an unwavering confidence in their ability to find solutions and reach goals. They prefer to base their decisions on hard data and quantitative information rather than gut feeling.

Let's say their IT project hits a major setback, because the legacy system is more complicated than anticipated. You won't find them pacing up and down the room. You won't hear them raising their voice. They quietly go to work. They systematically consider various options until they've found the optimal solution.

Their quiet demeanor hides a strong inner core. That's why we've called them The Veiled Strength. They don't reveal all their inner thoughts (that's their primary Mystique Advantage), but as leaders they are firmly in control (that's Power).

Archetype Twin
The Mastermind (page 140)

The Veiled Strength's Top 5 Adjectives

1. Realistic—They analyze facts before making decisions. When faced with a project delay, they won't act on impulse. They carefully consider the options before deciding whether to commit extra resources or to accept a delay.

2. Intentional—They communicate with a clear purpose. Their business updates are clearly structured around key performance indicators. They don't ramble on. When they speak, they have a clear message.

3. To the point—They pare their message to the core. They edit out unnecessary fluff. Their emails, for instance, are direct and businesslike. They express with clarity why they're emailing you and what they expect from you.

4. Orderly—They explain their ideas clearly in a no-nonsense manner. They, for instance, prepare a well-structured induction program for each new starter to give them the best chance to start their job well.

5. Multilayered—They are complex characters. They restrain their emotions and rarely reveal their innermost thoughts. Sometimes their response may surprise you.

"Highest and Best Value" of The Veiled Strength

They set high goals with a methodology to reaching them. Nothing is random. They approach objectives in a focused, systematic manner.

The Veiled Strength doesn't push too forcefully, or show strength too overtly. They lead in an understated way. You won't find them boasting about achievements. They have a quietly pragmatic attitude, and they direct their team with confidence.

They help team members by showing how a job is done. You'll find them mentoring junior staff by explaining processes step by step. They ask questions to help them learn.

Veiled Strengths have a subtle ability to lead.

What Is Not the "Highest and Best Value" of The Veiled Strength?

Veiled Strengths are many things, but they are not the life of the party at your annual get-together. They are not natural networkers.

It may take you time to get to know your Veiled Strengths. But you'll come to appreciate their analytical and problem-solving skills.

How to Work with a Veiled Strength

They remain focused and in command even in high-pressure environments.

Rather than being swayed by popular opinion, they carefully do their research before giving a project the go-ahead and committing resources. They are fact-finders.

They are equally at ease in dynamic start-ups and large, mature organizations. You get the most out of them in positions of leadership where their analytical abilities are appreciated.

Archetypes That Can Optimize The Veiled Strength

Like Veiled Strengths, Architects (page 212) have a quiet manner. They add a strong focus on details and the quality of results.

The People's Champion (page 152) leads by building strong emotional connections.

A Lesson That Everyone Can Learn from The Veiled Strength

You can be a strong leader in an understated manner.

One-Minute Coaching to My Veiled Strengths

Your presentations are intelligently crafted. You present your ideas in a logical and straightforward manner. If you can also make your presentations more vivid and passionate, then it becomes easier for your audience to remember your message.

Try to include short stories that illustrate your arguments. Stories keep your audience captivated. Also, use more sensory and emotional words, because they activate more brainpower of your listeners. That'll make your presentation more persuasive and more memorable.

Example of an Anthem for The Veiled Strength

REALISTIC LEADERSHIP

How The Veiled Strength Might Apply This Anthem

Alex knows what has worked in the past. When his clients come to him with unrealistic expectations, he guides them back on course. His advice is efficient and matter-of-fact, without gimmicks or glitz. He effectively finds the right solution, at the right time. He keeps everything to the point, without veering off on wild tangents. He adds value to clients by helping them set realistic goals so they can ultimately stay focused and intentional.

THE ROYAL GUARD: MYSTIQUE + PRESTIGE

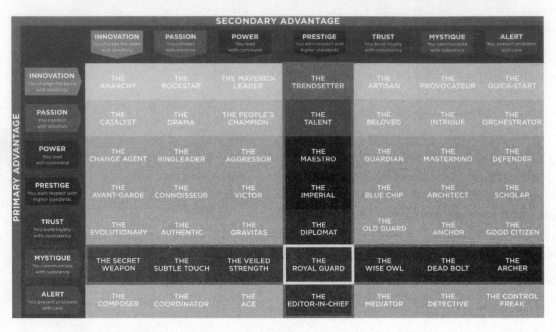

		SECONDARY ADVANTAGE					
	INNOVATION You change the game with creativity	**PASSION** You connect with emotion	**POWER** You lead with command	**PRESTIGE** You earn respect with higher standards	**TRUST** You build loyalty with consistency	**MYSTIQUE** You communicate with substance	**ALERT** You prevent problems with care
INNOVATION You change the game with creativity	THE ANARCHY	THE ROCKSTAR	THE MAVERICK LEADER	THE TRENDSETTER	THE ARTISAN	THE PROVOCATEUR	THE QUICK-START
PASSION You connect with emotion	THE CATALYST	THE DRAMA	THE PEOPLE'S CHAMPION	THE TALENT	THE BELOVED	THE INTRIGUE	THE ORCHESTRATOR
POWER You lead with command	THE CHANGE AGENT	THE RINGLEADER	THE AGGRESSOR	THE MAESTRO	THE GUARDIAN	THE MASTERMIND	THE DEFENDER
PRESTIGE You earn respect with higher standards	THE AVANT-GARDE	THE CONNOISSEUR	THE VICTOR	THE IMPERIAL	THE BLUE CHIP	THE ARCHITECT	THE SCHOLAR
TRUST You build loyalty with consistency	THE EVOLUTIONARY	THE AUTHENTIC	THE GRAVITAS	THE DIPLOMAT	THE OLD GUARD	THE ANCHOR	THE GOOD CITIZEN
MYSTIQUE You communicate with substance	THE SECRET WEAPON	THE SUBTLE TOUCH	THE VEILED STRENGTH	THE ROYAL GUARD	THE WISE OWL	THE DEAD BOLT	THE ARCHER
ALERT You prevent problems with care	THE COMPOSER	THE COORDINATOR	THE ACE	THE EDITOR-IN-CHIEF	THE MEDIATOR	THE DETECTIVE	THE CONTROL FREAK

(PRIMARY ADVANTAGE shown along left axis)

HOW THE WORLD SEES THE ROYAL GUARD

Royal Guards execute projects with precision.

They have a stoic exterior and they rarely show their innermost thoughts. Even in volatile situations they remain calm.

At work or when playing sports, they are intensely competitive. They want to achieve the best quality, the highest level, and the most excellent results. They strive to improve.

As you'd expect from a Royal Guard, they can assess a situation quickly (as if they have to protect a queen or king!). They are part of the elite in their profession, and bring a certain dignity.

Archetype Twin

The Architect (page 212)

The Royal Guard's Top 5 Adjectives

    1. Elegant—They bring a subtle, understated dedication to each aspect of their life. When presenting an idea to the board, they choose their words carefully. Their emails reflect sophistication as they explain in precise words what they need. There's no fluff. You might be impressed by their extensive vocabulary. Royal Guards think before speaking.

2. Astute—They're able to quickly, and usually accurately, assess situations. When joining a company as interim CEO, they know within a few days the key issues facing the company. They draw up a change program and execute it with care and determination.

3. Discreet—They earn attention with a quiet voice rather than a shrill yell. In sales, they're not driven by ego, but earn respect from customers for their ability to listen. They don't make wild claims they can't back up. They close a deal by offering measured advice based on facts.

4. Particular—They know what they're looking for, and don't jump on ideas immediately. In brainstorming sessions, they don't contribute a jumble of half-baked ideas, but they excel at picking the right ideas that add value to the company.

5. Measured—Their actions and words are carefully chosen. Even under high pressure, they keep a calm composure. They are quiet observers who get their message across at the right time, with the right words.

"Highest and Best Value" of The Royal Guard

Conscientious and dedicated, Royal Guards tend to be focused on one task at a time. They can work with intense concentration to get minute details right.

You can find them in their office examining their monthly report and polishing each sentence before sending it out. Their PowerPoint slides for a sales presentation are accurate, factual, and relatively brief. They focus on essentials. And present with minimal fuss.

Royal Guards are perceptive. They notice subtle changes in people's behavior. Discerning and observant, they know exactly what's going on.

What Is Not the "Highest and Best Value" of The Royal Guard?

Don't expect them to be front and center. Royal Guards don't like putting the spotlight on themselves.

They are competitive, but not in a *big ego* way. They don't bang the drum for themselves. They let their achievements speak. They deliver first-class results.

How to Work with a Royal Guard

They enjoy working privately and independently.

They're able to remain coolheaded when everyone else frantically goes around in circles. They keep their attention focused on executing their plan with a keen eye for detail.

Is your boss a Royal Guard? They probably have a minimalist communication style, and that's why you might not always know exactly what your responsibilities are. Be sure to ask questions for clarification. Remember that you're expected to deliver superior results at all times. When you make mistakes, a Royal Guard won't make a fool out of you in front of your co-workers. They call you into their office to have a quiet word with you.

Never sloppy and never heavy-handed, Royal Guards are clearheaded, confident leaders who expect their team to deliver high standards.

Archetypes That Can Optimize The Royal Guard

The Rockstar (page 244) will generate lots of fresh ideas, while The Royal Guard selects the best ideas and implements them.

The Avant-Garde (page 196) is an enterprising leader who adds creativity to the team.

A Lesson That Everyone Can Learn from The Royal Guard

Your achievements speak for you.

One-Minute Coaching to My Royal Guards

When leading your team, you tend to keep your meetings short and to the point. But sometimes you need to spell out the details, because not everyone gets what you mean.

Take a little more time to ensure everyone understands what is required of them. If people don't fully grasp their tasks, they may disappoint you.

Famous Royal Guard

Malcolm Gladwell

Example of an Anthem for The Royal Guard

ASTUTE ATTENTION TO DETAIL

How The Royal Guard Might Apply This Anthem

Dale is a trainer inside a large service-oriented corporation. He's earned expert status within and among his peers. When faced with a problem, he looks closely at the data to find solutions. He can come across as reserved, and is unlikely to gush or have warm-and-fuzzy conversations, yet his crisp intellectual elegance helps him remain objective even when politics get complicated. To ensure that his trainings are successful, he carefully documents the process and records recommendations and feedback so that future sessions will go even smoother.

THE WISE OWL: MYSTIQUE + TRUST

HOW THE WORLD SEES THE WISE OWL

They carefully analyze situations before making decisions. Even in high-pressure environments, they don't feel overwhelmed, and they don't get stressed. They're able to find the most effective path toward a goal.

When there's a crisis at home because their aging mother has fallen ill, the family relies on a Wise Owl to tell them what to do. And when a project hits a major problem, their co-workers look at them for direction. Employers and friends appreciate their loyalty and commitment.

During a job interview, you'll find that Wise Owls remain composed even when asked tough questions. On a manic day just before a product launch, they remain coolheaded, checking off their to-dos one by one.

They are Wise Owls because others rely on their thoughtful advice. They communicate with little fuss. They're dignified, discreet, and well-informed.

Archetype Twin
The Anchor (page 284)

The Wise Owl's Top 5 Adjectives

1. **Observant**—Wise Owls are always aware. They notice from your behavior when something is up. They spot obstacles that put projects at risk before everyone else notices them. Attentive and alert, they recognize subtle diversions from standard processes.

2. **Assured**—They are confident in their ability to make the right decisions on behalf of the team. They don't act impulsively. Thoughtful and steadfast, they rely on their experience and analytical skills to make the right decisions. When faced with a quality issue, for instance, they'll point out how the problem was solved last time.

3. **Unruffled**—They remain even-keeled in the midst of project setbacks and tough challenges. When the whole team panics about a major product recall, they prepare press releases and instruct the team on how to deal with negative feedback on social media. You can rely on them to keep cool even in the most chaotic circumstances.

4. **Nuanced**—They bring a delicate touch to interactions. Before meeting a prospective client, they carefully do their own research. They check out the company's social media presence, website, and blog. They find out whether the company has recently been in the news. Modest and unpretentious, they build credibility with rational arguments.

5. **Logical**—They make their decisions by weighing pros and cons. When discussing where to go on vacation, they mention the pluses and minuses of going to Hawaii versus Florida. You'll also find they have a checklist of what to get done before they go away.

"Highest and Best Value" of The Wise Owl

They are watchful of the details. They systematically approach problems to find the best solutions.

They efficiently work through their daily to-do lists. You won't find them coming to a meeting unprepared. They can present a detailed status update on any of their projects at any time. They never miss an action point.

What Is Not the "Highest and Best Value" of The Wise Owl?

They rarely make an impassioned plea or over-the-top sales pitch. Instead,

Wise Owls carefully outline rational arguments for their ideas. They have an understated style.

How to Work with a Wise Owl

Wise Owls are able to work independently. They don't reveal all their thoughts. They tend not to show their emotions. Businesslike in most situations, they have a calm sense of purpose.

You get the most out of Wise Owls if they can work in a structured way. At a busy start-up, they'll bring order to the chaos. You'll find you come to rely on their steadiness and thoughtful advice.

Archetypes That Can Optimize The Wise Owl

The Quick-Start (page 264) brings a strong drive to implement ideas according to the plan.
A Mastermind (page 140) leads the team with a sense of authority.

A Lesson That Everyone Can Learn from The Wise Owl

Steady wins the game.

One-Minute Coaching to My Wise Owls

Over the last few years, you've become a valued member of the team. You remain focused on goals, and you're steadfast in the face of major challenges. Your colleagues appreciate your unassuming manner. But sometimes you need to speak up for yourself and contribute your valuable opinions. Don't wait to be asked.

You don't like to promote yourself, but in some situations you need to highlight what you've accomplished. To further your career, you need to ensure you receive the credit you deserve for your achievements.

Famous Wise Owls

Stephen Hawking and Confucius

Example of an Anthem for The Wise Owl

SUBTLE SOLUTIONS

How The Wise Owl Might Apply This Anthem

As an audiologist, Gerry helps people deal with hearing loss. It's not an easy job, because most of his patients are resistant to getting hearing aids. To help overcome this obstacle, Gerry takes the time to carefully learn about each patient's needs. In a calm and unruffled voice, he spends extra time to go over a five-point overview of his recommended solutions. This reassures his patients, making it more likely that they will end up with a better solution, and continue to return to him for service going forward.

THE ARCHER: MYSTIQUE + ALERT

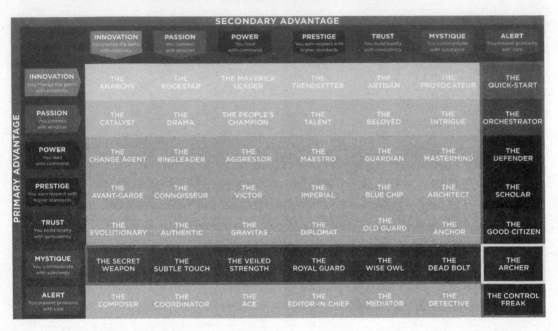

HOW THE WORLD SEES THE ARCHER

This focused communicator finds accurate solutions to complex problems.

Their analytical skills are exemplary. As factory directors, they analyze processes to find ways to improve productivity when everyone thinks optimum productivity has already been reached. As marketing analysts, they know exactly how each campaign performs, and they understand why, for instance, Twitter was a good source of Web traffic in one campaign and not in another. As finance directors, they're able to uncover ways to save costs.

During an argument about resource allocation, they support their request for extra man-hours with facts and hard data. You'll find that they probably have a file at hand with all the required information. They point out exactly how long a project took last year. They highlight pitfalls that may cause delays. Unwavering and steadfast, they will not back down easily. They present logical arguments without raising their voice.

They are goal-oriented and determined. They precisely aim at reaching desired results (hence their name). They have exceptional attention to detail.

Archetype Twin
The Detective (page 240)

The Archer's Top 5 Adjectives
   1. On-Target—They formulate their ideas with clarity. They are particular about archiving their emails. Their office is neatly organized. They pay attention to the fine print. They're able to follow procedures in a methodical way.
   2. Reasoned—They work hard, acting with purpose rather than folly. Sometimes, in the world of this Mystique personality, chitchat is just a waste of their time ("Enough with the pleasantries, let's talk business").
   3. Pragmatic—They are logical and practical, and prefer working with quantitative information. You'll find their budget proposal for next year is neatly summarized in an Excel document. Resources are carefully considered based on forecasted sales. They build in a buffer for unforeseen problems.
   4. Sharp—They focus intensely on key problems. They analyze data to find the root causes of problems. That's how they come up with smart solutions.
   5. Under-the-radar—They get things done without drama. They don't draw attention to their achievements. During a job interview they may even undersell themselves. They're competitive, but they don't flaunt their successes.

"Highest and Best Value" of The Archer
They don't rest until they've completed a task and delivered the desired result.
   They are highly principled. They work hard to uphold values. They like to do things the right way.
   When writing a status update, they are succinct and deliberate. They don't waste time with unnecessary discussions. They steer the meeting to complete the full agenda within the agreed time.
   They are cautious leaders who avoid risky new ventures. Their forecasts are never overoptimistic. They prefer to play it safe.

What Is Not the "Highest and Best Value" of The Archer?
Archers carefully plan and execute their communication, getting to the substantive center matter. They're rarely audacious in words, mind-set, or dress.

Archers tend to be reserved, but their mild manners hide a steely determination. They are strong achievers who rarely come out behind.

How to Work with an Archer

They are methodical people who are happy to work on their own. They carefully work through potential consequences before making decisions.

They are quick to understand how to get from A to B. If the company objective is to increase profitability by 30%, they can quickly compare the various scenarios and recommend whether to increase prices, grow the sales team, or reduce overheads.

You get the most out of your Archers when you take advantage of their analytical skills and allow them to work in a systematic way.

Archetypes That Can Optimize The Archer

The Gravitas (page 276) is a firm leader who naturally exudes authority.
The Orchestrator (page 168) helps to inspire other people to get desired results.

A Lesson That Everyone Can Learn from The Archer

Skillful solutions can be found through sheer hard work and careful analysis.

One-Minute Coaching to My Archers

Your analytical skills are excellent. You make a sound contribution to the company's performance. Sometimes you seem to struggle to leverage the creative skills in your team.

You are a cautious person, but the company needs to take considered risks to meet its growth targets. Take advantage of the creative people on your team to come up with fresh ideas for new products, new market channels, or new business models. Use your analytical skills to pick the most promising ideas—even if they sometimes seem outlandish to you.

Famous Archers

Michael Crichton and SEAL Team Six

Example of an Anthem for The Archer
ON TARGET ANALYSIS

How The Archer Might Apply This Anthem

Rather than leading through sheer power, The Archer knows how to hit the bull's-eye. He isn't a social butterfly. But behind the scenes, he has established a contingency plan. Hans is a master of organization. His files are impeccable, as are his calendar, his drawers, and even his laundry room. He is the company record keeper. He collates and catalogues efficiently, becoming the go-to person within the entire corporation. He manages data with a pragmatic system, providing a reliable and reasoned structure. Want to find that contract from 1998? Hans has your answer.

THE PRESTIGE ADVANTAGE

THE PRESTIGE ADVANTAGE IS ACHIEVING SUCCESS WITH HIGHER STANDARDS.
PRESTIGE PERSONALITIES SPEAK THE LANGUAGE OF EXCELLENCE.

THE AVANT-GARDE: PRESTIGE + INNOVATION

		SECONDARY ADVANTAGE						
		INNOVATION You change the game with creativity	PASSION You connect with emotion	POWER You lead with command	PRESTIGE You earn respect with higher standards	TRUST You build loyalty with consistency	MYSTIQUE You communicate with substance	ALERT You prevent problems with care
PRIMARY ADVANTAGE	INNOVATION You change the game with creativity	THE ANARCHY	THE ROCKSTAR	THE MAVERICK LEADER	THE TRENDSETTER	THE ARTISAN	THE PROVOCATEUR	THE QUICK-START
	PASSION You connect with emotion	THE CATALYST	THE DRAMA	THE PEOPLE'S CHAMPION	THE TALENT	THE BELOVED	THE INTRIGUE	THE ORCHESTRATOR
	POWER You lead with command	THE CHANGE AGENT	THE RINGLEADER	THE AGGRESSOR	THE MAESTRO	THE GUARDIAN	THE MASTERMIND	THE DEFENDER
	PRESTIGE You earn respect with higher standards	THE AVANT-GARDE	THE CONNOISSEUR	THE VICTOR	THE IMPERIAL	THE BLUE CHIP	THE ARCHITECT	THE SCHOLAR
	TRUST You build loyalty with consistency	THE EVOLUTIONARY	THE AUTHENTIC	THE GRAVITAS	THE DIPLOMAT	THE OLD GUARD	THE ANCHOR	THE GOOD CITIZEN
	MYSTIQUE You communicate with substance	THE SECRET WEAPON	THE SUBTLE TOUCH	THE VEILED STRENGTH	THE ROYAL GUARD	THE WISE OWL	THE DEAD BOLT	THE ARCHER
	ALERT You prevent problems with care	THE COMPOSER	THE COORDINATOR	THE ACE	THE EDITOR-IN-CHIEF	THE MEDIATOR	THE DETECTIVE	THE CONTROL FREAK

How the World Sees The Avant-Garde

Avant-Gardes are forward-thinking and enterprising leaders.

As marketers, they come up with the next big campaign idea. As designers, they know what will be popular next year. As entrepreneurs, they have an ambitious vision of where they want to take the company in the next five or ten years.

Their creativity makes them excellent contributors to brainstorming sessions. They're able to generate a lot of ideas. But they also choose the right ideas and implement them with attention to detail. They look for the highest quality. And that's how they earn respect.

Avant-garde artists are the people who experiment with new ideas. Avant-Garde personalities have a similar talent for developing experimental concepts. They have a gift for looking ahead, for predicting how things are going to develop.

Archetype Twin
The Trendsetter (page 252)

The Avant-Garde's Top 5 Adjectives

1. Original—They're "one-of-a-kind." In brainstorming sessions, they generate ideas that only they can come up with. When presenting, they utter phrases that only they use. Their social media profiles show unusual photos only they can present. Their innovative approach gives them an edge.

2. Enterprising—They have an uncanny ability to spot opportunity and turn it into success. As serial entrepreneurs, they may have developed and sold several successful businesses. As employees in large companies, they've instigated various new projects. They never sit still. They are always looking to create the next big thing.

3. Forward-thinking—They inspire others to look ahead. When you point out in a board meeting that clients are happy with your products, they'll ask to consider whether they'll still be happy next month or next year when a competitor brings out a more advanced model. Never complacent, they push a company to innovate.

4. Dashing—Their bold thinking and dramatic style make people take notice. Even their weekly status meetings are fun and uplifting. They inspire their team with their enthusiasm and ideas.

5. Commendable—They are strong leaders. They are competitive and successful. Even as junior sales executives, their peers watch their actions carefully because they know they can learn from Avant-Gardes.

"Highest and Best Value" of The Avant-Garde
Their minds works quickly to develop unconventional solutions.

They are prolific idea generators. They bring fresh interpretations of the *same old thing.* They tweak the game. They change the rules.

Stuck with a project? Or is your company struggling to innovate? An Avant-Garde will bring new ideas and execute them to a high standard. You can expect her to deliver high quality in whatever she does (that's her primary Prestige Advantage).

What Is Not the "Highest and Best Value" of The Avant-Garde?

If you force your Avant-Garde to follow the same routine over and over again, they'll become bored and demoralized. They enjoy experimenting. They reinterpret the status quo.

Don't let your Avant-Gardes do monotonous work. You get the most out of them if they can tweak procedures, reinvent the rules, and create new business models.

How to Work with an Avant-Garde

Is your company facing an uncertain future? Need new ideas to reinvigorate sales? An Avant-Garde has a natural ability to find new business opportunities, new partnerships, and new product ideas. They're nonlinear thinkers who see opportunities wherever they go. And thanks to their Prestige Advantage, they also aim to have the best ideas implemented.

Avant-Gardes thrive in dynamic organizations, where their creativity is most useful. Employ them to breathe new life into a stale organization or to ensure an innovative organization takes advantage of future opportunities.

Archetypes That Can Optimize The Avant-Garde

The cautionary approach of The Detective (page 240) provides a balance to The Avant-Garde's creativity and push for progress.

The calm presence of The Gravitas (page 276) provides reassurance that not everything is subject to change. The Gravitas also adds a methodical way of working.

A Lesson That Everyone Can Learn from The Avant-Garde

In business you don't need to know what's popular today; you need to know what will sell tomorrow.

One-Minute Coaching to My Avant-Gardes

You are naturally plugged in to new business prospects, trends, and opportunities to meet new people. But sometimes you need to stay a little more grounded.

Take time to be in the moment. Focus on connecting with the people around you. See how they react to your ideas. Listen to their concerns. Capture your energy and use it to persuade others. Focus on company goals to show how you add value.

Famous Avant-Gardes

Pablo Picasso and Steve Wynn

Example of an Anthem for The Avant-Garde

FORWARD-THINKING CREATIVITY

How The Avant-Garde Might Apply This Anthem

Emily is a graphic designer working for an advertising agency. Her agency has recently taken on a client, and the new business will help add much-needed revenue to the agency's bottom line. Only problem is, this client is stuck on an outdated design. They are resistant to change. Emily is concerned they could become irrelevant if they don't change, fast.

Applying her Advantages, Emily immediately begins developing cutting-edge ideas to refresh the brand. She takes cues from respected but progressive industry leaders who are on the forefront, figuring out a way to communicate the client's message in a visually engaging way. With her primary Prestige Advantage, she knows how to raise standards. She develops a new series of images for the client website, making small but creative adjustments that transform the stale image into a modern brand.

THE CONNOISSEUR: PRESTIGE + PASSION

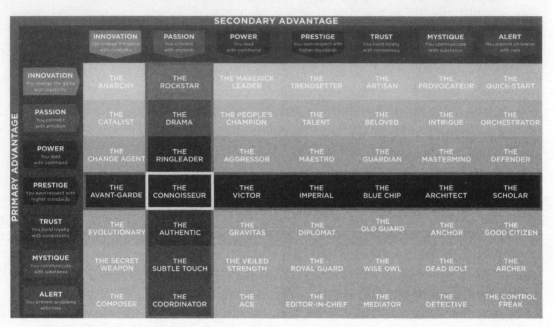

HOW THE WORLD SEES THE CONNOISSEUR

Insightful and knowledgeable, Connoisseurs are highly appreciated by colleagues, employees, and customers.

Connoisseurs enjoy a wide social circle. Need an editor for your next book? Need a chic interior designer for your new house? Want a table for two at that new impossible-to-get dinner spot? Ask a Connoisseur, because he probably knows someone who can make it happen.

They have a natural glow. When presenting, they have a light in their eye. Their excitement comes across in their Twitter stream, their profile pictures, and in the way they talk to people. They make others feel confident. They give them praise. They show them what to do next.

Like a connoisseur of fine wines, they appreciate subtleties. They understand minute differences. They are respected experts.

Archetype Twin
The Talent (page 156)

The Connoisseur's Top 5 Adjectives

1. **Insightful**—They communicate their ideas with clarity and conviction. You'll find that they quickly obtain buy-in from their audience—whether they're "selling" their idea for a new project in a board meeting or launching a new loyalty program at a huge dealer conference. They're confident, articulate, and sharp.

2. **Distinguished**—They know how to choose the right style, approach, and words appropriate for each situation. They encourage a nervous interviewee. They guide a naughty child. They strike the right tone when lobbying the governor. They're good communicators who meticulously prepare meetings.

3. **In-the-know**—They keep themselves informed on the latest industry trends, new business practices, and relevant news. You may find that they are sought-after speakers in their specialized area. A conference audience appreciates their expertise and vivid presentation style.

4. **Admired**—They're respected for their knowledge, and they are highly valued for their sophistication. They prefer to excel in a limited number of things rather than spread themselves too thin. They are competitive spirits who continuously strive to meet higher goals. They want to get better at what they do. They set high expectations.

5. **Desirable**—Their emotional intelligence makes them fascinating. You'll find them the center of attention at cocktail parties commenting on the latest news. At networking events and office parties, people naturally gravitate to them to listen to their opinions. Knowledgeable and astute, they are good conversationalists.

"Highest and Best Value" of The Connoisseur

They intuitively understand what others need. Almost effortlessly, they excel at selling products and ideas. When talking, they build vivid images of the positive impact new products will have on clients.

They get inspired by making new connections. They enthusiastically share their knowledge. They are warm personalities thanks to their Passion Advantage. Their Prestige Advantage brings a keen eye for detail and a drive to deliver quality results.

Networking comes easily to them both at business meetings and private gatherings. They connect people to each other and have a wide sphere of influence—especially as they progress in their career.

Charming and eloquent, they know how to win over doubters. They cultivate their own image as an admired pro.

What Is Not the "Highest and Best Value" of The Connoisseur?

With a keen focus on getting things right, Connoisseurs may not always embrace change. Trying new ideas may lead to failure, which they carefully try to avoid.

You get the most out of Connoisseurs in people-focused roles like customer-experience management. In both start-ups and larger organizations, they raise quality standards and ensure your products and services are top-notch.

How to Work with a Connoisseur

Need to sell a new service to a difficult customer? Ask a Connoisseur to join your customer meeting. Their enthusiasm for your new service is contagious. Without being pushy, they present a persuasive case for how your customer will benefit from switching to a new product. Leaving no stone unturned, they point out each benefit with a twinkle in their eye.

Are quality standards slipping in your firm? With his attention to detail, a Connoisseur will quickly focus workers' attention on getting things right. His enthusiasm gets workers motivated to actively participate in a better solution or system.

Archetypes That Can Optimize The Connoisseur

The Evolutionary (page 268) will carefully push for change.
The Ace (page 228) ensures that projects are finished on time and under budget.

A Lesson That Everyone Can Learn from The Connoisseur

Subtle details make the difference between good and extraordinary. Small changes generate exponential results.

One-Minute Coaching to My Connoisseurs

You have an intense drive to increase standards and improve performance. This is great. You have carefully engineered your personal image, but be careful to maintain consistency.

You excel at connecting with new people, but don't forget to maintain strong bonds with existing suppliers and clients.

Famous Connoisseurs

Heidi Klum and John F. Kennedy

Example of an Anthem for The Connoisseur

IN-THE-KNOW OPINIONS

How The Connoisseur Might Apply This Anthem

Among his friends, people look to Jaime to learn what to buy, where to go, what to do (and how to do it). People look to Jaime for recommendations on the best of everything. He intuitively identifies social cues. When he writes Facebook status updates, Jaime shares his favorites in all areas: where to find the freshest kale at the local farmer's market, or which dry cleaner will offer speedy delivery in a pinch. He's tapped into trends, and has an innate ability to identify the next big meme.

He knows the best of the best. His insightfulness, coupled with his ability to see what others want, makes him valuable to his peers and co-workers.

THE VICTOR: PRESTIGE + POWER

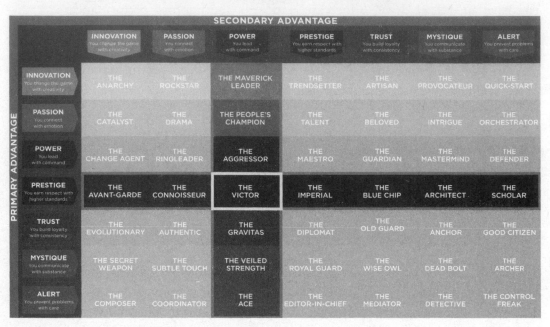

		SECONDARY ADVANTAGE					
	INNOVATION You change the game with creativity	**PASSION** You connect with emotion	**POWER** You lead with command	**PRESTIGE** You earn respect with higher standards	**TRUST** You build loyalty with consistency	**MYSTIQUE** You communicate with substance	**ALERT** You prevent problems with care
INNOVATION You change the game with creativity	THE ANARCHY	THE ROCKSTAR	THE MAVERICK LEADER	THE TRENDSETTER	THE ARTISAN	THE PROVOCATEUR	THE QUICK-START
PASSION You connect with emotion	THE CATALYST	THE DRAMA	THE PEOPLE'S CHAMPION	THE TALENT	THE BELOVED	THE INTRIGUE	THE ORCHESTRATOR
POWER You lead with command	THE CHANGE AGENT	THE RINGLEADER	THE AGGRESSOR	THE MAESTRO	THE GUARDIAN	THE MASTERMIND	THE DEFENDER
PRESTIGE You earn respect with higher standards	THE AVANT-GARDE	THE CONNOISSEUR	THE VICTOR	THE IMPERIAL	THE BLUE CHIP	THE ARCHITECT	THE SCHOLAR
TRUST You build loyalty with consistency	THE EVOLUTIONARY	THE AUTHENTIC	THE GRAVITAS	THE DIPLOMAT	THE OLD GUARD	THE ANCHOR	THE GOOD CITIZEN
MYSTIQUE You communicate with substance	THE SECRET WEAPON	THE SUBTLE TOUCH	THE VEILED STRENGTH	THE ROYAL GUARD	THE WISE OWL	THE DEAD BOLT	THE ARCHER
ALERT You prevent problems with care	THE COMPOSER	THE COORDINATOR	THE ACE	THE EDITOR-IN-CHIEF	THE MEDIATOR	THE DETECTIVE	THE CONTROL FREAK

(left axis label: **PRIMARY ADVANTAGE**)

HOW THE WORLD SEES THE VICTOR

Victors are strong leaders who set big goals. They pursue excellence across the board.

Victors express themselves with confidence. Is there a problem with an underachieving member of the staff? Victors don't waste time. They'll have a firm word to point out what's expected. Have a conflict in the team? They deal with it resolutely; they keep the team on track.

Victors are results-oriented. In a chaotic world they maintain a sharp focus on objectives. Ambitious and competitive, they constantly seek ways to improve their products, procedures, and ways of working.

You may think they've delivered a flawless presentation to a prospect, but next time they'll have fine-tuned it even further.

Victors are admired achievers with an impressive track record. They are winners (a victor is a winner—as in victorious).

Archetype Twin

The Maestro (page 132)

The Victor's Top 5 Adjectives

1. **Respected**—Their impeccable presentation style earns them immediate respect from employees, clients, and colleagues. They never turn up for a meeting underprepared.

2. **Competitive**—They are ambitious. Their résumés show a clear progression. They know what they want to achieve in their career. They are classic overachievers who enjoy being publicly recognized for their contributions to the company.

3. **Results-oriented**—They don't just want to get the job done. They want to excel. As entrepreneurs they want their new app to get more media coverage than their competitor's app. They want to get higher customer satisfaction scores each year. They want each product upgrade to surpass the previous upgrade in terms of sales. They never rest because things can always be improved.

4. **Concentrated**—They keep their eyes firmly on company goals and their personal objectives. They don't get distracted. They know what they want to achieve.

5. **Exemplary**—They are strong leaders regardless of their position in an organization. Their peers look to them as examples of success. They set the tone in meetings.

"Highest and Best Value" of The Victor

They excel in their work. They exceed expectations. And they expect high standards from their team, too.

In sales they impress clients with a superb presentation and detailed product knowledge. In marketing they focus on generating high-quality leads. As buyers they seek suppliers who can meet their high expectations.

Victors achieve excellent results in the career they choose to pursue.

What Is Not the "Highest and Best Value" of The Victor?

Victors play to win. They quickly become frustrated when others on their team do not share their goals. They lose respect when people seem wishy-washy or uncommitted. Don't put your Victor in a position in which they must tread water. Because they play to win, they dislike playing not to lose.

Victors exude a natural authority. They impress with their direct communication style. They put their energy into generating results and retaining a strong command.

How to Work with a Victor

Is your boss a Victor? You'll be well aware of your goals, but you may need to ask what exactly is expected from you. Make sure you exceed the quality standards you're set. You won't be able to get away with sloppy work.

Is a Victor working for you? Remember that they thrive on recognition. Be sure to thank them for their contribution to the company. If they've excelled (as they usually do), mention them publicly in your next company update.

You get most out of your Victors if they are in a leadership position. Their commitment to high standards and natural ability to lead will quickly earn them respect from their team.

Archetypes That Can Optimize The Victor

The quiet Wise Owl (page 188) builds a loyal team.
The Archer (page 192) finds skillful solutions to complex problems.

A Lesson That Everyone Can Learn from The Victor

Don't let anything stand in your way to reach your goals.

One-Minute Coaching to My Victors

You've successfully led your team to launch an excellent new product. Congratulations. You're developing a strong and effective leadership style.

Be careful that you don't get too wrapped up in your goals and successes. Remain aware of how others perceive you. Remember to spend more time listening than talking. Bring in the Passion Advantage to build devotion among your team. Share your excitement about team performance or plan an evening out with the team to nurture team spirit.

Famous Victors

Enzo Ferrari and Michael Bloomberg

Example of an Anthem for The Victor

RESULTS-ORIENTED EXECUTION

How The Victor Might Apply This Anthem

Meet Rachel, scratch golfer. She's accomplished, perhaps intimidatingly so. She's not concerned about other players' feelings. She doesn't play favorites, because favorites don't result in a bottom-line victory. She's competitive—and proud of it. Trophies line her mantel (and they're not for "most improved"). She brings an elegance and power to the field whenever she plays. To ensure that she attains her best, Rachel practices her swing at least fifty times a day to ensure that she always knows precisely where the ball will go.

THE BLUE CHIP: PRESTIGE + TRUST

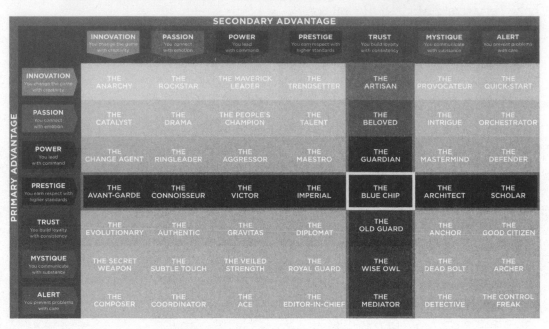

		SECONDARY ADVANTAGE					
	INNOVATION You change the game with creativity	**PASSION** You connect with emotion	**POWER** You lead with command	**PRESTIGE** You earn respect with higher standards	**TRUST** You build loyalty with consistency	**MYSTIQUE** You communicate with substance	**ALERT** You prevent problems with care
INNOVATION You change the game with creativity	THE ANARCHY	THE ROCKSTAR	THE MAVERICK LEADER	THE TRENDSETTER	THE ARTISAN	THE PROVOCATEUR	THE QUICK-START
PASSION You connect with emotion	THE CATALYST	THE DRAMA	THE PEOPLE'S CHAMPION	THE TALENT	THE BELOVED	THE INTRIGUE	THE ORCHESTRATOR
POWER You lead with command	THE CHANGE AGENT	THE RINGLEADER	THE AGGRESSOR	THE MAESTRO	THE GUARDIAN	THE MASTERMIND	THE DEFENDER
PRESTIGE You earn respect with higher standards	THE AVANT-GARDE	THE CONNOISSEUR	THE VICTOR	THE IMPERIAL	THE BLUE CHIP	THE ARCHITECT	THE SCHOLAR
TRUST You build loyalty with consistency	THE EVOLUTIONARY	THE AUTHENTIC	THE GRAVITAS	THE DIPLOMAT	THE OLD GUARD	THE ANCHOR	THE GOOD CITIZEN
MYSTIQUE You communicate with substance	THE SECRET WEAPON	THE SUBTLE TOUCH	THE VEILED STRENGTH	THE ROYAL GUARD	THE WISE OWL	THE DEAD BOLT	THE ARCHER
ALERT You prevent problems with care	THE COMPOSER	THE COORDINATOR	THE ACE	THE EDITOR-IN-CHIEF	THE MEDIATOR	THE DETECTIVE	THE CONTROL FREAK

(Left axis label: **PRIMARY ADVANTAGE**)

HOW THE WORLD SEES THE BLUE CHIP

Their reputation for quiet excellence stretches far and wide.

As R&D managers, they will deliver excellent new products. Their eye for detail is unmatched. Developing an OEM product for a specific client? You can rely on their contribution in client meetings. Unfazed by difficult clients and their demands, their calm demeanor reassures everyone. Their direct communication style breeds trust.

As CEOs you can expect them to meet or exceed the agreed budget year in and year out. They are quiet overachievers who continuously find ways to generate tremendous results.

As with *blue-chip* stocks, others have confidence in their stability and high value. They are calm leaders who earn respect for their impeccable presentations, their outstanding results, and their composed response to challenges.

Archetype Twin
The Diplomat (page 280)

The Blue Chip's Top 5 Adjectives

    1. Classic—Their style is timeless. They are usually unaffected by fads and trends. They tend to speak in familiar words rather than jargon and buzzwords. They carefully form ideas based on their own criteria.

    2. Established—Friends and co-workers depend on them. You'll find they often represent their companies at trade organizations and conferences. Their quiet demeanor and distinguished reputation earn them trust.

    3. "Best in class"—Their performance is consistently outstanding. Even as junior team members you won't find them cutting corners. They follow a step-by-step process to managing projects. They get their job done—and do it extremely well.

    4. Safe—They tend to avoid risk. They prefer the familiar path. As marketers they prefer optimizing campaigns rather than trying out unproven tools and tactics. They are, for instance, excellent at improving pay-per-click performance by paying attention to keyword groups and ad text.

    5. Punctual—They are precise and value routine. They arrive at meetings on time and appreciate it if others do, too. When leading a Skype call with an overseas client, they carefully adhere to an agenda to ensure all points are covered.

"Highest and Best Value" of The Blue Chip

Blue Chips constantly seek ways to improve, and to raise standards.

    In customer service they carefully review and enhance scripts to reduce call times. In marketing they monitor campaigns to improve marketing effectiveness. In factories they pay attention to details to reduce defects and improve reliability.

    Blue Chips exude a quiet confidence. Their mild manners and no-nonsense communication style gain them the respect of suppliers, clients, and staff. You can rely on them to deliver results.

What Is Not the "Highest and Best Value" of The Blue Chip?

Don't expect a dog-and-pony show from these established communicators.

    Blue Chips are coolheaded, trusted leaders. While they don't dominate the conversation, their quietness lets you know that they know what they're doing. They excel in their job by following the path that they know has worked in the past.

How to Work with a Blue Chip

Need to present your business plan to the bank? Blue Chips will present your plan without fuss. Their straightforward slides increase confidence in your plan, and they'll impress your bankers with their detailed knowledge of the market and in-depth understanding of your financial forecast.

Blue Chips are outstanding leaders. Their Prestige Advantage gives them an eye for detail and drives them to deliver high-quality results. Their Trust Advantage brings stability and calmness to any situation. Their dependability earns them the loyalty of their employees. They lead by example.

Archetypes That Can Optimize The Blue Chip

The Secret Weapon (page 172) will add a touch of creativity and provide clever solutions to problems.

The Coordinator (page 224) will nurture a team spirit and keep everyone focused on deadlines.

A Lesson That Everyone Can Learn from The Blue Chip

You don't need drama to make a good impression.

One-Minute Coaching to My Blue Chips

You deliver excellent results—which is much appreciated by our shareholders. You've earned the loyalty of staff and suppliers.

But as a leader you should also learn to get more emotionally involved. Your calm demeanor is often good, but sometimes you can build relationships quicker by showing your passion for the company.

Famous Blue Chips

Ralph Lauren and Princess Diana

Example of an Anthem for The Blue Chip

CLASSIC EXPERTISE

How The Blue Chip Might Apply This Anthem

From the time he was trained at Cordon Bleu, Daryl has helped others find the beauty in time-honored traditions. He hones his cooking technique relentlessly, maintaining standards even when cooking brunch for family. He relies on carefully chosen ingredients and timeless techniques. Unlike many of his peers, he refuses to rely on trends or the latest fad. Quite literally, he avoids becoming the flavor du jour. He takes this approach very seriously, having an almost prejudicial attitude toward trends. He puts in the extra effort to explain the background on why he chooses certain ingredients, utensils, and methods. He increases the perceived value of his menu, helping his patrons understand and appreciate the history behind his work, by continuing to implement the best traditions and techniques.

THE ARCHITECT: PRESTIGE + MYSTIQUE

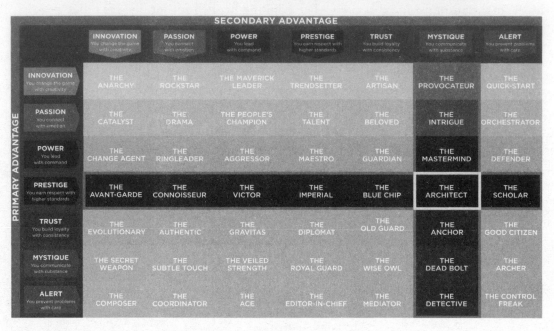

		SECONDARY ADVANTAGE						
		INNOVATION You change the game with creativity	**PASSION** You connect with emotion	**POWER** You lead with command	**PRESTIGE** You earn respect with higher standards	**TRUST** You build loyalty with consistency	**MYSTIQUE** You communicate with substance	**ALERT** You prevent problems with care
PRIMARY ADVANTAGE	**INNOVATION** You change the game with creativity	THE ANARCHY	THE ROCKSTAR	THE MAVERICK LEADER	THE TRENDSETTER	THE ARTISAN	THE PROVOCATEUR	THE QUICK-START
	PASSION You connect with emotion	THE CATALYST	THE DRAMA	THE PEOPLE'S CHAMPION	THE TALENT	THE BELOVED	THE INTRIGUE	THE ORCHESTRATOR
	POWER You lead with command	THE CHANGE AGENT	THE RINGLEADER	THE AGGRESSOR	THE MAESTRO	THE GUARDIAN	THE MASTERMIND	THE DEFENDER
	PRESTIGE You earn respect with higher standards	THE AVANT-GARDE	THE CONNOISSEUR	THE VICTOR	THE IMPERIAL	THE BLUE CHIP	THE ARCHITECT	THE SCHOLAR
	TRUST You build loyalty with consistency	THE EVOLUTIONARY	THE AUTHENTIC	THE GRAVITAS	THE DIPLOMAT	THE OLD GUARD	THE ANCHOR	THE GOOD CITIZEN
	MYSTIQUE You communicate with substance	THE SECRET WEAPON	THE SUBTLE TOUCH	THE VEILED STRENGTH	THE ROYAL GUARD	THE WISE OWL	THE DEAD BOLT	THE ARCHER
	ALERT You prevent problems with care	THE COMPOSER	THE COORDINATOR	THE ACE	THE EDITOR-IN-CHIEF	THE MEDIATOR	THE DETECTIVE	THE CONTROL FREAK

HOW THE WORLD SEES THE ARCHITECT

Architects are leaders with a clearly defined opinion.

They earn the respect of their team with their determination to deliver high-quality results. They can be competitive in their quest to improve results. Don't show up without serious prep work to a meeting with The Architect.

Intellectual and soft-spoken, Architects are able to formulate their ideas in a clear and articulate manner. They are principled in their work and home life, deviating little from their intentions.

When a difference of opinions arises among the management team, an Architect observes how others are digging in their heels. Even when others raise their voices, the Architect remains calm. By posing questions and pointing out facts, he is able to defuse heated discussions.

Like actual architects, they have a keen eye for detail and are happy to find solutions to challenging problems by themselves. The quality of their work is excellent.

Architects are quietly proud of their achievements. Their mild manner hides a determination to succeed.

Archetype Twin
The Royal Guard (page 184)

The Architect's Top 5 Adjectives
1. **Skillful**—They prefer to learn how to master specific skills at a high level rather than leapfrogging from one hobby to the next. You'll find them concentrating deeply to learn how to play the violin or repeatedly practicing their tennis serve. They avoid taking on work that they feel they're not qualified to do.

2. **Restrained**—They have a quiet but firm speaking style. In meetings, they won't be a dominant voice, but when they speak up, everyone listens. They carefully articulate their ideas. They think things through before talking.

3. **Polished**—They keep their motives and opinions to themselves until they've decided the time has come to share. They don't make rash decisions. They carefully consider their responses. When it's time for them to share, people know it will be a well-thought-out plan.

4. **For insiders only**—They are selective when making friends. Architects prefer to keep themselves at a distance, and you may find they avoid socializing with colleagues after work. On Twitter you'll find them tweeting links to useful articles rather than tweeting about their personal life.

5. **Sterling**—Their work is known to be first-rate. Whether writing code or a business report, they're committed to submitting top-notch, error-free work. They are meticulous.

"Highest and Best Value" of The Architect
They are excellent listeners and observers. Thoughtful and analytical, they remain coolheaded under pressure and won't be rushed into decision-making.

In team meetings they only speak when they can add value to a discussion. This doesn't mean they're afraid to speak up. They make their points and speak with conviction when they feel it is required.

What Is Not the "Highest and Best Value" of The Architect?

Don't expect them to throw themselves into the limelight, because they don't like drama and fuss.

Their achievements are likely to be widely respected, but they don't let it go to their heads. If you watch carefully, you can see them becoming fed up with braggadocio colleagues, they prefer to let their achievements do the talking.

How to Work with an Architect

Quiet and unassuming, they present their ideas matter-of-factly.

They impress clients with their sensible responses. They influence their staff with rational arguments and firm leadership. They're admired by your bankers with their in-depth market knowledge and grasp of financials.

You get the most out of your Architects if you allow them to work independently. They're able to concentrate intensely on the task at hand, and work in a deliberate, systematic way.

Archetypes That Can Optimize The Architect

Defenders (page 144) are strong, driven leaders who create momentum to get a project done.

The Guardian (page 136) is a sure-footed leader with sound long-term vision.

A Lesson That Everyone Can Learn from The Architect

An unassuming leadership style can be as effective as bold leadership.

One-Minute Coaching to My Architects

You've quietly won several new clients since joining us last year. Congratulations. You impress with your in-depth understanding of our products, and you listen well to prospects and are able to quickly sense what they require.

You tend to win business with rational arguments, but some clients need to feel you are passionate about our products. You don't need to gush with passion, but try to express your enthusiasm for our products by giving examples and by painting a more vivid picture of how our products can help customers. You might even share a little more about your experience of working here.

Famous Architects
James Bond and Ansel Adams

Example of an Anthem for The Architect
SKILLFUL STRUCTURE

How The Architect Might Apply This Anthem
Raoul quickly built a respected reputation as a programmer, because his work is as polished as he is. He carefully thinks through the structure and process of his information design, right from the start. Unlike sloppier programmers, he takes the time to investigate all possible solutions. Because he has a restrained personality, he tends not to draw attention to himself and his ideas. For this reason his past clients and supervisors haven't always realized how intricately his projects are planned out. However, now Raoul gets rapid "buy-in" from his team by clearly detailing his proposed structure right from Day One.

THE SCHOLAR: PRESTIGE + ALERT

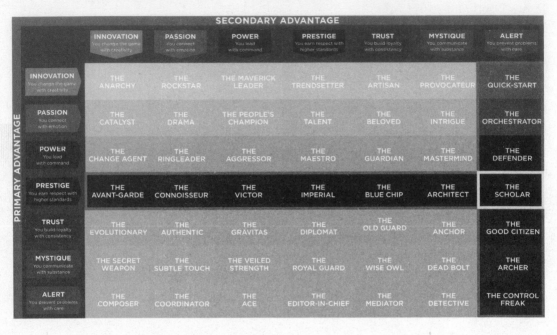

HOW THE WORLD SEES THE SCHOLAR

They are admired leaders with impressive track records.

They set the bar high for themselves, and for their team. Co-workers know that they are particular about how plans are executed. They sense the urgency and the importance of coming out on top.

Their constant drive to improve gains them ample recognition. Clients are impressed by continuous product or service upgrades. Suppliers are kept on their toes with requests for even higher-quality standards and more accurate deliveries.

Scholars expect the highest quality at all times (of course!), and they want action to be taken promptly.

Archetype Twin
The Editor-in-Chief (page 232)

The Scholar's Top 5 Adjectives

1. **Intellectual**—They are competitive and ambitious. Their résumés usually boast a list of achievements, awards, and membership in professional bodies. Receiving recognition for their work is important because they strive to be at the top of their game. Their knowledge base is admirable.

2. **Disciplined**—They are committed to their goals. When others start to tire because it's been a long day, The Scholar will remain focused and tick off one more task from their to-do list. When studying the piano, they're able to concentrate on practicing the same few notes until they've mastered them completely.

3. **Systematic**—In their pursuit of perfection, they usually don't make concessions. They don't settle for next best. When writing their first book, they want everything to be flawless—the cover, the grammar and spelling, and most of all the reviews. To be the best, they leave nothing to chance. Everything they do has a purpose. Their work is organized and measured.

4. **Relentless**—They don't give up easily. As entrepreneurs, they have a boundless drive. They may tweak their product, they may pivot their business, but they'll work damn hard to make their start-up a success.

5. **Standard-bearer**—They follow a strict internal compass. They're comfortable with enforcing regulations—whether health and safety rules, or best practices. They define procedures and set the norm. They're highly principled and respected by employees, suppliers, and clients.

"Highest and Best Value" of The Scholar

Conscientious and highly motivated, they keep their eye on minute details. They know how to set goals, and then go on to achieve them.

As CEOs they expect their team to work hard and to improve their own performance. They have little time for slackers. When reviewing résumés for a new VP, they'll disregard résumés with spelling errors immediately. They look for proof of a candidate's achievements—scanning the résumé for numbers that quantify performance.

Scholars are the people to turn to when your team is getting a little complacent. They point out the negative consequences of underperformance. They put pressure on sloppy employees to deliver better quality. They get latecomers to improve their punctuality.

What Is Not the "Highest and Best Value" of The Scholar?

You won't find a Scholar dashing off a quick email or social media update just to get it done on time. They give everything their full attention and avoid making mistakes.

Scholars tend to be risk-averse. They prefer a steady company improvement rather than a risky new venture.

How to Work with a Scholar

Scholars can be intensely driven to deliver results. They thrive on the recognition they receive for excelling in their jobs.

In a client meeting, they'll point out the company's good reputation with well-known brands. On their social media profiles they proudly list that they have an MBA and were once a tennis champion.

Their paperwork is always up-to-date. They are usually hyperorganized—even when under high pressure.

Hardworking and conscientious, Scholars are an asset to any company seeking highly detailed expertise.

Archetypes That Can Optimize The Scholar

Like The Scholar, Royal Guards (page 184) keep an eye on detail, but they do so in a more understated way.

The Artisan (page 256) will add creativity to problem-solving.

A Lesson That Everyone Can Learn from The Scholar

You should always strive to do better.

One-Minute Coaching to My Scholars

You know how to raise the quality of work done in your department, so that fewer mistakes are happening. You're protecting our reputation, which is great. Sometimes you need to open your approach to experimentation. Try to devote a small part of your work to testing new tactics. It doesn't matter if small experiments fail. You'll learn from them and find new ways to improve.

Famous Scholars

Gordon Ramsay and Anna Wintour

Example of an Anthem for The Scholar

DISCIPLINED VISION

How The Scholar Might Apply This Anthem

Jacob isn't the manager of his company, but his co-workers hold him in high regard. They respect his dedication to excellence and his disciplined vision for the business. Even his managers come to him for advice. Whenever a project goes into crunch mode, his team knows they can count on his leadership. He rallies the team and talks with members to see how he can help. Once he has a clear idea of what needs to be done, he lists out all of the deliverables and tracks who is responsible for each. He also checks in with each teammate periodically to make sure everyone is on schedule. The team knows that if they follow Jacob's lead, they can avoid last-minute all-nighters.

THE ALERT ADVANTAGE

THE ALERT ADVANTAGE IS CAREFUL PRECISION.
ALERT PERSONALITIES SPEAK THE LANGUAGE OF DETAILS.

THE COMPOSER: ALERT + INNOVATION

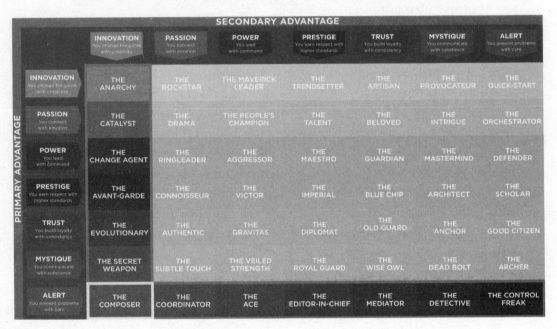

		SECONDARY ADVANTAGE					
		INNOVATION You change the game with creativity	**PASSION** You connect with emotion	**POWER** You lead with command	**PRESTIGE** You earn respect with higher standards	**TRUST** You build loyalty with consistency	**MYSTIQUE** You communicate with substance	**ALERT** You prevent problems with care
PRIMARY ADVANTAGE	**INNOVATION** You change the game with creativity	THE ANARCHY	THE ROCKSTAR	THE MAVERICK LEADER	THE TRENDSETTER	THE ARTISAN	THE PROVOCATEUR	THE QUICK-START
	PASSION You connect with emotion	THE CATALYST	THE DRAMA	THE PEOPLE'S CHAMPION	THE TALENT	THE BELOVED	THE INTRIGUE	THE ORCHESTRATOR
	POWER You lead with command	THE CHANGE AGENT	THE RINGLEADER	THE AGGRESSOR	THE MAESTRO	THE GUARDIAN	THE MASTERMIND	THE DEFENDER
	PRESTIGE You earn respect with higher standards	THE AVANT-GARDE	THE CONNOISSEUR	THE VICTOR	THE IMPERIAL	THE BLUE CHIP	THE ARCHITECT	THE SCHOLAR
	TRUST You build loyalty with consistency	THE EVOLUTIONARY	THE AUTHENTIC	THE GRAVITAS	THE DIPLOMAT	THE OLD GUARD	THE ANCHOR	THE GOOD CITIZEN
	MYSTIQUE You communicate with substance	THE SECRET WEAPON	THE SUBTLE TOUCH	THE VEILED STRENGTH	THE ROYAL GUARD	THE WISE OWL	THE DEAD BOLT	THE ARCHER
	ALERT You prevent problems with care	THE COMPOSER	THE COORDINATOR	THE ACE	THE EDITOR-IN-CHIEF	THE MEDIATOR	THE DETECTIVE	THE CONTROL FREAK

HOW THE WORLD SEES THE COMPOSER

Creative and goal-focused, Composers come up with innovations that contribute to your company's bottom line.

When others suggest quick wins, a Composer will consider long-term consequences. Unwavering, they defend their long-term vision even if that means losing revenues in the short term. They know they can make up for potential losses. They have a clear vision for the company and they focus on implementing it.

Composers are open to new ideas, but they don't act on impulse. They carefully evaluate fresh ideas before implementing them in a methodical way.

Skilled and creative, they are strong project managers. They don't just run projects; they work toward their vision of the required results—just like composers and artists have an image in mind when creating music or artwork. That's why we've called them Composers.

Archetype Twin
The Quick-Start (page 264)

The Composer's Top 5 Adjectives

1. Strategic—Composers have a vision for the distant future. As CEOs, they evaluate projects based on their contribution to the bottom line and fit with the overall vision. You won't find them choosing to implement a vanity project. They make practical choices that positively impact long-term goals.

2. Fine-tuned—They deftly maneuver, finding fine-tuned solutions to problems. You'll find they adjust processes to improve productivity. They tweak product specifications to gain more market share. They implement customer service experiments to test the market.

3. Judicious—They are open to new ideas, but carefully evaluate them to ensure they support their goals. As world-wise leaders, they won't jump to implement radical ideas. They first evaluate and test how ideas can contribute to the bottom line.

4. Rational—Composers communicate their ideas with clarity and respond to problems with careful reasoning. When proposing to test a freemium model, they'll provide a clear explanation of how users of a free app will be converted into paying users.

5. Immediate—They may carefully consider their reactions, but this doesn't stop them from taking quick action and producing results. They are keen to avoid delays and get projects delivered on time.

"Highest and Best Value" of The Composer
They have a rare combination of creative talent and the ability to work in a methodical way. They don't just dream up new ideas; they're keen to implement them, too.

Their Innovation Advantage helps Composers come up with creative solutions. Their dominant Alert Advantage pushes them to implement the best ideas on time and within budget. They're always aware of what could go wrong, and work hard to prevent problems and delays.

Equally at ease in small start-ups and global conglomerates, they challenge a stale organization to change and they help innovative companies to implement ideas.

What Is Not the "Highest and Best Value" of The Composer?

Composers have an entrepreneurial streak. While they're able to work in a methodical way, too much routine may wear them down.

You get the most out of Composers if you give them free rein to suggest and implement innovative ideas. They enjoy exploring new opportunities.

How to Work with a Composer

In brainstorming sessions Composers come up with plenty of ideas, but they're also able to pick the best ideas and push forward to get them implemented. They are pragmatic problem-solvers with a keen eye for detail.

As entrepreneurs, they have an innovative vision. They prefer creating a new market rather than emulating competitors. They enjoy testing the market to obtain customer feedback, and then tweak products to get optimal results.

Archetypes That Can Optimize The Composer

A Composer works well with an Orchestrator (page 168). They share a keen eye for detail, and an Orchestrator increases team spirit with warmth and a focus on relationship building.

Alternatively, team a Composer up with an Intrigue (page 164), who relates to people and projects in both an intellectual and emotional way.

A Lesson That Everyone Can Learn from The Composer

Long-term goals are reached through creativity and determination.

One-Minute Coaching to My Composers

You come up with great ideas and you know how to implement them, too.

You work independently, which is good. But sometimes you can give people the impression that you prefer to do things all by yourself.

To cement bonds with teammates, use the Trust Advantage to add warmth and encourage loyalty. You know how to respond quickly, and the addition of Trust will let people know. Use Mystique to *listen* before offering advice. You have very good ideas for managing the group, so think about how your listener will receive your feedback. It's important that people listen with the respect you deserve.

Famous Composers
Ralph Nader and Paul Revere

Example of an Anthem for The Composer
FINE-TUNED INSPIRATION

How The Composer Might Apply This Anthem
Brenda likes to think out-of-the-box. But she also realizes that her ideas need to be executable. Whenever her team has a brainstorming session, she makes a point to take careful notes. Next, she researches their client more thoroughly to see what ideas could work best in their situation. Because she always wants to be fine-tuned in her approach, she doesn't just throw every idea in their direction and hope that one sticks. Clients appreciate her strategic business savvy and they know they can count on her to collaborate with them to create the best game plan.

THE COORDINATOR: ALERT + PASSION

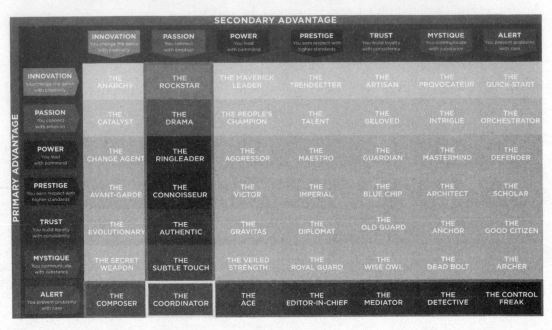

	SECONDARY ADVANTAGE						
	INNOVATION You change the game with creativity	**PASSION** You connect with emotion	**POWER** You lead with command	**PRESTIGE** You earn respect with higher standards	**TRUST** You build loyalty with consistency	**MYSTIQUE** You communicate with substance	**ALERT** You prevent problems with care
INNOVATION You change the game with creativity	THE ANARCHY	THE ROCKSTAR	THE MAVERICK LEADER	THE TRENDSETTER	THE ARTISAN	THE PROVOCATEUR	THE QUICK-START
PASSION You connect with emotion	THE CATALYST	THE DRAMA	THE PEOPLE'S CHAMPION	THE TALENT	THE BELOVED	THE INTRIGUE	THE ORCHESTRATOR
POWER You lead with command	THE CHANGE AGENT	THE RINGLEADER	THE AGGRESSOR	THE MAESTRO	THE GUARDIAN	THE MASTERMIND	THE DEFENDER
PRESTIGE You earn respect with higher standards	THE AVANT-GARDE	THE CONNOISSEUR	THE VICTOR	THE IMPERIAL	THE BLUE CHIP	THE ARCHITECT	THE SCHOLAR
TRUST You build loyalty with consistency	THE EVOLUTIONARY	THE AUTHENTIC	THE GRAVITAS	THE DIPLOMAT	THE OLD GUARD	THE ANCHOR	THE GOOD CITIZEN
MYSTIQUE You communicate with substance	THE SECRET WEAPON	THE SUBTLE TOUCH	THE VEILED STRENGTH	THE ROYAL GUARD	THE WISE OWL	THE DEAD BOLT	THE ARCHER
ALERT You prevent problems with care	THE COMPOSER	THE COORDINATOR	THE ACE	THE EDITOR-IN-CHIEF	THE MEDIATOR	THE DETECTIVE	THE CONTROL FREAK

PRIMARY ADVANTAGE

HOW THE WORLD SEES THE COORDINATOR

Coordinators bring a pragmatic, step-by-step approach to every project.

Have a Coordinator on your project team? He knows the critical path by heart. When a task is at risk of delay, he's quick to point out the negative consequences. He calculates required increase in investment due to the delay. And he tells you how much revenue may be lost if the launch is delayed by a month.

But Coordinators aren't just scrutinizing the pieces. They're loyal to the team. During their Monday team meetings you'll find there's some time to chat about the weekend. A Coordinator is genuinely interested in knowing whether everyone is well. But after the chitchat, there's a strong focus on what needs to happen in the week ahead, and potential bottlenecks will be discussed.

Coordinators do their utmost to avoid negative consequences. They are detail-oriented, work in an ordered manner, and focus on deadlines. They ensure that their team is in agreement and that everyone is happy. They update plans. They align resources. That's why they're Coordinators.

Archetype Twin
The Orchestrator (page 168)

The Coordinator's Top 5 Adjectives

1. Constructive—Coordinators are able to scan a situation quickly. As marketing manager, for instance, they're able to provide you a brief weekly report, including a table with key performance indicators and comments, a few bullet points on what was achieved the previous week, what milestones are coming up, and which issues need to be resolved. They carefully review marketing effectiveness to get the most out of the team and the available budget.

2. Organized—Coordinators are methodical workers. When packing their suitcase for a vacation, they do it in the same order each time—socks and underwear first, then trousers and shorts, shirts and T-shirts, before adding toiletries. Someone may remark that their suitcase content looks like a watchmaker's toolkit.

3. Practical—They consider the impact of each action and are always aware of the bottom line. When proposing a celebrity endorsement, for instance, they'll be clear about the potential benefits to the brand, but they'll also point out the costs and potential pitfalls (what if the celebrity is arrested for speeding?).

4. Safeguard—They are loyal to their team and take interest in the well-being of team members. When co-workers struggle with tasks, they lend a helping hand. When someone has problems with a sick child at home, The Coordinator will ensure their workload is reduced so they can leave early when needed.

5. Tuned in—They are careful observers. They are hyperaware of the progress each team member is making toward common goals.

"Highest and Best Value" of The Coordinator

Coordinators inspire small teams. They captivate their team members with their enthusiasm and drive, but they also keep projects on track with a strong focus on deadlines.

As HR managers they'll present a balanced view on why you need to implement an employee suggestion scheme, for instance. They explain how such a scheme empowers employees and makes them feel valued (thereby potentially reducing staff turnover). They give examples of how employee ideas may lead to revenue increases and cost savings. They also point out the time the senior team needs to commit to make the scheme a success.

Need to implement a cost-cutting exercise? A Coordinator will take into account the cost savings as well as the potential impact on the remaining team if employees are made redundant.

Coordinators are equally at ease with quantitative as well as qualitative information.

What Is Not the "Highest and Best Value" of The Coordinator?

Don't expect a Coordinator to challenge the status quo if it's not necessary. They are not usually the ones to spontaneously hit upon a new plan. They tend to be somewhat risk-averse, which helps their team stay on course.

Coordinators thrive in structured environments and love working in small teams.

How to Work with a Coordinator

Working with a Coordinator at a start-up? They can provide the necessary balance to a team that's strong on Innovation. They'll prevent the team from making hasty decisions by pointing out the risks and costs involved. And once projects are given the go-ahead, they'll plan how to maximize results with minimal resources. They'll be careful with the budget and won't overspend.

At larger organizations you may find Coordinators in managerial or project management positions. They make annual planning and budgeting look easy.

Is a Coordinator working for you? You'll find he's keen to please you and will provide regular, detailed progress reports. You'll always know what he's up to.

Archetypes That Can Optimize The Coordinator

A Coordinator tends to be risk-averse, so team him up with a Trendsetter (page 252) to look ahead and embrace the unknown. Together they weigh both downsides and upsides to ensure no new opportunities are missed.

A Coordinator tends to make pragmatic decisions. If quality is important for your business, consider teaming him up with a Blue Chip (page 208) to raise standards.

A Lesson That Everyone Can Learn from The Coordinator

Be aware of the negative consequences of your actions.

One-Minute Coaching to My Coordinators

You are a good project manager and you always keep your eye on deadlines. That's great. Sometimes, however, your focus on the ramifications of failure may be perceived as overbearing.

Instead of pointing out the negatives of failure, paint a picture of what success will look like. Rely more on your Passion Advantage to inspire and engage with your team.

Famous Coordinators

David Allen and Mary Poppins

Example of an Anthem for The Coordinator

PRACTICAL CREATIVITY

How The Coordinator Might Apply This Anthem

Sharon is the manager for community engagement for a small public relations firm. Their first big client has requested her team's help to garner buzz around a new product they're launching. Some people on her team are throwing out big ideas with a large reach that will cost the firm a lot out-of-pocket. Sharon uses her practical creativity to steer the conversation in a different direction. Instead of spending too much, and with no idea of what will work, she starts a grassroots campaign that connects with people emotionally. That way, the company stays on budget and it allows the customer base to implement the campaign for them.

THE ACE: ALERT + POWER

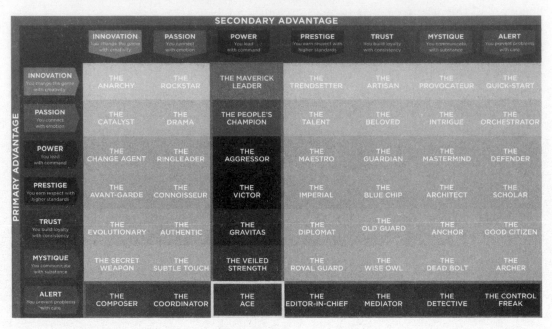

		SECONDARY ADVANTAGE					
		INNOVATION You change the game with creativity	PASSION You connect with emotion	POWER You lead with command	PRESTIGE You earn respect with higher standards	TRUST You build loyalty with consistency	MYSTIQUE You communicate with substance	ALERT You prevent problems with care
PRIMARY ADVANTAGE	INNOVATION You change the game with creativity	THE ANARCHY	THE ROCKSTAR	THE MAVERICK LEADER	THE TRENDSETTER	THE ARTISAN	THE PROVOCATEUR	THE QUICK-START
	PASSION You connect with emotion	THE CATALYST	THE DRAMA	THE PEOPLE'S CHAMPION	THE TALENT	THE BELOVED	THE INTRIGUE	THE ORCHESTRATOR
	POWER You lead with command	THE CHANGE AGENT	THE RINGLEADER	THE AGGRESSOR	THE MAESTRO	THE GUARDIAN	THE MASTERMIND	THE DEFENDER
	PRESTIGE You earn respect with higher standards	THE AVANT-GARDE	THE CONNOISSEUR	THE VICTOR	THE IMPERIAL	THE BLUE CHIP	THE ARCHITECT	THE SCHOLAR
	TRUST You build loyalty with consistency	THE EVOLUTIONARY	THE AUTHENTIC	THE GRAVITAS	THE DIPLOMAT	THE OLD GUARD	THE ANCHOR	THE GOOD CITIZEN
	MYSTIQUE You communicate with substance	THE SECRET WEAPON	THE SUBTLE TOUCH	THE VEILED STRENGTH	THE ROYAL GUARD	THE WISE OWL	THE DEAD BOLT	THE ARCHER
	ALERT You prevent problems with care	THE COMPOSER	THE COORDINATOR	THE ACE	THE EDITOR-IN-CHIEF	THE MEDIATOR	THE DETECTIVE	THE CONTROL FREAK

HOW THE WORLD SEES THE ACE

Aces are decisive, but cautious leaders.

They are thoughtful. Is a project getting delayed? They consider their options—whether to accept a delay in the launch or increase resources or perhaps find another way to catch up. They make up their mind, and then commit the resources required to get a project back on track.

Aces are usually go-getters. Hardworking and persistent, they're comfortable tackling big goals. They aren't afraid to do the real work that makes things happen. Even when a sales target for this quarter seems difficult, they do not get intimidated. For instance, rather than making excuses or becoming paralyzed with indecision, an Ace would look through her customer list, and determine which customers are most likely to give them the required increase to meet the target.

An Ace leads without being overly intimidating. They are respected because of their relentless pursuit of what they believe in.

Archetype Twin
The Defender (page 144)

The Ace's Top 5 Adjectives

1. **Decisive**—Aces make decisions efficiently. When they face a pile of résumés for a new quality manager, they're able to sift through these fast to provide a short list of the five candidates they want to interview. They don't waste time. They get on with the job that needs to be done.

2. **Tireless**—They are determined in their pursuit of what they believe is right. When they see a huge opportunity for your products in Asian markets, they actively promote their proposed export strategy to the senior management team. In the face of opposition they'll persevere and bring up new arguments, statistics, and case studies to show why exporting to Asia is such a good idea.

3. **Forthright**—Although their reactions are carefully considered, they are quick to take action and produce results. When a supplier goes into liquidation, they'll soon review their list of alternative suppliers and immediately get on the phone to the three preferred choices to avoid disrupting supply. They get right to the point.

4. **Goal-oriented**—Aces are focused on reaching whatever goals are set for them (or they have set for themselves). On social media platforms, for instance, they like to work toward clear goals such as a particular number of followers or a Klout score. And when their Klout score drops, they quickly think of a plan to get back on track.

5. **Shielded**—They always think before they act or embark on a new project. When your company wants to completely redesign an existing app, they'll point out the risks of alienating existing users. Their thoughtfulness helps avoid obstacles and errors.

"Highest and Best Value" of The Ace

Aces are strong leaders. They are assertive. They take charge.

Imagine a group of senior managers who've never met before. They're in a business management course preparing their input for a business case simulation. An Ace is likely to take control regardless of his seniority on the team.

He organizes the team and allocates various roles. He proposes an agenda so he's sure the team is ready with time to spare.

As business leaders, Aces tend to choose the least risky approach. They prefer a solid business case projecting steady growth, rather than a risky venture that could skyrocket profits but also might lead to failure.

Aces tend to be in command. Always aware of what could go wrong, they carefully prepare plans. They work in a structured way to meet company objectives.

What Is Not the "Highest and Best Value" of The Ace?

Don't expect Aces to make decisions based on impulse or gut feelings. Their style tends to be intellectual rather than emotional. They base their decisions on facts rather than anecdotal information.

Aces are strong, businesslike leaders who thrive in small and medium-sized organizations where their decisiveness is most appreciated.

How to Work with an Ace

Have an Ace as your manager? He's both a doer and a thinker. While typically described as a man of action, he will not carelessly make decisions. His biography boasts an impressive track record. He is the type of man who gets results wherever he goes.

When your company faces a new challenge, Aces step up to take the lead. For instance: A competitor launches a new product that attacks your product head-on. You risk losing market share and revenues. Aces don't get drawn into endless discussions about what to do next. They carefully consider their response before deciding to fast-track a product development program to win back market share.

Archetypes That Can Optimize The Ace

Since Aces tend to be risk-averse, it's useful for them to work with a Secret Weapon (page 172), who is more willing to take risks and who will spot new opportunities.

Do you need to recruit an assistant for an Ace? Consider an Intrigue (page 164). They soften an Ace's image while nurturing connections with team members.

A Lesson That Everyone Can Learn from The Ace

Being decisive doesn't mean you have no time to think through your options.

One-Minute Coaching to My Aces

You have achieved a lot since joining the company three years ago as a call center supervisor. You've hit your targets. You should be proud of that. If you'd like to further your career and become a senior manager, you need to learn how to use Passion and Trust to add warmth to relationships and to encourage loyalty.

Don't just focus on what will go wrong if people don't hit deadlines. Pay attention to how others are feeling. Be more enthusiastic about their contributions to keep them motivated. Maybe you can take your team out for lunch so you can get to know each other better.

Your ability to become a great manager depends on your ability to build rapport and use emotional intelligence.

Famous Aces

Jim Cramer and Chuck Norris

Example of an Anthem for The Ace

TIRELESS WORK ETHIC

How The Ace Might Apply This Anthem

As a recent college graduate, Henry knows the importance of working hard. He doesn't just want *any* job; he wants to jump-start the process to getting his dream job. Other graduates are taking a week off, but Henry is making a thorough list of the associations he needs to join to best position himself as a viable candidate. He pays his dues right away and plans his schedule around meetings. Henry is confident and forthright. He isn't afraid to jump in and start meeting people because he knows that they could be the doorway to his future. To prep for the networking events he makes sure that his résumé is up-to-date and error-free.

THE EDITOR-IN-CHIEF: ALERT + PRESTIGE

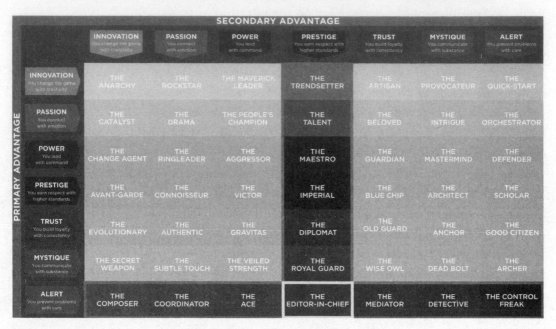

		SECONDARY ADVANTAGE					
	INNOVATION You change the game with creativity	**PASSION** You connect with emotion	**POWER** You lead with command	**PRESTIGE** You earn respect with higher standards	**TRUST** You build loyalty with consistency	**MYSTIQUE** You communicate with substance	**ALERT** You prevent problems with care
INNOVATION You change the game with creativity	THE ANARCHY	THE ROCKSTAR	THE MAVERICK LEADER	THE TRENDSETTER	THE ARTISAN	THE PROVOCATEUR	THE QUICK-START
PASSION You connect with emotion	THE CATALYST	THE DRAMA	THE PEOPLE'S CHAMPION	THE TALENT	THE BELOVED	THE INTRIGUE	THE ORCHESTRATOR
POWER You lead with command	THE CHANGE AGENT	THE RINGLEADER	THE AGGRESSOR	THE MAESTRO	THE GUARDIAN	THE MASTERMIND	THE DEFENDER
PRESTIGE You earn respect with higher standards	THE AVANT-GARDE	THE CONNOISSEUR	THE VICTOR	THE IMPERIAL	THE BLUE CHIP	THE ARCHITECT	THE SCHOLAR
TRUST You build loyalty with consistency	THE EVOLUTIONARY	THE AUTHENTIC	THE GRAVITAS	THE DIPLOMAT	THE OLD GUARD	THE ANCHOR	THE GOOD CITIZEN
MYSTIQUE You communicate with substance	THE SECRET WEAPON	THE SUBTLE TOUCH	THE VEILED STRENGTH	THE ROYAL GUARD	THE WISE OWL	THE DEAD BOLT	THE ARCHER
ALERT You prevent problems with care	THE COMPOSER	THE COORDINATOR	THE ACE	THE EDITOR-IN-CHIEF	THE MEDIATOR	THE DETECTIVE	THE CONTROL FREAK

(PRIMARY ADVANTAGE labels the left column.)

HOW THE WORLD SEES THE EDITOR-IN-CHIEF

An Editor-in-Chief maintains high standards without losing sight of deadlines.

They are usually hard workers who manage to get a lot done without cutting corners. Their work is always excellent.

They don't need to work as an editor. Picture, for instance, a guy on your Web development team. His work is meticulous. Even under stress he delivers flawless code. He's precise. And punctual. He never misses a deadline.

Like real editors who cross their *t*'s and dots their *i*'s, Editors-in-Chief produce error-free work. They're able to concentrate intensely on their own work. An open office doesn't faze them. They don't seem to notice what's going on around them, almost as if they live in their own world.

Archetype Twin
The Scholar (page 216)

The Editor-in-Chief's Top 5 Adjectives

1. **Productive**—Editors-in-Chief work hard, but also work smart. Rather than multitask, they focus on one job at a time. As your personal assistant, for instance, they can manage more work than most. Whether it's handling your invoices or posting social media updates, they accomplish many tasks quickly—one by one.

2. **Detailed**—They make sure every detail is correct. As your accountant, they produce comprehensive financial reports on the same day each month. They're never late. They follow an ordered process to ensure the best quality.

3. **Skilled**—Editors-in-Chief excel in the jobs they take on. They don't need much time to analyze a situation. When coaching new staff members, they can quickly gauge gaps in knowledge and skill. They work tirelessly to improve their own skills and those of their team.

4. **Immersed**—They channel their energy carefully, and can be superconcentrated. You see them in the office working on their latest Web design. You call them, but they don't pick up the phone. And when you walk over to see them, they won't notice you until you call their name.

5. **Results-driven**—Their focus is on producing a quality result. You might find them working late at night to hit a deadline. They won't submit their work until they know it's perfect.

"Highest and Best Value" of The Editor-in-Chief

Editors-in-Chief are unwavering leaders with a clear vision.

Discerning and determined, they define the path and set the standard. As project managers, they are keenly focused on deadlines and compel their team to act swiftly to avoid negative consequences. They don't compromise the quality of results. And they expect you won't cut corners to deliver on time.

As entrepreneurs they want to deliver the perfect app. They don't like the idea of launching beta versions.

What Is Not the "Highest and Best Value" of The Editor-in-Chief?

Editors-in-Chief don't take failure well. They work hard to minimize the risk of errors. They tend to prefer tried-and-tested methods over experimentation.

You'll get the most out of them if you allow them to do precise, high-quality work. Even under pressure they'll deliver.

How to Work with an Editor-in-Chief

Editors-in-Chief are happy to work independently and don't require strong management. They are often confident in their own skills. They probably won't take on projects that stretch beyond their expertise.

Editors-in-Chief are an excellent appointment to a news desk (of course!) thanks to their intense focus on details and deadlines. Their skills are suitable for any project where deadlines and high quality standards need to be met, such as software development.

Archetypes That Can Optimize The Editor-in-Chief

To encourage a more open approach to experimentation, creativity, and risk-taking, let them work together with a Trendsetter (page 252).

A Talent (page 156) maintains high standards just like an Editor-in-Chief. Thanks to their primary Passion Advantage, Talents are more engaging with co-workers and clients. They can help an Editor-in-Chief to keep sight of the needs and wishes of others.

A Lesson That Everyone Can Learn from The Editor-in-Chief

Meeting tight deadlines doesn't mean you need to let quality standards slip.

One-Minute Coaching to My Editors-in-Chief

You never miss deadlines and the quality of your work is excellent. But sometimes your focus on high standards can be perceived as inflexible.

Try to spend more time with your team members and ask for feedback. Pull back a little if you sense a negative reception. If you reach out, people will be more understanding and supportive of you.

Famous Editors-in-Chief

Dan Rather and James Cameron

Example of an Anthem for The Editor-in-Chief

DETAILED MANAGEMENT

How The Editor-in-Chief Might Apply This Anthem

It's important that a management team provide a stable work environment for its employees. And nobody understands that better than Bill. As a leader in his customer service department, Bill has to make sure that employees are getting enough hours, without feeling overworked. His style of management is skilled and detailed. He does this by watching over each employee and keeping a close eye on their monthly workload, time worked, and productivity levels. When he sees someone slipping, he meets with them to come up with the best game plan for getting back on track to meet their production targets on schedule, using detailed management.

THE MEDIATOR: ALERT + TRUST

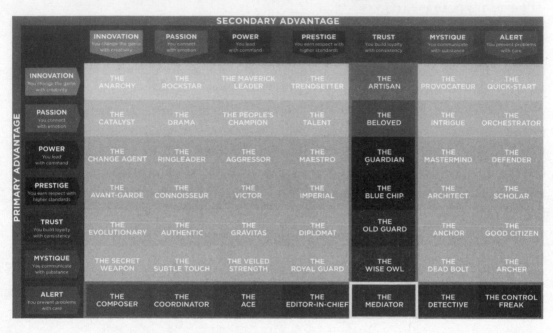

	SECONDARY ADVANTAGE						
	INNOVATION You change the game with creativity	PASSION You connect with emotion	POWER You lead with command	PRESTIGE You earn respect with higher standards	TRUST You build loyalty with consistency	MYSTIQUE You communicate with substance	ALERT You prevent problems with care
INNOVATION You change the game with creativity	THE ANARCHY	THE ROCKSTAR	THE MAVERICK LEADER	THE TRENDSETTER	THE ARTISAN	THE PROVOCATEUR	THE QUICK-START
PASSION You connect with emotion	THE CATALYST	THE DRAMA	THE PEOPLE'S CHAMPION	THE TALENT	THE BELOVED	THE INTRIGUE	THE ORCHESTRATOR
POWER You lead with command	THE CHANGE AGENT	THE RINGLEADER	THE AGGRESSOR	THE MAESTRO	THE GUARDIAN	THE MASTERMIND	THE DEFENDER
PRESTIGE You earn respect with higher standards	THE AVANT-GARDE	THE CONNOISSEUR	THE VICTOR	THE IMPERIAL	THE BLUE CHIP	THE ARCHITECT	THE SCHOLAR
TRUST You build loyalty with consistency	THE EVOLUTIONARY	THE AUTHENTIC	THE GRAVITAS	THE DIPLOMAT	THE OLD GUARD	THE ANCHOR	THE GOOD CITIZEN
MYSTIQUE You communicate with substance	THE SECRET WEAPON	THE SUBTLE TOUCH	THE VEILED STRENGTH	THE ROYAL GUARD	THE WISE OWL	THE DEAD BOLT	THE ARCHER
ALERT You prevent problems with care	THE COMPOSER	THE COORDINATOR	THE ACE	THE EDITOR-IN-CHIEF	THE MEDIATOR	THE DETECTIVE	THE CONTROL FREAK

PRIMARY ADVANTAGE

HOW THE WORLD SEES THE MEDIATOR

From the moment you meet a Mediator, it's easy to see why others describe them as loyal and hardworking.

As you might expect from their name, The Mediator's advantage lies in his ability to mediate, building harmony among teams. For instance, to create harmony on a project, a team, or a company's core principles. The Mediator calmly guides others to stay the course.

Professionally and personally, Mediators add value through their ability to uphold and support. People often turn to them as the "hub" of a group. Whenever there's a question, these organized thinkers always seem to know where, when, how, and who.

(Even their body language is efficiently minimal.)

Mediators don't often point the spotlight directly at themselves—but they often work extremely well with those who do.

Archetype Twin

The Good Citizen (page 288)

The Mediator's Top 5 Adjectives

1. **Steadfast**—Mediators are diligent, faithful, and dependable. They are highly committed to reaching agreed upon objectives and deadlines. On occasions when the rest of the team despairs because the project doesn't progress as expected, Mediators remain focused and committed to delivering results on time and within budget. Co-workers and clients alike appreciate their reliability.

2. **Composed**—Even in pressure-filled situations, they keep their cool, setting the tone for everyone else on the team. When you're grilling them in an interview with difficult questions about their résumé, they remain calm, consider their response, and respond in a logical way.

3. **Structured**—Mistakes live in fear of their fine-toothed comb! Mediators see all the moving parts that form the bigger picture and they keep them highly organized.

4. **Effectual**—Always a fan of following the game plan, they prefer to stick with proven solutions rather than experiment with a radical or untested approach. As HR managers, for instance, they compel senior managers to follow the detailed employee handbook at all times. You find they're quick to point out the negative consequences of not following the guidelines set out.

5. **Vigilant**—Before embarking on any pursuit (however big or small), they carefully think things through. This thoughtfulness guides them to correct errors (or better yet, avoid them entirely). You won't find them dashing off quick social media updates or thoughtlessly tossing out commentary. They think before clicking send, and carefully check grammar and spelling.

"Highest and Best" Value of The Mediator

Practical productivity.

I've heard many Mediators describe how much they relish the act of crossing items off their to-do list (and there's always a to-do list!). They combine the detail-orientation of Alert with the sincerity and stability of Trust.

In the office, Mediators are valued for their ability to stay on track and get things done. They're conscientious and keep an eye on details in any project, which can help them accurately accomplish successive tasks. They diligently review each piece.

You get the most out of your Mediators when you allow them to maintain a sense of calm order. This Archetype offers the greatest distinct value when allowed to get into a routine, and then keep things humming along smoothly. Mediators help others by evaluating daily risks and potential outcomes, managing details that can get others off track.

Office mates seek them out for assurance and backup. This helps bind the overall team together toward a common pursuit.

Rarely reckless or out of control, these folks want to do "the right thing" in the right way. Unlike the more flashy or creative Archetypes, Mediators don't get easily distracted. They take pride in a job well done, and know how to work hard from start to finish.

What Is Not the "Highest and Best" Value of The Mediator?

Mediators can become unsettled by chaos. They prefer to have a set schedule, with clearly defined roles and expectations. Are you asking a Mediator to ping-pong from one spot to another? This will likely weaken one of their key advantages: their grounded nature.

Side note: Although Mediators don't relish a great deal of change and upheaval, they can be extremely effective in crazy environments, if you allow them to instill order in the chaos.

How to Work with a Mediator

The more information you can give a Mediator, the more they can operate within the guidelines. Don't expect them to read your mind, unless they're already familiar with your process. Ensure they're familiar with processes; explain their role and what exactly is expected from them. You'll find that setting a schedule and following the plan helps them feel more secure, and work in a far more productive manner.

While they don't immediately gravitate to brainstorming or untraditional ideas, they add structure to those who do. In innovative environments Mediators can provide the much-needed framework for executing ideas. Get them involved in vetting ideas, and allow them to create procedures for implementing these. Mediators bring structure to complex projects. They keep your innovation program on track.

Archetypes That Can Optimize The Mediator

The Catalyst (page 148) will infuse creativity.

The Victor (page 204) will set ambitious goals and avidly pursue them.

A Lesson That Everyone Can Learn from The Mediator

Stick to the plan.

One-Minute Coaching to My Mediators

You excel in keeping things on track—yet occasionally rules are made to be broken. Conventional working methods aren't always the most efficient or effective. Try to tweak formulas to improve results. Gradually change procedures (or products) through small experiments.

Famous Mediator

Abraham Lincoln

Example of an Anthem for The Mediator

STRUCTURED INTERACTION

How The Mediator Might Apply This Anthem

Some jobs can be hectic, and Todd's is no exception. He works as an accountant for a growing computer engineering company. Their products are time-consuming and costly to create—so they need to make sure not to take on more business than they can handle.

Todd's boss is a big thinker. His focus is to keep moving forward but he doesn't always have the most cost-effective solution in mind. Always composed, Todd uses structured interaction with his boss to lay out a clear plan for the coming months. First, he studies a printout of the budget and then figures out how many man-hours it will take to complete their current projects. That way, when Todd's boss begins to protest—Todd has all the information close at hand so that he can help his boss make an informed decision.

THE DETECTIVE: ALERT + MYSTIQUE

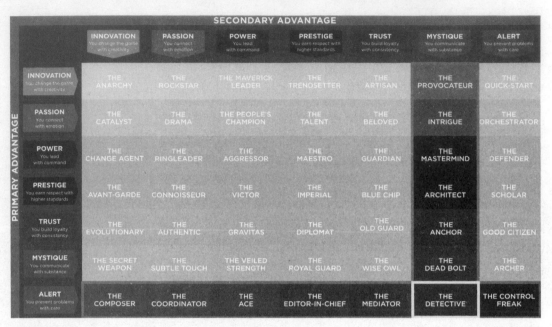

		SECONDARY ADVANTAGE					
	INNOVATION You change the game with creativity	**PASSION** You connect with emotion	**POWER** You lead with command	**PRESTIGE** You earn respect with higher standards	**TRUST** You build loyalty with consistency	**MYSTIQUE** You communicate with substance	**ALERT** You prevent problems with care
INNOVATION You change the game with creativity	THE ANARCHY	THE ROCKSTAR	THE MAVERICK LEADER	THE TRENDSETTER	THE ARTISAN	THE PROVOCATEUR	THE QUICK-START
PASSION You connect with emotion	THE CATALYST	THE DRAMA	THE PEOPLE'S CHAMPION	THE TALENT	THE BELOVED	THE INTRIGUE	THE ORCHESTRATOR
POWER You lead with command	THE CHANGE AGENT	THE RINGLEADER	THE AGGRESSOR	THE MAESTRO	THE GUARDIAN	THE MASTERMIND	THE DEFENDER
PRESTIGE You earn respect with higher standards	THE AVANT-GARDE	THE CONNOISSEUR	THE VICTOR	THE IMPERIAL	THE BLUE CHIP	THE ARCHITECT	THE SCHOLAR
TRUST You build loyalty with consistency	THE EVOLUTIONARY	THE AUTHENTIC	THE GRAVITAS	THE DIPLOMAT	THE OLD GUARD	THE ANCHOR	THE GOOD CITIZEN
MYSTIQUE You communicate with substance	THE SECRET WEAPON	THE SUBTLE TOUCH	THE VEILED STRENGTH	THE ROYAL GUARD	THE WISE OWL	THE DEAD BOLT	THE ARCHER
ALERT You prevent problems with care	THE COMPOSER	THE COORDINATOR	THE ACE	THE EDITOR-IN-CHIEF	THE MEDIATOR	THE DETECTIVE	THE CONTROL FREAK

(left axis label: PRIMARY ADVANTAGE)

HOW THE WORLD SEES THE DETECTIVE

Detectives examine each detail. Picture a boss who meticulously reviews your reports. He checks all figures to ensure your analysis is correct. He spots a comma or period in the wrong place.

Whether a Detective is complimenting or critiquing you, he will consider his response. You never know what he's really thinking. He keeps his thoughts to himself, and doesn't express his emotions openly.

Detectives scrutinize numbers. They focus on quantitative information. They carefully analyze data before making decisions. They don't act on gut feelings. They take all facts into account and only make decisions after reviewing the figures.

Archetype Twin
The Archer (page 192)

The Detective's Top 5 Adjectives

1. Clear-cut—Detectives are logical and practical. When board members disagree, for instance, on the merits of implementing employee hack days (where everyone can spend a day a month on their own projects), they'll provide their recommendations based on the positive results that other companies have seen. They quote facts and figures and tell it to you straight.

2. Accurate—They are able to quickly scan a situation and see how to get the best results. As salespeople, they'll know exactly which customers are most profitable. They compare sales in different towns or channels to know where there's an opportunity. Their competitiveness rarely leaves them behind.

3. Meticulous—They are precise in how they approach their responsibilities. When preparing a project plan, they'll list even the smallest of tasks, like organizing lunch for the product launch day. They consider each detail with care. Nothing escapes their attention.

4. Circumspect—They always think before they act or embark on a new project. They'll never tweet a link to a blog post unless they've read the whole post. And before they press *tweet*, they'll double-check their 140 characters really well. The care they take checking details helps them avoid mistakes.

5. Private—Detectives often choose to keep their emotions to themselves. They don't think aloud. You'll find they consider pros and cons, and make up their mind before communicating a well-organized plan.

"Highest and Best Value" of The Detective

Detectives are linear thinkers who analyze data to guide their decisions. They can see the most efficient way to solve a problem, and then implement a solution without errors.

As a supervisor in your factory, they are quick to understand the root causes of quality problems. They adapt procedures to improve reliability. As a personal assistant, they'll keep your diary in good order. They avoid appointment clashes, and ensure each day isn't jam-packed with appointments, so you have time to think, read, and prepare your own reports.

What Is Not the "Highest and Best Value" of The Detective?

Detectives tend to think through decisions rather than shooting from the hip. Don't expect them to say *I feel that's wrong*. They always base their advice on facts and careful consideration.

Allow them time to make up their mind. They'll carefully work through the possible consequences of their decision and then act accordingly.

How to Work with a Detective

Is your CEO a Detective? Make sure your reports are tip-top. Focus on quantitative rather than qualitative data. They want to know the effectiveness of each marketing campaign. They want to understand why Web traffic is up. Be sure to explain which traffic source is causing the upward trend.

You get the most out of your Detectives in a role where their analytical skills and eye for detail are appreciated, such as operations, finance, or quality control. They prefer a structured working environment, but can be valuable in a start-up as a balance to entrepreneurs who base decisions on intuition rather than facts.

Archetypes That Can Optimize The Detective

A Detective likes to work on his own and work out the best approach by himself. Team him up with an Authentic (page 272) to help him engage with the rest of the team.

If your situation requires slightly more risk-taking, quick decision-making, or out-of-the-box thinking, then get your Detective to work with a Rockstar (page 244). The Rockstar is an unorthodox, big-picture thinker, who is not afraid to make bold decisions.

A Lesson That Everyone Can Learn from The Detective

Think before you act.

One-Minute Coaching to My Detectives

You analyze problems well and you base your decisions on quantitative information. Your analytical skills are second to none. However, not all problems can be quantified, and sometimes risks have to be taken based on business instinct.

Try to gain input from team members who rely on experience and intuition to make the right decision.

Famous Detectives

Upton Sinclair and Oliver North

Example of an Anthem for The Detective

METICULOUS FOLLOW-THROUGH

How The Detective Might Apply This Anthem

As content manager for a busy entrepreneur, Kelly has to ensure that her projects are getting approved in a timely manner. The problem is that Kelly's boss gets almost two hundred emails daily and she is often out of the office. In order to be successful at her job, Kelly uses meticulous follow-through to make sure that none of her communications fall through the cracks. To do this, she creates a clear-cut list of deliverables that she will have reviewed and approved before she can move forward. Once Kelly's list is substantial enough, she sets a meeting with her boss and provides her with all of the appropriate materials. Now her boss can review everything at once and make all the edits that she needs to in one place. Once that is finished, Kelly implements all of the revisions and gets the projects into production without delay, using meticulous follow-through.

THE INNOVATION ADVANTAGE

THE INNOVATION ADVANTAGE IS NEW IDEAS AND SOLUTIONS.
INNOVATION PERSONALITIES SPEAK THE LANGUAGE OF CREATIVITY.

THE ROCKSTAR: INNOVATION + PASSION

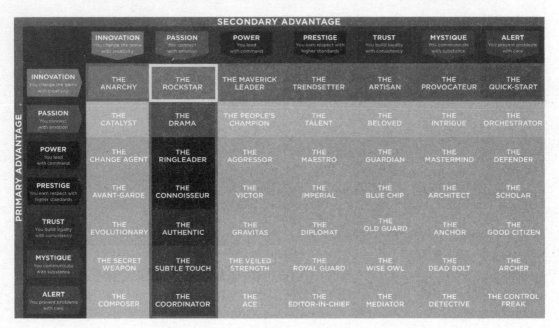

	SECONDARY ADVANTAGE						
	INNOVATION You change the game with creativity	**PASSION** You connect with emotion	**POWER** You lead with command	**PRESTIGE** You earn respect with higher standards	**TRUST** You build loyalty with consistency	**MYSTIQUE** You communicate with substance	**ALERT** You prevent problems with care
INNOVATION You change the game with creativity	THE ANARCHY	THE ROCKSTAR	THE MAVERICK LEADER	THE TRENDSETTER	THE ARTISAN	THE PROVOCATEUR	THE QUICK-START
PASSION You connect with emotion	THE CATALYST	THE DRAMA	THE PEOPLE'S CHAMPION	THE TALENT	THE BELOVED	THE INTRIGUE	THE ORCHESTRATOR
POWER You lead with command	THE CHANGE AGENT	THE RINGLEADER	THE AGGRESSOR	THE MAESTRO	THE GUARDIAN	THE MASTERMIND	THE DEFENDER
PRESTIGE You earn respect with higher standards	THE AVANT-GARDE	THE CONNOISSEUR	THE VICTOR	THE IMPERIAL	THE BLUE CHIP	THE ARCHITECT	THE SCHOLAR
TRUST You build loyalty with consistency	THE EVOLUTIONARY	THE AUTHENTIC	THE GRAVITAS	THE DIPLOMAT	THE OLD GUARD	THE ANCHOR	THE GOOD CITIZEN
MYSTIQUE You communicate with substance	THE SECRET WEAPON	THE SUBTLE TOUCH	THE VEILED STRENGTH	THE ROYAL GUARD	THE WISE OWL	THE DEAD BOLT	THE ARCHER
ALERT You prevent problems with care	THE COMPOSER	THE COORDINATOR	THE ACE	THE EDITOR-IN-CHIEF	THE MEDIATOR	THE DETECTIVE	THE CONTROL FREAK

PRIMARY ADVANTAGE

HOW THE WORLD SEES THE ROCKSTAR

Rockstars create new ideas with enthusiasm.

You'll find that all eyes turn to Rockstars when they enter your meeting room. They know it and enjoy it. They're quick-witted and energetic. You'll also enjoy reading their humorous tweets. They make the mundane funny.

Rockstar personalities love experimenting. They are risk-takers who have a knack for disrupting the status quo. (That's their Innovation Advantage.) When everyone is thinking about how to improve an existing product, The

Rockstar will propose something radically new. When everyone considers how to improve interaction on Facebook, your Rockstar will come up with a fantastic idea for an innovative Pinterest campaign instead.

As a job interviewee, they won't sit back. They answer your questions resolutely without much umming and ahhing. And they ask you daring questions without worrying about protocol.

They enjoy the limelight (of course). Their ability to captivate audiences is a distinct advantage. They dazzle their listeners whether they're on a big stage or in a stuffy boardroom.

Archetype Twin
The Catalyst (page 148)

The Rockstar's Top 5 Adjectives

1. **Bold**—When everyone gets nervous about the unexpected that lies ahead, Rockstars drive a team forward. Rockstars think BIG, thrive on uncertainty, and are unafraid to take risks.

2. **Artistic**—Rockstars are creative, unconventional thinkers. They associate freely to come up with amazing ideas.

3. **Unorthodox**—Rockstars enjoy the uncertainty of trying something new. They look for fresh approaches and innovative ideas. You can count on them to turn standard formulas into a surprising new twist.

4. **Revolutionary**—They challenge the status quo, see opportunities everywhere, and enjoy working against the grain. Rockstars stand out. They bring a dash of unexpected humor to liven up company meetings.

5. **Sensational**—They present ideas with genuine excitement and engage listeners with emotion and enthusiasm.

"Highest and Best Value" of The Rockstar
Influential leadership that breaks the mold.

Rockstars are unconventional thinkers. They don't think in a linear way. That's why they can come up with creative ideas and inventions.

They thrive in challenging environments. They reinvigorate the team with their energy and passion. They are active contributors to brainstorming sessions. They surprise everyone with their big ideas.

Rockstars are the people to turn to when your company is stuck in a declining market, or when the status quo needs to be shaken up.

What Is Not the "Highest and Best Value" of The Rockstar?

Rockstars might toe the corporate line for a while, but that's not their distinct value. Don't expect them to follow set procedures. They don't like to hear *that's how we do things here.*

These bold spirits excel when given opportunities to give fresh ideas to the table. You get the most out of your Rockstars if you allow them the freedom to experiment and to change things around.

How to Work with a Rockstar

Need to present a new idea to the board? Or want to convince customers to try out your new product? Ask a Rockstar to present your new concepts. They're animated sellers, and their enthusiasm for *what's new* is contagious.

They present in an expressive and visually vibrant way. They know exactly how to fascinate a big audience. They're full of life.

You'll get the most out of a Rockstar in creative environments like start-ups, marketing agencies, and companies that value innovation.

Archetypes That Can Optimize The Rockstar

The Good Citizen (page 288) will put a solid plan in place to implement innovative ideas.
The Veiled Strength (page 180) will temper risk-taking and add a healthy dose of reality.

A Lesson That Everyone Can Learn from The Rockstar

Be bold and brave to get ahead and win business.

One-Minute Coaching to My Rockstars

You present big ideas with fanfare. You are a performer, but sometimes you may forget that others need rational arguments to get on board.

Slow down to allow others to keep up. Present facts, specific details, and statistics to persuade those who are more rationally inclined.

Famous Rockstars

Salvador Dali and Madonna

Example of an Anthem for The Rockstar

UNORTHODOX TEAMWORK

How The Rockstar Might Apply This Anthem

Antonio is a VP within a large sales-based organization. Sales have been plummeting, and the culprit seems to be the team's internal dynamics. Processes are breaking down. There's a growing failure to communicate and collaborate effectively.

As The Rockstar, Antonio approaches this challenge with a fresh perspective on how to foster an emotional connection. He searches for ways to bring connection in innovative ways.

Antonio applies his Advantages by finding a bold solution: One afternoon, he surprises his team with an afternoon to a mini-golf course, where he pairs team members in creative ways. (Hey, when everyone is chasing little white balls around a course, it's easy to stop worrying about office politics for a while.) The burst of energy helps people return to the office with a jolt of shared excitement.

THE MAVERICK LEADER: INNOVATION + POWER

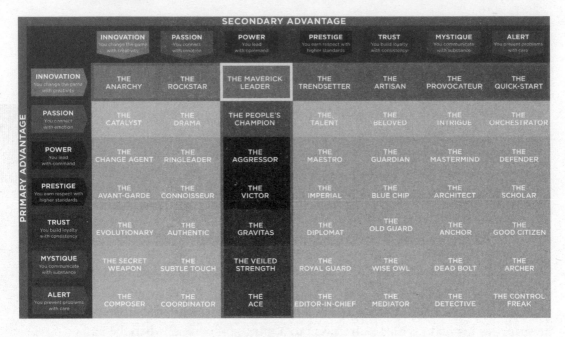

HOW THE WORLD SEES THE MAVERICK LEADER

Maverick Leaders lead with a bold and unconventional vision.

You recognize a Maverick Leader quickly. They're unafraid to take the lead and happy to propose a new direction for a product or market strategy. Even early in their career, they are confident enough to present their pioneering ideas to the board. And they do so with flair.

Do you have a Maverick Leader on your team? They're always full of new ideas, and almost a little restless. They definitely make sure there's no dull moment in your meetings. Whenever they detect a hint of apathy on the team, their energy and wit will energize everyone.

If something starts to feel familiar, Maverick Leaders will start experimenting to see whether higher goals can be achieved. They take their chances and depart from accepted strategies, processes, or tactics (they're mavericks!).

Archetype Twin

The Change Agent (page 124)

The Maverick Leader's Top 5 Adjectives

1. Pioneering—Always ready to challenge the familiar path, Maverick Leaders seek to discover new ways to attain goals. In large companies you'll find them coming up with ideas for new product features, alternative business directions, and radical marketing campaigns.

2. Irreverent—Their revolutionary thinking is coupled with a strong confidence and focus on attaining goals. They don't propose new designs only because they enjoy new things (although they do love them, of course!); they're also keen to use their fresh ideas to help achieve the company's goals.

3. Entrepreneurial—They are full of new ideas. They enjoy starting projects, and their energy drives them to implement ideas and complete projects.

4. Artful—Clever and charming in professional and social scenarios, Maverick Leaders respond to questions and detractions with sharp humor. Even in a rather formal interview setting, they're able to break the ice with a funny remark.

5. Dramatic—Maverick Leaders present their ideas vividly. They energize their message and keep their audience intrigued. When presenting, they use strong body language. They use energetic gestures to emphasize their points. They walk around the stage or boardroom. Their unusual stories and metaphors keep their listeners captivated.

"Highest and Best Value" of The Maverick Leader

Maverick Leaders are independent, confident, and perhaps a little eccentric. The Power Advantage tends to keep them on track to reach their goals, while their primary Innovation Advantage makes them creative, innovative, and sharp-witted.

They're able to think in both linear and nonlinear ways. Free association allows them to come up with fresh ideas, while their logical mind helps them to implement ideas in a methodical way.

They are natural leaders with an adventurous spirit. Unafraid to test new ideas, they're always keen to embark on new projects. They lead the team in uncharted territories.

What Is Not the "Highest and Best Value" of The Maverick Leader?

Maverick Leaders dislike routine tasks. They get bored when forced to follow predictable patterns.

You get the most out of your Maverick Leaders if you allow them to build their own path, find smart solutions to the usual rules, and find their own way to do things.

How to Work with a Maverick Leader

Need a fresh perspective on an existing market? Or is it time to change your business model? A Maverick Leader will resist the pull of inertia and implement change.

They're not constrained by *we've never tried that before* or *that's not how we do things here*. Allow them free rein to spot opportunities in new situations and new relationships.

You might find them at the helm of an organization that embraces their revolutionary spirit, or as a serial entrepreneur. Early in their career they function best in a flat organization—uninhibited by hierarchical structures.

Archetypes That Can Optimize The Maverick Leader

The Orchestrator (page 168) is grounded in detail and reality.
The Defender (page 144) watches over customers and co-workers, keeping everyone protected against risks.

A Lesson That Everyone Can Learn from The Maverick Leader

New projects are exciting. You can learn from their success and failure.

One-Minute Coaching to My Maverick Leaders

Your energy is contagious and your contribution to a brainstorming session is great. Sometimes others may feel overwhelmed by your unstoppable flow of ideas.

Try to calm down to allow others to catch up. Explain your ideas in finer detail. Make it clear that your innovations aren't frivolous but purposeful.

Famous Maverick Leaders
Jeff Bezos and Albert Einstein

Example of an Anthem for The Maverick Leader
PIONEERING IDEAS

How The Maverick Leader Might Apply This Anthem
Fred is a partner in a top law firm. The firm has an incredible reputation in the community; however, the firm is losing new business due to the market's changing needs. The Maverick Leader is unfazed by this challenge. Although the firm's philosophy is conservative and traditional, Fred applies his differences in order to drive revenue. He strategically looks for new growth opportunities. Is there an area where the firm already thrives, so they change their strategy to focus on only taking on those sorts of cases? Is there an emerging area of law that would be a good fit based on the firm's current knowledge and expertise? The Maverick Leader constantly creates new ideas, and then confidently leads the team to accomplish novel goals.

THE TRENDSETTER: INNOVATION + PRESTIGE

		SECONDARY ADVANTAGE					
PRIMARY ADVANTAGE	INNOVATION You change the game with creativity	PASSION You connect with emotion	POWER You lead with command	PRESTIGE You earn respect with higher standards	TRUST You build loyalty with consistency	MYSTIQUE You communicate with substance	ALERT You prevent problems with care
INNOVATION You change the game with creativity	THE ANARCHY	THE ROCKSTAR	THE MAVERICK LEADER	THE TRENDSETTER	THE ARTISAN	THE PROVOCATEUR	THE QUICK-START
PASSION You connect with emotion	THE CATALYST	THE DRAMA	THE PEOPLE'S CHAMPION	THE TALENT	THE BELOVED	THE INTRIGUE	THE ORCHESTRATOR
POWER You lead with command	THE CHANGE AGENT	THE RINGLEADER	THE AGGRESSOR	THE MAESTRO	THE GUARDIAN	THE MASTERMIND	THE DEFENDER
PRESTIGE You earn respect with higher standards	THE AVANT-GARDE	THE CONNOISSEUR	THE VICTOR	THE IMPERIAL	THE BLUE CHIP	THE ARCHITECT	THE SCHOLAR
TRUST You build loyalty with consistency	THE EVOLUTIONARY	THE AUTHENTIC	THE GRAVITAS	THE DIPLOMAT	THE OLD GUARD	THE ANCHOR	THE GOOD CITIZEN
MYSTIQUE You communicate with substance	THE SECRET WEAPON	THE SUBTLE TOUCH	THE VEILED STRENGTH	THE ROYAL GUARD	THE WISE OWL	THE DEAD BOLT	THE ARCHER
ALERT You prevent problems with care	THE COMPOSER	THE COORDINATOR	THE ACE	THE EDITOR-IN-CHIEF	THE MEDIATOR	THE DETECTIVE	THE CONTROL FREAK

HOW THE WORLD SEES THE TRENDSETTER

A Trendsetter senses what the next big thing will be.

Whether it's fashion or gadgets, consumer or business trends, Trendsetters know what will be hot tomorrow. They are competitive and ambitious. They are able to influence company direction with their fresh interpretation of market opportunities.

Is your Trendsetter a marketer? He's always up-to-date with the latest tactics in social media. For instance, when you hadn't even heard of Pinterest, he already had an account with a few hundred followers. He'll devote a relatively large part of the marketing budget to experimenting with new tactics.

Is your Trendsetter a Web developer? He'll be the first to produce an HTML5 infographic with parallax scrolling, embedded tweets, and animated pictures.

The Trendsetter is a trailblazer (of course) who guides others in often uncharted territories.

Archetype Twin
The Avant-Garde (page 196)

The Trendsetter's Top 5 Adjectives

1. **Cutting-edge**—They have a natural feeling for what'll be "the next big thing." Always a step ahead, they have a strong sense of what will be interesting and important tomorrow.

2. **Elite**—Their ambitious and creative approach put Trendsetters ahead of the pack. They are often admired, and sometimes envied, for their inventive approach. In meeting such people, listen to their ideas. You'll find yourself thinking, *Wow, I've never thought about it that way, but I love it.*

3. **Imaginative**—Their bold, creative ideas make others take notice. They present them in their own unique way.

4. **Edgy**—Trendsetters break new grounds. They enjoy working against the grain. They'll insist, for instance, on selling insurance directly to the public even when everyone else says you can't cut out the middleman.

5. **Progressive**—Trendsetters are always looking ahead. They inspire those around them to move forward and drive change. They like to see their business come out ahead of the competition, and they aren't afraid to tweak expectations to make it happen.

"Highest and Best Value" of The Trendsetter

Trendsetters prefer breakthrough to incremental innovation. Their ability to reformulate products, processes, and business models is a distinct advantage. They impress with their intellect and inventiveness.

You'll like to turn to Trendsetters in uncertain times. They are able to see opportunities where others see only threats. They're able to turn a company's weakness into a strength by adapting your product offering to changing conditions.

Trendsetters implement change with determination. They have an ability to see things in a different light. They change your perception of what business you're in.

What Is Not the "Highest and Best Value" of The Trendsetter?

Sometimes a Trendsetter gets so wrapped up in what's new, others can't keep up. Picture a CFO rolling his eyes or a CEO questioning whether we really need to invest in the latest firewall software. *Isn't the old one okay?*

You get the most out of your Trendsetters if you allow them to develop and implement their unique visions.

How to Work with a Trendsetter

They are naturally plugged in to new business prospects, trends, and opportunities to meet new people. Trendsetters flourish in rapidly changing industries like IT, marketing, and fashion. They're equally suited for start-ups and large companies—as long as they're able to run with their ideas.

Expect a newly recruited Trendsetter to contribute fresh ideas from their first day. They don't act on impulse. They're quite methodical in their approach.

Archetypes That Can Optimize The Trendsetter

A Mediator (page 236) keeps a Trendsetter grounded.
A Good Citizen (page 288) prevents mistakes and balances overeagerness.

A Lesson That Everyone Can Learn from The Trendsetter

Standing still often means moving backward.

One-Minute Coaching to My Trendsetters

Your ideas contribute to the company's vision of the future, but sometimes others struggle to keep up with them. Explain carefully how your ideas add value for customers. Illustrate your ideas with concrete examples of how specific customers will benefit. Remember: What's clear to you is not always immediately clear to others.

Famous Trendsetters

Amelia Earhart and Don Draper

Example of an Anthem for The Trendsetter
CUTTING-EDGE STRATEGIES

How The Trendsetter Might Apply This Anthem
Teddy is a consultant for high-profile clients, helping them develop cutting-edge email strategies. He knows that even if a client's content is good, they still need to build a process to optimize their contact list. The Trendsetter always looks forward, never back. Teddy is constantly developing imaginative ways to take processes to the next level. Teddy looks to user behavior to creatively segment the list in a way that's never been done before, so that his client's content gets better open rates and click-throughs. From there, he looks at weekly email reports, and constantly tweaks the campaigns in new ways to achieve better results.

THE ARTISAN: INNOVATION + TRUST

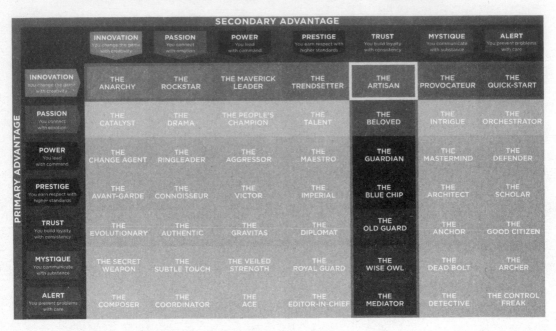

	SECONDARY ADVANTAGE						
	INNOVATION You change the game with creativity	**PASSION** You connect with emotion	**POWER** You lead with command	**PRESTIGE** You earn respect with higher standards	**TRUST** You build loyalty with consistency	**MYSTIQUE** You communicate with substance	**ALERT** You prevent problems with care
INNOVATION You change the game with creativity	THE ANARCHY	THE ROCKSTAR	THE MAVERICK LEADER	THE TRENDSETTER	THE ARTISAN	THE PROVOCATEUR	THE QUICK-START
PASSION You connect with emotion	THE CATALYST	THE DRAMA	THE PEOPLE'S CHAMPION	THE TALENT	THE BELOVED	THE INTRIGUE	THE ORCHESTRATOR
POWER You lead with command	THE CHANGE AGENT	THE RINGLEADER	THE AGGRESSOR	THE MAESTRO	THE GUARDIAN	THE MASTERMIND	THE DEFENDER
PRESTIGE You earn respect with higher standards	THE AVANT-GARDE	THE CONNOISSEUR	THE VICTOR	THE IMPERIAL	THE BLUE CHIP	THE ARCHITECT	THE SCHOLAR
TRUST You build loyalty with consistency	THE EVOLUTIONARY	THE AUTHENTIC	THE GRAVITAS	THE DIPLOMAT	THE OLD GUARD	THE ANCHOR	THE GOOD CITIZEN
MYSTIQUE You communicate with substance	THE SECRET WEAPON	THE SUBTLE TOUCH	THE VEILED STRENGTH	THE ROYAL GUARD	THE WISE OWL	THE DEAD BOLT	THE ARCHER
ALERT You prevent problems with care	THE COMPOSER	THE COORDINATOR	THE ACE	THE EDITOR-IN-CHIEF	THE MEDIATOR	THE DETECTIVE	THE CONTROL FREAK

PRIMARY ADVANTAGE

HOW THE WORLD SEES THE ARTISAN

Artisans both generate and implement new ideas.

Their multifaceted personality provides a clear advantage. They value both new ideas as well as tried-and-tested methods. They welcome change but not just for the sake of it. They tend to rely on trusted, methodical ways of working, but they are flexible when they need to change course because of obstacles.

When your new product development project gets stuck and no one knows how to progress, you can trust Artisans to come up with a creative solution— probably while scribbling notes or drawing pictures on a sheet of paper late at night. They're resourceful and practical.

Artisans take pleasure from creating something new (hence their name). They tend to design new products or new work procedures by follow- ing a trusted method. They possess a strong work ethic, and they are loyal employees.

Archetype Twin
The Evolutionary (page 268)

The Artisan's Top 5 Adjectives

1. **Deliberate**—Artisans quickly gain the confidence of clients, co-workers, and peers thanks to clear communication. Whether they're presenting a new work procedure to their team or a new product to clients, they impress with their rational approach. Their demeanor is just right—not overly boisterous, but not subdued, either. Their communication always has a specific purpose.

2. **Thoughtful**—They have a clear vision on implementing their creative ideas. When they propose a clever solution to a niggling quality issue, you can be certain their idea will work.

3. **Flexible**—They relish new experiences and relationships; and are comfortable with change. You'll find that they're happy to try out new social media platforms, but they'll observe carefully how others use them rather than jumping in immediately.

4. **Resourceful**—They come up with novel solutions to implement change, but they are not *pie-in-the-sky* thinkers. In brainstorming sessions you'll find they contribute practical ideas.

5. **Composer-like**—Artisans enjoy creating results from challenging circumstances like designing a new product while taking a lot of constraints into account. Projects that require care and focus appeal to them.

"Highest and Best Value" of The Artisan

They are talented innovators. They balance a rational approach with an ability to think outside of the box.

As creative directors at an ad agency, they'll follow a structured approach to generating new ideas, selecting the best ones, and preparing a pitch for a client. They choose ideas that are realistic. They're mindful of a client's needs and wishes. Their presentation is respectful and logical.

At a start-up you'll find they take a methodical approach to pivoting the business. They'll carefully think through the consequences of a change of direction and implement their plan step by step.

What Is Not the "Highest and Best Value" of The Artisan?

Artisans are open-minded, but their independent spirit may lead them to search for solutions all by themselves.

They're self-sufficient; they make up their own mind and like to be in control. You get most out of your Artisans in an environment that values innovation.

How to Work with an Artisan

Need someone to take charge of your change program? Artisans embrace change, but they're also empathetic to those who resist change. They communicate clearly; they use rational arguments, and they consider the concerns of the team. Their ability to reassure their team and peers will be hugely beneficial to your change program.

Artisans excel in roles such as creative director, architect, and account or project manager that take advantage of their combined skills of planning and creative thinking.

Archetypes That Can Optimize The Artisan

The Connoisseur (page 200) raises the quality of results.
The warmth and expressive character of a People's Champion (page 152) engages team members.

A Lesson That Everyone Can Learn from The Artisan

Creating new products is about both innovation and implementation.

One-Minute Coaching to My Artisans

You have a talent for coming up with great ideas. You have a pragmatic approach appreciated by your co-workers and peers. Occasionally you need to assume more authority to drive your colleagues forward toward a goal. Explain negative outcomes if deadlines aren't met. Show your passion for the success of the program to nurture a productive team spirit.

Famous Artisans

Johnny Carson and Frank Lloyd Wright

Example of an Anthem for The Artisan

THOUGHTFUL ORIGINALITY

How The Artisan Might Apply This Anthem

Maggie is a chief operations officer for a large financial company. Employees have been working overtime for the past couple of weeks, and morale is beginning to slip.

The Artisan excels at examining the past while looking toward the future. Maggie applies her distinct qualities by looking at all resources available to improve employee morale. Perhaps it's bargaining the extra work for extra time off. Perhaps it's using the firm's connections to get highly coveted tickets to sports games or concerts as a reward to employees for a job well done when it counts. She then consistently delivers on her promises, with her thoughtful originality, to make sure employees get the time they need to recharge and be successful.

THE PROVOCATEUR: INNOVATION + MYSTIQUE

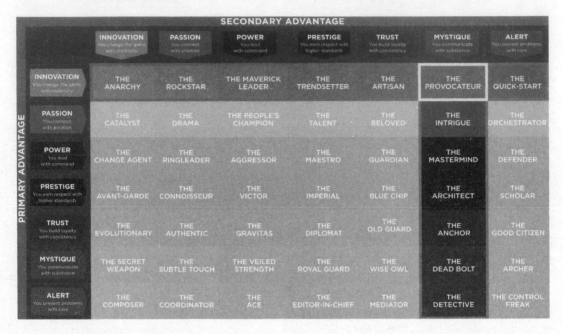

		SECONDARY ADVANTAGE					
	INNOVATION You change the game with creativity	PASSION You connect with emotion	POWER You lead with command	PRESTIGE You earn respect with higher standards	TRUST You build loyalty with consistency	MYSTIQUE You communicate with substance	ALERT You prevent problems with care
INNOVATION You change the game with creativity	THE ANARCHY	THE ROCKSTAR	THE MAVERICK LEADER	THE TRENDSETTER	THE ARTISAN	THE PROVOCATEUR	THE QUICK-START
PASSION You connect with emotion	THE CATALYST	THE DRAMA	THE PEOPLE'S CHAMPION	THE TALENT	THE BELOVED	THE INTRIGUE	THE ORCHESTRATOR
POWER You lead with command	THE CHANGE AGENT	THE RINGLEADER	THE AGGRESSOR	THE MAESTRO	THE GUARDIAN	THE MASTERMIND	THE DEFENDER
PRESTIGE You earn respect with higher standards	THE AVANT-GARDE	THE CONNOISSEUR	THE VICTOR	THE IMPERIAL	THE BLUE CHIP	THE ARCHITECT	THE SCHOLAR
TRUST You build loyalty with consistency	THE EVOLUTIONARY	THE AUTHENTIC	THE GRAVITAS	THE DIPLOMAT	THE OLD GUARD	THE ANCHOR	THE GOOD CITIZEN
MYSTIQUE You communicate with substance	THE SECRET WEAPON	THE SUBTLE TOUCH	THE VEILED STRENGTH	THE ROYAL GUARD	THE WISE OWL	THE DEAD BOLT	THE ARCHER
ALERT You prevent problems with care	THE COMPOSER	THE COORDINATOR	THE ACE	THE EDITOR-IN-CHIEF	THE MEDIATOR	THE DETECTIVE	THE CONTROL FREAK

(left axis label: PRIMARY ADVANTAGE)

HOW THE WORLD SEES THE PROVOCATEUR

While Provocateurs tend to not draw attention to themselves, their ideas can be very attention-getting. Unorthodox and independent, these creative intellectuals bring novel approaches and smart thinking to companies.

Their work is cutting-edge. They find unexplored niches for existing products. They dream up new business models in mature industries. They change the rules of how to do business.

Provocateurs are less overtly creative than other Innovation personalities, but make no mistake, they know how to evoke a response from others around them. They don't overcommunicate, which adds to the curiosity they provoke. You might see them working in their office combining research with brainstorming, and you know something new and exciting is coming up. They combine Mystique and Innovation, for the best of both worlds.

Archetype Twin
The Secret Weapon (page 172)

The Provocateur's Top 5 Adjectives

1. Clever—Provocateurs create novel solutions. Their energy drives them forward to implement their ideas. When you think a product is at the end of its life cycle, they find a new market to keep it selling.

2. Adept—They're one of the smartest people in the room. A Provocateur is an expert in their field and highly skilled at what they do. For them, proficiency is a key component to everything they do.

3. Contemporary—They stay relevant. If their products or services start to fall behind the times, they'll do their best to give them a fresh look.

4. State-of-the-art—Progressive and pioneering, Provocateurs are rarely constrained by orthodoxy. Self-confident, they participate actively in board meetings and propel company offerings into the future.

5. Surprising—Provocateurs are irreverent. They surprise their co-workers with unconventional ideas. You'll enjoy their Facebook updates. Never boring, they share original ideas, jokes, and edgy pictures.

"Highest and Best Value" of The Provocateur
Pioneering entrepreneurs who break new ground.

Provocateurs are independent thinkers. They don't follow the "party line." Autonomous and adventurous, they're quick to respond to obstacles.

They thrive in a challenging environment where they're able to try new approaches. You'll find them testing out a new social media platform, rather than tweaking an existing marketing campaign.

You'll see them bringing the call center back in-house just when everyone else outsources. And when overseas companies are considered a threat, they see the opportunity of sourcing products abroad.

You'll find that Provocateurs are quick to grasp alternative viewpoints. They're able to look at the same old thing from a new perspective. That's how they drive change.

What Is Not the "Highest and Best Value" of The Provocateur?

Don't expect Provocateurs to follow the beaten path or adhere to protocol. They prefer to explore new ways of doing business.

They are most valuable to a company when they're allowed to run with their revolutionary ideas.

How to Work with a Provocateur

Don't manage your Provocateurs rigidly. They're at their best when they can define their own path from the get-go. Allow them to rethink the way things are done. Use their intellect to create exciting new opportunities for the company.

Is your manager a Provocateur? Make sure you understand their vision. Ask them for explanations and how they'd like you to contribute. Provocateurs enjoy working on their own, so you need to carefully manage upward.

Archetypes That Can Optimize The Provocateur

Connoisseurs (page 200) add in-the-know expertise with discerning observations. The Diplomat (page 280) brings carefully worded finesse to sticky situations.

A Lesson That Everyone Can Learn from The Provocateur

If the game doesn't suit you, change the rules. Or, invent a new game.

One-Minute Coaching to My Provocateurs

You have great ideas that can benefit the company. You enjoy working on your own.

Sometimes you need to slow down to invest your energy in obtaining buy-in for your projects. Try helping others to visualize your ideas.

Try to involve your co-workers to contribute by sharing your ideas earlier. Their involvement can help get them on board.

Famous Provocateurs

Lady Gaga and David Letterman

Example of an Anthem for The Provocateur

CLEVER APPROACH

How The Provocateur Might Apply This Anthem

Craig is a dentist, and a large portion of his patients are children. Many of them have deep-seated anxieties about going to the dentist. Others just don't want to sit still long enough for him to do his work. Craig knows this, so he uses an intelligent and unexpected approach with his young clients. He provides each child with an iPad that's stocked with popular games like Angry Birds and Minecraft to occupy the children, which redirects their focus long enough for him to adeptly work.

Rather than focusing on their nervousness, the children focus on their games. The kids are so entertained, the procedure seems done before they know it. As The Provocateur, Craig has found a contemporary solution to a dreaded problem.

THE QUICK-START: INNOVATION + ALERT

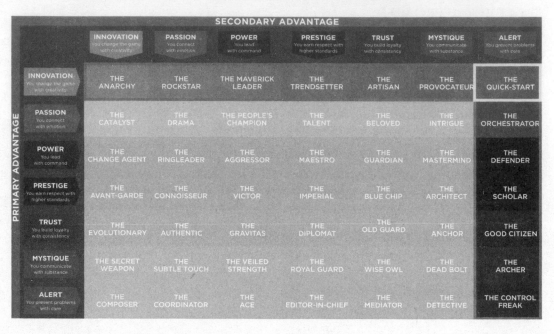

		SECONDARY ADVANTAGE					
	INNOVATION You change the game with creativity	PASSION You connect with emotion	POWER You lead with command	PRESTIGE You earn respect with higher standards	TRUST You build loyalty with consistency	MYSTIQUE You communicate with substance	ALERT You prevent problems with care
INNOVATION You change the game with creativity	THE ANARCHY	THE ROCKSTAR	THE MAVERICK LEADER	THE TRENDSETTER	THE ARTISAN	THE PROVOCATEUR	THE QUICK-START
PASSION You connect with emotion	THE CATALYST	THE DRAMA	THE PEOPLE'S CHAMPION	THE TALENT	THE BELOVED	THE INTRIGUE	THE ORCHESTRATOR
POWER You lead with command	THE CHANGE AGENT	THE RINGLEADER	THE AGGRESSOR	THE MAESTRO	THE GUARDIAN	THE MASTERMIND	THE DEFENDER
PRESTIGE You earn respect with higher standards	THE AVANT-GARDE	THE CONNOISSEUR	THE VICTOR	THE IMPERIAL	THE BLUE CHIP	THE ARCHITECT	THE SCHOLAR
TRUST You build loyalty with consistency	THE EVOLUTIONARY	THE AUTHENTIC	THE GRAVITAS	THE DIPLOMAT	THE OLD GUARD	THE ANCHOR	THE GOOD CITIZEN
MYSTIQUE You communicate with substance	THE SECRET WEAPON	THE SUBTLE TOUCH	THE VEILED STRENGTH	THE ROYAL GUARD	THE WISE OWL	THE DEAD BOLT	THE ARCHER
ALERT Your prevent problems with care	THE COMPOSER	THE COORDINATOR	THE ACE	THE EDITOR-IN-CHIEF	THE MEDIATOR	THE DETECTIVE	THE CONTROL FREAK

(PRIMARY ADVANTAGE)

HOW THE WORLD SEES THE QUICK-START

Quick-Starts combine creative thinking with a strong drive to implement ideas according to plan.

They have the rare ability to rapidly identify opportunities and execute a plan with focus and determination. It's the Innovation Advantage that makes them creative and imaginative, while the Alert Advantage helps them to follow through and get a project delivered on time.

When interviewing Quick-Starts, you'll find their CV shows strong achievements and is put together with a keen eye for detail, but perhaps in a slightly unconventional way. They may have chosen unusual words, used a rare font, or created a slightly different layout. During the interview they may surprise you with unexpected but clever answers.

Quick-Starts are able to take swift action (of course, they're Quick-Starts!) and to think on their feet. Their complex personality allows them to consider their decisions carefully when time allows, and to come to sensible conclusions quickly when under time pressure.

Archetype Twin
The Composer (page 220)

The Quick-Start's Top 5 Adjectives

1. **Prolific**—Quick-Starts are creative in thought and action. Rather than getting stuck, they come up with ingenious solutions to obstacles. They're able to devise a plan quickly and get a job done. You'll find they're in their element if they have to give an impromptu speech.

2. **Thorough**—Don't be fooled by their ability to think quickly—Quick-Starts implement their tasks with care. They're ever aware of the status of each detail. When presenting a new project plan to their team, you'll find they communicate with clarity and ensure everyone knows exactly what the consequences are if they don't deliver their project tasks on time.

3. **Diligent**—They make decisions carefully and follow through on what they say they will do. When they promise clients a delivery the next day, you can be sure they'll make it happen. Clients appreciate their frank and conscientious approach to solving problems.

4. **Can-do**—They quickly grasp alternative viewpoints and perspectives. They are clever, unconventional, and sometimes irreverent. And when faced with new challenges, they know that they'll succeed. No obstacle is unbeatable.

5. **Reliable**—It's not in the nature of Quick-Starts to let people down. Co-workers and customers can depend on their promise to deliver.

"Highest and Best Value" of The Quick-Start

Independent and always in control, Quick-Starts add value by generating and implementing fresh ideas. They're not dreamy thinkers. They combine creativity with a drive to reach goals.

Need a manager for a complex or creative project? You can rely on The Quick-Start to get the project delivered. Conscientious and hardworking, they ensure no detail escapes their attention. They adapt their plans if required, they find innovative solutions to problems, and they keep their eye firmly on the deadline.

They work best if given a license to think outside of the box. You can leave Quick-Starts to get on with their job because they're determined to succeed.

What Is Not the "Highest and Best Value" of The Quick-Start?

Their style of interaction tends to be more intellectual than warm and enthusiastic. They manage teams in a rational way—focusing on tasks, responsibilities, and deadlines.

Despite their ability to improvise, they are rational thinkers who tend to rely on facts rather than gut feelings.

How to Work with a Quick-Start

Quick-Starts thrive in environments where quick action is appreciated. Whether it's a busy call center, an airport, a factory, or an emergency room, they function extremely well in high-pressure environments where they can use their experience and detailed knowledge to improvise. They prosper under time pressure and are unafraid to take immediate action when required.

They can make major contributions in most environments. In highly structured organizations you may find they push for change and experimentation to drive the company forward. In more chaotic environments they will focus on creating order, developing clear plans, and improving accountability.

Archetypes That Can Optimize The Quick-Start

The Beloved (page 160) helps nurture relationships.
The Ringleader (page 128) motivates the team and puts forward compelling arguments to obtain buy-in.

A Lesson That Everyone Can Learn from The Quick-Start

Creative thinking doesn't need to be pie-in-the-sky.

One-Minute Coaching to My Quick-Starts

You manage your team with clarity. You allocate tasks resolutely. But not everyone is as rational as you. Some people rely on emotional energy to get involved in your project.

A dose of Passion will help you get others on board and to work together toward a goal. Try to build emotional relationships with your team with occasional chitchat. Show your team your enthusiasm. Paint a picture of what success will look like.

Example of an Anthem for The Quick-Start

DILIGENT RESOURCEFULNESS

How The Quick-Start Might Apply This Anthem

A big project is due tomorrow, and Mei is finishing the details. Suddenly, the client calls, upset. He's talked to the committee overseeing the project, and they want significant changes to the project's scope.

Mei is in a tricky spot: These changes are outside the scope of the original agreement, but she knows that if she doesn't make them, the client won't ultimately be happy with the work. This could compromise future opportunities for her company.

Instead of becoming overwhelmed, Mei goes to work. As a Quick-Start, she is a fixer. She quickly brainstorms available options. What are the resources available, and how can they be used in this situation? Is there a reserved co-worker who has been waiting on the sidelines, waiting for the opportunity to shine? Is there a vendor she can pull in, and barter services for a future project? Can the timeline be lengthened, by telling the client that she can enthusiastically undertake this new direction if he works with you to adjust the timeline? By quickly looking at all resources available to her, Mei saves the day.

THE TRUST ADVANTAGE

THE TRUST ADVANTAGE IS BUILDING LOYALTY OVER TIME.
TRUST PERSONALITIES SPEAK THE LANGUAGE OF STABILITY.

THE EVOLUTIONARY: TRUST + INNOVATION

PRIMARY ADVANTAGE	SECONDARY ADVANTAGE						
	INNOVATION You change the game with creativity	PASSION You connect with emotion	POWER You lead with command	PRESTIGE You earn respect with higher standards	TRUST You build loyalty with consistency	MYSTIQUE You communicate with substance	ALERT You prevent problems with care
INNOVATION You change the game with creativity	THE ANARCHY	THE ROCKSTAR	THE MAVERICK LEADER	THE TRENDSETTER	THE ARTISAN	THE PROVOCATEUR	THE QUICK-START
PASSION You connect with emotion	THE CATALYST	THE DRAMA	THE PEOPLE'S CHAMPION	THE TALENT	THE BELOVED	THE INTRIGUE	THE ORCHESTRATOR
POWER You lead with command	THE CHANGE AGENT	THE RINGLEADER	THE AGGRESSOR	THE MAESTRO	THE GUARDIAN	THE MASTERMIND	THE DEFENDER
PRESTIGE You earn respect with higher standards	THE AVANT-GARDE	THE CONNOISSEUR	THE VICTOR	THE IMPERIAL	THE BLUE CHIP	THE ARCHITECT	THE SCHOLAR
TRUST You build loyalty with consistency	THE EVOLUTIONARY	THE AUTHENTIC	THE GRAVITAS	THE DIPLOMAT	THE OLD GUARD	THE ANCHOR	THE GOOD CITIZEN
MYSTIQUE You communicate with substance	THE SECRET WEAPON	THE SUBTLE TOUCH	THE VEILED STRENGTH	THE ROYAL GUARD	THE WISE OWL	THE DEAD BOLT	THE ARCHER
ALERT You prevent problems with care	THE COMPOSER	THE COORDINATOR	THE ACE	THE EDITOR-IN-CHIEF	THE MEDIATOR	THE DETECTIVE	THE CONTROL FREAK

HOW THE WORLD SEES THE EVOLUTIONARY

Evolutionaries have a clear vision and follow through on their word.

Is your personal assistant an Evolutionary? You'll find she knows the rules about carry-on luggage, change fees, and frequent-flyer miles for each airline (that's her Trust Advantage).

But she doesn't panic when you miss a flight.

She can think on her feet (that's her Innovation Advantage). She'll quickly come up with alternative solutions, like using the same airline from another airport or trying a different airline at the airport where you're currently stuck.

Evolutionaries have a rare combination of talents. They like to work in a structured way and prefer creating routine in their day. But they're also open to change.

They have a creative mind, and use their imagination wisely. They prefer steady improvements to radical new ideas. That's why they're Evolutionaries.

Archetype Twin
The Artisan (page 256)

The Evolutionary's Top 5 Adjectives

1. Curious—They delight in understanding how things work. When meeting a brain surgeon at a cocktail party, you find them asking probing questions about how the brain repairs itself after injury. And when an engineer arrives to repair their oven, they want to know exactly what was wrong and how the fault was solved.

2. Open-minded—They don't get locked into one way of doing or thinking. When the sales remuneration system, for instance, doesn't seem to improve sales performance, they're happy to experiment with abolishing commission and get the team to work on higher basic salary. They're intelligent and willing to try new ideas.

3. Adaptable—They allow themselves to evolve. Whether they're early in their career or at a more senior position, an Evolutionary is keen on professional development. They'll take a course at least once a year to keep up-to-date with industry trends and to improve their personal skills.

4. Incremental—They learn why things are the way they are; and then make a difference by improving. For instance, rather than rethink the new-product development process from the ground up, they will improve it step by step. First they may change how suppliers are involved in product design, and then they may change how prototypes are built. They are pragmatic innovators.

5. Devoted—They remain dedicated to the people and projects they commit to. As CEOs they're driven to change the way the company does business, but they prefer to keep the existing team to go through the journey together.

"Highest and Best Value" of The Evolutionary
Evolutionaries have leadership potential.

As CEOs you see them driving change by continuously tweaking procedures and updating products. Rather than introduce radically new products, they make some small changes and seek customer feedback.

You'll find these CEOs are very inquisitive. When they meet clients, they ask them detailed questions about their experience with your customer service, how they're using your product, and whether they have suggestions for product or service improvements.

They like "management by walking around" and they may take their employees off guard by asking detailed questions about what they're up to at work. That's how they learn and develop their vision.

They're equally at ease with the big picture and the nitty-gritty stuff.

What Is Not the "Highest and Best Value" of The Evolutionary?

Don't expect Evolutionaries to rule their peers. As managers, for instance, they don't fire their employees quickly; instead, they will look to find a more peaceful and gradual solution.

Evolutionaries are calm leaders who implement change at a steady pace.

How to Work with an Evolutionary

Evolutionaries value traditions. You might find them getting together with the same group of high school friends once a year to go bowling and have dinner at the same Italian restaurant afterward. They appreciate familiarity and are loyal employees.

At the same time Evolutionaries will push for change. They understand that innovation is required in a competitive world.

Evolutionaries are usually independently minded, and you will get the most out of them if you allow them to create their own routines and don't impose strict guidelines. Use their creativity to adjust your company strategy, to tweak traditional working methods, and to update your product range.

Archetypes That Can Optimize The Evolutionary

The Guardian (page 136) has a more commanding approach to managing the team.

The Blue Chip (page 208) will ensure that the quality of results is excellent.

A Lesson That Everyone Can Learn from The Evolutionary

Radical change is not always required. Incremental innovation can get you far.

One-Minute Coaching to My Evolutionaries

Your approach to problems is gentle and easygoing. Your team members appreciate your talent to solve issues in a creative way. However, sometimes you need to use your authority to push toward an end goal.

Your team will respect you more when you communicate your opinions strongly and decisively. Be clear about the targets that have to be met. Challenge people who are lagging behind.

Famous Evolutionaries

Mahatma Gandhi and Betty White

Example of an Anthem for The Evolutionary

ADAPTABLE DIRECTION

How The Evolutionary Might Apply This Anthem

Cynthia is the project manager for a creative company. Senior management makes an announcement that the company is taking a new direction with its marketing strategy. The Evolutionary's laid-back style collaborates easily with team members in a quickly changing landscape. They can spin on a dime, seamlessly changing direction mid-process, while still staying true to the long-term vision. Others are having trouble accepting the new vision, but Cynthia applies her Advantages. She brainstorms new ways for the company to market their firm. How have they boosted results in the past? What new technologies could be applied? Are there employees who are not excelling in their role who may bring fresh creativity in this situation? By being adaptable in her direction, Cynthia adds distinct value.

THE AUTHENTIC: TRUST + PASSION

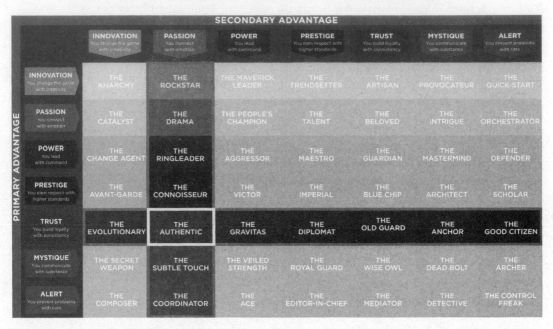

		SECONDARY ADVANTAGE					
		INNOVATION You change the game with creativity	**PASSION** You connect with emotion	**POWER** You lead with command	**PRESTIGE** You earn respect with higher standards	**TRUST** You build loyalty with consistency	**MYSTIQUE** You communicate with substance	**ALERT** You prevent problems with care
PRIMARY ADVANTAGE	**INNOVATION** You change the game with creativity	THE ANARCHY	THE ROCKSTAR	THE MAVERICK LEADER	THE TRENDSETTER	THE ARTISAN	THE PROVOCATEUR	THE QUICK-START
	PASSION You connect with emotion	THE CATALYST	THE DRAMA	THE PEOPLE'S CHAMPION	THE TALENT	THE BELOVED	THE INTRIGUE	THE ORCHESTRATOR
	POWER You lead with command	THE CHANGE AGENT	THE RINGLEADER	THE AGGRESSOR	THE MAESTRO	THE GUARDIAN	THE MASTERMIND	THE DEFENDER
	PRESTIGE You earn respect with higher standards	THE AVANT-GARDE	THE CONNOISSEUR	THE VICTOR	THE IMPERIAL	THE BLUE CHIP	THE ARCHITECT	THE SCHOLAR
	TRUST You build loyalty with consistency	THE EVOLUTIONARY	THE AUTHENTIC	THE GRAVITAS	THE DIPLOMAT	THE OLD GUARD	THE ANCHOR	THE GOOD CITIZEN
	MYSTIQUE You communicate with substance	THE SECRET WEAPON	THE SUBTLE TOUCH	THE VEILED STRENGTH	THE ROYAL GUARD	THE WISE OWL	THE DEAD BOLT	THE ARCHER
	ALERT You prevent problems with care	THE COMPOSER	THE COORDINATOR	THE ACE	THE EDITOR-IN-CHIEF	THE MEDIATOR	THE DETECTIVE	THE CONTROL FREAK

HOW THE WORLD SEES THE AUTHENTIC

Who doesn't enjoy working with an Authentic? These folks are peaceful team players, and easy to talk to. You'll find that they give everyone a listening ear. They keep an open-door policy.

Their pleasant personality builds strong emotional connections. They earn the loyalty of their staff by being dependable, genuine, and generous. You'll find them asking after your children because they'll remember they were ill last week. You'll also see them bringing in a homemade cake for their colleague's birthday.

Authentics usually speak in a direct manner, but they rarely raise their voice. Their management style is supportive and engaging.

Archetype Twin
The Beloved (page 160)

The Authentic's Top 5 Adjectives

1. Approachable—They're rarely confrontational, and they're open and transparent. When you struggle with a personal or business issue, you happily turn to Authentics for advice. You feel free to speak your mind in a conversation with them.

2. Dependable—Their steady-going attitude keeps everyone on a stable path—even in a volatile and competitive environment. When everyone panics about a new competitor entering the market, they'll keep calm and point out the long-standing and valuable connections your company has with existing customers.

3. Trustworthy—People are attracted to the safety and generosity that Authentics bring. They make new recruits feel welcome. They help interns find their way. Whatever your problem or concern, an Authentic will be there to watch your back.

4. Agreeable—Their harmonious personality makes everyone feel comfortable. They're well liked—with few exceptions. You won't find them gossiping behind your back.

5. Benevolent—They genuinely care about their team, their family, and causes that are close to their heart. You'll find them keeping in touch with old friends using Facebook, email, and regular phone calls.

"Highest and Best Value" of The Authentic

Their commitment inspires the team.

Authentics are the people you love to have on your team. You can rely on them. They're hardworking, committed, and popular.

You'll find they create a friendly team atmosphere. They make newcomers feel at ease. They treat them like family members. They inspire others to join in and to work together.

Authentics build strong networks thanks to their loyalty and warmth.

What Is Not the "Highest and Best Value" of The Authentic?

Authentics rely on their personality to make connections and get things done. They're unlikely to be disciplinarians at work or at home. They prefer using the carrot rather than the stick. They lead by example rather than using their authority.

Authentics aren't solitary workers. You get the most out of them if they can work with a team and nurture relationships both inside and outside the company.

How to Work with an Authentic

Struggling to build a strong relationship with your most important customer, because the buyer is awkward? Allow an Authentic to manage the account. Even the most difficult characters appreciate their support. Over time they build long-lasting partnerships.

Are politics getting in the way of good company management? Hire an Authentic to create a better team spirit at senior level. Their people focus and dedication will make their peers work closer together.

Archetypes That Can Optimize The Authentic

The Change Agent (page 124) will focus the team on achieving big goals.
The Evolutionary (page 268) will help embrace the unknown.

A Lesson That Everyone Can Learn from The Authentic

People are a company's most valuable asset.

One-Minute Coaching to My Authentics

You're building a great, dedicated team, but don't forget you need to meet deadlines, too. To ensure your team performs, you need to occasionally point out the negative consequences of failing to hit target.

People love working for you because of who you are, but don't let them get away with average work. Don't be afraid to use harsh words when required.

Famous Authentics

Mother Teresa and Walt Disney

Example of an Anthem for The Authentic

APPROACHABLE ENGAGEMENT

How The Authentic Might Apply This Anthem

Lilly knew that she wanted a career that dealt directly with people. That's why she was excited when she was offered a position in the learning and development department of her office. Her boss quickly noticed a change in the interoffice dynamics. Suddenly, many employees were more productive and working better as a team. That's because Lilly did extensive research into what established businesses in her field had done to boost employee engagement. If it worked for her bigger competitors, it could work for her team as well. Next, she created a dependable system to engage employees in learning and drew them in with her approachable and kind nature. Lilly made a point to reach out to each person under her leadership and let them know that they could always come to her for approachable engagement if they were having problems.

THE GRAVITAS: TRUST + POWER

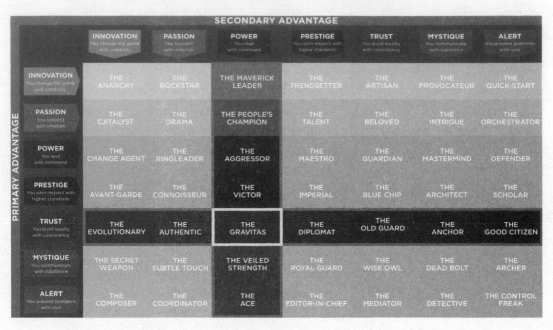

HOW THE WORLD SEES THE GRAVITAS

Employees instinctively respond to the leadership of a Gravitas.

Committed and loyal, a Gravitas naturally exudes authority. When a team is stuck with a difficult problem, they turn to a Gravitas for advice (even if he's not appointed as team leader).

Whether it's an unexpected new entrant to the market or an internal procedure that causes issues, a Gravitas will think through the best course of action, and recommend it with conviction.

The word *gravitas* means dignity or seriousness. You'll find that a Gravitas is respected for his long-standing industry experience and his firm leadership. Always in control, they manage their team in a relatively unassuming style but with a strong focus on what needs to be achieved.

Archetype Twin
The Guardian (page 136)

The Gravitas's Top 5 Adjectives

1. Dignified—They respond to problems with careful reasoning. They communicate with confidence. People respect their advice because they know a Gravitas doesn't act on impulse.

2. Stable—Even in chaotic surroundings, they keep a steady demeanor. Clients and co-workers depend on their sound judgment. For instance, when your company's Twitter account gets hacked, everyone will look to a Gravitas for guidance. You'll find he thinks through a plan carefully before recommending actions with confidence.

3. Hardworking—Guided by high principles, they have a strong work ethic. Their team members quickly adopt their diligent work mentality. A team managed by a Gravitas will find little time for chitchat, because they're focused on getting the job done.

4. Seemingly invincible—Unfazed by challenges, they motivate their employees to overcome setbacks. When a competitor beats them by introducing a new product first, they double their efforts to get their version to market as soon as possible.

5. Straightforward—They communicate their ideas with clarity and conviction. At sales presentations their no-nonsense approach quickly earns the admiration of potential new clients.

"Highest and Best Value" of The Gravitas

A Gravitas thinks in a linear way. They approach challenges methodically. They cope well under pressure. Problems may even reinforce their commitment to reaching the targets they've set.

In an entrepreneurial environment, they keep everyone grounded. Their ability to think clearly in a hectic atmosphere is a distinct benefit. When your start-up is planning to pivot, they'll ensure you don't make any hasty changes. They keep your business on track. They keep your ultimate goal in mind (and in the mind of the team, of course).

You'll find the substantial but calm presence of a Gravitas reassuring. Your customers, suppliers, and employees will also welcome their solid performance.

What Is Not the "Highest and Best Value" of The Gravitas?

Don't put your Gravitas in a position that requires her to be showy, because for her this will feel flamboyant. She does not want to seem reckless, so does not usually come to conclusions quickly.

They approach problems in a logical and rational way. They think before they act.

How to Work with a Gravitas

Need to present an investment plan to the bank? Ask a Gravitas to do the presentation. They're the type of person who puts a banker's mind at rest when they need to increase a loan. They'll reassure them that they'll achieve the plans that they set out. Their nonflashy, confident manner impresses all.

Gravitas personalities are natural leaders who set ambitious but realistic targets. They follow through and don't get easily swayed from the agreed direction. If you're working for them, they'll expect you to work hard and they'll reward your commitment fairly.

Archetypes That Can Optimize The Gravitas

A Composer (page 220) will increase focus on meeting deadlines.
Maestros (page 132) keep reaching for higher goals, even in the face of challenges.

A Lesson That Everyone Can Learn from The Gravitas

Authority is developed through commitment and knowledge.

One-Minute Coaching to My Gravitas

Clients and employees respect your authority. People value your ability to rationally reach conclusions. Yet, in certain situations, you can attract prospects more quickly by communicating with feeling.

Use stronger body language to make your points. Use vivid and emotional words to paint a clear picture of your company vision. A dash of drama can give you a sense of warmth and help you win over prospects and employees more quickly.

Famous Gravitas
Sam Walton

Example of an Anthem for The Gravitas
DELIBERATE CERTAINTY

How The Gravitas Might Apply This Anthem
Shannon is a wealth management advisor for a financial company. The end of the fiscal year is fast approaching, and clients are nervous to learn where they stand. They want deliberate certainty.

Shannon starts preparing for these meetings months in advance. Her workflow is incredibly deliberate. When she speaks with clients, Shannon calmly breaks their profile down item by item to show them exactly where they showed consistent improvement, and references these past successes to make authoritative portfolio recommendations for the future.

THE DIPLOMAT: TRUST + PRESTIGE

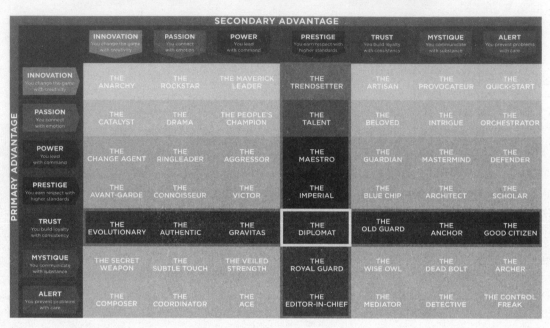

HOW THE WORLD SEES THE DIPLOMAT

Their commitment to high principles reassures customers and gives employees great confidence in the leadership of Diplomats.

Diplomats lead by example. Their thoughtful words and considerate actions inspire their team to do its best work. They seldom use high-pressure tactics. They prefer to maintain a consistent approach of encouragement with an understated leadership style.

At a client meeting, they quickly gain respect for their clear presentation. Well dressed and well prepared, they're able to answer all questions and address objections in an assured manner. In the rare case they don't know an answer, they've brought their file so they can quickly find the required details.

Diplomats are able to persuade clients and critics with their soft-spoken but confident approach. Their ability to win the admiration of others is a distinct advantage when others cross the line with a harsh remark or thoughtless response.

Archetype Twin
The Blue Chip (page 208)

The Diplomat's Top 5 Adjectives

1. **Levelheaded**—They are unfazed by setbacks. They bounce back quickly to keep their team motivated to achieve objectives. When a new product has failed a test, they adjust resources and put a plan in place to pass the test next time. You'll never see them lose their cool.

2. **Subtle**—They work toward goals in a steady way. They keep their attention, and their co-workers' attention, focused on the ultimate goal. Despite their relatively quiet demeanor, Diplomats won't allow others to digress from the agenda when they are chairing a meeting.

3. **Capable**—Co-workers and higher-ups don't question their ability to deliver results and to exceed expectations. When the company's future depends on the success of a particular project, you'll find yourself putting a Diplomat in charge. You know they'll deliver high-quality results.

4. **Impeccable**—Everything about their performance and presentation reflects their attention to detail. When you receive a written report from a Diplomat, you can trust that all facts have been scrutinized. You'll find a document written in clear and precise language, and carefully spell-checked (of course!).

5. **Prudent**—They communicate their ideas with clarity and conviction. Their confident, no-nonsense approach quickly earns the admiration of their audience.

"Highest and Best Value" of The Diplomat

Methodical and steadfast, Diplomats produce quality results. They have clear aspirations, and they can map the most efficient plan to get there. They push themselves hard to attain higher and higher goals.

In a job interview you'll find they know their own strengths. Their answers carefully highlight what they've achieved—just as their CV focuses on achievements rather than responsibilities.

You'll find they arrive at the first interview better prepared than most. They've researched the company meticulously. They've checked financials, read press releases, and requested a brochure. The questions they ask you are to the point.

They have a purposeful vision for their personal life, their career, and for the company they work for. Never complacent, they are high achievers.

What Is Not the "Highest and Best Value" of The Diplomat?

Surprise can make Diplomats uncomfortable, as do unpredictable schedules and people. Because they carefully think through their communication, they dislike being put on the spot. They value conventional wisdom, developed over time, instead of inventing untested or unproven ideas.

Diplomats are rational and precise. You get the most out of them in a relatively stable environment.

How to Work with a Diplomat

Need to leave someone in charge during your vacation? You'll feel you can safely go away when a Diplomat runs the company for a few weeks. You won't find any surprises on your return. They'll keep the ship steady during your absence.

You can entrust critical projects to Diplomats. They won't let you down. They're more likely to exceed your expectations. Diplomats are conscientious employees. They are trustworthy, reliable, and steady-going.

Archetypes That Can Optimize The Diplomat

A Ringleader (page 128) has a natural ability to connect team members with big goals.
A Trendsetter (page 252) will help guide the team through uncharted territories.

A Lesson That Everyone Can Learn from The Diplomat

Meticulous planning helps to achieve ambitious goals.

One-Minute Coaching to My Diplomats

Your work is of excellent quality. You're good at working independently. Sometimes you can delegate more. Even when you feel you can do things better yourself, it's still good to get others involved. Try to learn how to use your team to reach your goals.

Ensure team members fully grasp your ultimate objective. Use vivid details to paint a picture of the goal you want to reach so your team members can understand how to support you. Remember: Effective leadership is about influencing others to join a shared mission.

Famous Diplomats
Dr. Oz and Norman Rockwell

Example of an Anthem for The Diplomat
LEVELHEADED EXPERTISE

How The Diplomat Might Apply This Anthem
As a business coach, Jennifer puts an extensive amount of prep work into her one-on-one coaching sessions. Her methods have been tested and she knows that as long as the client is willing to put in the effort, they will be effective. When she meets with a client for the first time, she has a clear plan for how she will support their long-term growth. She researches the client and gets to know their field. She strives for excellence, so she doesn't want to encounter any surprises that she won't be able to overcome. She does not strive for overnight success stories; instead, she has tried-and-true methods that have worked for many of her clients, along with statistics on how their businesses benefited from her expertise. If a potential client is skeptical about her traditional approach, Jennifer can point them to the extensive online testimonials about her levelheaded expertise.

THE ANCHOR: TRUST + MYSTIQUE

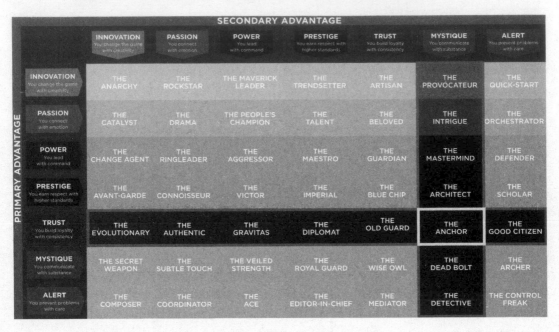

HOW THE WORLD SEES THE ANCHOR

Anchors earn a good reputation for their solid thinking.

You'll find that in moments of crisis, their peers look to Anchors for advice. Usually quiet, they have a distinct advantage because they keep their cool even under high pressure. They're able to come up with a workable solution when everyone else gets agitated.

In team meetings they are plainspoken and businesslike. They don't reveal their innermost thoughts. Their quietness, however, doesn't stop them from making major contributions, because everyone listens when they speak. What they say makes sense and has been carefully evaluated.

You'll find that Anchors communicate their recommendations with solid, rational arguments. You know you can depend on their well-considered advice. Their co-workers appreciate their no-fluff, no-nonsense approach.

They keep their ideas and opinions firmly rooted in reality. That's why they're called Anchors.

Archetype Twin

The Wise Owl (page 188)

The Anchor's Top 5 Adjectives

　1. **Protective**—Anchors are watchful over projects and people. If they're on a team, they'll do their best to ensure that everyone is taken care of. People respect them for their dedication.

　2. **Purposeful**—They do not act rashly or randomly. Over time, both their co-workers and their bosses come to depend on their balanced approach. You can trust that they deliver what they promise.

　3. **Analytical**—Anchors communicate their ideas with clarity and respond to problems with careful reasoning. You'll find they arrive at a job interview well prepared, and they briefly think before answering your questions. They don't get flustered when you grill them.

　4. **Calm**—They remain calm in the face of challenges. In an overheated management meeting—for instance, when the company's reputation is on the line due to a major product recall and bad press—you'll notice that people listen to the reasonable approach of an Anchor.

　5. **Steady**—They take a low-key approach. In a sales situation, they're attentive. Certainly not flamboyant, they support their pitch with rational arguments.

"Highest and Best Value" of The Anchor

Pragmatic and focused, Anchors can contribute to any company's success. Their co-workers value their loyalty and down-to-earth attitude. Their peers appreciate their sensible solutions. Their bosses welcome their intelligence and their analytical approach.

　Their slightly subdued demeanor doesn't mean they're laid-back. They just think before they speak. They don't act on impulse and provide a good balance in a team of high-strung entrepreneurs.

What Is Not the "Highest and Best Value" of The Anchor?

Anchors tend toward smaller groups for conversation and friendship, rather than haphazardly jumping around as the center of attention. They're at their most influential when working in the background. Their analytical skills and intellect are admired by those who've worked with them for some time.

How to Work with an Anchor

Anchors thrive in both mature and new industries, in large and small companies. Their practical approach is a distinct advantage. You'll find their contribution remains rock solid—even in chaotic times.

Anchors remain steady and keep on the right path, when others around them lose sight of the company's vision.

Archetypes That Can Optimize The Anchor

Avant-Gardes (page 196) will set a bolder, more radical company vision. The Beloved (page 160) will help nurture stronger relationships.

A Lesson That Everyone Can Learn from The Anchor

Influencers can also be quiet and steady.

One-Minute Coaching to My Anchors

You think through your recommendations carefully. Your advice is valuable. But sometimes you're not heard because you're too quiet.

Communicate your ideas with more emotional arguments for those who are less rational than you. Describe your ideas with vivid words. Don't keep your arms stiffly by your side. Use stronger body language to show your enthusiasm.

Famous Anchors

The Dalai Lama and Clint Eastwood

Example of an Anthem for The Anchor

PROTECTIVE SOLUTIONS

How The Anchor Might Apply This Anthem

In today's world of instant communication, one slipup can have a costly effect. Terry works with companies to re-create their websites and branding.

Sometimes his customers want to create a totally different voice for their content. Terry makes sure that his customers understand what they're doing. He knows that if it worked in the past, then it can work now; it just might need a little makeover. Terry's mission is to protect the reputation of his customers through a purposeful and research-backed plan. He creates an action plan around what worked on their website originally, what created the most engagement. And then he researches what is the best way to improve the features that are lagging. He never takes an idea at face value because he understands that every redesign could change how loyal customers view the company. Once the site has been redesigned, Terry works with his clients to monitor any changes in engagement, continuing to apply protective solutions.

THE GOOD CITIZEN: TRUST + ALERT

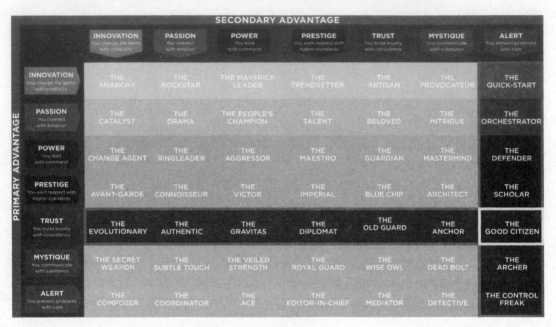

HOW THE WORLD SEES THE GOOD CITIZEN

Everyone knows a Good Citizen will handle all details and guide you to your goal.

As team leaders, they inspire others to follow plans. They push them to execute their tasks with attention to detail. As customer service managers, for instance, they'll provide strong guidelines and scripts for the team to follow. They'll implement an extensive checklist and work through it in a methodical way. Nothing escapes their attention—whether it's a misplaced box or an incomplete report.

As you'd expect from Good Citizens, they take care of their circle of people. They help as required. They offer support to co-workers and friends. Their life revolves around certain people, practicalities, and principles.

Archetype Twin
The Mediator (page 236)

The Good Citizen's Top 5 Adjectives

1. **Principled**—Even when obstacles arise, they stay on course. They don't want to let the team or customers down. They are keen to accomplish the tasks agreed upon. When your computer system breaks down and they can't do their work, you'll find they'll stay late (or arrive at the office early the next day) to get the jobs done that they've promised to do.

2. **Prepared**—They anticipate problems and aim to eliminate any chance for error or unpleasant surprise. For recurring tasks you'll find they quickly settle into a routine to reduce mistakes, and when they're doing something new they'll draw up a detailed plan.

3. **Conscientious**—They are thorough and thoughtful. They take pride in doing their job well. Whether they're organizing a nice lunch for a product launch meeting or preparing a major brochure update, you find that Good Citizens take pleasure in getting details right.

4. **Modest**—Personal glory isn't their main goal. Once they are committed to a team you'll find they put team needs above their own. You won't find them engaging in political games for their own good. They have a strong sense of purpose.

5. **Detail-oriented**—They review tasks and situations with a fine-toothed comb. When reviewing a project plan, they won't brush over any details. They take their time in order to understand the critical path. They'll prepare detailed checklists for each milestone so nothing escapes their attention.

"Highest and Best Value" of The Good Citizen

Good Citizens are loyal workers. They carefully weigh risks and rewards of projects before recommending whether or not to go ahead. Once they're committed to a project they'll ensure it gets executed well.

They're not afraid to explain the negative consequences for poor results. They can be taskmasters who push their team to finish projects on time.

Good Citizens set high expectations and are strongly focused on delivering what has been promised.

What Is Not the "Highest and Best Value" of The Good Citizen?

Good Citizens can be particular about how plans should be executed. They can be slow to embrace experimentation and untested ways of working. They prefer to follow known procedures to eliminate the risk of mistakes.

You get the most out of Good Citizens in a structured environment or if you allow them to create order in a chaotic environment.

How to Work with a Good Citizen

Good Citizens are able to carry out routine tasks with diligence. If a routine doesn't exist, they'll create a step-by-step guide.

Have a Good Citizen as your personal assistant? Count yourself lucky. They'll make you feel secure. They handle your travel arrangements and present you a detailed itinerary the day before you leave. They monitor your diary to help manage your workload. They'll remind you of your children's birthdays. You can trust them to carry out their responsibilities with care and attention.

Is your project manager a Good Citizen? Make sure you prepare for each project team meeting well. Know the status of your tasks. Expect detailed questions on how to catch up if you're slightly behind with one of your to-dos. Be sure to provide a warning if you see problems arising.

Good Citizens enjoy working with a team that's familiar to them. They like to know what to expect. That's why they're good planners. You can rely on them to execute their tasks and gain good results. They're hard workers.

Archetypes That Can Optimize The Good Citizen

With their warm personality, Talents (page 156) will quickly win over team members.
The Quick-Start (page 264) will rapidly identify new opportunities and push for innovation and experimentation.

A Lesson That Everyone Can Learn from The Good Citizen

Follow the plan to reduce risks. Set routines to eliminate mistakes.

One-Minute Coaching to My Good Citizens

You have a keen eye for detail and you are particular about implementing your plan. Pushing people to act is good, but building emotional bonds will help you get your project delivered, too.

You tend to be more reserved. Assess other people's reactions. Look for cues on how they're feeling and try to react appropriately Create a stronger team spirit by showing your excitement about the project. Building a wider network of contacts will also help you further your career.

Famous Good Citizens
Walter Cronkite and Alan Greenspan

Example of an Anthem for The Good Citizen
CONSCIENTIOUS AWARENESS

How The Good Citizen Might Apply This Anthem
Donovan is the project coordinator for an architecture firm. Business is booming, and the firm is receiving an influx of new clients. Donovan uses his CONSCIENTIOUS AWARENESS to make sure each client receives a consistent and thorough orientation.

He creates a checklist of materials all new clients need to complete to make sure their needs are identified and met. He also creates a questionnaire for each new client to fill out with the project goals and vision. Donovan immediately makes clients feel heard and helps them clarify their goals, so there is no confusion on how these goals are going to be implemented. Donovan brings comfort to the client by then walking them through the process they've co-created to make sure there are no surprises.

DOUBLE TROUBLES: WHEN ONE ADVANTAGE BECOMES TOO MUCH OF A GOOD THING

Your primary Advantage has natural advantages. But be careful. There is such a thing as *too much* of a good thing. Here's why.

Your personality normally uses two Advantages: primary and secondary. These two Advantages balance each other and help your Archetype communicate within a healthy range.

Primary Advantage + Secondary Advantage = Archetype

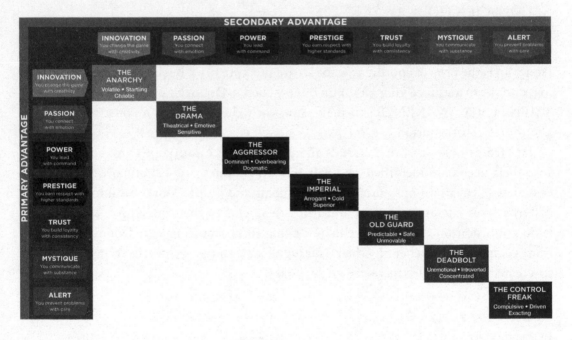

Yet when you feel unusually stressed, overwhelmed, or fearful, your normal positive attributes can turn into weaknesses. In these situations, your combined strengths get thrown out of equilibrium, and you begin using only your primary Advantage.

In this case, you're in "Double Trouble" mode. Your normal range of communication disappears, and you start using one Advantage to an exaggerated degree.

On the color Matrix of Personality Archetypes (on the inside front and back covers), you might have noticed a row of negative traits, in a diagonal line from the upper left corner to the lower right.

Your Archetype blends the best of two different Advantages. When you communicate with these top two Advantages, you embody the strongest advantages of each of them. However, when you communicate with only *one* Advantage, pitfalls begin to outweigh advantages. This is when you're at risk of becoming Double Trouble.

You might not realize that you're in Double Trouble mode, and thus it's a potential blind spot. It's important to be aware of these blind spots, because they can build negative impressions.

When you rely too much on one Advantage, your personality becomes one-dimensional, and rather than fascinate others, you can potentially turn them off.

Let's say you have a manager at work, and she's known for being social and expressive. Customers value her warm and approachable personality, and she effortlessly builds connections among her staff, helping everyone share their ideas. But one day, she suffers a romantic breakup. Just as she shared her positive emotions with the world before, now she shares her heartbreak. The theatrics make you a little uncomfortable, and shed a different light on her personality. People feel a little awkward. It's like having a raw nerve ending in the office.

In this situation, the Passion Advantage totally overrides the other facets of her communication. She's temporarily turned into The Drama (Passion + Passion). Her Advantage has temporarily become a pitfall.

Here's an example with the Trust Advantage. Trust seems like an Advantage that everyone would aspire to embody. But not always. While these personalities are stable and dependable, there's also a potential pitfall: Trust can become overly predictable, or even locked in a rut. In this situation, a Trust personality becomes The Old Guard (Trust + Trust).

Let's look at another example with the Power Advantage. People with a primary Power Advantage are confident and goal-oriented. With an overuse of Power, they can be seen as dominant, overbearing, or dogmatic. As the expression goes: Absolute power corrupts absolutely.

When someone has a primary Mystique Advantage, they are seen as observant, strategic, and coolheaded. This is an advantage, and allows these personalities to excel in situations with complex problems and delicate negotiations.

Yet if someone allows Mystique to totally consume their communication, without also weaving in other Advantages such as Passion or Power, they can be perceived as unemotional, introverted, or mechanical.

For instance, imagine that you are The Authentic (Trust + Passion). You combine the qualities of Trust (stable, reliable, familiar) and Passion (expressive, intuitive, affectionate). However, if you only communicate using the Trust Advantage, you could become The Old Guard (predictable, safe, unmovable).

In these examples, the value of your communication is overtaken by unbalanced delivery. If you are in Double Trouble mode, it means that one attribute is totally consuming your communication. It's too much of a good thing. Just as every Advantage has certain *advantages*, it also has certain *pitfalls*. And when you rely too heavily on a single Advantage, you're more likely to be perceived as Double Trouble.

Fascination is based upon hardwired responses. You want to create a healthy and dimensional response, not a simplistic or fixated one.

In your Fascination Advantage report, you will see the degree to which your own personality uses all seven of the Advantages. You will see how you score on Power, Passion, Mystique, and so on. Think of this combination as a recipe. Blend more than one ingredient, in order to avoid an imbalanced concentration of a single ingredient. It's the difference between eating a mouthful of flour versus a mouthful of cake. Combine your Advantages in different ratios to create a more dimensional and appealing response from others.

The Seven "Double Trouble" Modes

The Aggressor = Power + Power

The Drama = Passion + Passion

The Deadbolt = Mystique + Mystique

The Imperial = Prestige + Prestige

The Control Freak = Alert + Alert

The Anarchy = Innovation + Innovation

The Old Guard = Trust + Trust

DOUBLE TROUBLE FOR POWER

The Aggressor: Power + Power

	SECONDARY ADVANTAGE						
	INNOVATION You change the game with creativity	PASSION You connect with emotion	POWER You lead with command	PRESTIGE You earn respect with higher standards	TRUST You build loyalty with consistency	MYSTIQUE You communicate with substance	ALERT You prevent problems with care
INNOVATION You change the game with creativity	THE ANARCHY	THE ROCKSTAR	THE MAVERICK LEADER	THE TRENDSETTER	THE ARTISAN	THE PROVOCATEUR	THE QUICK-START
PASSION You connect with emotion	THE CATALYST	THE DRAMA	THE PEOPLE'S CHAMPION	THE TALENT	THE BELOVED	THE INTRIGUE	THE ORCHESTRATOR
POWER You lead with command	THE CHANGE AGENT	THE RINGLEADER	THE AGGRESSOR	THE MAESTRO	THE GUARDIAN	THE MASTERMIND	THE DEFENDER
PRESTIGE You earn respect with higher standards	THE AVANT-GARDE	THE CONNOISSEUR	THE VICTOR	THE IMPERIAL	THE BLUE CHIP	THE ARCHITECT	THE SCHOLAR
TRUST You build loyalty with consistency	THE EVOLUTIONARY	THE AUTHENTIC	THE GRAVITAS	THE DIPLOMAT	THE OLD GUARD	THE ANCHOR	THE GOOD CITIZEN
MYSTIQUE You communicate with substance	THE SECRET WEAPON	THE SUBTLE TOUCH	THE VEILED STRENGTH	THE ROYAL GUARD	THE WISE OWL	THE DEAD BOLT	THE ARCHER
ALERT You prevent problems with care	THE COMPOSER	THE COORDINATOR	THE ACE	THE EDITOR-IN-CHIEF	THE MEDIATOR	THE DETECTIVE	THE CONTROL FREAK

(Left axis label: PRIMARY ADVANTAGE)

Power personalities are natural leaders, comfortable with being in command. This is a positive attribute and makes them decisive leaders. Yet in certain situations, a Power personality can be seen as overly opinionated, forceful, or dominant.

HOW POWER ADVANTAGES CAN BECOME A WEAKNESS

A Power personality exudes a natural authority. Yet taken to the extreme, without blending in a secondary Advantage, this person becomes dominant and forceful. When he steps into a room, others become deferential, waiting for him to give his opinion first. Taken too far, the Power Advantage can crush creativity in others and silence the group's voices.

When a Power personality starts acting as an Aggressor, you'll find them dominating the discussion, speaking in absolute terms as if there's no alternative possible. Decisions become facts. Co-workers may feel belittled or even bullied into accepting a decision. Rather than building consensus, they order their subordinates (that's how they see them) to do as they are told.

Leaning too much on Power creates a sense of dictatorial leadership, distilling fear rather than nurturing loyalty in their team.

EXAMPLE OF A PERSONALITY IN "AGGRESSOR" MODE

Normally, Katrina is an effective decision-maker. She uses Power in a positive way, and is willing to consider alternate points of view. However when she gets worked up, watch out. When Katrina starts to over-rely on her power Advantage, she becomes unreasonably overbearing. Barking orders and hurling insults, she doesn't consider the affect of her actions on other team members.

Katrina speaks Power, the language of *confidence*. Yet in Double Trouble mode, she only speaks the language of *dominance*. She becomes overbearing and dogmatic.

When Katrina recognizes that she's in Double Trouble mode, she can balance the need to control her environment with the need to involve other team members in the decision-making process. Once she cools down, she's fine. With some emotionally intelligent thinking, Katrina can return to a balanced communication style.

COACHING FOR ANYONE IN "AGGRESSOR" MODE

Use Passion to inspire participation from the team. Gain buy-in by making people feel part of the decision-making process.

Use Trust to develop a loyal team. Show that your decisions will benefit the team and not just yourself.

Use Mystique to observe the team's reaction. Have you noticed how they go quiet when you enter the room? Coax them out of their shells by asking questions.

Use Prestige to recognize your team for their efforts. Show that you've noticed their hard work. Praise them for the quality of their work. Tell them you appreciate their input.

Use Alert to focus on the nuts and bolts of your projects. Don't just focus on the ultimate goal. Be sure to understand the milestones involved in getting to your destination.

Use Innovation to break through hierarchical barriers. Dissenting voices will help you make better decisions.

The Drama: Passion + Passion

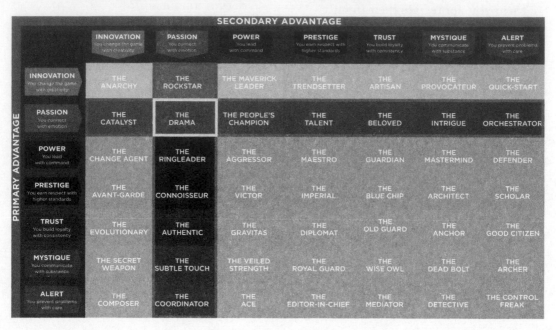

	SECONDARY ADVANTAGE						
PRIMARY ADVANTAGE	**INNOVATION** You change the game with creativity	**PASSION** You connect with emotion	**POWER** You lead with command	**PRESTIGE** You earn respect with higher standards	**TRUST** You build loyalty with consistency	**MYSTIQUE** You communicate with substance	**ALERT** You prevent problems with care
INNOVATION You change the game with creativity	THE ANARCHY	THE ROCKSTAR	THE MAVERICK LEADER	THE TRENDSETTER	THE ARTISAN	THE PROVOCATEUR	THE QUICK-START
PASSION You connect with emotion	THE CATALYST	THE DRAMA	THE PEOPLE'S CHAMPION	THE TALENT	THE BELOVED	THE INTRIGUE	THE ORCHESTRATOR
POWER You lead with command	THE CHANGE AGENT	THE RINGLEADER	THE AGGRESSOR	THE MAESTRO	THE GUARDIAN	THE MASTERMIND	THE DEFENDER
PRESTIGE You earn respect with higher standards	THE AVANT-GARDE	THE CONNOISSEUR	THE VICTOR	THE IMPERIAL	THE BLUE CHIP	THE ARCHITECT	THE SCHOLAR
TRUST You build loyalty with consistency	THE EVOLUTIONARY	THE AUTHENTIC	THE GRAVITAS	THE DIPLOMAT	THE OLD GUARD	THE ANCHOR	THE GOOD CITIZEN
MYSTIQUE You communicate with substance	THE SECRET WEAPON	THE SUBTLE TOUCH	THE VEILED STRENGTH	THE ROYAL GUARD	THE WISE OWL	THE DEAD BOLT	THE ARCHER
ALERT You prevent problems with care	THE COMPOSER	THE COORDINATOR	THE ACE	THE EDITOR-IN-CHIEF	THE MEDIATOR	THE DETECTIVE	THE CONTROL FREAK

Passion personalities easily make emotional connections with co-workers, customers, and suppliers. They build strong networks and deep relationships because their communication demonstrates their emotion for others. They have positive interactions with co-workers, suppliers, and clients.

HOW PASSION CAN BECOME A PITFALL

Passion makes people intimately attuned to the feelings of others. But taken too far, without blending in a secondary Advantage, Passion personalities become too delicate. They become overly sensitive and vulnerable. The wrong glance or words can lead to a heated reaction.

Strong demonstrations of feelings can make you seem temperamental and a little unpredictable. Being authentic is usually an advantage, but it doesn't mean that people want to know exactly what's going on with your relationship, your problems at home, and your frustrations with the boss.

Too much Passion in negotiations can also weaken your position. Showing disappointment or eagerness can quickly ruin a sale.

A one-dimensional focus on Passion can make people act like drama queens. They start wearing their hearts on their sleeves too much.

EXAMPLE OF A PERSONALITY IN "DRAMA" MODE

David is appealing and friendly, and when in a good mood, the life of the party, with a personality that's engaging and playful. However, when stressed, he becomes moody and unpredictable, swinging between extremes. His mood drives his actions, rather than his responsibilities. People don't know how to interact with him for fear of being caught in the vortex of ups and down. This is unappealing to customers, co-workers, and friends, and adds tension to the office.

David speaks Passion, which is the language of *relationship*. Yet in Double Trouble mode, he only speaks the language of *theatricality*. He becomes overly sensitive and irrational.

When David recognizes that he's falling into Double Trouble mode, he can balance his emotions with the other Advantages in his bag of tricks. With a little clearheaded thinking, David can return to his normal balanced communication.

COACHING FOR ANYONE IN "DRAMA" MODE

Use Trust to build loyal relationships. Be more consistent in your voice and attitude. Don't be too swayed by the mood of the day.

Use Mystique to shade your feelings from view. Reduce your boundless energy and take a more rational approach to choices and setbacks.

Use Prestige to emphasize your achievements. Your Passion allows you to build quick connections with potential customers. Don't forget to point out the reputation of your company, and use rational as well as emotional arguments to close a deal.

Use Power to radiate authority. The exuberance and emotion of Passion can make you unintimidating. Use Power to organize teams and to focus on goals.

Use Alert to get projects finished on time. Don't just rely on your "can do" attitude to get tasks completed. Try to implement a more methodical approach and be aware of potential pitfalls.

Use Innovation to channel emotion into creativity. This will help you contribute fresh ideas and experiment with new ways of working.

The Deadbolt: Mystique + Mystique

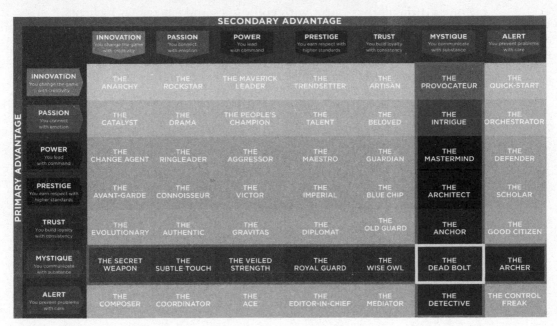

		SECONDARY ADVANTAGE						
		INNOVATION You change the game with creativity	**PASSION** You connect with emotion	**POWER** You lead with command	**PRESTIGE** You earn respect with higher standards	**TRUST** You build loyalty with consistency	**MYSTIQUE** You communicate with substance	**ALERT** You prevent problems with care
PRIMARY ADVANTAGE	**INNOVATION** You change the game with creativity	THE ANARCHY	THE ROCKSTAR	THE MAVERICK LEADER	THE TRENDSETTER	THE ARTISAN	THE PROVOCATEUR	THE QUICK-START
	PASSION You connect with emotion	THE CATALYST	THE DRAMA	THE PEOPLE'S CHAMPION	THE TALENT	THE BELOVED	THE INTRIGUE	THE ORCHESTRATOR
	POWER You lead with command	THE CHANGE AGENT	THE RINGLEADER	THE AGGRESSOR	THE MAESTRO	THE GUARDIAN	THE MASTERMIND	THE DEFENDER
	PRESTIGE You earn respect with higher standards	THE AVANT-GARDE	THE CONNOISSEUR	THE VICTOR	THE IMPERIAL	THE BLUE CHIP	THE ARCHITECT	THE SCHOLAR
	TRUST You build loyalty with consistency	THE EVOLUTIONARY	THE AUTHENTIC	THE GRAVITAS	THE DIPLOMAT	THE OLD GUARD	THE ANCHOR	THE GOOD CITIZEN
	MYSTIQUE You communicate with substance	THE SECRET WEAPON	THE SUBTLE TOUCH	THE VEILED STRENGTH	THE ROYAL GUARD	THE WISE OWL	THE DEAD BOLT	THE ARCHER
	ALERT You prevent problems with care	THE COMPOSER	THE COORDINATOR	THE ACE	THE EDITOR-IN-CHIEF	THE MEDIATOR	THE DETECTIVE	THE CONTROL FREAK

Mystique personalities restrain their emotions. Their air of mystery piques curiosity. They are independent, analytical, and systematic in their way of working. They can be formidable negotiators as they keep their cards close to their chest. They always think two steps ahead.

HOW MYSTIQUE CAN BECOME A PITFALL

Mystique personalities tend to be secretive. They rarely share information about themselves, but too much secrecy can negatively impact their trustworthiness. You may wonder whether they have something to hide.

When a Mystique personality gets into Deadbolt mode, they may struggle to work as part of a team. They can become outsiders and loners. They don't join in the gossip at the water cooler. They eat lunch in their own room. You might not even know whether they have a partner or live on their own. They can come across as inaccessible, or even antisocial.

Too much Mystique can make people cold fishes. They become aloof and standoffish. Their lack of warmth may make them seem disinterested. And it becomes difficult to connect with colleagues and engage with clients.

EXAMPLE OF A PERSONALITY IN "DEADBOLT" MODE

Anton's co-workers know that he is insightful and thoughtful. But sometimes, Anton can appear secretive and standoffish. He becomes so withdrawn into himself; he can be seen as aloof or even hostile. In this Double Trouble mode, Anton appears secretive, which makes people around him less likely to communicate with him. His personality can't shine through, and he is seen as reclusive. Often this can create a snowball effect; the more he withdraws from others, the less likely they are to connect with him.

When Anton recognizes that he's in Double Trouble mode, he can balance the need for isolation with the need to interact and socialize with others.

Anton speaks Mystique, which is the language of *listening*. Yet in Double Trouble mode, he only speaks the language of *introversion*. He becomes unemotional and concentrated. With a little expressive thinking, Anton can return to his normal balanced approach.

COACHING FOR ANYONE IN "DEADBOLT" MODE

Use Passion to open yourself up a little, and to add warmth to your relationships. It will help you to gain buy-in for your projects.

Use Trust to gain the confidence of others, and to become a valued member of the team.

Use Prestige to promote your distinct value. Show what you've achieved and gain recognition from others.

Use Power to stamp your authority on the team. Don't shy away from taking disciplinary action. Take a more forceful approach to underperformance.

Use Alert to create urgency and to work out a solid plan of action with your team.

Use Innovation to generate ideas. Complement your analytical skills with creativity and inventiveness.

The Imperial: Prestige + Prestige

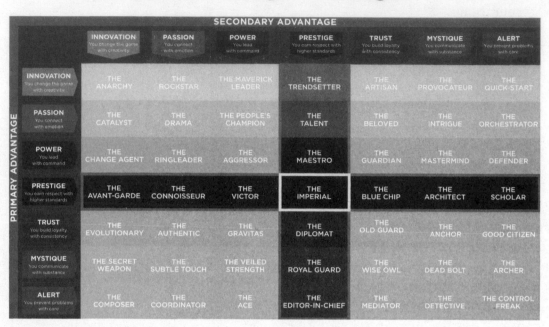

Prestige personalities are admired achievers who set high standards. They are ambitious, goal-oriented, and determined. They keep an eye on details and excel in each project they take on. They continuously strive to improve performance.

HOW PRESTIGE CAN BECOME A PITFALL

Prestige personalities thrive on public recognition. But too much focus on their achievements can make them look pretentious. Unafraid to promote themselves, they may show off their awards, proudly talk about their expensive car, and boast about their accomplishments.

When Prestige personalities forget to blend in a second Advantage, they start flaunting their successes, and they can make others feel inferior. Their fierce competitiveness starts to damage the team spirit. They constantly strive to win and to triumph over other people. They don't allow anything to stand in their way on the road to success.

Their intense focus on quality may come across as needlessly perfectionistic and uncompromising. Their relentless drive to be successful can make them look like pushy careerists.

Too much Prestige can turn people into big egos who become overly individualistic in their pursuit of success.

EXAMPLE OF A PERSONALITY IN "IMPERIAL" MODE

Devin has high standards, which is usually a good thing. This has helped him rise in his career, and contributed greatly to how he is regarded by his family and co-workers. Yet when Devin slips into Double Trouble mode, his Prestige Advantage becomes a disadvantage. He comes across as arrogant. Even a little righteous. In this mode, nobody else can possibly measure up. Nobody wants to get involved and contribute, because nothing they do will be good enough. His attitude alienates him from others, because he seems pompous, pretentious, and patronizing.

Devin speaks Prestige, which is the language of *excellence*. Yet in Double Trouble mode, he only speaks the language of *perfection*. He becomes perfectionistic and egotistical.

When Devin recognizes that he's in Double Trouble mode, he can balance the needs for excellence with the need to build and maintain healthy relationships that value the contribution of others. With a little down-to-earth thinking, Devin can return to a more normal, balanced communication.

COACHING FOR ANYONE IN "IMPERIAL" MODE

Use Passion to become warmer and less intimidating. Show others you care about their achievements, too.

Use Trust to become a valued partner of suppliers, clients, and co-workers. You can achieve even more success by building consensus and loyal partnerships.

Use Mystique to tone down your public display of achievements. You don't have to tell everyone about your successes. Step back now and then. There's no need to be center stage all the time.

Use Power to gently guide your team members and encourage them to take action. You are respected by your team—use this to your advantage by implementing a mild leadership style (just like a father coaxes his daughter to do her homework).

Use Alert to rally the team, and learn how to compromise to avoid conflicts with other team members.

Use Innovation to become more open-minded. Invigorate the team by injecting a sense of adventure and creativity.

The Control Freak: Alert + Alert

PRIMARY ADVANTAGE	SECONDARY ADVANTAGE						
	INNOVATION You change the game with creativity	PASSION You connect with emotion	POWER You lead with command	PRESTIGE You earn respect with higher standards	TRUST You build loyalty with consistency	MYSTIQUE You communicate with substance	ALERT You prevent problems with care
INNOVATION You change the game with creativity	THE ANARCHY	THE ROCKSTAR	THE MAVERICK LEADER	THE TRENDSETTER	THE ARTISAN	THE PROVOCATEUR	THE QUICK-START
PASSION You connect with emotion	THE CATALYST	THE DRAMA	THE PEOPLE'S CHAMPION	THE TALENT	THE BELOVED	THE INTRIGUE	THE ORCHESTRATOR
POWER You lead with command	THE CHANGE AGENT	THE RINGLEADER	THE AGGRESSOR	THE MAESTRO	THE GUARDIAN	THE MASTERMIND	THE DEFENDER
PRESTIGE You earn respect with higher standards	THE AVANT-GARDE	THE CONNOISSEUR	THE VICTOR	THE IMPERIAL	THE BLUE CHIP	THE ARCHITECT	THE SCHOLAR
TRUST You build loyalty with consistency	THE EVOLUTIONARY	THE AUTHENTIC	THE GRAVITAS	THE DIPLOMAT	THE OLD GUARD	THE ANCHOR	THE GOOD CITIZEN
MYSTIQUE You communicate with substance	THE SECRET WEAPON	THE SUBTLE TOUCH	THE VEILED STRENGTH	THE ROYAL GUARD	THE WISE OWL	THE DEAD BOLT	THE ARCHER
ALERT You prevent problems with care	THE COMPOSER	THE COORDINATOR	THE ACE	THE EDITOR-IN-CHIEF	THE MEDIATOR	THE DETECTIVE	THE CONTROL FREAK

Alert personalities are natural project managers. They go to great lengths to avoid problems and to deliver on time. They are reliable, practical, and perceive the details with great clarity. They keep the team safe by steering clear of negative consequences.

HOW ALERT CAN BECOME A PITFALL

Alert personalities provide a strong dose of harsh reality and are good at poking holes in ideas and theories. They can be a helpful *devil's advocate*. Taken too far, they become a negative influence and they can put up a barrier and block attempts at innovation.

In Control Freak mode, when Alert personalities forget to use their secondary Advantage, their negative energy can make them unpleasant company. They forget to look at the bright side of life. Instead, they point out glitches, complications, problems, and potential conflicts. They warn you not to trial something new for fear of making a fool of yourself. They suggest not taking on that exciting new role you've been offered, because you might not be up for it.

Their team may get irritated or frustrated by their micromanagement. They constantly check whether you've completed your tasks on time. They call you first thing to ensure you know what needs to be done that day.

When they get into Double Trouble mode, they might be perceived as detail-mongers, or potentially even neurotic. They hamper progress for fear of making mistakes.

EXAMPLE OF A PERSONALITY IN "CONTROL FREAK" MODE

Huang is attentive to deadlines, which is a key way he adds value. His primary Advantage is Alert. Yet when he gets in Double Trouble mode, he becomes obsessive about details at the expense of reasonable interaction. He squelches optimism and creativity in both himself and others. He's seen as nitpicky, obsessively focused on the details. His pessimism becomes exhausting and a negative force at work. The nitpicking drives everyone crazy. He fails to look for the reason behind a policy, and rigidly adheres to the letter of the law. In this mode, the customer is never right— the rulebook reigns supreme.

If Huang backs off and looks at the bigger picture, he can see beyond the rule to the reason behind it. When Huang recognizes that he's in Double Trouble mode, he can balance the need to follow the rules with the need to work cohesively with more creative partners.

Huang speaks Alert, the language of *details*. Yet in Double Trouble mode, he only speaks the language of *compulsion*. He becomes driven and exacting. With a little open-minded thinking, Huang can return to his normal, balanced communication.

COACHING FOR ANYONE IN "CONTROL FREAK" MODE

Use Passion to soften your harshness. Don't just focus on the practical side of your project. Build a friendlier team spirit.

Use Trust to build a committed team. Earn respect because of your dependability.

Use Mystique to tone down your strong focus on meeting deadlines.

Observe the reaction of your teammates when you point out deadlines and responsibilities.

Use Prestige to motivate others. Tell your team what the successful completion of a project will do for their career. Explain how much recognition they'll receive.

Use Power to become an authoritative voice. Get your team to want to work for you rather than executing their tasks out of fear of negative consequences.

Use Innovation to see the positive side of new opportunities. You tend to weigh the negative consequences more heavily than the potential success new opportunities can bring.

The Anarchy: Innovation + Innovation

	SECONDARY ADVANTAGE						
PRIMARY ADVANTAGE	**INNOVATION** You change the game with creativity	**PASSION** You connect with emotion	**POWER** You lead with command	**PRESTIGE** You earn respect with higher standards	**TRUST** You build loyalty with consistency	**MYSTIQUE** You communicate with substance	**ALERT** You prevent problems with care
INNOVATION You change the game with creativity	THE ANARCHY	THE ROCKSTAR	THE MAVERICK LEADER	THE TRENDSETTER	THE ARTISAN	THE PROVOCATEUR	THE QUICK-START
PASSION You connect with emotion	THE CATALYST	THE DRAMA	THE PEOPLE'S CHAMPION	THE TALENT	THE BELOVED	THE INTRIGUE	THE ORCHESTRATOR
POWER You lead with command	THE CHANGE AGENT	THE RINGLEADER	THE AGGRESSOR	THE MAESTRO	THE GUARDIAN	THE MASTERMIND	THE DEFENDER
PRESTIGE You earn respect with higher standards	THE AVANT-GARDE	THE CONNOISSEUR	THE VICTOR	THE IMPERIAL	THE BLUE CHIP	THE ARCHITECT	THE SCHOLAR
TRUST You build loyalty with consistency	THE EVOLUTIONARY	THE AUTHENTIC	THE GRAVITAS	THE DIPLOMAT	THE OLD GUARD	THE ANCHOR	THE GOOD CITIZEN
MYSTIQUE You communicate with substance	THE SECRET WEAPON	THE SUBTLE TOUCH	THE VEILED STRENGTH	THE ROYAL GUARD	THE WISE OWL	THE DEAD BOLT	THE ARCHER
ALERT You prevent problems with care	THE COMPOSER	THE COORDINATOR	THE ACE	THE EDITOR-IN-CHIEF	THE MEDIATOR	THE DETECTIVE	THE CONTROL FREAK

Innovation personalities are creative. They enjoy experimenting. They trial new procedures, reimagine products, and envision new business models. Because they communicate with creativity, they can be valuable assets in any organization that seeks to improve and innovate.

HOW INNOVATION CAN BECOME A PITFALL

Innovation personalities provide a strong dose of creative energy to any organization. But in excess, they can become unruly and insubordinate. When they forget to blend in a secondary Advantage, they start to resist being told *that's how we do things here.* They interrupt a meeting with a seemingly crazy idea. They become troublemakers.

People in Anarchy mode don't like routine. They may challenge everyone to shelve proven methods and experiment with new ways of working. They may ignore the potential disruption that innovation can bring to an organization. They don't understand why others may be resisting change.

They see new opportunities everywhere and forget that company performance can be improved by fine-tuning and by serving existing customers better. They jump from idea to idea, sometimes without ever finishing a project.

Too much Innovation leads to unnecessary risk-taking. Ideas can become wildly successful, but they can lead to catastrophic failures, too.

EXAMPLE OF A PERSONALITY IN "ANARCHY" MODE

Marcella develops fantastically brilliant creative ideas. Yet sometimes, her creative thinking becomes a little *too* creative. She has trouble staying on track. Her Innovation Advantage becomes a disadvantage, leaving a startling whirlwind of chaos and confusion all around her. She exhausts her friends because she starts a parade of projects without actually finishing any of them. In this mode, she flip-flops, jumping from one thing to the next with what seems like accelerated ADD. She has a tattoo she regrets, and a credit card bill to show for her impulsive Double Trouble mode.

Marcella speaks Innovation, the language of *creativity*. Yet in Double Trouble mode, she only speaks the language of *chaos*. She becomes volatile and startling.

When Marcella recognizes that she's letting her creativity get the best of her, she can balance the exploration with structure, and can get projects done. With some practical thinking, Marcella thinks ahead and works within a productive structure. She returns from daredevil back to being the visionary that her clients and co-workers look to for big ideas.

COACHING FOR ANYONE IN "ANARCHY" MODE

Use Passion to build warm connections with the team. Use your positive energy to gain buy-in for your ideas.

Use Trust to improve consistency. Your creative idea generation makes it difficult for others to keep up. Slow down a little and focus on your most important ideas.

Use Mystique to tame your irreverence. You don't always have to take center stage. Stand back occasionally and observe how others react.

Use Prestige to select your best ideas and to carefully plan their implementation.

Use Power to explain how your plans can contribute to the company's overall goals.

Use Alert to take calculated risks. Weigh the negative as well as the positive consequences of new opportunities.

The Old Guard: Trust + Trust

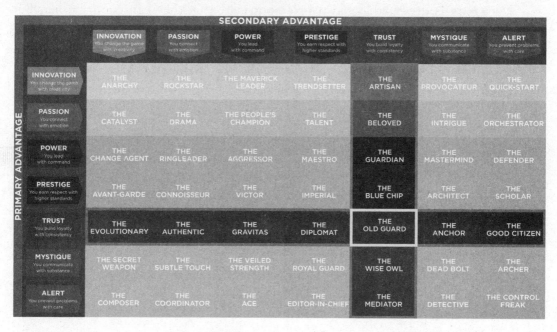

		SECONDARY ADVANTAGE					
		INNOVATION You change the game with creativity	**PASSION** You connect with emotion	**POWER** You lead with command	**PRESTIGE** You earn respect with higher standards	**TRUST** You build loyalty with consistency	**MYSTIQUE** You communicate with substance	**ALERT** You prevent problems with care
PRIMARY ADVANTAGE	**INNOVATION** You change the game with creativity	THE ANARCHY	THE ROCKSTAR	THE MAVERICK LEADER	THE TRENDSETTER	THE ARTISAN	THE PROVOCATEUR	THE QUICK-START
	PASSION You connect with emotion	THE CATALYST	THE DRAMA	THE PEOPLE'S CHAMPION	THE TALENT	THE BELOVED	THE INTRIGUE	THE ORCHESTRATOR
	POWER You lead with command	THE CHANGE AGENT	THE RINGLEADER	THE AGGRESSOR	THE MAESTRO	THE GUARDIAN	THE MASTERMIND	THE DEFENDER
	PRESTIGE You earn respect with higher standards	THE AVANT-GARDE	THE CONNOISSEUR	THE VICTOR	THE IMPERIAL	THE BLUE CHIP	THE ARCHITECT	THE SCHOLAR
	TRUST You build loyalty with consistency	THE EVOLUTIONARY	THE AUTHENTIC	THE GRAVITAS	THE DIPLOMAT	THE OLD GUARD	THE ANCHOR	THE GOOD CITIZEN
	MYSTIQUE You communicate with substance	THE SECRET WEAPON	THE SUBTLE TOUCH	THE VEILED STRENGTH	THE ROYAL GUARD	THE WISE OWL	THE DEAD BOLT	THE ARCHER
	ALERT You prevent problems with care	THE COMPOSER	THE COORDINATOR	THE ACE	THE EDITOR-IN-CHIEF	THE MEDIATOR	THE DETECTIVE	THE CONTROL FREAK

Trust personalities build a loyal team. They are even-tempered, committed, and dependable. Cool under pressure, they offer stability in times of stress. They follow through on what they promise, use tried-and-tested methods, and deliver on time.

HOW TRUST CAN BECOME A PITFALL

Trust builds consistency and loyalty. But when Trust personalities forget to use their secondary Advantage, they can become too predictable, and perhaps a bit boring. You don't need to ask their opinion; you know exactly what they'll say.

People in Old Guard mode can get stuck in traditions. A strong dependence on proven methods can lead to rigidity. They become overly resistant to change. You'll find they unwaveringly insist *that's how we do things here*. Occasionally, they can even be perceived as obsessive-compulsive because they adhere too strictly to patterns.

A strong focus on Trust can make people boring old fogies. They become stuck in their ways. Their aversion to experimenting and risk-taking can lead to staleness. New opportunities may be missed.

EXAMPLE OF A PERSONALITY IN "OLD GUARD" MODE

Kristy is dependable and people appreciate that they can count on her. But when Kristy becomes tense or fearful, she comes across as narrow-minded. In this mode, she gets locked into fixed routines and is not open to the possibility of alternatives. As a manager, she becomes shut down to opportunity, losing the ability to consider alternatives or new ideas. In this one-dimensional mode, she's only open to one way of thinking (the way it's always been done). People perceive her as stale. For example, when faced with a big change at work or at home, Kristy refuses to even think about new possibilities. This makes it difficult for her to adapt, and difficult for others to evolve and grow in their relationships with her.

Kristy speaks Trust, which is the language of *stability*. Yet in Double Trouble mode, she only speaks the language of *predictability*. She becomes safe and immovable.

When Kristy recognizes that she's in Double Trouble mode, she can balance the need for routine with a positive openness to change. With a little creative thinking, Kristy can return from that state of immobility, and move in sync with her surroundings.

COACHING FOR ANYONE IN "OLD GUARD" MODE

Use Passion to inject impulsiveness into your routine. Passion will also help you to build rapport quickly with new team members or prospects.

Use Mystique to pause for a moment, and see if you should reevaluate your patterns. Take your time to work out thoughts for yourself.

Use Prestige to encourage your team to achieve better results and strive for excellence.

Use Power to take control of a new team. It takes time to build loyalty, so when you need to be in command quickly, use your authority to set goals and motivate your team.

Use Alert to focus your team on hitting deadlines. Nurturing good working relationships is good, but sometimes you need to point out the negative consequences of failure to meet objectives.

Use Innovation to accept new ways of doing things. Experiment a little. Tweak processes to see how you can improve current work practices.

WHEN PERFECTION ISN'T GOOD ENOUGH

Among top colleges, the application process can become ridiculously competitive.

For students applying to Princeton or Stanford, it's not enough to merely be smart. Smart is a given. That 4.0 GPA might have earned valedictorian honors at a local high school, but in the elite pond it's practically passé.

When *everyone* is smart, smart is no longer a competitive edge. Perfection is a commodity. You can't out-perfect perfect.

At this point in the competition, other factors come into play. In any crowded market, *"different" is better than "better."*

Instead of obsessing over improving test scores by a fraction, how could a student find a different way to stand out in a sea of academic excellence? Many applicants can rattle off a list of sports or clubs or volunteer work. An untraditional leadership role might stand out, as can travel adventures and early career victories. Better yet, a student can demonstrate how he applies natural abilities to stand out and build influence. That's what is required to succeed in the real world. He can point to how he has built stronger relationships, persuaded his peers, and mobilized groups of people to action.

As competition rises, strengths matter less than differences.

If a team only rewards one or two types of strengths, most people will fail. To win, you need differences.

Every single person you know has natural Advantages. Once you identify the differences among employees, you can get off the endlessly spinning hamster wheel and start to make real progress.

IDENTIFY ADVANTAGES IN OTHERS

By now you have a pretty good idea of the two Advantages that you use most often. You see how you add value. How about the people around you? How do they add value *to you*?

Are you starting to wonder about your manager, and which Advantages she's using? How about your college professor, your airline gate agent, or the date sitting on the other side of the table? Yes? That's good, because it means you're ready to step it up a notch.

THE ARCHETYPES | 317

You've probably already begun to recognize the Advantages and patterns of those around you. At networking events, for instance, you'll recognize the warm personalities that quickly make strong connections (that's Passion). In brainstorming sessions you'll notice who invents ideas (that's Innovation). In meetings, you'll observe the cautious co-worker who carefully keeps projects on track (that's Alert).

This is a little like bird-watching. A bird-watcher has already studied the sounds, movements, and characteristics of each bird species. Similarly, you can begin to spot which Advantage someone is using, even in the first moments of an interaction.

Here's a quick look at identifying the Advantages of the people around you. You can begin to "read" the Advantages someone is using in their communication, so that you can more quickly build rapport. I'll give you a few fast tips for beginning the process of identifying how others add value through their Advantages.

HOW DIFFERENT PERSONALITIES ADD VALUE

A quick look at the building blocks to the patterns behind how a personality is most likely to add value:

The Power Advantage: Leading Through Authority

The Passion Advantage: Creating warm emotional connections

The Mystique Advantage: Thinking before speaking

The Prestige Advantage: Achieving success with higher standards

The Alert Advantage: Careful precision

The Innovation Advantage: New ideas and solutions

The Trust Advantage: Building loyalty over time

A FEW TIPS TO "READ" OTHER PEOPLE

How can you identify the Advantages in clients and customers, even if they have not taken the Fascination Advantage assessment?

This question presents a big topic, and the answers encompass an entire training curriculum. Yet, I do want to give you a few specific tips to get you started, below.

Leaders, you will want to learn how to identify the Advantages in your team members, so you can adapt your style to support their best, and to help different personalities better perform in their role. By mentally cataloguing your contacts according to which Advantages they use, you can gain a huge edge in building rapport. You can more quickly dial into which frequency they are most likely to use on their communication radio.

Begin by noticing the "language" that your conversational partner is speaking.

POWER

Power personalities speak the language of CONFIDENCE.

You'll recognize a Power personality when they communicate with strength and command. Do they tend to take control of a situation? Do they often speak with a definite point of view? Do they come across as decisive? Power personalities actively lead situations rather than passively sitting back. They communicate and inspire with intensity. They get involved, and often command the direction of a group. You'll find they shape opinion and guide their peers, and they tend to confront problems to clear the path for progress. They're able to quickly make decisions by weighing facts and opinions. They usually listen to the advice of others, but ultimately design the action plan.

PASSION

Passion personalities speak the language of RELATIONSHIP.

They quickly build rapport and relationships. They tend to have a wide social network. They do business by treating others like friends, or even like family. In a car showroom, for instance, they can win the sale solely based upon their personal connection with people walking through the door. Is someone expressive? Do they often use vivid and emotional words? Do they use strong body language? These are hints that someone has a strong Passion Advantage. With exuberance and enthusiasm, Passion boosts presenters of ideas and information. They're able to adjust messages in real time based on the reaction of their audience. Passion personalities shine in face-to-face situations. They boost other team members' motivation and build a team spirit.

MYSTIQUE

Mystique personalities speak the language of LISTENING.

By listening, they can think things through rather than jumping in too quickly. You'll find that you have a hard time "reading" what they are thinking. They rarely show strong emotions and are able to remain calm in situations of mounting pressure. Does someone prefer to stand back and observe rather than be in the spotlight? Do they carefully think through an issue before voicing their opinion? Do they remain unruffled under pressure? Mystique personalities carefully choose what to reveal and share. They communicate selectively, and they present their ideas in an objective, factual manner. They're unlikely to ramble, overstate, or make claims that they cannot back up. They prefer to immerse themselves in analysis and problem-solving.

PRESTIGE

Prestige personalities speak the language of EXCELLENCE.

These overachievers earn respect with higher goals. Prestige is ambitious and focused on improving the outcome. Is someone fiercely competitive? Do they have a keen eye for detail? Are they frequently unsatisfied? Is *good enough* never good enough for them? Prestige personalities seek consistent improvement and tangible evidence of their success. You'll find they're motivated by clear rewards and the respect of their peers. In sales, they are usually able to persuade others to buy by elevating the perceived value of the sale, which makes the idea or service more enticing to the purchaser.

ALERT

Alert personalities speak the language of DETAILS.

People who use the Alert Advantage have a natural ability to handle the details and stay focused on outcomes. They usually approach tasks in a linear and rational way, focusing on concrete deliverables such as schedule and budget. As managers they set clear expectations and establish consequences. That's how they create action and heighten performance. Teams with a high ratio of Passion and Innovation can often benefit from a greater use of Alert to keep projects on track, avoid mistakes, and get the job finished.

INNOVATION

Innovation personalities speak the language of CREATIVITY.

With an entrepreneurial approach, they help a group brainstorm new solutions. You'll find they surprise you with unconventional ideas, and they may advocate an untraditional point of view. In sales they transform the humdrum into something that feels unique. By using their natural creativity, they keep the buying party interested—even in commoditized markets. Innovation personalities love experimenting and they prevent a company from going stale. They seem to enjoy starting a new project more than finishing it.

TRUST

Trust Personalities speak the language of STABILITY.

These folks are dependable, always following through on what they promise. They feel familiar, as though you already know them. Does someone tend to follow the same routine, day in and out? Do they follow tried-and-true methods rather than experiment with new ways of doing things? Are they traditional in their dress and style? You'll find that Trust personalities don't like change. They keep the ship steady.

Here's a quick guide to review before your next important meeting with new customers.

Our clients find that as they begin to understand the seven Advantages, and can apply them in their own communication, something really interesting begins to happen: They can pick up which Advantages others are using.

As a result, our clients learn how to tailor their delivery and message to more quickly create rapport with the Advantage they identify in their listener.

IDENTIFYING A PERSON'S PRIMARY ADVANTAGE

CLUES TO LOOK FOR	HOW THEY OPERATE	HOW THEY FASCINATE	THEIR PRIMARY ADVANTAGE IS
Creative, Visionary, Entrepreneurial	You change the game.	Invent creative solutions that tweak tradition.	**INNOVATION**
Expressive, Intuitive, Engaging	You immediately create connections.	Apply your natural optimism and energy to instantly build relationships.	**PASSION**
Confident, Goal-Oriented, Decisive	You're in command of the environment.	Become the opinion of authority.	**POWER**
Ambitious, Results-Oriented, Respected	You immediately earn respect for your results.	Use admiration to raise the value of yourself and your company.	**PRESTIGE**
Stable, Dependable, Familiar	You build loyalty with stability and dependability.	Repeat and reinforce patterns.	**TRUST**
Independent, Logical, Observant	You reserve yourself and your communication for "best and highest" use.	Keep the focus on results, not drama. Carefully select what you reveal.	**MYSTIQUE**
Proactive, Organized, Detailed	You incite immediate and urgent action.	Keep your team focused on deadlines, structure, and potential negative consequences.	**ALERT**

Download this image at HowToFascinate.com/Resources

They can identify when a prospective customer has a Passion Advantage. On the other hand, if they have trouble "reading" someone during a first meeting, they understand it might be because of the Mystique Advantage. By recognizing the Mystique Advantage, they can know to tone down the body language and give a little extra space before getting too comfortable.

What about the people that you "click" with, and those you don't so much? How can your Advantages better complement *theirs*, and theirs *yours*?

How are your co-workers and employees positioned to excel? Which Advantages are they using while greeting customers, or making field visits, or resolving conflict? Know your team member's Advantages so you can understand how they uniquely contribute.

For instance, say your marketing department has a tight budget. Someone with primary Alert will add value by carefully planning the exact steps to finish within the budget. Alternatively, someone with primary Innovation is naturally suited to inventing an unexpected idea for a grassroots campaign or social media initiative. Two different personalities, two different ways to solve the problem.

It's extremely helpful to identify the Advantages within a group. For instance, before my team and I lead a Fascination Laboratory discovery session, each of our participants takes the Fascination Advantage assessment. This allows us to customize the group's content and experience around their Advantages. In other words, if this group scores highly on Power, then the presentation will be structured with clear directives, strong words, and even black-or-white absolutes. If they score highest on Trust, we make sure they understand the long-term history behind our research, and how they can gradually apply it bit by bit over time.

Understanding your co-workers and employees will allow you to predict how they are most likely to interpret and apply your communication.

RECOGNIZING COMMUNICATION PATTERNS AROUND YOU

In this next section, I'll give a few colorful examples of how different people approach challenges differently. By seeing this variety of approaches, you can begin to recognize these patterns in others.

Just for fun, we'll start with an example from family life. (After all, clients and customers can be much easier to convince than your own kids!) Let's say your kids aren't so keen on eating their green vegetables. As a parent, you have a challenge: *Get your kids to eat broccoli.*

How could you persuade your kids to eat their broccoli by experimenting with different languages of fascination?

You could use the **Power** Advantage, and be an authority: "Eat your vegetables now."

You could delight them with the **Passion** Advantage, turning the broccoli into a visual experience: Make a face out of the broccoli (perhaps using cheese sauce to draw the smile).

You could motivate them with curiosity by communicating with **Mystique**: "I have a great game to play. But I'm not going to tell you what it is until you eat the broccoli."

With **Prestige**, you might spark a little competitive spirit: "Okay, kids, who's going to be tonight's broccoli-eating champion?"

With **Alert,** you'd establish a structure: "If you don't eat the broccoli, then you don't get dessert."

With the **Innovation** Advantage, you'd use creativity to surprise them: "No problem, don't eat the broccoli. Brussels sprouts for everybody!!"

Finally, with **Trust,** you could draw upon a familiar tradition. For instance, you could promise that if they eat their broccoli, you'll read their favorite story at bedtime.

One of these options will feel natural for you, and others will not. It's productive to consider your options. You don't want to get in a communication rut, always hammering away with the exact same Advantage, over and over.

EXAMPLE: USING THE SEVEN ADVANTAGES TO CLOSE A SALE

Let's say you're meeting a potential client. You've already met this guy a few times. You're ready to make the offer, but he keeps finding excuses, never making a decision. Ergh! Which do you use to get someone to take action, now? Seven ways to close a sale:

POWER: Demonstrate how you can push your client's success.
PASSION: Express your true enthusiasm to build the relationship.
MYSTIQUE: Allow them to discover your product benefits with a product trial.
PRESTIGE: Impress them with higher goals.
ALERT: Offer time-limited savings by signing up today.
INNOVATION: Excite with what's new and creative about your product.
TRUST: Show how your product is tried-and-true.

EXAMPLE: USING THE SEVEN ADVANTAGES TO SOLVE A TEAM CONFLICT

Conflict can rip a team apart, skyrocketing resentment against management or even pitting co-workers against each other.

We frequently hear from our clients how office conflicts can calm down or even dissolve entirely, once people understand each other's differing Advantages. Once you know someone's Advantages, you can see past the exterior, and see what's really going on.

Each Advantage speaks a different "language." (For instance, Alert is the language of *details*, Mystique is the language of *listening*, and Innovation is the language of *creativity*.)

When you understand what language your team members are speaking, you can better understand why discord is happening in the first place. Each team member is suited to solve a conflict in a different way.

Conflict can encourage alternative points of view, spark creativity, and provoke discussion—as long as there is a positive way to deal with it. Here's how the Advantages can each deal with conflict in a positive way:

POWER: Think through points before taking a strong stand.
PASSION: Be considerate, care for feelings and emotions involved.
MYSTIQUE: Ask questions to understand underlying issues.
PRESTIGE: Verbally recognize the ways in which others make contributions.
ALERT: Organize in advance to prevent unproductive conflicts.
INNOVATION: Think outside the box to offer a completely new solution.
TRUST: Nurture relationships so the focus is on *team* rather than individual.

A diverse mix of Advantages can provide balance for a team. (To learn more about how teams can become conflicted and imbalanced when there's a pronounced use of one particular Advantage among team members, see "When a Team's Advantage Becomes a Disadvantage" on page 387.)

EXAMPLE: USING THE SEVEN ADVANTAGES TO MOTIVATE YOUR TEAM

Ever wanted your team to get motivated . . . pronto? Let's say you've got a big deadline coming up. The pressure is on and you have to deliver the goods. But the amount of work is scary. And your project is only one item on everyone's looooong to-do list. How to get your team pumped and moving?

POWER: Use authority to emphasize the importance of the goal.
PASSION: Give emotional support and praise for everyone's efforts.
MYSTIQUE: Offer a secret reward when the project is delivered on time.

PRESTIGE: Emphasize how this project's success will enhance the team's reputation.

ALERT: Keep everyone on track with specific details and deadlines.

INNOVATION: Present the project as a challenging experiment—almost an adventure.

TRUST: Remind them how you've consistently reached difficult goals together.

Think of the challenges facing your team right now. Go through the Advantages, one by one, and see how you could solve the challenge in new ways to get better results.

I have yet to find a profession that can't apply the seven Advantages to improve results, whether the industry is hearing aid distributors or dental equipment manufacturers, accountants or software developers, restaurant owners, kitchen supply manufacturers, or spa owners. Sometimes an industry is an obvious fit, for instance, you can quickly imagine how a travel agent can apply the seven Advantages to offering seven types of vacations. Or a hairstylist can apply the seven Advantages to fashion. Other times, however, the application isn't quite so obvious. For example, the challenges facing family physicians can be literally life or death.

A recent study by the Texas Medical Association found that 1 in 3 physicians experiences burnout at any given time. This growing burnout leads to increased risk for liability. Worse, it can lead to mistakes in medication dosing. To solve this problem, the study outlined the top three strategies for lowering stress and risk:

The first recommendation: *Enhance the patient-physician relationship.*

The second recommendation: *Improve communication.*

The third: *Avoid medication errors.*

By now you can probably already see how fascination could help a physician achieve the first and second strategies, because they're tied to relationships and communication. But what about the third, "avoid medication errors"?

When I presented to thousands of doctors at the American Academy of Family Physicians, I joked that although I didn't go to medical school, I would gamely show them how to apply their individual Advantages to get patients to pay attention when being prescribed a particular medication, and then remember to take it as directed.

Here were my seven Advantages for helping family physicians make sure that patients take their medication:

EXAMPLE: USING THE SEVEN ADVANTAGES TO IMPROVE PATIENT MEDICATION RESULTS

POWER: Give strong, clear direction for why and how to take the medication.

PASSION: Get the patient emotionally involved in the treatment.

MYSTIQUE: Listen to concerns before offering research and objective information.

PRESTIGE: Highlight how this medication will improve quality of life or help them reach a goal.

ALERT: Identify problems that can arise if medication is not taken as instructed.

INNOVATION: Offer a variety of treatment options, and let them get involved.

TRUST: Shift their perspective to the long term, such as their family history or future.

UNDERSTANDING CO-WORKERS AND EMPLOYEES

In addition to helping you finding the *right people for a role*, you also want to find the *right role for each person.**

An employee with a **Power Advantage** is probably feeling ready for a promotion, because she tends to feel most comfortable in a position of authority. Don't micromanage this person unless you want to see her either backlash or

---

*Here's a way to more accurately identify your next team members, based on your needs. Go to the Archetype Matrix (it's the color chart on the inside front and back covers of this book). Look across the horizontal rows. Those are the seven different Advantages. Ask yourself: Which adjectives describe the qualities I am seeking? Do I want the adjectives associated with Trust, or Alert, or Prestige? Prescreen applicants to find candidates who possess those Advantages.

leave for another job. Instead, give her room to prove herself, and then evaluate results together.

Employees with a **Passion Advantage** want to be right in the heart of the activity. Properly motivated and coached, they'll engage customers because they naturally understand how to relate to people's emotional needs. They excel in introductions and presentations, because they can form bonds more quickly than Advantages such as Mystique and Alert. Make sure that they understand your expectations, because their expressive nature and intuitive skill mean they might tend to "wing it" rather than follow protocol. A recommendation: They thrive on face-to-face human contact. Give them plenty of opportunity to collaborate. Ignored, their naturally high energy will putter out.

Mystique Advantage means that this employee wants to focus on the results without a lot of fuss or drama. You won't always know what he is thinking or doing; however, you will see all the "proof in the pudding." Stand back, advise as needed, but direct with a light touch. He doesn't want to belabor discussions about process, and usually shies away from on-the-spot group brainstorming. His skill at complex mental assignments means he often excels in information-driven roles, usually behind the scenes.

An employee with a **Prestige Advantage** aims for tangible evidence of success. Because she seeks to exceed expectations, it's important to help her by giving clear goals, with clearly outlined expectations and a way to self-check progress. Incentive programs will work extremely well to inspire exceptional efforts; these don't necessarily need to be extravagant, but rather, symbolic demonstrations that the employee is overdelivering for you. One last word of caution: She will be demoralized, if not wounded, by public criticism. Reprimand her carefully, and praise as often as warranted.

For employees with the **Alert Advantage**, you'll want to provide plenty of structure with a predictable schedule and policies. If you suddenly change your own vacation plans, or schedule a last-minute presentation, you might see them feeling flustered and struggling to regain balance. They succeed when allowed to map out a plan, with desired results and contingencies, and then get a group to adhere to the plan. These employees often work well in HR, billing, and other jobs that require control of details.

Want to empower employees with an **Innovation Advantage**? Steer their natural creative energy into productive places. Coach them with clear rules when necessary, but also give room to explore. Give them space to show you what could be improved, and how you can rethink your company's old habits. They have the ability give you solutions you'd never have dreamed possible. They'll work best in roles that encourage forward-thinking invention, such as design or new business outreach. Many entrepreneurs have a high use of Innovation.

With a primary **Trust Advantage**, employees want to buy in for the long haul. These folks are not looking for the quick win at work; they want stable, lasting relationships. While their personalities might not be as expressive as those with the Passion or Prestige Advantages, they do exude stability, so customers become comfortable with them. These employees will deliver dependable results, on time, completed as planned. You might find, however, that they are uncomfortable with change, or with being pushed to perform at a higher level. They're built for consistency and repetition.

If hiring someone new isn't an option, that's okay. Get a clear look at what Advantages already exist on your team, so you can maximize those. Also get a clear look at the pitfalls, so you can take steps to prevent them. Here's an example of preventing pitfalls.

I'm a Catalyst, and my husband, Ed, is a Maverick Leader. That means we both have Innovation as part of our top two Advantages. We are *very* good at developing ideas, and also *very* good at misplacing house keys. Sometimes neither one of us carries a key, and we've been known to lock ourselves out of a house or two. Before we depart our house, we'll say: "Do you have the house key? . . . Are you sure?" (If you and your spouse both have a high use of Trust or Alert, you don't need to ask twice, because you probably both have two sets of house keys!)

INCREASE THE ADVANTAGES OF YOUR TEAM

Rather than trying to get employees to change (which doesn't work for long), there's another way. Help them become more of who they already are. Once you identify the Advantages that your team is using, you can help each person succeed by dialing up their existing traits. Rather than training people to follow a formula (and trying to force-fit them into a mold), you can support them in adding value in the way that is most effective and natural for them.

There are seven Advantages, but one does not trump another. They each bring a different benefit. Each Advantage follows a distinct pattern. Each has pros and cons. Each has potential blind spots. There is no right or wrong here, but it's important to align people's natural inclinations with the goals of a team.

You wouldn't want to build a team with *only* Power, or *only* Trust. When a group has an extremely high concentration of just one or two Advantages, it tends to be exaggeratedly strong in specific areas, but very weak in others. (When it comes to Advantages, there can definitely be "too much of a good thing." Learn about a personality's potential downside in the section on "Double Troubles.")

Every Advantage has an important role within an organization. Just as employers should seek diversity in gender and backgrounds, so should they also understand the Advantages used by their existing team members and potential hires, in order to build teams with a balanced and healthy interplay of perspectives.

PREDICTING A TEAM'S COLLECTIVE ADVANTAGE

With a high concentration of this Advantage . . .	. . . the group will be most likely to succeed in these situations:
Power	When given a shared goal with plenty of room.
Passion	When building relationships, empathizing with others, and encouraging the team.
Mystique	When "cracking the code" on complex, technical projects.
Prestige	When given clear expectations and ambitious standards (such as exceeding a sales quota).
Alert	When given careful, practical execution that doesn't get off track.
Innovation	When tasked with developing groundbreaking solutions.
Trust	When consistently and gradually building results over time.

When two people work together, their primary Advantages will combine and communicate according to certain patterns. What follows are guidelines for pairing people with different primary Advantages.

HOW PRESTIGE TEAMS WITH OTHERS

HOW PRESTIGE PERSONALITIES RELATE TO OTHER ADVANTAGES

INNOVATION	Working with Innovation types can be very productive when they inspire better results through creativity.
PASSION	You generally find it easy to bond with Passion personalities. Together, you can build a team spirit to achieve results for the group.
POWER	A natural combination. Join with energetic Power leaders to achieve big goals together.
PRESTIGE	Cooperating with other Prestige personalities may feel like a perfect fit. Too much, however, can make your organization brittle and overly competitive.
TRUST	While you can become frustrated with the consistency of Trust, these partners will add stability.
MYSTIQUE	Be careful not to overshadow Mystique personalities. They're astute thinkers who can help you achieve your objectives.
ALERT	You share your attention to detail with Alert personalities. They help you stay grounded in pursuit of a goal.

HOW PASSION TEAMS WITH OTHERS

HOW PASSION PERSONALITIES RELATE TO OTHER ADVANTAGES

INNOVATION	You share a creative spirit with an Innovation personality, inspiring each other to develop new ideas.
PASSION	You quickly bond with other Passion personalities—just be careful to stay focused on company objectives.
POWER	You share an energetic approach to your job, and steered in the right direction, can make a highly productive team.
PRESTIGE	You'll enjoy working with Prestige personalities when they help you stay focused on a goal, and improve your quality of deliverables.
TRUST	A Trust personality will help you build consistent messages and develop loyal relationships.
MYSTIQUE	It may take time to build rapport with Mystique personalities, but their rational communication is a useful balance to your spontaneity.
ALERT	You might resist having someone watch over your impulsive nature, but partnering with the Alert Advantage can help you watch the details and stay on schedule.

HOW TRUST TEAMS WITH OTHERS

HOW TRUST PERSONALITIES RELATE TO OTHER ADVANTAGES

INNOVATION	To change and innovate, work with a person who uses Innovation. They help you see new approaches.
PASSION	While you might initially find the Passion types to be overly enthusiastic, on a team you can feed off their positive outlook to support the group.
POWER	Power leaders tend to take command more quickly than you. Join with them as long as they do not try to dominate you.
PRESTIGE	By partnering with a Prestige type you can raise standards of the team and exceed rather than just meet objectives.
TRUST	Working with other consistent Trust types will feel natural to you. Just be careful you don't get stuck in a rut together.
MYSTIQUE	Like the Mystique personalities, you are not showy or aggressive, and prefer facts to emotion.
ALERT	Working with an Alert personality will help you motor through difficult projects and avoid issues along the way.

HOW MYSTIQUE TEAMS WITH OTHERS

HOW MYSTIQUE PERSONALITIES RELATE TO OTHER ADVANTAGES

INNOVATION	Put someone on your team with Innovation whose creativity can help you discover new approaches.
PASSION	The Passion Advantage is valuable to you because it sparks warmth and enthusiasm within the team and with clients.
POWER	You can be a formidable team with Power types. Just be careful they don't overshadow you.
PRESTIGE	You'll profit from working with the Prestige Advantage, since they can help you get recognition for your work.
TRUST	Trust types prefer working in the background, like you. Make sure you have a "front man."
MYSTIQUE	In teams with other Mystique types, you tend to work independently and not collaborate closely. Make sure you benefit from each other's ideas and experiences.
ALERT	An Alert personality is focused, like you. Together you will keep your eyes on the practical side of things. Just make sure you are inclusive of others such as Passion.

HOW POWER TEAMS WITH OTHERS

HOW POWER PERSONALITIES RELATE TO OTHER ADVANTAGES

INNOVATION	You may find the Innovation type disruptive at times, because they want to explore. Yet their perspective can bring innovation to your outcome.
PASSION	You form an energetic team with Passion personalities. Together you motivate the team to reach higher goals.
POWER	Join with other Power types to exponentially increase your momentum as you feed off each other's energy, as long as you don't get in a struggle.
PRESTIGE	You share a strong self-motivation with Prestige types. Together you can go after serious goals.
TRUST	Trust personalities can help you build ongoing and dependable loyalty with clients, suppliers, and staff.
MYSTIQUE	Your strong opinions may overshadow Mystique personalities. Be careful to listen when they make observations.
ALERT	You have a lot of energy and momentum; working with an Alert personality will help you fine-tune execution.

HOW ALERT TEAMS WITH OTHERS

HOW ALERT PERSONALITIES RELATE TO OTHER ADVANTAGES

INNOVATION	Having someone with the Innovation Advantage on your team will keep the ideas flowing. It's up to you to keep them grounded.
PASSION	Passion types may seem too "in the moment" for your careful style, but take advantage of their positive spirit to win buy-in for your projects.
POWER	Join forces with the Power Advantage to accomplish big tasks on time and within budget.
PRESTIGE	Partnering with Prestige personalities will accelerate your performance. Together you'll deliver faster results.
TRUST	You share a preference for tried-and-true with Trust personalities. Be sure to tweak processes to achieve even better results.
MYSTIQUE	It's an easy fit for you to work with Mystique personalities, because you both make pragmatic decisions.
ALERT	While it seems easy to run projects with other Alert types, don't forget to watch for opportunities as well as risks.

HOW INNOVATION TEAMS WITH OTHERS

HOW INNOVATION PERSONALITIES RELATE TO OTHER ADVANTAGES

INNOVATION	Working with fellow Innovation types will be invigorating for you. But be sure to stay on track and on budget.
PASSION	You feed off energetic Passion types, and they share your zest for the creative process. Be careful to remain focused on objectives.
POWER	Teaming up with Power types can be stimulating for you, but be careful that their strong personality doesn't stifle your creativity.
PRESTIGE	You can thrive when working with Prestige personalities because they implement your ideas with an energetic force.
TRUST	Trust types can seem stuck or traditional for you. They prefer tested methods. Yet together, you can combine consistency with out-of-the-box thinking.
MYSTIQUE	Like Mystique types, you are constantly thinking of solutions. The difference is, yours might feel surprising or even challenging.
ALERT	You may find their attitude tiring, but the natural cautiousness of Alert types helps you consider your ideas more carefully.

HIRING BASED ON ADVANTAGES

Consider new hires in terms of Advantages, rather than just skills and experience.

> **HINT: On the Archetype Matrix, find the adjectives that describe the qualities you are seeking in a job applicant, a committee seat, or other role. Then fill the role with a preference for those Advantages. If you want detail, you might screen prospects to find someone for Alert. If you want a big personality who can quickly draw in prospects, you might search for an applicant with Passion or Power.**
>
> **What's the ROI of hiring based on Advantages? CommonWealth Planning, a financial services firm, began using the Fascination Advantage for hiring, to identify each candidate's highest value during the hiring process.**
>
> **Two years before, the firm interviewed 530 potential hires, and of those, hired just sixteen employees (3%). But after identifying each candidate's Advantages, and honing the talent pool, they doubled the percentage of hires. In fact, they interviewed less than half the number of recruits in the first place, because they could then hire smarter based on each candidate's highest and best contributions to the firm.**
>
> **Joe Counts, the firm's president, says that the team-based selling process has saved his company countless hours in hiring—and has boosted sales by almost 50%.**

When you're in charge of hiring for a position, make sure you're not biased toward someone with whom you feel an immediate connection. The qualities that make it difficult for you to "click" with someone could very well be the attributes you most need. If you only hire people whom you like in an interview, you could be building a lopsided team.

When I recruit and interview for office staff, before looking at résumés, I look at the candidate's Fascination Advantage report. For day-to-day operations, I seek out people with Alert, Trust, and Mystique. Why do I seek these

Advantages for my staff? I score low on Alert, Trust, and Mystique. Here is the average population of dormant Advantages.

TRUST

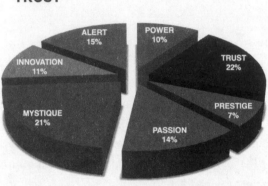

My dormant **advantage** is TRUST

22% of the people who took the Fascination Advantage test also have **TRUST** as their dormant advantage.

Alert is the language of *details*. Mystique is the language of *listening*. And Trust is the language of *stability*. On a team, these Advantages are well-suited to execute and implement.

An example is The Defender personality:

The Defender = Power + Alert
The Defender's three adjectives: *proactive, cautionary, strong-willed*

As their name suggests, Defenders add value by defending others. They are *proactive* in seeing what's on the horizon. They are *cautionary* in watching over their team, company, and clients. And they're *strong-willed*, unafraid to take steps to protect the greater good.

If I hire a Defender as an executive assistant, the more that she can *defend* me from getting stuck in the weeds, the more valuable she becomes. This complements my Passion + Innovation Advantages. I'm a Catalyst, and therefore most productive when developing big ideas. My staff helps me make sure that

I can stay focused on high-level vision rather than getting so wrapped up in details that I lose the bigger picture.

When I support my staff in applying their own Advantages, they become more valuable—and they help me become more valuable, too.

Do I enjoy working with other Passion personalities? Yes! But it's not necessarily productive. When Passion personalities work together, they tend to focus more on the relationship than the result. When I hire for Passion, I'm replicating myself, rather than optimizing my company's outcome. Are you unintentionally building teams that replicate you?

If your team is not getting the outcome you desire, and you're unsure why, find out the Fascination Advantage of each person in your group by having them take the assessment. Map these Advantages on the "do-it-yourself heat map" found in Part III. It's entirely possible that your group lacks certain Advantages.

By supporting and accentuating each person's natural traits, companies can increase engagement. Engaged employees are more satisfied, and more likely to satisfy customers, which in turn leads to greater revenue and higher goals.

UP NEXT: CREATE YOUR ANTHEM

So far, you've learned about Advantages, and how the world sees you. You've begun to understand your peers, so you can set up your whole team for success. Now roll up your sleeves, and pull out a pen and paper. Be thinking about this in very practical terms. Get ready to experiment and discover.

We're about to enter the doors of the Fascination Laboratory. Inside, you'll explore new ways to see yourself, through the science of fascination.

YOUR ANTHEM: THE TAGLINE FOR YOUR PERSONALITY

THE FASCINATION LABORATORY

We're about to enter the Fascination Laboratory. Together, we'll discover your highest distinct value through the science of fascination.

A laboratory is a place to research and experiment, test and retest, and ultimately, create breakthroughs. During the next steps of our journey, we'll be collaborating side by side, identifying how to communicate most persuasively by applying your natural personality Advantages.

This is *your* laboratory. You'll be experimenting with new ways to describe yourself, and what makes you different than everyone else. I'll give you the tools and research you'll need to make it simple and enlightening (not to mention fun). Together, we'll pinpoint the best of how the world sees you.

As with any laboratory, our goal is to achieve a breakthrough. This will happen when you discover your own highest distinct value. Apply this value throughout your work and life, and you will grow your business, create better relationships, rise above the competition, and become intensely valuable to those who matter most.

Welcome Inside Our Fascination Laboratory Headquarters

My company, How To Fascinate, discovers how the world sees you at your best, so that you can become more valuable every time you communicate.

Our team applies the science and art of fascination by combining proprietary market research with communication and branding principles.

We work with high performers: the individuals, leaders, teams, trainers, and organizations that want to become most valuable in their area of expertise. This book includes two core pieces of our curriculum: First, the Fascination Advantage online assessment, which measures your key points of difference, and the Anthem method, which highlights your defining personality differences. You'll create your Anthem in just a few pages.

Our ongoing research includes different industries and professional levels, from global corporations to university students to CEO mastermind groups. Every day, we're developing new ways to grow your business and career around your key points of difference. Find our newest discoveries and programs at HowToFascinate.com.

You can become a more influential communicator by tapping into your personality Advantages. Whether or not you realize it, you've probably had these Advantages your entire life, ready for you to discover and use. They help you become the most valuable you.

YOUR MOST VALUABLE .1%

As much as we might like to think that we're all 100% special and unique, we're not. We're 99.9% average. Your human DNA is 99.9% the same as everyone else's. Only a minuscule amount defines our differences. As the *New York Times* puts it, "our individuality hangs on only .1 percent."

From a genetic perspective, you and I are astonishingly similar. Your eyes might be *blue* while mine are *brown*, but we both have two of them, and they're located on approximately the same spot on our body. And yet, hidden within a vast expanse of genetic monotony, small details have the ability to make us dramatically different. Idiosyncrasies might seem trivial at first, but they have extraordinary implications over the long run.

The same is true of our personalities. Like our genes, we have only a few truly singular characteristics. The other 99.9% is more of a commodity. Yet while there's not much that distinguishes you from everyone else, there is something. And it turns out, that something is more than enough.

YOUR LITTLE ZONE OF GENIUS

Your .1% is your distinct value. It describes the best of how the world sees you, and how you are most likely to rise above and stand out. It's your own little zone of genius.

This is good news and bad news.

First, the bad news. Struggling to marginally improve the less valuable parts of yourself won't work. At least, it won't work without a lot of strain and expense.

For example, if you're not a naturally gifted athlete, it's easy to see why you shouldn't spend decades pursuing a career as a tennis pro or downhill skier. Likewise, in your career, struggling to improve your areas of averageness can only take you so far—and it can cost you years of wasted effort and opportunity.

Much about you is a commodity. These are your *least* valuable traits—unlikely to ever lead you to a wellspring. In these areas, *increased effort* will not yield substantially *increased results*—at least, not increased enough to overcome the three threats. (Your commodity traits are usually linked to your *dormant* Advantage.)

Now the good news: Your built-in Advantages hold real promise for the way you can become invaluable and irreplaceable to others. Small details make you different, and in the right circumstances, they make you *better*. Your Advantages reveal how you will be most likely to build a prosperous and fulfilling career.

Instead of trying to "fix" the parts of yourself that are a commodity, you can achieve more by just feeding that tiny but extraordinary streak. Don't change who you are, become *more* of who you are.

If you're feeling frustrated by trying to be all things to all people, this is a relief. You can stop trying to be that. Instead of making major changes, you can tweak the pieces that will give you maximum leverage. Find one or two details that distinguish you from other people, and then clearly communicate those details, over and over. The more that you can identify your .1% difference and apply it in the right places, the more valuable you become.

FASCINATION NIRVANA

If you could build a fascination nirvana, here's what it would look like: Your career would be built entirely around your .1% of uniqueness. Work would feel like an endless source of inspiration. You'd constantly be in the flow. You'd be intensely valuable. You'd live inside your primary and secondary Advantages. This would energize and elevate you. You could raise your prices and attract all the right clients. In this idealistic world, you'd never be forced to call upon your dormant Advantage, which means you'd be less exhausted. Imagine . . . no quicksand to pull down your efforts!

In reality, we don't live in a vacuum. It's unrealistic to hope for this nirvana (just as it's unrealistic to hope for germ-free jungle gyms, or garbage cans that merrily float themselves to the curb). We have to deal with situations that drain us and people who irk us.

Yet you can fine-tune your work and your life around your Advantages. Professionally, these are your most attractive personality features.

Physically, you probably already know your "best feature" (perhaps hazel eyes or wavy hair). You can play up your most attractive feature with certain styles or colors. When you do, people probably compliment you on this feature. The rest of you might be 99.9% average, but when you pinpoint your defining traits, you can showcase them. The same is true for your personality.

> You don't need to change into a *different person*.
> You just need to be different than *other people*.

Earlier, I described that by applying your highest distinct value, you can stand out in a crowded market and leverage your natural Advantages. These small but critical details differentiate you from everyone else.

The more you can elevate these characteristics, the higher you rise on the value chain. This is your most valuable you.

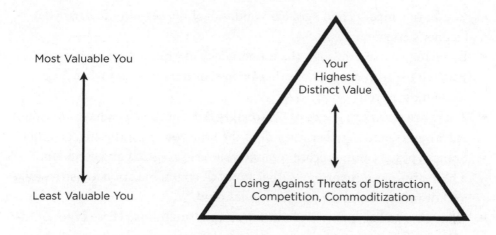

Your personality is more valuable than any possession, more valuable than your stock portfolio or home or retirement plan.

For instance, if you're a business owner, your personality helps you grow your business without spending more money on marketing, without getting a new lease on an office space, without hiring more people. Your personality doesn't depreciate over time. It doesn't require overhead or management because it's built right into you. Yet to fully monetize your personality, you must fully apply it.

In this section, we'll start to see how you can become most worthy of attention, and triumph over the three threats by applying your highest value.

We've covered a lot in Parts I and II. If you'd like to review the background about the major trends shaping communication, turn back to Part I. For an in-depth review on the Fascination Advantage system, go to Part II. Let's take a quick look back at the highlights we've covered so far:

- It's not enough to only know *how you see the world*. You also have to realize the signals that you're intentionally or unintentionally sending to the world, because that shapes how the world sees you.
- Every time you communicate, you face three threats: *distraction*, *competition*, and *commoditization*. You can overcome these threats if you fascinate your listener by adding distinct value.

- You have a nine-second "golden window" of opportunity to earn your listener's attention.
- By seeing yourself through the modern lens of branding, you can see yourself through the eyes of other people, and understand what they value most in you.
- There are seven categories of personality Advantages. You have two main Advantages, and together, they describe how you naturally engage others.
- Some types of communication make you feel energized and confident. These are your *wellsprings*. Other types of communication are stressful and draining, and these are your *quicksand*.
- Your personality is custom-built for certain situations. These types of interactions give you a prime opportunity to impress and influence others, because they allow you to accentuate your main Advantages.
- To become more successful, you do not have to change who you are. You have to become *more* of who you are.

Readers of my book *Fascinate* will remember the research around how fascination drives connection and communication. When you fascinate someone, they're more likely to remember you, like you, and buy from you. Once you capture their interest, they become focused on you, which allows you to more effectively sway the outcome of your interaction.

How is your personality likely to get others into this state of focused attention? There's no one *right* way to fascinate. Over the long run, shy or low-key personalities can be as fascinating as the most charismatic ones. For instance, the steady Trust personalities have an edge over the vibrant Passion personalities in situations that call for accountability. Those with Mystique have an upper hand over those with Power in environments that demand an intellectual touch with surgical precision.

By now you've already done your Fascination Advantage assessment and viewed your online report (and if you haven't, turn to the end of the book for your private invitation code). Take a moment to review your customized online report detailing your Advantages and Archetype.

Your Primary, Secondary, and Dormant Advantages

A quick refresher on the pieces of your Fascination Advantage report:

Your *primary* Advantage: This is your most compelling mode of communicating. When you communicate using your primary Advantage, you're more likely to make a positive impression.

Your *secondary* Advantage: Every person mostly uses two Advantages. Your *secondary* Advantage is the one that describes how you use your primary Advantage.

Your *dormant* Advantage: This is your most exhausting form of communication. It's how you are least likely to surpass others. Tread carefully in these areas, because this form of communication will cost you a disproportionate amount of time and energy.

Your Archetype: Your top two Advantages combine, forming your Archetype. This is how the world sees you.

Archetype = Primary Advantage + Secondary Advantage

Your Archetype identifies your differentiating qualities. Each Archetype has different patterns, and different ways of adding value.

Once you know your Archetype, you can quickly unlock the formula for your personality's tagline, also known as your **Anthem**.

YOUR ANTHEM

You do not have to be perfect at *everything*. But you do have to be extraordinary at *something*. Your Anthem lights the way to your most extraordinary qualities, so that you can focus on what you naturally do best.

Successful brands distinguish themselves from the competition, often with only a mere sliver of a competitive difference. Similarly, we will distill your personality's key defining qualities into just a few words, summarizing your key benefits.

The Perfect 9-Second Communication

Taglines are an exquisitely efficient piece of communication. They can convey a mammoth volume of information, distilling the essence of an entire company into a micro statement. Taglines offer a bite-size snack version of the buffet meal.

Overtly or subtly, a tagline can communicate the product benefit, the company's priorities, or what a consumer will think or feel as a result of buying the product. They can even encapsulate the unspoken insecurities or aspirations behind a purchase. For instance, L'Oréal hair color has used the same tagline for many years: "Because I'm worth it." This deceptively simple phrase actually speaks to much more than hair color. At the time this tagline launched in the 1960s, most ads were narrated by men. Women had a more subservient role in advertising. With a cheeky dash of unapologetic narcissism this tagline gave women permission to flaunt their self-worth. Note the wording of "I'm worth it" rather than "you're worth it." The product is worth more, as is the woman who buys it.

Taglines tell you why to invest your time and money in a certain product. They establish what makes one brand different from another.

You probably have a few taglines emblazoned onto your memory from your youth, even if they've been long retired from actual use. Remember how M&Ms promised to "melt in your mouth, not in your hands"? Lucky Charms were "magically delicious." The state of Virginia claimed, "Virginia is for lovers."* I described earlier that BMW has been "The Ultimate Driving Machine," while MINI Cooper wants us to get out and explore, with "Let's Motor."

Brands understand the importance of telling a big story in a small sound bite. In a distracted, competitive, and commoditized world, people don't have time to read a wordy letter or sit through a drawn-out presentation. You might prefer to introduce yourself with a full-length résumé, but in reality, your audience probably has the same attention span as a goldfish: nine seconds.

Your Anthem solves this problem. This very short phrase is usually just

---

*Which is a little ironic, considering that Queen Elizabeth I was "the Virgin Queen."

two or three words. It describes *how you are different*, and *what you do best*.

A *tagline* is a shortcut to how a brand is most likely to add distinct value to its consumers. In the same way, an *Anthem* is your shortcut to how you are most likely to add distinct value to your co-workers, customers, and your company.

Since the start of my career, when I was an advertising copywriter, taglines have been a big part of how I've delivered my highest value. I'm no longer in advertising, but I still write taglines. Today, instead of writing taglines for brands, I'll help *you* write your own tagline.

Few people know how to front-load their value. I want you to be one of those who do.

For instance, before a crucial webinar, many people will spend hours reviewing the numbers in the slide deck, yet not give a thought to how they'll hold their listeners' attention during the call. In the days leading up to a job interview, applicants obsess over the "skills" section of their résumé, yet fail to even consider the more critical need to let their most outstanding and desirable personality traits shine through.

It's Not Their Responsibility; It's Yours.

It's not your manager's responsibility to figure out how you can help solve a problem. It's not your client's job to know what makes you different. Same goes for your co-workers, your customers, and your audience. Don't expect them to automatically recognize your value. It's not their job. It's yours. Cut to the chase. Get to the bottom line. Make it easy for your listener to understand what you're offering.

If this news makes you feel stressed or confused, that's understandable. Now the pressure is on *you*, rather than on your *listener*.

Your Anthem is immediate shorthand for how your personality is primed to add value. This is the heart of a strong first impression, and lasting loyalty.

Psst . . . Here's a Secret Shortcut

Ever struggled to find the exact words to describe yourself? Most of us do. It's easy to feel paralyzed when pressured to find the *perfect* words.

To make it very easy to for you to communicate your highest and best value, I'll give you the words and phrases to illustrate who you are, at your best. In Part II, you'll find dozens of useful phrases to help you describe yourself, based on your top two Advantages and your Archetype. The videos inside your online report are especially helpful in pointing out catchphrases that capture the best of your personality.

In a few pages, we'll use these words to create your Anthem.

Unlike an elevator pitch, your Anthem is not a "pitch." Unlike a mission statement, your Anthem is not a projection of who you hope to become at some point. It's who you already are, today, at your most valuable.

At one point or another, you will need to communicate your credibility in some way: in an interview, or on a proposal. That's where the Anthem method comes in. If you are an employer, this method will help employees to establish clearer roles, and build credibility with customers.

My certified trainers and I have done this exercise with all types of organizations, from major global corporations to intimate executive groups. It has been included in coursework for colleges and universities, and with community-based nonprofits including YMCA and the Red Cross. No matter how big the organization or how small the team, everyone faces the same problem: *How do I fascinate my listeners?*

The ability to fascinate is at the heart of influence. Robert Cialdini describes this principle in his book *Influence: The Psychology of Persuasion*: "You and I exist in an extraordinarily complicated stimulus environment, easily the most rapidly moving and complex that has ever existed on this planet. To deal with it, we need shortcuts. We can't be expected to recognize and analyze all the aspects in each person, event, and situation we encounter in even one day. We haven't the time, energy or capacity for it. . . . As the stimuli saturating our lives continue to grow more intricate and variable, we will have to depend increasingly on our shortcuts to handle them all."

Your Anthem is this shortcut to maximizing your influence.

You can apply your Anthem to update your social media profiles. Reinforce why you deserve a promotion. Fill out a job application. Introduce yourself in a way that makes listeners eager to hear what you'll tell them next.

Yet on a higher level, your Anthem can steer your entire career, and your life.

Here's how we'll create your Anthem.

THE ANTHEM METHOD

STEP 1: Pick one adjective (how you are different)
STEP 2: Pick one noun (what you do best)
STEP 3: Bring the words together to create your Anthem

With an Anthem as your tagline, you'll make better use of what you already have, and who you already are.

CHAPTER 6

DISCOVER YOUR DIFFERENCES

Earlier, I described how a 3-D movie screen looks like a chaotic swirl of confusing images—until you put on those plastic glasses, and everything whips into focus. In this section, we'll be putting on those 3-D glasses, seeing your personality through a new lens, revealing the hidden patterns behind how the world sees you.

Every Archetype has a favorable position in certain scenarios, and disadvantages in others. In the coming pages, we'll identify the types of situations in which you are most likely to excel, and find ways to re-create those situations as often as possible.

First, we'll identify the adjectives most strongly associated with your Archetype. These adjectives indicate where you are most likely to be a high performer. By concentrating on these attributes, you are more likely to positively influence how the world sees you. Think of these as your built-in specialty.

YOUR SPECIALTY ADJECTIVES

A specialty is an area of highest distinction and performance. For instance, a doctor might have a specialty in orthopedics or internal medicine. A restaurant's specialty is the dish for which they are most famous or acclaimed. An artist's specialty describes their area of greatest expertise, such as oil painting or engraving.

Whether you realize it or not, your personality has a specialty. You can find your specialty by looking at the Archetype Matrix, and seeing which adjectives are linked to your Archetype.

If your Archetype is The Guardian (Power + Trust), for example, you are naturally suited to add value in situations in which you can be *prominent, genuine, sure-footed.*

For The Blue Chip (Prestige + Trust) you're most likely to communicate clearly and effectively when your communication is *classic, established, best-in-class.*

The Editor-In-Chief (Alert + Prestige) can best support her team when she can focus on being *productive, skilled,* and *detailed.*

THE EDITOR-IN-CHIEF
Productive • Skilled
Detailed

As an example of how different Archetypes compare and contrast, let's take a look at two job candidates interviewing for the position of project manager.

The first candidate, Laura, is a Change Agent, which means she has a primary Power Advantage (she communicates with strength) and secondary Innovation Advantage (she shares untraditional ideas). As you can see on the Archetype Matrix, Laura's three top attributes are: *inventive*, *untraditional*, and *self-propelled*. These adjectives describe how she communicates differently than others. Even during Laura's interview, she can use these adjectives to separate herself from the herd of other candidates. She describes how her *inventive* spirit led her to a faster process to develop new products. People admired her *untraditional* solutions, and she was selected to spearhead new ventures. In meetings and conversations, her *self-propelled* work ethic meant that her boss didn't need to babysit her progress. The more Laura's role allows her to be *inventive*, *untraditional*, and *self-propelled*, the more pronounced her distinct value.

The next candidate, Josh, is a Beloved. His primary is Passion, so he interacts with warmth. His secondary is Trust, so he's stable and reliable. Josh's adjectives on the Matrix: *nurturing*, *loyal*, and *sincere*. Those who've worked with Josh report that he is a true team player, with an even-keeled approach that makes everyone comfortable. Like Laura, Josh could also apply his adjectives during his interview to describe his style of interaction. By *nurturing* his team's projects from beginning to end, he builds *loyal* relationships with co-workers. Even though his workplace can become a pressure cooker as deadlines approach, Josh's *sincere* approach binds the team together through tough stages of the project.

Laura is creatively feisty, while Josh is more agreeable and conservative. Laura wants to take the ball and run independently, while Josh is a solid team player. Each will contribute different benefits to the team, even if they are technically doing the same job.

Neither is necessarily a "better" hire than the other—it all depends on what this company wants to achieve with this particular project management position. Does the company want an imaginative force, or someone who can execute according to the prescribed plan? Different specialties achieve different results.

If she tried really hard, Laura could probably adapt her spirited style to mimic Josh's approach, but it would make her feel awkward and unfulfilled. Same for Josh. He cannot out-Laura Laura. If his manager wanted him to frequently rattle off new ideas in meetings, that would be exhausting and inauthentic for him.

Employees are most fulfilled and successful when their company doesn't try to change who they are, but rather, supports them in becoming more of who they naturally are, at their best.

Here's another example, with a commercial real estate advisor named Craig. His Archetype is The Good Citizen. Craig has a modest demeanor, rarely jumping into the center of attention. He's *principled* in his approach with his clients, acting according to a strong moral compass. He's *prepared* for every meeting. He's *conscientious* about delivering for his clients.

These snapshots might seem like a random assortment, but they all point to a consistent framework. Craig is The Good Citizen (Trust + Alert). His three attributes are *principled*, *prepared*, and *conscientious*. He excels when given the opportunity to build a long-term plan, and then execute it. That's his distinct value, and his clients treasure him for it. If you want a real estate advisor with the moral ballast to stay on track during tricky negotiations, someone you can rely upon through the ups and downs of a volatile market, Craig is your guy.

Unlike opinionated Archetypes such as The Maestro, or cutting-edge Archetypes such as The Trendsetter, Craig's communication will be prudent. He never overpromises or oversells. Don't ask him for razzle-dazzle showmanship.

Craig's team will set him up for success by knowing what his specialized value is. Your team will set *you* up for success by doing the same thing. Before anyone can know your value, however, you have to identify exactly what your value is.

Do you know your intrinsic highest value? You're about to find out. These "warm-up exercises" will get you ready to write your Anthem, beginning the process of distilling your personality down to its essence. Take out a pen and paper, and we'll get started.

WARM-UP EXERCISE 1: YOUR ADJECTIVES

Flip to the color Archetype Matrix (inside the front and back covers). Take a look at your own Archetype. You'll see three adjectives.

These adjectives describe your Archetype's key differences—how the world is likely to see you as different than other Archetypes, and more valuable, in your own way.

In the above examples, for instance, the three adjectives of Laura's Archetype are *inventive, untraditional,* and *self-propelled.*

Josh's adjectives are *nurturing*, *loyal*, and *sincere*. Here is what these adjectives look like on the Matrix:

THE
BELOVED
Nurturing • Loyal
Sincere

Now let's make a quick list of your adjectives. Go to the Matrix, and write down the three adjectives for *your* Archetype:

Adjective #1: _____

Adjective #2: _____

Adjective #3: _____

You've begun to uncover your key differences, to see how you can avoid blending in. Let's go a little further, and see how you are *already* applying these adjectives in your work and life.

WARM-UP EXERCISE 2: APPLY YOUR ADJECTIVES

In the following exercise, you'll start to see how these three adjectives already describe your interactions around the office, with clients, or even with your family. As an example, let's return to Laura, The Change Agent we met earlier. Her primary is Power, secondary Innovation. We'll see how her three adjectives describe how she adds distinct value at work as The Change Agent:

Inventive: She brings unexpected ideas to each meeting.

Untraditional: She can shortcut a traditional process by finding the "back door."

Self-propelled: She doesn't require management; she is self-directed with goals and projects.

Certain personality traits hold your greatest potential. How do your differences make you singularly suited to solve certain problems, and overcome certain challenges? How do you help co-workers on projects, or add your own touch to special occasions?

For each adjective in your Archetype, write down one way in which this describes how you communicate at work.

How adjective #1 describes your distinct value: _____

_____

How adjective #2 describes your distinct value: _____

_____

How adjective #3 describes your distinct value: _____

_____

You might not immediately see the ideal adjective. That's fine. In the upcoming sections, we'll explore different options.

HINT: It's helpful to also know which adjectives do *not* describe your specialty. To see yours, go to the Archetype Matrix, and look at the adjectives in the horizontal row of your *dormant* Advantage (the Advantage you are *least* likely to use). Those are very different than the ones you've been looking at so far, aren't they? Most people look at the adjectives in their dormant Advantage and say, "That is definitely *not* me!"

WARM-UP EXERCISE 3: DESCRIBE YOURSELF

You probably already know the ways in which you are similar to your peers. But how are you different? We'll continue the process of selecting the adjectives that best describe how you communicate *differently* than others, so that you can accentuate this quality in the most positive way.

Pick ONE adjective from the three. (Remember, we want to describe your most singular personality traits, so that you can quickly explain how you stand out.) Find the one adjective that mostly closely sets you apart from everyone else.

Then, use your adjective to complete these sentences:

"People can always count on me to be . . ."
Fill in your adjective: _____

"I can solve certain problems better than anyone else because I am . . ."
Fill in your adjective: _____

"I am better suited to serve my customers because I deliver solutions that are . . ."
Fill in your adjective: _____

You're starting to see how you do things a little differently, right? Now we're ready to take a step closer to pinpointing how you'll actually use this new approach in describing yourself. We're ready to create your Anthem.

Your Anthem is a short phrase that describes how you are different, and what you do best. This makes it easy for people to understand why they should work with you. They can quickly "get" you, because they immediately grasp what you do best.

Now on to the Anthem method. This is the tagline for your personality.

CHAPTER 7

THE ANTHEM METHOD

We're ready to customize a tagline that communicates the most valuable you, right from the very start.

In the previous Anthem warm-up exercises, you identified a collection of adjectives that describe how you communicate most naturally and effectively.

Now we will narrow down to the one adjective that is most distinct, and most unlike others in your market. This adjective best describes *how you are different.*

Next we'll select a noun that describes *what you do best.*

Finally, we will combine your adjective with your noun.

The result is a short phrase, usually only two or three words long. Those words might seem simple, but just like a tagline, they encapsulate your greatest chance of winning your listener's time and attention.

I'll show you the absolute *fastest*, hands-down *easiest* Anthem method. Then, later, I'll show you how to fine-tune your wording.

We'll be using the "How to Create Your Anthem" worksheet in this section of the book. Visit us at HowToFascinate.com/Anthem, where you can download a color version along with more Anthem training materials.

Ready? Here we go. We'll start with those three adjectives built right into your Archetype on the Matrix.

HOW TO CREATE YOUR ANTHEM

Your Anthem is a very short phrase, usually just two words long. It describes *how you are different*, and *what you do best.* This is the fastest and easiest way to describe your distinct value. Think of it like a tagline for your personality.

- FIND AND CIRCLE YOUR **ARCHETYPE**
- THEN, FIND AND CIRCLE YOUR **TWIN**

Notice the six adjectives inside those circles.
Which adjective describes *how you are different?*

 STEP 1

PICK ONE ADJECTIVE FROM THE MATRIX
(Your adjective describes how you are different)

_____

 STEP 2

PICK ONE NOUN FROM THE SAMPLE LIST IN THE BOOK
(Your noun describes what you do best)

_____

 STEP 3

NOW, COMBINE YOUR ADJECTIVE AND NOUN TOGETHER
Finish this sentence: My distinct value is my ability to deliver...

_____   _____
(adjective)   (noun)

FOR COMPLETE INSTRUCTION ON THE ANTHEM METHOD,
PLEASE VISIT: HowToFascinate.com/Anthem OR
EMAIL US: Hello@HowToFascinate.com

HOWTOFASCINATE
DISCOVERED BY SALLY HOGSHEAD

STEP 1: PICK ONE ADJECTIVE (HOW YOU ARE DIFFERENT)

Look at the adjectives you wrote down in the warm-up exercises. Pick *one* adjective, and write it down.*

(You already picked this adjective a moment ago, in the previous warm-up exercises. Just in case you need a review: Look at your Archetype on the Matrix. See that list of three adjectives? They describe how your personality is different, and most likely to be admired by others. Pick one.)

For example, if you are The Maestro, your three adjectives are *ambitious*, *focused*, and *confident*. When selecting one defining trait of her personality, someone who is a Maestro might pick *focused*.

Now look at your Twin on the Archetype Matrix. You'll see three adjectives describing your Twin. Do you prefer one of these adjectives?

Remember, your Twin is the Archetype most similar to yours, with the same top two Advantages. For instance: A Maestro's primary Advantage is

---

* Gentle reminder: As you go through these steps, don't feel boxed in by the exact wording. The examples in your Archetype report are not rigid doctrine; they point you in a flexible direction. Feel free to explore different words. After all, your Anthem should be distinctly yours.

Power, secondary Advantage is Prestige. The Maestro's Twin is The Victor, with the same top two Advantages (Prestige + Power). These two Archetypes resemble each other very closely in what makes them valuable.

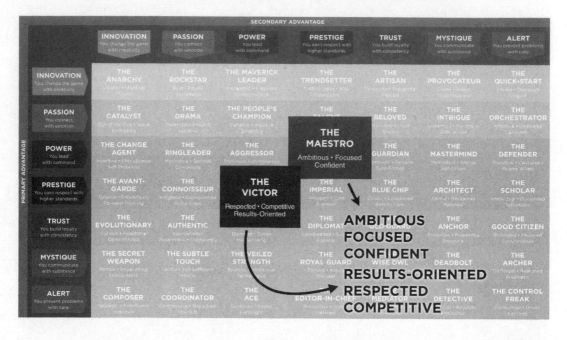

Write down the adjective that describes your Twin (for instance, if you are The Maestro, you might pick from The Victor's adjectives: *respected*, *competitive*, or *results-oriented*).

Write down ONE adjective on your worksheet.

Our goal is to narrow down to just one adjective, for now. Don't worry, you can always go back and change it. We're not engraving it in marble. (It's a worksheet, not a tombstone.)

STEP 2: PICK ONE NOUN (WHAT YOU DO BEST)

You do many things *well*. But what do you do *at your best*? When you are making a real difference on an assignment or task, what exactly are you giving to others?

This word is a *noun*, and forms the second half of your Anthem. It describes what you do best.

Write down that word on your worksheet.

To get you started, below is a list of nouns. This will help you envision your value in a more tangible way. Read through the list. Then ask yourself: *Which noun best describes what I do best?*

EXAMPLES OF NOUNS

ACCURACY	EXPERIENCE	PROBLEM-SOLVING
ACTION	EXPERTISE	RELATIONSHIPS
ATTENTION TO DETAIL	FLEXIBILITY	REPUTATION
ATTITUDE	FOLLOW-THROUGH	RESULTS
BRAINSTORMING	IDEAS	SKILL SET
CHARACTER	INFLUENCE	SOLUTIONS
COMMUNICATION	INSIGHTS	TEAM-BUILDING
CREATIVITY	MANAGEMENT	TENACITY
CREDENTIALS	MIND-SET	THOUGHT-LEADERSHIP
EFFICIENCY	NETWORK	VISION
ENERGY	PRECISION	WORK ETHIC

You will probably be able to cross a few off the list right away, because they are not what you do best. For example, when I look at this list, it's easy for me to immediately cross off nouns such as *follow-through*, *attention to detail*, and *precision*. It's not that I can't provide these things, but they are not what I do best. What can you cross off the list? On the other hand, which feel like a perfect fit for what you do best?

The bank of nouns above represent popular choices for the Anthem exercise. Want something different? You can also choose a noun related specifically to your expertise, your industry, or from your career highlights. I've collected an extended list of options for you at HowToFascinate.com/Anthem.

STEP 3: BRING THE WORDS TOGETHER TO CREATE YOUR ANTHEM

Combine your adjective with your noun, to create a pairing of two words.

This is your Anthem: The tagline for your personality.

Your Anthem is the simplest way to describe your distinct value. It's the essence of your communication. You can use this phrase as a guidepost, pointing all of your communication in this direction.

Our goal here is not to write your Anthem, but to apply it, every day. Let's get right into application.

Now you have it!

Here's an example of how to apply. If you are The Victor, you might select *results-oriented* as your adjective, and *action* as your noun. Pairing these two together, your Anthem is RESULTS-ORIENTED ACTION. This is what you stand for. It's your promise to co-workers and clients. You want results, rather than just pats on the back. You keep things moving forward, always in action, rather than passively observing. With your team, you clearly convey the intended outcome that each project will accomplish. Your clients appreciate that you're not just looking for touchy-feely good vibes. You prioritize RESULTS-ORIENTED ACTION in everything you say and do. When working with someone who does not want to be *results-oriented*, or does not want *action*, you will quickly become discouraged because it doesn't allow you to focus on your core promise.

Imagine that you take your new Anthem, and describe it like this:

- "If you need someone who delivers [fill in your Anthem], I can help."
- "Even when things get tough, I promise to give [fill in your Anthem]."
- "If you're like me, you want someone who can give [fill in your Anthem]."

Your Anthem is a promise of what you can be counted on to provide to the others. The next time you have an important interaction, think ahead: How can the promise behind your Anthem solve this person's needs, or give them more opportunity? (You don't literally need to use the words of your Anthem; it is the way in which you are most likely to add value.) Imagine that you are communicating this: "I can solve your needs better than anyone else because I provide [insert your Anthem here]." "I can solve your problem better than anyone else because I deliver [insert your Anthem here]."

Once you know your Anthem, you can apply it in a very practical way, every day. It's the hub of your communication. Everything else builds outward from this hub. An Anthem gives you more than just a snappy introduction. Many people find that it becomes their own rallying cry, a phrase that they can return to over and over.

A MORE CUSTOMIZED APPROACH TO CREATING YOUR ANTHEM

Want to include two adjectives, or two nouns? Sure. Now that you've pared down to the essence, you can choose to build upon that with additional descriptions. (In fact, the original Anthem exercise used three word pairings, and was a lengthy sentence. We saw that this was harder to remember, and the additional words didn't necessarily make it better. Now we advise paring it down to one adjective and one noun; however, yours can be the length that works best for you.)

Want to "go shopping" for more words to distinguish yourself? Inside this book, you'll find dozens of statements and benefit-oriented phrases for you to customize. You can always search for your own adjectives that describe your personality's most attractive professional traits.

Here's how to hand-select words that distinguish your defining qualities:

- Return to Part II and read your Archetype overview. Review your Archetype's list of "Top 5 Specialty Adjectives."
- At the beginning of Part II, reread the sections about your primary and secondary Advantages. Use the language that best defines your top traits.
- Go into your Fascination Advantage online account and peruse your complete online report. It includes a variety of refined descriptors.
- Watch your Archetype video, also included in your report. Take special note of the words that appear on screen.
- Read the overview for your Twin (that's the Archetype that has the same top two Advantages, but in reverse order). This is the Archetype that most closely resembles your own.

Still want more adjectives?

- Find your primary Advantage on the Matrix. Look along that horizontal row, to the left and right of your own Archetype. Those Archetypes share your primary Advantage, and have many things in common with you. Look at the other Archetypes in your primary Advantage. Those adjectives are also fair game. If you are The Wise Owl, for instance, you have primary Trust. Look to the adjectives in The Authentic or The Diplomat descriptions.

Finally, if you still want more words . . . there's a guy named Roget who wrote a neat thesaurus to help with that.

WHAT ANTHEMS ARE ON YOUR TEAM?

Individuals on your team have a range of communication styles and problem-solving abilities. The Anthem highlights these critical benefits.

The more that you can identify the differences among your team, the more likely you are to get the right people in the right seats. You can also understand how to better allocate tasks and responsibilities. For instance, if one employee's Anthem is BOLD BRAINSTORMING, they are promising to deliver big ideas. Yet exactly how will those ideas be executed? Hmm. That's a different specialty. In this case, it's easy to see why someone with BOLD BRAINSTORMING would be wise to find a co-worker who delivers PRECISE EXECUTION or DETAILED EXECUTION.

Which Anthem examples are most *unlike* yours? Would this ability help you accomplish your own goals? You might be a perfect match for certain types of projects. Even if someone doesn't seem like your cup of tea, they might provide the missing puzzle piece you need.

ANTHEMS IN ACTION

It's useful to see Anthem examples that are *similar* to your own; however, it's far more instructive to see examples that are very *unlike* your own. That's how you'll recognize the ways in which others add value differently than you. This is a key to building communication diversity on your team.

When you can see how you are *different* than other people, it helps you to zoom in and focus on your own specialized abilities, and what you need from others. (In Part II, you saw one Anthem example for each Archetype, and examples of how this type of personality is most likely to improve results through distinct value. To find these application examples, go to the end of each of the Archetype descriptions.)

I'll give a few examples of contrasting Anthems, so that you can see how two people can approach the same task from a different perspective. We'll start with two very different Anthems: STABLE WORK ETHIC and UN-ORTHODOX VISION.

Two examples of word pairings:

Example 1: STABLE WORK ETHIC
Example 2: UNORTHODOX VISION

You can imagine that an employee who selects the word pairing STABLE WORK ETHIC will be rock-steady and unlikely to radically change. You might want this person to be in charge of daily tasks that require a steady hand and experience. Yet this person won't frequently blow your mind with a new idea. For that, you'd have more success with an employee with UN-ORTHODOX VISION.

A few more examples to help you get the hang of how Anthems can potentially apply:

Example 1: NURTURING RELATIONSHIPS
Example 2: DISCIPLINED PRECISION

Say you own a day-care center, and are looking at potential hires. Which person would you pick: Someone who adds value through NURTURING RE-LATIONSHIPS? Or, someone with DISCIPLINED PRECISION? If you said NURTURING RELATIONSHIPS—not so fast. If your child-care center has a hopelessly disorganized back office, and you need to bring some structure to the organization in order to keep your doors open, your best hire might be an administrator to get the business back on track with DISCIPLINED PRECISION.

HINT: You can also "reverse-engineer" this exercise, to help you more accurately select team members. Which adjectives do you want in your company, and on your team? Screen for those traits when interviewing candidates. Learn more at HowToFascinate.com/Resources.

Remember: This is about you, at your highest and best. Your Anthem should capture the essence of who you are. Play around with the words to create your own Anthem. Sleep on it. Discuss it with a colleague or friend. Make it your own. Handcraft it. Then live by it.

When you feel confused, and not sure exactly how to communicate, you can always come back to your Anthem. When you need a compass to navigate through tricky communication waters, your Anthem lights the way to how you are most likely to succeed. Are you walking into a job interview, and not sure what type of person they're looking for? Are you joining a new organization, and don't know anyone yet? When negotiations deteriorate, or your career throws you a curve, come back to your Anthem. It's home base.

Here's an example. Many financial advisors are in an unenviable position, selling the exact same products and services as their competitors. It's very difficult for clients to see why one advisor is better than another. As a result, advisors face the daunting challenge of setting themselves apart. How would you impress and excel in this situation?

When the stakes are high, you have one priority: Focus on your Anthem.

A TALE OF TWO PRESENTATIONS

Introducing Mr. and Mrs. Martin. They are an ideal client: empty-nesters, in a secure financial position, ready to invest more heavily in their retirement planning. They are a financial advisor's dream.

Yet the Martins are feeling a little overwhelmed by all the planning options so they will work with a financial advisor. They have face-to-face meetings with two financial advisors, Andy and Simon, and they plan to choose one.

Andy and Simon have similar levels of experience and similar backgrounds. Most of all, they have similar planning services. On paper, they're evenly matched, and their services are virtually identical. But there's a critical difference. One of them knows how to instantly communicate value.

Andy is not what most would describe as a charming personality. He's shy, a self-described introvert. He dislikes the obligatory small talk at the start of a meeting, and wants to listen rather than generate discussion. Most would call him intense. Yet Andy has an ace in the hole. He asks astute questions, and he listens keenly. He perceptively parses through the jumble of what the Martins describe. When he does finally speak, he articulates a vision for what the Martins actually want for their retirement, bringing structure and clarity to their confusion about their own financial goals.

Andy's personality Advantages are Prestige + Mystique.

His Archetype is The Royal Guard. This Archetype is not flashy or gimmicky. Like the royal guards outside Buckingham Palace, he is reserved and watchful, minimalist in conversation, with carefully thought-out words and actions. His Anthem is ASTUTE QUESTIONS, because he has an unusual ability to listen skillfully, and discern details that others would miss.

If Andy only does *one thing* during his meeting with the Martins, he must deliver value through ASTUTE QUESTIONS. This is his number-one priority, and everything else is secondary. Here's why. His questions are impressive, but more importantly, the Martins' *answers* to those questions will reveal everything Andy knows to win their business. If Andy fails to focus on his Anthem, he will miss his best shot at earning their business.

Even from Andy's first meeting, he is quietly intense. Not warm or chatty. Unlike many financial planners, he doesn't sound like a brochure. Instead, Andy has come to this meeting knowing that he will succeed through ASTUTE QUESTIONS. His discussion reflects careful prior thinking and research. This impresses the Martins, because Andy had clearly focused his prep time around their needs rather than selling himself. The Martins are already thinking about how to apply Andy's structure to their investments. There is no guarantee that Andy will close the deal, but Andy *has* attained his highest likelihood of doing so.

The other financial advisor, Simon, has a very different effect. Though Simon is selling almost exactly the same service as Andy, he is not nearly as persuasive. Simon begins each meeting exactly as he has been trained to do, following a conversational script. His words feel a little forced as he delivers a canned presentation. He gives the Martins the obligatory flurry of brochures and corporate literature. His information does explain why someone should invest . . . but does not explain why they should invest *with Simon.*

How do the Martins respond? Mrs. Martin's eyes glaze over, and Mr. Martin becomes vaguely irritated. They disengage, shifting in their chairs. Both begin thinking of all the reasons why they could delay the whole retirement planning process altogether.

You might not be surprised to hear that Andy is still working with the Martins today.

Why did one planner fascinate the prospect, and the other did not? Andy and Simon are both selling a commodity service—in fact, the exact *same* service. Simon is more charismatic and conversational than Andy, so how did Andy fascinate the Martins?

The Lesson: The higher the stakes, the more important it becomes to deliver value. Your Anthem is your single most important objective. If nothing else, you must deliver your Anthem, or you will miss your key opening. Don't get pulled in a hundred directions. Plan ahead. Think through the meeting, and all the ways that your words and actions will fulfill your Anthem's promise. You are the ideal person for this opportunity because you deliver [insert your Anthem here].

NOW APPLY YOUR ANTHEM

Your Anthem guides all your communication. In fact, it guides all your day-to-day interaction with the world around you.

I've already given you an example of an Anthem for your Archetype. You can use this as your Anthem, or create your own. This example is already right in your Archetype description, back in Part II. Feel free to use this one and give it your own twist.

Like an elevator pitch, your Anthem very specifically guides your introductions. But it doesn't just live in introductions. It should guide all your actions and activities and plans for your business—drawing upon your natural Advantages, rather than just arbitrary aspirations.

The higher you rise within your organization, the more crucial it is to add your highest distinct value.

My team worked closely with a CEO of a fast-growing technology firm, named Daniel. As The Maestro, his word pairing is AMBITIOUS IDEAS. This describes his highest and best use. When Daniel can deliver AMBITIOUS IDEAS—in other words, when he's assertive and proactive and pushing toward a higher level of performance—he's in his zone of genius. Same goes for when he develops original thinking around new product concepts. But when he gets stuck in the weeds, he's mired in fine points, and less likely to add value to his team or clients.

Yet unfortunately, Daniel was often stuck in the weeds, failing to centralize himself around AMBITIOUS IDEAS. He'd get deep into the daily minutiae and technical details.

We took a step back and began to apply Daniel's Anthem throughout his work, from his meetings to his office décor. A few examples:

- Presentations: When pitching investors, he demonstrated how his firm was more competitively positioned to bring AMBITIOUS IDEAS to market.
- Status meetings: Rather than starting Monday morning staff meetings with dry "housekeeping," he started with the AMBITIOUS IDEAS that would be accomplished over the course of the week.
- Hiring: When hiring, he described his performance-oriented company culture, to make sure that nobody was surprised by the intense deadlines required to implement his AMBITIOUS IDEAS.
- Workplace environment: His own office had been decorated in a stiff and formal style, as if a harp performance were about to commence, so he traded the carved mahogany for sleek furnishings and stark walls where AMBITIOUS IDEAS could be pasted around the room.

HOW WILL YOU APPLY YOUR ANTHEM?

Like a tagline, you can incorporate your Anthem throughout your marketing and communication. Make it the intro for your LinkedIn profile. Add it to your email signature. Put it above your desk, reminding you to always live to your fullest potential. Include it at the top of your "about" page on your website, or on your bio. Use the wording in social media profiles.

Knowing your Anthem gives you a sense of confidence when you introduce yourself. Beyond the first impression, however, it can also help you orient around one solid purpose and message. That way, you're not running in all different directions, and spreading yourself too thin.

Imagine you're a travel writer, and your Anthem is EXPRESSIVE IDEAS. Your enthusiasm is evident in everything you say and do, from wearing bold designs, to punctuating your articles with vibrant words. You paint a colorful picture for your reader to visualize your experiences. You should seek opportunities that allow you to be as expressive as possible. And you should deliver as many ideas as possible. You chafe under strict management or regimented parameters (that feels like quicksand!). When possible, take care to avoid assignments that do not allow you to succeed through EXPRESSIVE IDEAS.

Now a different scenario. Imagine you are a travel writer, but this time, your Anthem is PRECISE COMMUNICATION. In this case, every word you write reflects the intense detail and research you've invested. Your topics are chosen with great care, and you stick to the facts. You never use more words than required. In person, your demeanor may be subdued, but you instill confidence with intelligent questions. You pride yourself on delivering precision without embellishment. The readers who most appreciate your work are those who want a to-the-point summary of information. You should not seek to deliver EXPRESSIVE IDEAS. In fact, you might feel uncomfortable if expected to execute in that manner.

Those two examples use the same profession (travel writer) and the same goal (providing information to readers), but with very different process and results. One is not better than the other. They might both publish articles about Hawaii or Palm Desert, but you would probably not confuse their writing styles, and they probably have divergent recommendations.

How else can you apply your Anthem? A range of applications to get you going:

Written Communication
- Business card
- Email writing style
- Email signature
- Your résumé

- Logo and letterhead
- Points you outline for an agenda for a meeting

Let's apply your Anthem to your communication.

If your Anthem is RESULTS-ORIENTED ANSWERS, your emails clearly outline *why* you're sending someone an email, and precisely *what* you expect the receiver to do. You add value by offering solutions with the end goal in mind.

Imagine your Anthem is ENTREPRENEURIAL THOUGHT-LEADER; the content of your emails might be more thought-provoking rather than results-driven. Your communication points to where your industry is heading next—in a year, five years, and beyond.

Our company's Anthem is FASCINATING COMMUNICATION. When my team created our business card, I knew the card had to instantly engage the recipient. (The pressure was on to create something truly fascinating!) My team developed an incredible idea: My business card immediately shows you how your personality is most likely to fascinate.

Now consider that one of my business cards costs $2 to print. That might sound insanely expensive—until you find out the ROI. We've met a lot of new clients through this $2 card, because people want to show it to their friends. As a result, we earn about $48 in revenue for every $2 card we give away. Want to check it out for yourself? Visit HowToFascinate.com/ Resources to see.

Presentations and Speeches

Getting more specific for a moment, see how you would apply your Advantages to your presentations. The bar is higher in these situations. You must instantly prove why you deserve attention.

People might have the same topic, but depending on their Anthem, they might present in remarkably different ways. Consider the following for your next presentation:

- The way you enter the stage (do you zip onstage with a flourish, or quietly slip behind the podium?)

- What is your opening (a humorous story, a question, or a hard-hitting fact?)
- How you interact with your audience (Twitter feed, or Q&A?)
- Emotional tone of presentation (neighborly congeniality, or strong sense of urgency?)

How could two speakers deliver a speech on the same topic, in totally different ways, according to their Anthems?

Say your Anthem is RATIONAL INSIGHTS, and you are giving a speech on economics. What would your presentation be like? You share facts and figures to establish and bolster your case. Your slide design is relatively simple; you focus on *what* you say, not *how* you say it. You add value through new information, giving the data your own expert insights. Even skeptical audience members would have trouble discounting your well-researched points on the economy. You carefully answer questions from your audience, and your last slide summarizes the hard-hitting statistics you've raised in your presentation. People are still tweeting the facts you presented in your slides.

If you are an economist with an Anthem such as IMAGINATIVE INFLU-ENCE, your speech would be quite different. You open with a riveting story to engross your audience, bringing the news headlines to life with striking impact. Immediately, you make a strong point that emotionally engages the crowd. You keep them captivated with graphics and anecdotes. Your slides use evocative pictures rather than words. When you finish your presentation with an inspiring battle cry to take action, the audience swells with excitement.

Around the Web

Considering that the Internet and social media are driving forces in our shortening attention span, it's important to apply your Anthem online:

- Social media profile (especially the "about" section)
- Social shares, tweets, updates, likes
- Personal website (your URL, and your choice of fonts, colors, words, and images)
- Your blog and newsletter

If your Anthem is DYNAMIC NETWORKER, you might want to reach out to new LinkedIn connections asking them how you can help them by connecting them to someone in your network. You generously offer networking tips. You probably have a photo with a warm smile, making you look approachable. You add value by helping others grow their networks (as well as your own).

Now, let's say your Anthem is IRREVERENT INNOVATOR instead. Your photos are not standard posed head shots, but something a little unexpected. Your tweets and shares will highlight your interest in new trends and ideas, with the occasional witty remark thrown in. You add value through the surprise of provocative new perspectives.

Among team members at How To Fascinate, our email signature line includes our own Anthem, explaining the value that each of us delivers for our clients. One of our clients lists every employee's Anthem underneath each person's photo on the company website.

In your office and other work environments, how can you incorporate your Anthem? This can be an extremely effective way to help people feel more connected to the workplace. In our own Fascination Laboratory headquarters, each team member has their Anthem hanging outside their office door.

After a day of training, we give participants a certificate highlighting their own Anthem, so they can display it in their office.

Even your office décor can convey your Anthem. Whether explicit or subtle, you can shape a visitor's perception of your company. It can even influence your decorating. As I said, our company Anthem is FASCINATING COMMUNICATION. In our offices, we have seven different wall colors— representing the seven different Advantages. Each wall has artwork that expresses the concept behind that wall's Advantage.

How could you bring Advantages and Anthems to life as a living, breathing part of your company?

Around the Office and More

- The design of your reception area (the colors, welcome message, music, office furniture, even the choice of magazines in a waiting area)
- Greeting from receptionist; hold music; voicemail greeting

- The table shape and size; how chairs are arranged
- Refreshments served (basic water and coffee, or exotic concoctions?)

Let's say you're the CEO and your Anthem is CAUTIONARY MANAGE-MENT. What would your office environment be like? You probably err on the side of caution with health and safety rules. You play it safe with muted wall colors and traditional furniture and office art, and you take clients for lunch to a moderately priced chain restaurant for food that everyone can agree on. You watch the details to make sure nothing ever goes awry, and that means that in the office, *uneventful* is far preferable to *remarkable*.

Now imagine that instead your Anthem is OUT-OF-THE-BOX MO-MENTUM. You might wow visitors immediately upon their entrance. Your location is definitely not a standard office park; you're in a cool refurbished former warehouse, or a place with quirky character such as a renovated fire station. You serve a variety of bottled refreshments, in handmade glasses. Every aspect of the interaction is to break convention, and challenge employees and clients alike to push into new ways of thinking.

EXAMPLES OF EXTENDED ANTHEMS

You have your Anthem's starter base. If you want to keep things simple, just hold there. Sometimes, simple is better, because it's easier to apply in multiple areas.

On the other hand, if you want a few nifty add-ons, you can tweak your Anthem with more specific language. Some people want more than two words, so that they can articulate their Anthem in a more traditional tagline format. A few examples:

- A Maverick Leader (Innovation + Power): "I create *bold solutions* with a *pioneering mind-set*."
- A Guardian (Power + Trust): "No matter what, I can be counted on for my *established relationships*."
- A Connoisseur (Prestige + Passion): "With clients, co-workers, and friends, I deliver *astute insight* based on my *in-the-know expertise*."
- A Composer (Alert + Innovation): "I'm not the usual *strategic thinker*. I always bring a *progressive mind-set* so I can stay open to change."

To personalize your Anthem, and find more ways to apply it, check out HowToFascinate.com/Anthem for ideas and tools.

You probably already realize this, but don't feel like you must literally use the exact words from your Anthem. It's a concept. This will help you find openings to answer the other person's needs. It will give you a clearheaded confidence in how you are most likely to add value to your conversational partner.

When you create an Anthem that truly resonates with your prospects, they respond immediately. For instance, here's how an entrepreneur named Dawnna described herself before doing the Anthem exercise:

BEFORE: *"Women's diversity inclusion and empowerment expert."*

That's a little confusing, right? It doesn't really explain why someone should work with Dawnna. This statement focuses on *what she does* but doesn't explain how she adds value.

Curious to know what Dawnna changed it to say? Her Archetype is The Avant-Garde (Prestige + Innovation). For her adjective, she chose *forward-thinking*. Here's what she wrote within a few minutes of doing the Anthem exercise:

AFTER: *"The forward-thinking game-changer that promotes women in business."*

Dawnna's marketing response rate tripled in the twenty-four hours after using this Anthem.

Why? Her new tagline very clearly articulates the opportunities that she is uniquely suited to address. You can improve results when you fascinate your target audience of prospective clients, immediately showing them why they should work with you. (I can't promise that you'll triple your income, but I can bet that you'll experience an improvement.)

How about your company? As your business grows, how can you recruit and hire more effectively? Does your group lack certain Advantages? As you'll see, smart businesses match Advantages to specific goals.

HOW TO BUILD MORE VALUABLE TEAMS

Help your employees feel more *fascinating* at work, and they're likely to feel more *fascinated* by work. The more a company understands and celebrates each person's highest value, the more likely employees are to give more of that value.

When everyone on a team understands how their co-workers are likely to add value, your organization becomes more efficient, with less conflict, and fewer overlapping roles.

We've watched this firsthand, as previously conflicted groups bond and establish new goals. The key is to have each person identify their own signature abilities, and to recognize the abilities of each person on their team, by collectively creating their own Anthems.

If you're on a team, you'll find that it's incredibly useful and rewarding to see how your co-workers individually add value.

When we do Fascination Laboratory workshops, every participant creates their own Anthem tagline on Day One. At the end of that first day, we collect them all (but don't tell them why). When they reconvene for Day Two, we have a surprise waiting: Each person receives a name badge featuring their own Anthem.

My clients always impress me with brilliant ways to build their team around Anthems.

Hyatt incorporated the Anthem method throughout their 2014 national sales meeting. We trained eighteen internal How To Fascinate certified trainers, and then those eighteen leaders trained 350 of their peers. Each person had their own Anthem, helping them identify and apply their highest value. The process continues today.

For a recent national convention, AutoTrader invited 1,200 employees to take the Fascination Advantage assessment before their national conference. Then, at the conference itself, they created a "Fascination Station" photo booth where employees could get professional photos of themselves holding up an icon representing their Advantages. Passion personalities wore bright feather boas, while those with primary Prestige wore golden crowns.

Here's an example of the difference this can make within an organization. Daina Middleton is the global CEO of Performics, one of the world's largest search and performance media agencies. She's also the author of *Marketing in the Participation Age*. When she first contacted me, Daina had just moved from Hewlett-Packard, and had a clear vision for what she wanted to achieve in her new position. Here is what Daina described to me in our first conversation:

Performics had long been a brilliant and successful company. Yet it had no clear point of difference in a highly competitive space. The sales team wasn't effectively communicating with clients and prospects. As a result, employees became demoralized, which led to further communication challenges.

Within a month after we delivered this team training, Performics saw a tremendous jump in results. They literally signed more new business in the first month after training than all of the previous year. And they landed more sizable business than in the last four years.

How could your group develop smart ways to create and share your Anthems, and become more valuable?

GROUP ACTIVITIES WITH ANTHEMS
A few cool ways your team and business can apply Anthems to increase engagement:

- A theme for your company's next off-site meeting: Create your Anthems together in the morning, apply with small group exercises in the afternoon, and host a fascinating activity that evening. (Get creative! When my husband, Ed, and I got married, we had Advantage-themed drinks. Alert was a jalapeño martini, and Trust was champagne.)
- At the start of a new project or client relationship, identify how each person is uniquely suited to contribute to the outcome through their Advantages.
- For an immediate icebreaker at a conference, have everyone do the Anthem exercise in advance. Print name tags showing their Advantages and Anthem to get people connecting and buzzing.

- At the beginning of a meeting, when people first introduce them-selves to the group, rather than asking them the usual question, such as "What's your hometown" or "What's your most embarrassing moment," invite people to share their Anthem for a faster and more authentic connection.
- At a luncheon or dinner party, get people to open up by inviting each person around the table to share how they apply their Anthem at work or at home.
- In the first few slides of a presentation deck, include your Anthem so that people know ahead of time how you will deliver value in that presentation.
- List each employee's Anthem on the company phone list, so people know how the other person on the other end of the phone can add value on the call.
- When hosting a conference call with a group of strangers, help people develop rapport more quickly by inviting each person to include his or her Anthem in their introduction.
- At a conference, invite every speaker to incorporate their Anthem at the start of their presentation, so that the audience can have a better sense of the outcome, right from the start.
- Have Anthem or Advantage T-shirts printed for team events.
- Have a group contest with categories such as "Most Creative Anthem" and "Most Accurate Anthem."
- Invite attendees at an event to collaborate in small groups and create one overall Anthem for the event.

Just as each person on your team has an Anthem, your team can share one collective Anthem, like a group tagline.

YOUR TEAM'S ANTHEM

You can develop an Anthem to describe the highest value of your team, your department, or your entire company. It's better than a mission statement, be-cause it's based on the inherent Fascination Advantages of the group.

In fact, you can write a different Anthem for your department or company. You can write one for your racquetball club, your study group, your Rotary club, your Twitter followers, your faith-based study group, your political party, or your group of fishing buddies.

Your goal is to show others the value of working with your team. For instance, if you're looking for donors, your Anthem can showcase your highest value for donors. You could write an Anthem to excite prospective members. Or help investors understand why they should get involved. Or make the media curious to call you and learn more.

Here is a quick sample process to write your team's Anthem:

1. Measure your team's Advantages. Which represent your core traits? Are there two most common Advantages among your group? As a group, which Advantages represent what you most specifically want to achieve? For instance, if your group rallies around the need to deliver exceptionally high standards, even those who do not have a primary or secondary Prestige Advantage can uniquely support this goal.
2. Go back to the Archetype Matrix and find the two Archetypes with your team's top two Advantages. For instance, if your team's top two Advantages are Trust and Mystique, then you'd choose adjectives from The Anchor (*protective, purposeful, analytical*) and The Wise Owl (*observant, assured, unruffled*).
3. Write your group's Anthem based on what you deliver at the highest value. For instance, if you are an IT department, with high use of Mystique and Trust, your Anthem might be: *We protect your data with* PURPOSEFUL INSIGHT. *For those who need their data protected with* PURPOSEFUL INSIGHT, *they will know exactly how and why they should invest their time and energy with us.*

A team Anthem can guide you internally as an encouraging way to rally people around a collective cause. If you take on new members or new hires, and grow and expand your team, it can guide you like a north star for your purpose.

THE BEST ADVANTAGES FOR A ROLE (AND THE BEST ROLES FOR AN ADVANTAGE)

When hiring, the Archetype Matrix indicates which personality is best suited to deliver the specific traits you need. On the Archetype Matrix, scan across the seven different primary Advantages (the horizontal rows). Which row identifies what you need in the role? Do you want someone who delivers the adjectives of Trust? Or, do you want someone who makes an emotional Passion connection?

Have your prospective hire create their own Anthem, so that you can get to know their key qualities. Send a signal from the start that you are a supporter of that person's highest potential.

A team or organization's culture often reflects the concentration of Advantages among the people on that team. What Advantages do you want to emphasize within your organization? Go through the Archetype Matrix at the front and back of this book, and read the adjectives. Then, list the adjectives that would be most beneficial to your business.

Look at your list of adjectives. What do they have in common? Did you pick adjectives from the primary Trust row? Or Power? Or one of the others? Do you already have employees that fit these Advantages?

Support people in using their inherent communication style. For instance, if you want more creativity and energy, look for Innovation or Passion. If you want logical and step-by-step communication, tap into Mystique or Alert.

If hiring new folks isn't an option, or isn't your desired move, that's okay. Identify the Advantages you already have on your team, and help each team member concentrate on their innate specialties.

PREDICTING A TEAM'S COLLECTIVE ADVANTAGE

Just as a group can succeed in predictable ways according to Advantages, there can also be disadvantages. When a group has an extremely high concentration of one Advantage, those qualities can become exaggerated and unbalanced.

When the members of a group share a very high concentration of similar traits, problems can potentially arise if those traits run amok. For instance, with too much Trust, the group can become rigid, or overly set in their ways, or stuck in ruts. With too much Power, the group can become so focused on goals that nobody is actually executing.

WHEN A TEAM'S ADVANTAGE BECOMES A DISADVANTAGE

If your team has a high use of this Advantage…	Your team can become disadvantaged in this way…
INNOVATION	Distracted, Unlikely to Complete Projects
PASSION	Hyper or Moody
POWER	Overly Intense
PRESTIGE	Competitive
TRUST	Dull, Out-of-Date
MYSTIQUE	Disconnected From Others
ALERT	Anal Retentive, Micromanaging

To learn more about how Advantages become disadvantages, see the section in Part II on "Double Troubles."

A high concentration of one Advantage is not necessarily a bad thing in an individual. The point is to understand what you have, and apply it strategically.

Now we'll apply your Advantages, and your Anthems, to strengthen and engage your entire organization.

CHAPTER 8

TEAMS, ADVANTAGES, AND ANTHEMS

Advantages are like a Ferrari engine: They can quickly get you where you want to go, but you need a map and a steering wheel. To give your organization a map and steering wheel, know what you've already got under the hood.

This starts by identifying each team member's Advantages. Next, see how people cluster in certain areas. With this data, you can help each employee rise in value, and collaborate to improve overall results.

When my team and I work with an organization, we build a pie chart of the group's primary Advantages, such as the one below, and compare it to our average population.

On the left you'll see the average results of the first two hundred thousand participants in the Fascination Advantage assessment. See how this compares with the pie chart on the right, from an Internet start-up company.

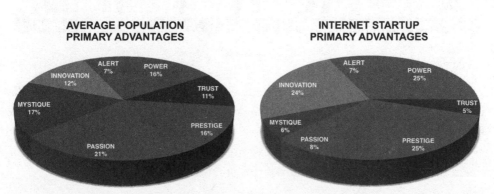

AVERAGE POPULATION PRIMARY ADVANTAGES

ALERT 7%
POWER 16%
INNOVATION 12%
TRUST 11%
MYSTIQUE 17%
PRESTIGE 16%
PASSION 21%

INTERNET STARTUP PRIMARY ADVANTAGES

ALERT 7%
POWER 25%
INNOVATION 24%
TRUST 5%
MYSTIQUE 6%
PASSION 8%
PRESTIGE 25%

As you might expect from an online start-up, this company is intensely creative and entrepreneurial, with a remarkably high dose of Innovation. The average result is 12% primary Innovation, but in this start-up company, it's more than double that, at 24%. This fuels their innovation process. They have less than half the usual percentage of Alert and Trust.

Here's why this is not surprising: Innovation usually has an inverse relationship with Alert and Trust. People and groups that rank very high in Innovation usually score low on Alert and Trust, because they resist following standard instructions or time-tested procedures. That means this group will be extremely productive in the quest for finding fresh solutions, but not as productive when it comes to day-to-day tasks.

Here is how this particular group looks in terms of their seven Advantages:

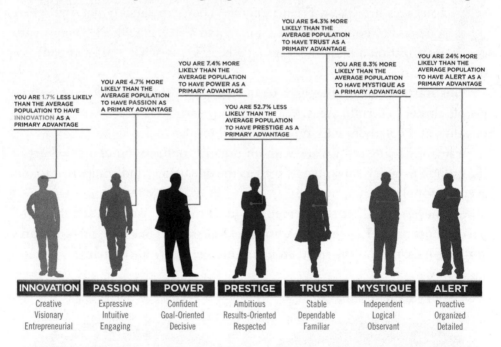

These numbers are decidedly different than a company that hires for traditional personalities; however, it can make perfect sense for a company driven by Innovation.

In our analysis of groups, we next turn the group's overall metrics into a "heat map." Here's the heat map of this start-up company:

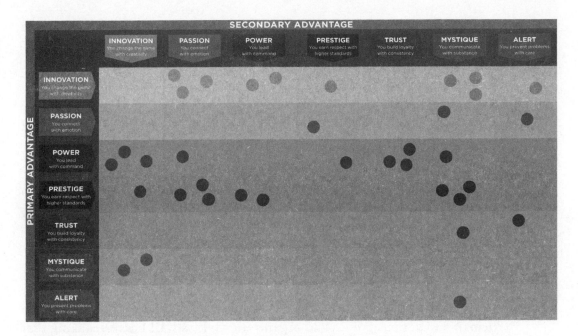

Because they have such a low use of Alert and Trust, they'll want to hire more people for those roles that require organization and implementation. They are less likely to maintain the structure of the company as it grows.

If the organization changes over time, and they hire more Trust and Alert to provide more stability, their heat map will change along with it. Mature organizations are more likely to have a balance of Advantages that will perpetuate the systems that are in place.

Let's compare this Internet start-up with the participants of a dramatically different group: a Fortune 100 life insurance company. This company focuses on delivering promises fifty years into the future (after all, this is life insurance). As a result, the group has less likelihood of untraditional thinking, but it enjoys higher loyalty among customers and long tenures among employees.

If you want to be more like a start-up, you will probably want high Innovation and Power. If you want to function more like a traditional life insurance company, then you should recruit, promote, and retain Trust.

To highlight your brand's value, look no further than your employees. *Employees are the living, breathing representation of your brand.* The system you're using right now in this book was originally built for brands to use in their marketing. It extends from the individual personality all the way to the overall brand.

IDENTIFY THE HIDDEN PATTERNS IN YOUR TEAM'S ADVANTAGES: YOUR HEAT MAP

When two people work together, their primary Advantages will combine and communicate according to certain patterns. Larger groups follow similar patterns. You can map your organization's primary Advantages in order to predict how you are most (and least) likely to solve problems, deal with conflict, and reach conclusions.

What are your own team's formulas of communication? Do you have one dominant Advantage, or are you evenly balanced? Do you have a fantastic core ability, or potentially even a disadvantage?

Here's a tool to help find the answers.

Over the past several years, I've studied hundreds of thousands of participants in various groups and organizations. In 2011 I began realizing that every group has hidden patterns according to job title, industry, gender, and of course, Advantages.

When we analyze a group's strong suits and potential pitfalls, we chart them out on a "heat map." You can learn more about our heat map data in the Appendix section, "Inside the Research."

Your goal for this exercise is to learn and leverage the Advantages of your organization (whether it is a corporate department, or your family). This exercise will help you complete your do-it-yourself heat map. A heat map is a visual summary of your entire group's Fascination Advantages. On one page, it charts the entire spectrum of scores in your group on the Archetype Matrix.

My team and I have created heat maps for groups as large as five thousand people.

If you'd like to create your own heat map, here's how.

1. **Have each group member describe themselves:**
- Name
- Primary Advantage

- Secondary Advantage
- Archetype

2. **Have each group member introduce themselves, along with their Advantages, and their Archetype.**

    Example: "My name is John. My primary Advantage is Innovation, and my secondary Advantage is Power. My Archetype is The Maverick Leader."

3. **Create a DIY Team Heat Map.**
    With each introduction, write the member's name in the appropriate box in the do-it-yourself Heat Map that corresponds to their primary and secondary Advantages.

    Here is a blank DIY heat map. Below that, you'll see an example of how a team filled in their heat map with their names.

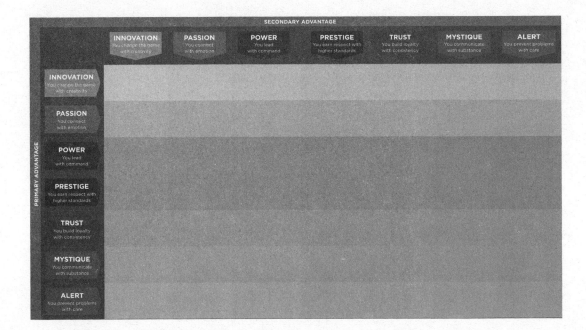

	SECONDARY ADVANTAGE						
	INNOVATION You change the game with creativity	PASSION You connect with emotion	POWER You lead with command	PRESTIGE You earn respect with higher standards	TRUST You build loyalty with consistency	MYSTIQUE You communicate with substance	ALERT You prevent problems with care
INNOVATION You change the game with creativity		Steph B.	Patrick J.				
PASSION You connect with emotion	Jodie H.					Daniel V.	
POWER You lead with command				Michael J. Rohan Q.			Ellie L.
PRESTIGE You earn respect with higher standards			Jack B.				
TRUST You build loyalty with consistency				Jeanne M.			
MYSTIQUE You communicate with substance	Ryan A.						
ALERT You prevent problems with care				Del S.			

For example, here are a few of the names that you'll see above in this heat map:

Ryan A. = Mystique + Innovation
Rohan Q. = Power +Prestige
Del S. = Alert + Trust
Jeanne M. = Trust + Prestige

To download your own free DIY heat map template, visit HowToFascinate .com/Resources.

AFTERWORD

The greatest gift you can give someone is to show them their own highest value.

The greatest way to empower someone is to show them their highest value. Once someone understands how they naturally add value, they blossom. They become more confident, more persuasive, and more influential.

Wouldn't the world be a better place if more people could realize their own highest value?

Now that you've read this book, how could you "pay it forward" to help someone else see her own true value?

We have scholarship programs available. We also have discounts available for nonprofits, faith-based organizations, military and veteran associations, and other groups who can change the world by discovering their highest value.

ACKNOWLEDGMENTS

My husband, Ed, is a Maverick Leader. On our first date in 2008, I was working on the manuscript for my last book, *Fascinate*, and literally showed up with a laptop. Despite this totally lame move, he's been my partner and best friend ever since. Ed is the one who developed the concept of a personality assessment based on the science of fascination. He's been by my side the whole way, literally traveling around the globe with me so I could research the principles of fascination, and share them. We're rarely apart. This past year, he quit his highly successful twenty-five-year career as a trial lawyer to officially take on the role of president of our company. Suffice to say, he fascinates me.

Thank you to our eight amazing children, each fascinating in their own way. To our Azalea, who is busily working on creating a kids' version of this system. To Quinton, who memorized every Archetype by heart. To Ian Normand, The Maestro, who performed our wedding ceremony. To Lura, The Maestro. To Max, The Change Agent. Gunnar, The Intrigue. Karli, The Secret Weapon. And to Isabelle, our little Connoisseur. I love you and I'm so proud of you.

My team at How to Fascinate is beyond brilliant. (Thank goodness for the Alert Advantage!) You make the whole system possible. My fullest Passion appreciation to Elizabeth Rissman, Emily Johnson, Melinda Graham, Corey Stewart, Beth Martin, Rosemary Oldendorf, Teddy Garcia, Gary Wong, Kathy Zader, Andrea Memenas, Alex Nghiem, Linda Jeo Zerba, and Cynthia Gaskin. And to Andrea Driesson, a Rockstar, for years of bold ideas and unconventional events.

This book was an intense three-year partnership with HarperCollins, with Hollis Heimbouch in the lead. Hollis is The Maestro, and without her ambitious ideas and focused leadership, this book would not have made it into your hands. My associate editor, Colleen Lawrie, is a Talent. Her emotionally intelligent comments helped shape the writing and topic. And John Jusino brought it all together in production.

My literary agent, Jud Laghi, is an Avant-Garde. He was forward-thinking enough to see the vision.

The speaking management team at SpeakersOffice is a godsend, allowing me to focus on my wellspring (fascinating communication) rather than my quicksand (expense reports!). Holli Catchpole, a Talent, never fails with her in-the-know expertise. Cassie Glasgow, a Diplomat, gives me levelheaded expertise. If you need the crème de la crème in speakers, go to them.

Thank you to my visionary clients, including AT&T, Cisco, Intuit, Unilever, Wells Fargo, General Electric, Hyatt, GKIC, and so many more extraordinary companies for being part of the research and learning in this book. To Daina Middelton, and the whole team at Performics, for being instrumental in our training development.

To my insanely brilliant friend John Gerzema and his strategic brand team at BAV Consulting, for refining our strategic personality research findings.

To Henneke Dustermat, a Maverick Leader, for enchanting words. Thank you to Dan Kennedy, a Mastermind. To Marie Forleo, a Talent. Thank you also to Mark Sanborn, Bob Burg, Larry Winget, Victoria Labalme, Clint Greenleaf, and everyone at the National Speakers Association for teaching me what it truly means to be a professional speaker.

Thank you to Stephanie Cary, our Life Assistant, for being the superglue that holds our work and life all together. Thank you to Rich Johnson, a Secret Weapon, for nimble creativity.

I am grateful to everyone in our community on Facebook and Twitter, and the blog at HowToFascinate.com. Your insights, ideas, and comments have brought this concept to life in a way that I could not have imagined.

Finally, thank you to everyone who has participated in the Fascination Advantage over the past years. I'm forever grateful to you for sharing your Advantages, your stories, and your experiences with me. I hope you've learned a fraction from me what I have learned from you.

And to you, the reader: Thank you. Here's to becoming more of the best of who you already are.

GLOSSARY

Advantage: The way in which you are most likely to add distinct value. There are seven Advantages: Power, Passion, Mystique, Prestige, Alert, Innovation, and Trust. Each of these speaks a different "language" and has a different way of standing out in business and life.

Anthem: The tagline for your personality. This quick statement is only two or three words, yet instantly communicates how you add value. Your Anthem is shorthand for how your personality is primed to create value for your team or organization.

Archetype: Your Archetype is how the world sees you, at your best. It reflects the combination of your primary and secondary Advantages. For example, if your top two Advantages are Prestige + Alert, then you are The Scholar. If your top two Advantages are Mystique + Trust, then you are The Wise Owl.

Archetype Matrix: The complete collection of Archetypes is printed in full color inside the front and back covers of this book. It includes 42 Archetypes and 7 Double Troubles, for a total of 49 Archetypes. This Archetype Matrix is your main piece of reference when comparing Advantages, and creating your Anthem. You can also download a copy at HowTo Fascinate.com/Matrix.

Commoditization: The threat of becoming so similar to your competition that you are no longer distinct. Once commoditized, you're in a vulnerable position, because you'll probably have to compete on the basis of price.

Competition: The threat of losing in a crowded environment in which others are competing for the same resources, recognition, or rewards.

Distraction: The threat of divided attention. Today, shortened attention spans make it increasingly difficult to capture and retain the attention of your listener.

Dormant Advantage: This is the form of communication that's least likely to play to your Advantage. In this area, you do not have a competitive advantage over others. You do not need to increase your use of this Advantage. Instead, you should avoid being evaluated purely on the basis of this form of communication.

Double Trouble: When you use one Advantage to an exaggerated degree, it becomes a disadvantage. For instance, when you feel highly stressed, overwhelmed, or fearful, your combined strengths get thrown out of equilibrium, and you "double up" on one Advantage rather than keeping a healthy balance.

Fascination: A state of intense focus. When you fascinate your listener, they become completely engrossed so that they're not distracted. In this neurological state, they are more likely to listen to you, remember you, and take action.

Fascination Advantage: The assessment you'll take as part of this book. It measures how the world sees you.

Heat Map: A one-page visual summary of a team or organization's Advantages, mapped out in the Archetype Matrix. This makes it easy to see where your group's Advantages cluster in certain areas. It also indicates where you have a lack of Advantages.

Pitfall: In certain situations, you will have a disadvantage in communicating with others. Your pitfall describes your disadvantage. It's the potential downside of your personality Advantages. To avoid pitfalls, focus on those opportunities that maximize your Advantages. In this book, you can find your Archetype's pitfall in your report. It's described as "What's Not the Highest and Best Value." You don't know it yet, but you have certain blind spots when it comes to how the world sees you. Those are not necessarily negatives, and the key is not to "fix" those, but instead to be aware of the areas where you are least likely to have leverage.

Primary Advantage: The way in which you are most likely to impress and influence people when you communicate. This is your strongest Advantage, the one that makes you most able to uniquely add value. When you communicate using your primary Advantage, people are more likely to hear and remember you.

Quicksand: A type of interaction in which a positive outcome is difficult and exhausting for your personality. In these situations, you feel awkward, or even trapped. Situations become quicksand for you if they don't allow you to play to your Advantages. (See also: WELLSPRING)

Secondary Advantage: Every person mostly uses two Advantages. Your secondary Advantage is the one that describes how you use your primary Advantage. Together, your primary and secondary Advantages form your Archetype.

Trigger: A hardwired response in communication. When you feel fascinated, something or someone is triggering this response. In my previous book, *Fascinate*, I described how brands influence behavior with Triggers. When applied to your personality, your Triggers become Advantages.

Twin: Your Twin is the Archetype that's most similar to your own. It has the same top two Advantages as you do, just in reverse order. (For example, The Victor is the twin of The Maestro.) By learning about your Twin, you gain a more dimensional view of how others see you.

Wellspring: A situation that allows you to fully apply your natural Advantages, so that you can become your most valuable. In these moments, you feel energized and focused. (See also: QUICKSAND)

HOW I DEVELOPED THE FASCINATION ADVANTAGE SYSTEM

Until 2010, I helped brands become more fascinating. But soon, I noticed something curious. Whenever I talked with people about their company's brand, afterward they would approach me. One by one, shyly or with bravado, they asked me this same question:

"So . . . what makes *me* fascinating?"

After a while, I decided it was time to shift my focus from how the world sees *products* to how the world sees *people*. How does your individual communication style determine your ability to capture attention and influence decisions? In other words, how do *you* fascinate?

I'm fascinated by psychology, but I'm not a psychologist, and this test is not based on psychology. Along those lines, I'm very interested in Myers-Briggs, DISC, and other systems, but I don't want to replicate what they have already done so well: showing you how you see the world.

New answers require a new perspective, one that looks from a different point of view. I developed this system the way I would develop advertising for Remy Martin, or Target, or PowerAde, or any other of my campaigns: by combining research, best practices, and experienced intuition. After decades working with the top brands and agencies in the world, I was able to see how millions of people respond to certain types of messages, and not others. I was able to watch what actually moved the needle for results—how brands communicate value to consumers, and how companies earn sales. I then extrapolated that marketing research, combined it with my own studies, and learned how individuals are seen by others.

The result is a methodology that combines both personality *and* marketing. That's new. By combining personality and marketing, your Anthem will convey your most desirable traits—or, as a marketer would say, your "unique value proposition," or your "benefits."

Rather than looking at other tests and profiles and assessments that show *how you see the world*, this turns the mirror into a window, revealing *how the world sees you*, and how you can use that insight to improve your communication.

By focusing on how you add distinct value, this method allows you to build your career and your life around *differences* rather than *strengths*.

Seeing yourself through this lens represents a new approach. But as I showed in Chapters 1 and 2 of this book, being *good* or even being *better* is no longer enough. To be noticed and to make a difference in your life, the value you add must be *distinct*.

As you also learned in this book, your Archetype is a reflection of your personal communication style. It tells you how you're most likely to engage and persuade people. By recognizing your Archetype's unique attributes and accentuating them, you learn how to become more persuasive. You learn how to fascinate by becoming more of yourself.

My team and I examined the inner team workings of large corporations, small businesses, and start-ups. A few examples of the ways we learned how individuals add value:

- We measured large groups within companies to find out how the employees of a company can positively (or negatively) drive a company's overall brand.
- We compared competing companies in the same industry, to see how they differed in their use of the seven Advantages.
- We measured high-performing talent, and how they applied certain personality Advantages to win business and get results.
- We guided tens of thousands of people through the Anthem method.

Over the past three years, we've learned how employees and leaders become more valued, more respected, and more fascinating to everyone around them. In every case, we searched for answers to improving performance:

- How team members can add more distinct value for their clients and company
- The highest and best use of an individual's personality Advantages
- How a leader influences outcomes by leveraging a well-defined point of difference

The resulting findings were based on both numbers and on experience. Part science, part art.

Visit HowToFascinate.com for our most recent findings, and how you can apply this insight to your company or group.

INSIDE THE RESEARCH: HOW WE DEVELOP OUR FASCINATING FINDINGS

I wouldn't call myself a numbers geek. But I do kind of geek out when looking at the numbers behind how different personalities fascinate. One of my favorite parts of my job is the moment when I first open the spreadsheet of numbers revealing the clusters of Archetypes within a group.

If you read my last book, *Fascinate*, you know that originally I studied what makes brands and products fascinating. As I explored the patterns in how customers behave when they're fascinated, I realized that it's far more interesting to study those customers themselves. People, rather than products. (You, for example.)

By 2010 my team and I had developed the first algorithm in the world to measure what makes someone fascinating—in other words, how he is most likely to deliver his highest value. Today we can map an entire organization. We've mapped groups within companies such as AT&T, New York Life, California Pizza Kitchen, Cisco, Intel, Qualcomm, State Farm, and shown them how to apply their unique Advantages with customers. Next, we began to show groups how they compare to our average test population, so they can further differentiate themselves from their competition.

This is our most exciting area of study, and in this section, you'll get a top-line look inside our new research. By the end of this section, you'll probably be fascinated to learn more about your own group's results (even if you're not a numbers geek!).

HOW OUR TESTING PROCESS WORKS FOR GROUPS

Before we begin training or coaching a group, everyone in that group takes the same assessment that you're taking as part of this book. My team dissects their results, identifying the patterns in how they apply the Advantages and comparing them to our previous findings.

First, we look at the group's distribution of Advantages. Here's an example of what that looks like:

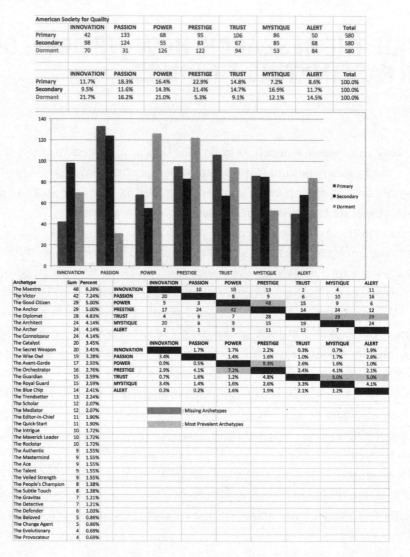

American Society for Quality

	INNOVATION	PASSION	POWER	PRESTIGE	TRUST	MYSTIQUE	ALERT	Total
Primary	42	133	68	95	106	86	50	580
Secondary	98	124	55	83	67	85	68	580
Dormant	70	31	126	122	94	53	84	580

	INNOVATION	PASSION	POWER	PRESTIGE	TRUST	MYSTIQUE	ALERT	Total
Primary	11.7%	18.3%	16.4%	22.9%	14.8%	7.2%	8.6%	100.0%
Secondary	9.5%	11.6%	14.3%	21.4%	14.7%	16.9%	11.7%	100.0%
Dormant	21.7%	16.2%	21.0%	5.3%	9.1%	12.1%	14.5%	100.0%

Archetype	Sum	Percent
The Maestro	48	8.28%
The Victor	42	7.24%
The Good Citizen	29	5.00%
The Anchor	29	5.00%
The Diplomat	28	4.83%
The Architect	24	4.14%
The Archer	24	4.14%
The Connoisseur	24	4.14%
The Catalyst	20	3.45%
The Secret Weapon	20	3.45%
The Wise Owl	19	3.28%
The Avant-Garde	17	2.93%
The Orchestrator	16	2.76%
The Guardian	15	2.59%
The Royal Guard	15	2.59%
The Blue Chip	14	2.41%
The Trendsetter	13	2.24%
The Scholar	12	2.07%
The Mediator	12	2.07%
The Editor-in-Chief	11	1.90%
The Quick-Start	11	1.90%
The Intrigue	10	1.72%
The Maverick Leader	10	1.72%
The Rockstar	10	1.72%
The Authentic	9	1.55%
The Mastermind	9	1.55%
The Ace	9	1.55%
The Talent	9	1.55%
The Veiled Strength	9	1.55%
The People's Champion	8	1.38%
The Subtle Touch	8	1.38%
The Gravitas	7	1.21%
The Detective	7	1.21%
The Defender	6	1.03%
The Beloved	5	0.86%
The Change Agent	5	0.86%
The Evolutionary	4	0.69%
The Provocateur	4	0.69%

	INNOVATION	PASSION	POWER	PRESTIGE	TRUST	MYSTIQUE	ALERT
INNOVATION		10	10	13	2	4	11
PASSION	20		8	9	6	10	16
POWER	5	3		48	15	9	6
PRESTIGE	17	24	42		14	24	12
TRUST	4	9	7	28		29	29
MYSTIQUE	20	8	9	15	19		24
ALERT	2	1	9	11	12	7	

	INNOVATION	PASSION	POWER	PRESTIGE	TRUST	MYSTIQUE	ALERT
INNOVATION		1.7%	1.7%	2.2%	0.3%	0.7%	1.9%
PASSION	3.4%		1.4%	1.6%	1.0%	1.7%	2.8%
POWER	0.9%	0.5%		8.3%	2.6%	1.6%	1.0%
PRESTIGE	2.9%	4.1%	7.2%		2.4%	4.1%	2.1%
TRUST	0.7%	1.6%	1.2%	4.8%		5.0%	5.0%
MYSTIQUE	3.4%	1.4%	1.6%	2.6%	3.3%		4.1%
ALERT	0.3%	0.2%	1.6%	1.9%	2.1%	1.2%	

: Missing Archetypes

: Most Prevalent Archetypes

Then we find what Archetypes are most common or rare in their group. This is where it really starts getting interesting. Because just like a forensic scientist can look at a fingerprint and see details that seem invisible to an untrained eye, we can look at the distribution of Archetypes and immediately deduce a wide range of conclusions about the group.

This chart might just look like numbers to you, but to me, those numbers capture the face of an organization as clearly as a team photograph. In fact, probably better than a photograph.

A photo can capture demographic info such as age and gender, as well as psychographic insights ranging from lifestyles to hairstyles. But these numbers describe what's really going on inside their communication and interactions, their relationships and goals. By studying the proportion of Archetypes within a group, I can get a very clear idea of what this organization is all about: how they hire and promote, what they value internally, how they are likely to market themselves, even their insecurities and blind spots.

Once we review the group's Advantages, and their Archetypes, our next step is to build a heat map based on this data. This heat map shows how their group clusters in certain Archetypes within their organization.

PRIMARY ADVANTAGE \ SECONDARY ADVANTAGE	INNOVATION You change the game with creativity	PASSION You connect with emotion	POWER You lead with command	PRESTIGE You earn respect with higher standards	TRUST You build loyalty with consistency	MYSTIQUE You communicate with substance	ALERT You prevent problems with care
INNOVATION You change the game with creativity		1.7%	1.7%	2.2%	0.3%	0.7%	1.9%
PASSION You connect with emotion	3.4%		1.4%	1.6%	0.9%	1.7%	2.8%
POWER You lead with command	0.9%	0.5%		8.3%	2.6%	1.6%	1.0%
PRESTIGE You earn respect with higher standards	2.9%	4.1%	7.2%		2.4%	4.1%	2.1%
TRUST You build loyalty with consistency	0.7%	1.6%	1.2%	4.8%		5.0%	5.0%
MYSTIQUE You communicate with substance	3.4%	1.4%	1.6%	2.6%	3.3%		4.1%
ALERT You prevent problems with care	0.4%	0.2%	1.6%	1.9%	2.1%	1.2%	

We create heat maps in preparation for virtual or online training. Often, a member of my team meets this group in person or over the phone. In addition to seeing the quantitative data behind the group, we also gain anecdotal, qualitative learning about them. By now, having done this several hundred times, I can look at the numbers and before meeting one person from the organization and can predict how they'll dress, what points will make them say "a-ha!" and even how to make them laugh.

I look forward to learning about a group by looking at their scores, and then meeting that group in person. It's like getting a glimpse of facial details in a baby's ultrasound image. Here's how that works. I usually receive these analytics about thirty-six hours before meeting a group in person. By that point, just about everyone has completed the assessment (and I tease those who don't that they score highest on the "Slacker" Advantage). I open the email immediately, because I'm always curious to learn their patterns. Sometimes it's easy to predict the results. Other times, I'm surprised. My team and I will dig more deeply into the industry or specific corporation to understand communication within this group.

As you'll see, group results can often be even more telling than an individual's report.

BACKGROUND ON OUR RESEARCH

We interviewed entrepreneurs and solopreneurs, HR managers and prospective hires, CEOs and CIOs and CMOs. We helped major corporations such as Cisco and Intuit to recruit better talent and help each person rise to their highest potential on the team.

We scored hundreds of different groups and hundreds of thousands of participants, with the Fascination Advantage (the same assessment in this book).

I shared this system with thousands of AT&T sales executives, helping them fascinate customers and prospects, then went on to develop a program to help their support staff learn how to communicate and get better results. Leaders within global corporations and hundreds of small businesses have learned this method. I coached global sales teams, solopreneurs, and elite leadership retreats, in industries ranging from health care to salon management to real estate, showing professionals how to win by tapping into the way they naturally fascinate. From this system grew our training curriculum for leaders, corporate teams, and entrepreneurs, which is now inside companies around the world.

Recently, we've been digging more deeply into the numbers, uncovering the patterns linking Advantages to gender, level of seniority, industries, and age. Some of the findings surprised us. Others confirmed what we already knew to be true but hadn't yet measured. And the results paint an even more vibrant picture of how your career is shaped by how the world sees you.

WHEN ADVANTAGES CORRELATE TO LEVEL OF SENIORITY

There is a strong and consistent relationship between three Advantages and level of seniority. These three Advantages are Alert, Trust, and Prestige.

The higher you go in the ranks of a company, the less likely people are to have a primary Alert Advantage. This inverse relationship between Alert and seniority can be seen in the hiring process. For instance, administrative assistants are hired to prevent problems, whereas VPs and managers are usually recruited to pursue opportunities.

Within the finance industry, for instance, a staff member is 300% more likely to have primary Alert than a CEO.

The findings for the Trust Advantage are similar. The higher you go in an organization, the less likely employees are to have Trust as a primary Advantage. On average, a company's staff members score twice as high on primary Trust Advantage as their C-level counterparts. This makes sense, because staff members are more likely to succeed by maintaining daily routines and schedule. The higher people rise in an organization, the more likely they are to have a primary Prestige Advantage.

This is consistent with our involvement with high performers inside top organizations. For instance, recently we studied an elite team within one of the most successful and respected brands in the world. This was the company's crème de la crème, intensely high performers, handpicked from around the world. This team was 191% more likely than the average population to have a primary Prestige Advantage. Within this group:

39% had primary Prestige

only 5% had primary Passion

only 3% had primary Innovation (77% less than our average population)

This group isn't focused on change or emotional connection, but on pure performance.

Interestingly, there is not a strong correlation between Passion and level of seniority. The same is true of Mystique: A senior executive is not more or less likely to use Mystique. However, there is a strong correlation between both Passion and Mystique and *industry*.

HOW DIFFERENT INDUSTRIES USE DIFFERENT ADVANTAGES

As a whole, people in creative fields score extremely high on Passion and Innovation. They succeed through exploring new paths and discovering fresh solutions. They typically have a very low use of Alert, because they're not focusing their communication on practical, nitty-gritty details.

Marketers, it's no surprise, score very high on Passion. They create emotional connections between products and people.

Who scores lowest on Passion? Employees in information technology, and finance.

Engineers, on the other hand, score high on Mystique. This makes sense. Most engineers prefer to think through problems and processes independently, rather than participating in rowdy group brainstorming. Engineers also have the ability to design, develop, and analyze rational processes through scientific theory.

So, what if an engineer doesn't score high on Mystique, and instead scores highly on Passion? Does that mean she can't be a good engineer? No, not at all. It means that she has an uncommon Advantage when it comes to connecting with people, so she should leverage this unusual way of adding value in engineering. For instance, if she's a civil engineer, she might design buildings with an intuitive and open feeling that makes visitors feel an emotion, or use emotion to more effectively sell her ideas.

Let's compare this with sales. Salespeople are more likely to use Power and Passion, because they get results by building strong relationships and driving the decision-making process. Yet these folks usually score very low on Mystique, because they naturally want to jump in and start a conversation rather than coolly observing their prospect.

We work closely with different areas in human resources, because this department usually recruits and manages the talent within an organization. To improve our relationship with HR managers, we studied them. We found that they have a higher use of the Passion Advantage than other departments, because this personality is usually a "people person," both literally and figuratively. For instance, HR leaders are 300% more likely to have primary Passion Advantage than those in IT.

When we looked at the data, we also found the very highest use of Trust Advantage among finance managers. This holds true in our extensive work with dozens of groups of financial advisors and managers. When we studied four separate groups of senior advisors from the same Fortune 50 company, we found that they were 2.5 times more likely than the average population to have Trust as a primary Advantage.

These advisors were also four times more likely to be the Archetype The Diplomat (Trust + Prestige) than the average population, reflecting their skillful ability to diplomatically steer a discussion with high-end investment clients.

Who had the lowest use of the Trust Advantage? Marketers. (Now, before you laugh and make jokes about marketers being untrustworthy, remember that the Trust Advantage is about consistency and routine in their communication. A marketer typically communicates both personally and professionally with engaging new approaches, which means they are less likely to apply the Trust Advantage.) In fact, finance managers are *six times* more likely to have primary Trust than a marketing CEO.

By comparison, finance managers score low on Passion. They don't connect through emotion, color, imagery, and body language. Marketing leaders are very likely to connect through emotion—they are twice as likely to use Passion than finance managers. Among staff, those in marketing use twice as much Passion as those in IT, while these two groups share the same use of Power.

How about age? Older generations have a more equal distribution of the Advantages. However, Millennials have a higher concentration of Passion and

Prestige. And here's a surprising fact: Millennials have a lower use of Innovation than their older counterparts. (Picture a baby boomer riding his Harley motorcycle, and you might see why.)

GENDER AND ADVANTAGES

Compared to women, men are more likely to have a primary Mystique or Innovation Advantage. In fact, men have 4 out of the 5 top frequencies of Innovation. (The exception? Female CEOs.)

In one batch of findings, we looked at our numbers for 12,390 CEOs and business owners. These included CEOs of corporations, leaders and owners of small to medium-sized businesses, and solopreneurs. We found that among CEOs, men and women both have strong use of Prestige. Female CEOs lead with almost three times more Passion than their male counterparts. Male CEOs, in contrast, are twice as likely to have primary Power than the women.

Here's an important point for women to know. The use of the Power Advantage increases with rank within an organization, but the lift is even more pronounced for women. Power as a primary Advantage is *three times* more frequent among female VPs than among female staff members.

If you want to rise within your organization, it's important to understand the Power Advantage. This is not to say that everyone should communicate through Power—you should communicate authentically according to your own Advantages. However, even if you score low on Power, you should understand how others around you and above you are using it so that you can build rapport. You probably also want to know how to selectively and strategically use this means of communication, so that you can be more likely to reach your potential.

Our newest research is in the area of hiring, teams, and leadership. What Advantages does your group lack, and do you need to recruit that Advantage? As a leader, what types of employees are most likely to help you focus on delivering your Anthem, rather than trying to do everything yourself? Which types of people will balance out your own Advantages? To access our freshest results and insights, visit HowToFascinate.com/Resources.

THE 49 ARCHETYPES

ARCHETYPE DESCRIPTIONS

The Ringleader: Power + Passion (page 128)

You are motivated, and motivating. People feel confident when you encourage them. Your excitement and drive are contagious.

The Guardian: Power + Trust (page 136)

Prominent and genuine, you are an authority in your field. You lead others with a steady yet gentle approach. People consider you the "rock" of any group and follow you because of your dependability.

The Mastermind: Power + Mystique (page 140)

In a world of uncertainty, you remain rational and grounded. You bring a quiet power to the table and are always one step ahead of the competition. People respect your expertise and your no-nonsense approach to life. You are a self-reliant and collected leader.

The Maestro: Power + Prestige (page 132)

Confidence is one of your greatest resources, and you waste no time in accomplishing your goals. Never wanting to settle, you are ambitious and always looking for ways to improve. You are a strong leader and people admire your unwavering conviction. As a Maestro, you face any obstacle head-on.

The Defender: Power + Alert (page 144)

People respect your strong leadership and by-the-book attitude. You are always on the lookout for potential problems, and your proactive nature is a welcome addition to any team. You approach every situation cautiously, but once you've made a decision you implement changes swiftly. You get the job done.

The Change Agent: Power + Innovation (page 124)

You lead with a fresh outlook and are always thinking of new and inventive ideas. People enjoy your untraditional and vibrant personality. In business and in life, you are unafraid to challenge the status quo and you like shaking things up. People respect that you are not afraid to be different.

The Beloved: Passion + Trust (page 160)

Passion and Trust make you a welcome presence on any team. People quickly connect with you and often seek your guidance in times of distress. Your nurturing nature and loyalty gradually win over customers and co-workers.

The Intrigue: Passion + Mystique (page 164)

Sometimes reserved and sometimes excited, you mix the best of both worlds. You assess situations carefully before getting emotionally invested. People are drawn in by your enigmatic personality. Your analytical skills and discernment are an important addition to any team.

The Talent: Passion + Prestige (page 156)

Often a role model of an engaging personality, you know how to get others involved. You entertain with panache. Though some may chalk it up to natural talent, you intensely focus on improving your presentation style, and you are always striving for excellence. Good enough is never good enough.

The People's Champion: Passion + Power (page 152)

Most enjoy your company because you're naturally supportive of the group. Your dynamic personality and conviction can make you a great leader. People know that if you're on their side, everything will be okay. You get emotionally invested in others and you want to succeed as a group. You are an advocate of people and ideas.

The Orchestrator: Passion + Alert (page 168)

You are always mindful of a situation and you can quickly discern how to achieve the best results. People look to you for leadership because of your ability to command attention and inspire others. Though passion is important, you also make sure that projects are always on track and that the details are not forgotten. People know they can count on you.

The Catalyst: Passion + Innovation (page 148)

You dislike ordinary ideas and communication. When others can't find solutions to their problems, they come to you for out-of-the-box thinking. You're highly creative and your enthusiasm for inventing creative solutions is contagious. People gravitate toward your energizing personality.

The Subtle Touch: Mystique + Passion (page 176)

You prefer an understated excellence to outright flashiness. You're able to connect with others easily but sometimes you prefer to remain reserved. When others need guidance, they come to you for your analytical prowess and your profound ability to read between the lines.

The Wise Owl: Mystique + Trust (page 188)

Calm and collected, you don't buckle under pressure. You are an aid in times of struggle because you're usually one step ahead of the problem. People respect you for your modest yet unruffled style of leading. You easily meld into groups and you can also work independently.

The Royal Guard: Mystique + Prestige (page 184)

Sophisticated and elegant in nature, you are often respected. When you communicate with people you're astute and reserved. You enjoy working independently and you are always dedicated to whatever you're doing. People can count on you to make a keen choice for a complicated situation.

The Veiled Strength: Mystique + Power (page 180)

As a realistic and intentional individual, you have the ability to find the best solutions and reach the highest goals. You like to base your decisions on facts instead of a gut feeling. People respect you for your subtle yet strong leadership and your direct communication style. With you, they know what they're getting.

The Archer: Mystique + Alert (page 192)

You are reasoned and pragmatic, and you enjoy a well-organized workspace. Your sharp eye can spot problems before anyone else knows what's going on. You analyze situations with the utmost care, and your communication is always on target. When people talk with you they know you mean business.

The Secret Weapon: Mystique + Innovation (page 172)

Even under intense pressure, you produce creative solutions. Although you enjoy being commended for your achievements, you prefer to work quietly and independently. You fully test ideas before sharing them with a group but once you do they take notice of your ingenuity.

The Connoisseur: Prestige + Passion (page 200)

The people around you appreciate your insightful knowledge and your warm-hearted attitude. You like to lift others up and you help them feel confident in their own abilities. Always striving for improvements, you make a point of keeping yourself in the know on the latest trends and news. Even the toughest skeptics can be swayed by your enthusiasm and expertise.

The Blue Chip: Prestige + Trust (page 208)

Your eye for detail is unmatched and you have a reputation for quiet excellence. People trust you because of your calm leadership and your impeccable work. You are most comfortable with the familiar and people know that they can depend on your established expertise.

The Architect: Prestige + Mystique (page 212)

High-quality results are your standard and you really do your research. Your communication with others is restrained and polished, and you don't lose your cool. You can defuse heated situations by focusing on the facts and helping others talk it out. Even though you prefer to be quiet, when you speak, people listen.

The Victor: Prestige + Power (page 204)

People look to you for leadership because you are confident and results-oriented. You aren't afraid of confrontation and you can easily resolve conflicts. Your ambition and competitive nature propel you to the front of the pack and gain you the respect of other leaders.

The Scholar: Prestige + Alert (page 216)

The bar is always set high for you and for those around you. You have a proven track record and you know how to get results through a systematic approach. You're intellectual, ambitious, and disciplined when it comes to reaching your goals. When others waver, you continue on.

The Avant-Garde: Prestige + Innovation (page 196)

Forward-thinking and enterprising, you lead and others follow. You're on top of the latest trends and always looking for ways to transition them into the future. Your original outlook on tough problems and bold style make you a captivating leader. Others take notice.

The Coordinator: Alert + Passion (page 224)

With practical skills and a discerning eye, you bring a constructive approach to every project. You keep everyone on their toes and remind them that failure isn't an option. You make sure that deadlines are met. Though you aren't as social as some personalities, you are loyal to those close to you and you make sure that everyone has what they need to succeed.

The Mediator: Alert + Trust (page 236)

Steadfast and composed, you are the hub of activity for those around you. Whenever there is a conflict, people look to you for guidance. Through your compassionate communication style and your efficient and structured work, you can be the glue that holds a team together.

The Detective: Alert + Mystique (page 240)

You focus on the details and expect your colleagues to follow suit. You consider your response to others carefully before giving it, and you prefer to work independently. Others appreciate your thought-out and rational approach to issues because you watch the details to solve the puzzle. Your meticulous approach can be essential to finishing important projects.

The Editor-in-Chief: Alert + Prestige (page 232)

Excellence is what you strive for and you keep projects on time and on budget. Your deliverables are detailed and usually error-free because you have an intense concentration while working. You prefer to focus on one thing at a time but you also work efficiently and quickly. You get results.

The Ace: Alert + Power (page 228)

You're a decisive and forthright leader. You command attention in an unintimidating way. People respect you for your tireless pursuit of what you believe in. You like to set clear goals for yourself and you stay focused until you've accomplished them. For you, familiarity is good and you consider carefully before trying something new.

The Composer: Alert + Innovation (page 220)

Although you enjoy routine, you aren't afraid to step out of your comfort zone and try something new, if it will help reach your goals. You stay focused on the big picture and help others reach the finish line. When problems arise, you think about them logically and respond carefully with feedback that is fine-tuned.

The Rockstar: Innovation + Passion (page 244)

When you enter a room you command attention (and know how to earn it). You help liven up any situation with your humor and bold personality. You love experimenting and you're not afraid to throw some unorthodox ideas out there. Like an actual rock star, you enjoy the limelight and enthralling those around you.

The Artisan: Innovation + Trust (page 256)

You are good at generating and implementing creative ideas. But you also appreciate the tried-and-true methods. You are thoughtful of situations and when you implement an idea it's because you're sure it will work. You enjoy brainstorming and you're flexible with change, but you make sure to remain practical.

The Provocateur: Innovation + Mystique (page 260)

Clever and adept is how most people would describe you. You generate a variety of fresh ideas and change the rules of how to do business. People are curious to learn more about you, and they can't wait to see what you'll come up with next.

The Trendsetter: Innovation + Prestige (page 252)

In every industry from fashion to gadgets, you can sense what will be hot tomorrow. People admire you because you're imaginative and ambitious. You bring a cutting-edge interpretation to the table and others are impressed by your ideas. You are happiest when working against the grain.

The Maverick Leader: Innovation + Power (page 248)

Pioneering and irreverent, you are a strong leader. You often have new ideas and you constantly excite others with your enthusiasm. You don't like slipping into routine and you are comfortable experimenting with new ideas, even in a high-stress environment. Others admire your entrepreneurial spirit.

The Quick-Start: Innovation + Alert (page 264)

Your ability to rapidly identify opportunities and execute a plan with determination makes you a vital addition to a team. You mix creativity with a thorough and diligent delivery. Your ability to think on your feet helps you make important decisions under pressure. You handle situations with care, and as a result, people know you're reliable.

The Authentic: Trust + Passion (page 272)

An approachable and dependable nature makes you easily likable. People know they can come to you if they need a shoulder to cry on. You also care passionately about the projects you do and those who work with you know you're trustworthy. You avoid confrontation and like to keep harmony in a group.

The Anchor: Trust + Mystique (page 284)

In moments of crisis, people come to you for advice. You like to take a quiet approach to problems and you keep your cool even in the toughest of situations. When everyone else is getting agitated, you're coming up with a workable solution. What you say makes sense and has been carefully evaluated. Once you're ready to share your thoughts, everyone listens. They rely on your purposeful and analytical way of working.

The Diplomat: Trust + Prestige (page 280)

Others have confidence in you because of your commitment to your principles. You lead others by example with a strong work ethic and ambition. You have a subtle yet confident approach to life. People know that the work you do will be solid and that you're capable of delivering quality results.

The Gravitas: Trust + Power (page 276)

Hardworking and dignified, you naturally exude authority. When people are stuck they often come to you for advice because you think through the best course of action and recommend it with conviction. You're respected for your lengthy experience and reliable stability. You are good in times of crisis, and unfazed by challenges.

The Good Citizen: Trust + Alert (page 288)

People know that you'll handle the details and guide others to their goals. You counsel people to execute their tasks with care and attention to detail. You are conscientious and loyal to those close to you. You do everything you can to help them succeed. People appreciate how prepared and dedicated you are.

The Evolutionary: Trust + Innovation (page 268)

You have a clear vision and follow through on your ideas. You think on your feet and can come up with alternative solutions to pressing problems. You have the ability to adapt when needed but you prefer to work in a structured environment. And you like implementing steady improvements over radical new ideas. Your methods evolve steadily.

DOUBLE TROUBLES: TOO MUCH OF A GOOD THING

The Drama: Passion + Passion (page 298)

Passion makes people intimately attuned to the feelings of others. But taken too far, without blending in a secondary Advantage, Passion can become too sensitive. Avoid becoming overly theatrical. And don't let yourself take things too seriously.

The Old Guard: Trust + Trust (page 313)

Trust builds consistency and loyalty. But when you don't combine Trust with a secondary Advantage, it can become too predictable, and perhaps a little boring. Avoid becoming too stuck in your own ways. Sometimes it's essential to try new things. Don't become so unmovable that people become frustrated by you.

The Deadbolt: Mystique + Mystique (page 301)

Mystique tends to be introspective. You rarely share information about yourself, but too much secrecy can negatively impact your trustworthiness. People may wonder whether you have something to hide. Avoid becoming so introverted and unemotional that you completely shut others out. This can make it hard for others to work with you.

The Imperial: Prestige + Prestige (page 304)

Prestige thrives on public recognition. But too much focus on your achievements can make you look pretentious. Being completely unafraid to promote yourself can cause others to be annoyed easily. Avoid thinking you are superior to others. This can make you seem arrogant and cold.

The Aggressor: Power + Power (page 295)

A Power personality exudes a natural authority. Yet taken to the extreme, without blending in a secondary Advantage, you can become too dominant and forceful. Avoid crushing the voices of others and silencing their contributions to the group discussion.

The Control Freak: Alert + Alert (page 307)
In Control Freak mode, when you forget to use your secondary Advantage, negative energy can make you unpleasant company. Don't be so compulsive and exacting that others don't want to work with you. Don't be such a downer that you constantly dismiss the ideas of others. Avoid micromanaging to such an extreme that you make it impossible to be productive.

The Anarchy: Innovation + Innovation (page 310)
Innovation provides a strong dose of creative energy to any organization. But in excess, you can become unruly and insubordinate. Out-of-the-box ideas can be great, but don't become a troublemaker or throw crazy ideas into the brainstorming session just for the sake of it. Avoid creating a volatile and chaotic workspace.

TWELVE INSPIRATIONS FOR YOUR FASCINATION ADVANTAGE

12 The greatest value you can add is to become more of yourself.

11 You will not make a difference by being quiet. You only make a difference by being heard.

10 To become more successful, don't change who you are. Become more of who you are.

9 Stand out, or don't bother.

8 Clients don't hire you because you are balanced. They hire you because you are extraordinary in some way.

7 You will never rise to your greatest potential by being all things to all people.

6 100% yourself trumps 100% perfect.

5 You don't learn how to be fascinating. You unlearn how to be boring.

4   You don't have to find the light. You are the light. And when you let your personality shine, you can light up the world.

3   Your personality is the greatest differentiator that you have.

2   The most powerful way to empower someone is to show them their own highest value.

1   The world is not changed by people who sort of care.

FAQ—FASCINATINGLY ASKED QUESTIONS

Q: When I look at my analytics, three Advantages have almost exactly the same percentage. What does that mean?

A: The algorithm measures your Advantages to a tenth of a percent, and your report shows the whole, rounded percentage. Your primary and secondary Advantages are determined by your top two scoring qualities. When you have more than two Advantages with the same score, it means that you can tap into that third Advantage as well.

Q: If the key is to understand how the world perceives me, why is this a self-test?

A: This is not a test built on psychology, it's built on branding. Just as a brand communicates to consumers, you communicate to listeners. Our algorithm measures how others are most likely to perceive you, based on the patterns of signals and cues that you communicate.

Q: How can this system help my team?

A: When each person on a team knows their most valuable differences, everyone can see each other at their best. When this happens, communication improves and productivity increases. Many teams find that it's motivating to learn each other's natural Advantages.

Q: What happened to "Triggers"? Did they become "Advantages"?

A: Triggers describe how brands are most likely to "trigger" a response in consumers. The seven Triggers were originally outlined in my book *Fascinate*. The word *Trigger* described how brands stand out, while *Advantage* describes how an individual stands out.

Q: Did you change the names "Alarm" and "Rebellion"?

A: We revised "Alarm" to "Alert," reflecting this personality's ability to quickly pick up on details. We also revised "Rebellion" to "Innovation," describing this personality's creative approach.

If you have other questions, don't hesitate to reach out: hello@HowToFascinate.com.

Every copy of *How the World Sees You* includes one complimentary Fascination Advantage® assessment.

Turn to the back of this book, and you'll find your individual scratch-off code. Take your assessment, and in just a few minutes, you'll find out how the world sees you.

This QR code will guide you through a quick video preview of what's inside your Fascination Advantage online report.

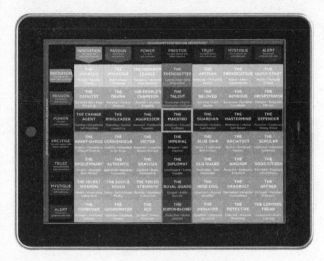

Online: *HowToFascinate.com/ FascinationReport*

Your customized report will describe how you are most likely to impress and influence others. You'll find out how to focus on what you're already doing right, so you can do more of it.

On a team, *differences* are more valuable than *similarities*. Find out your own team's different Fascination Advantages, so everyone can rise to their highest value.
Online: **HOW**TO**FASCINATE**.COM/RESOURCES

IF YOUR PRIMARY ADVANTAGE IS:	HOW OTHERS SEE YOU	ONE WAY TO ADD VALUE
INNOVATION	Creative Independent Entrepreneurial	Invent creative solutions that tweak tradition.
PASSION	Expressive Intuitive Engaging	Apply your natural optimism and energy to build relationships within the group.
POWER	Confident Goal-Oriented Decisive	Lead others by becoming an authority.
PRESTIGE	Ambitious Uncompromising Respected	Use admiration to raise the value of yourself and your company.
TRUST	Stable Dependable Familiar	Reinforce consistent patterns so people know they can depend on you.
MYSTIQUE	Understated Logical Observant	Focus everyone's communication on results, not drama.
ALERT	Proactive Organized Reliable	Keep the team on top of details and deadlines.

Download a free copy of this cheat sheet online at **HOW**TO**FASCINATE**.COM/RESOURCES

10 WAYS TO START APPLYING YOUR ANTHEM TODAY

1 Update your social media profiles (such as your LinkedIn profile and Twitter bio) to include your Anthem.

2 Share your Anthem with a few co-workers or clients, and ask for input on examples of how you are already applying your Anthem.

3 Post your Anthem on Facebook, and ask for input from friends and followers.

4 Identify one way that you are already living your Anthem at work and at home.

5 Identify one way in which your communication is NOT yet consistent with your Anthem.

6 Encourage other people on your team to create their own Anthem, so you can immediately identify how everyone in your group is uniquely suited to add value.

7 Before your next speech or presentation, include a slide with your Anthem, so your listeners can know how you are going to deliver value, right from the start.

8 Tweet your Anthem to me so my team and I can see. Here's an example: My Anthem is STRATEGIC ANSWERS cc: **@Sally Hogshead #AnthemInAction**

9 Post your Anthem outside your office, so that visitors can immediately know how to tap into who you are at your best.

10 Download your free PDF online at **How**To**Fascinate**.com/Anthem

PRECISE ATTENTION TO DETAIL

NURTURING RELATIONSHIPS

TIRELESS WORK ETHIC

METHODICAL STRATEGY

Your Anthem helps you feel confident and focused, so you're more likely to hold your listener's attention and get your message across.

Create your Anthem in Part III of this book, and then check out the online training materials to add more value every time you communicate.

When everyone on your team has an Anthem, communication improves, conflict is reduced, and productivity increases. Our Anthem tool kits are great for training, off-site meetings, and discovery sessions.

Scan this QR code to watch a video about creating your Anthem.

The world's most fascinating online training and workshops

For complete instructions on building your Anthem and creating Anthems with your entire organization, please visit:

Online: **HOW**TO**FASCINATE**.COM/ANTHEM | Email: **START**@**HOW**TO**FASCINATE**.COM

5 STEPS TO A MORE ENGAGED TEAM

DISCOVER HOW THE WORLD SEES YOU:
Begin with the Fascination Advantage® assessment. Have each person on the team discover how they are most likely to add distinct value.

LEARN YOUR TEAM'S PATTERNS:
With a "Heat Map" of your team's top Advantages, you'll see your team's patterns of communication.

ONLINE TRAINING:
Create a deeper understanding of core Fascinate principles in an interactive online environment. Build better teams, center your communication around your Anthem and discover the best of how the world sees you.

ANTHEM WORKSHOP:
Schedule an Anthem Workshop, so each person in the office can create an Anthem to immediately identify how they are most likely to add value.

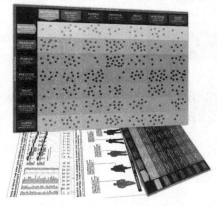

FREE RESOURCES:
Visit our website to access a range of free ways for everyone on the team to apply their Anthem around the office, in meetings, and with clients.

Online: **HOW**TO**FASCINATE**.COM/RESOURCES
Email: **START**@**HOW**TO**FASCINATE**.COM | Call: 855-**9SECOND**

The most successful teams allow individuals to focus on how they are different, rather than how they are similar.

Once everyone on your team has taken the Fascination Advantage assessment, review these questions as a group discussion. See how you are already applying the Advantages, and where you might tap into new Advantages among your group.

INNOVATION — What areas of your company could benefit from a new, more creative approach?

PASSION — In daily life around the office, how does your team build connections with each other?

POWER — What are different leadership styles within your team?

PRESTIGE — Give a few examples of goals or accomplishments that earn respect among your group.

TRUST — What types of activities build long-lasting bonds for your group?

MYSTIQUE — In meetings, does your group tend to interrupt and talk over each other? What would improve if you listened more?

ALERT — What types of details do you track most closely? Which fall through the cracks?

Online: **HOW**TO**FASCINATE**.COM/ANTHEM
Email: **START**@**HOW**TO**FASCINATE**.COM | Call: 855-**9SECOND**

Who do you need on your team to succeed? Which personality would be the perfect fit for your specific challenges? If you could describe exactly the type of person you need, what adjectives would you use to identify how they are different? Here are a few examples of our Anthems, organized by Advantage.

ANTHEM SAMPLES

▶ THE POWER ADVANTAGE
Confident Ambition
Engaging Relationships
Results-Oriented Ideas
Solid Expertise
Intense Work Ethic
Courageous Standards

▶ THE PRESTIGE ADVANTAGE
Modern Solutions
Elegant Attitude
Competitive Results
Spotless Credentials
Astute Attention to Detail
Detailed Expertise

▶ THE INNOVATION ADVANTAGE
Entrepreneurial Results
Creative Management
Original Communication
Deliberate Influence
Innovative Skillset
Sensational Focus

▶ THE PASSION ADVANTAGE
Bold Teambuilding
Compelling Relationships
Loyal Character
Thoughtful Influencer
Attentive Follow-through

▶ THE ALERT ADVANTAGE
Perfect Precision
Dedicated Expertise
Decisive Results
Productive Accuracy
Steadfast Results
Clear-cut Plan

▶ THE TRUST ADVANTAGE
Open-minded Problem Solving
Sincere Relationships
Enduring Values
Realistic Solutions
Genuine Relationships
Thoughtful Results

▶ THE MYSTIQUE ADVANTAGE
Inquisitive Mindset
Profound Results
Self-reliant Attitude
Sterling Insight
Assured Results
Sharp Leadership

Online: **HOW**TO**FASCINATE**.COM/ANTHEM
Email: **START**@**HOW**TO**FASCINATE**.COM | Call: 855-**9SECOND**

There's one marketplace that is more distracted, more competitive, and more commoditized than anywhere else. And that marketplace is... online dating.

Even if you've never done online dating, you can learn key lessons here. It's intimidating to describe yourself in an online dating profile, just like it's daunting to introduce yourself to a prospective customer or employer.

5 TIPS FOR CREATING AN ONLINE DATING PROFILE (OR ANY INTRODUCTION)

1 Think of your online dating profile like a "dating Anthem." Remember, your Anthem is the tagline for your personality. You can use this same exercise from Part III of this book for crafting the perfect intro.

2 Rather than describing yourself in terms of your interests or hobbies, bring your personality to life. Go back to your Fascination Advantage online report. Pick a few descriptive words and phrases to illustrate who you are.

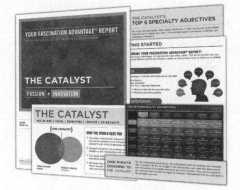

3 What type of personality are you looking for? Look at the Archetype Matrix, and pick three adjectives. Include those in your profile.

4 Remember: 100% yourself beats 100% perfect.

5 How To Fascinate is researching new ways to help you create more fascinating romance, marriage, and dating. Interested? Let us know!

Online: **HOW**TO**FASCINATE**.COM/ANTHEM
Email: **START**@**HOW**TO**FASCINATE**.COM | Call: 855-**9SECOND**

You might be curious about the people and purpose behind the Fascination Advantage assessment. A few words of introduction to my company, How To Fascinate:

WHAT IS HOW TO FASCINATE: We research and discover your personality's highest value, through the science of fascination.

OUR PURPOSE: We identify your most valuable traits, so you can become your most valuable you.

WHAT WE DO: We work with high-performing individuals, teams and companies, showing them how to communicate most persuasively by applying their natural personality Advantages.

HOW WE DO IT: We offer innovative programs, digital tools, online training, live presentations, home study courses, and train-the-trainer curriculum. Our core product is the Fascination Advantage assessment which measure your natural communication advantages, and the Fascination Anthem, a tool to pinpoint how you are different and what you do best.

WHY WE DO IT: We show you how you're naturally primed to succeed, so that you can become more fascinating and valuable every time you communicate.

WHY YOU SHOULD CARE: By applying our methods, you will grow your business, create better relationships, rise above the competition, and become intensely valuable to those who matter most.

HOWTOFASCINATE
DISCOVER YOURSELF THROUGH
THE SCIENCE OF FASCINATION

Online: **HOWTOFASCINATE**.COM/RESOURCES
Email: **START@HOWTOFASCINATE**.COM | Call: 855-**9SECOND**

ONLINE & ONSITE TRAINING

Get started today! Find out how each person in your organization can immediately add their highest value using the science of fascination. With our motivating and interactive online training, you will discover how each person is uniquely suited to contribute and get results. Build a better team with the Fascination Advantage. Online: **How**To**Fascinate**.com/Training

PERSONAL DEVELOPMENT

Get rewarded for what you naturally do best. Make a strong impression at your next client meeting, or your next job interview, with the Anthem. This step-by-step method gives you exactly the right words to describe yourself— why someone should work with you, hire you, and buy from you. This tool will help you build a stronger first impression, based on your authentic personality. Online: **How**To**Fascinate**.com/Anthem

COACHING

Create better teams, happier customers, and a smarter company! Instead of working harder or increasing overhead costs, grow your business around your built-in personality Advantages. This program is right for you if you want intensive, one-on-one coaching. You will get an accelerated understanding of how to grow your business around your core personality Advantages. Our coaches will give you application ideas based on your Fascination Advantage report, and ways to apply this insight to build your business. You'll get personalized coaching on one topic of your choice (for instance: your business path, your leadership style, or how to balance your team). Online: **How**To**Fascinate**.com/Advocates

HIRING & HR

When it comes to hiring new employees, it's important to understand how individual personalities contribute to a team dynamic. The lesson: When you hire an employee, you are hiring an outcome – and while we usually think of that outcome as being linked to tangible attributes such as skills, knowledge and experience, it is also directly linked to personality Advantages. Before the interview even begins, find out how candidates are naturally primed to succeed. Our Hiring & HR tool kit gives you a different perspective on your applicants, and leads to more meaningful and authentic conversations during the hiring and courtship process. Hire better, and build better teams with the Fascination Advantage. Online: **How**To**Fascinate**.com/HR

ABOUT THE AUTHOR

S ALLY HOGSHEAD believes the greatest value you can add is to become more of yourself. Hogshead rose to the top of the advertising profession in her early twenties, writing ads that fascinated millions of consumers. Her internationally acclaimed book *Fascinate: Your 7 Triggers to Persuasion and Captivation* has been translated into over a dozen languages. The science of fascination is based on Hogshead's decade of research with 250,000 initial participants, including dozens of Fortune 500 teams, hundreds of small businesses, and over a thousand C-level executives. She frequently appears in national media, including NBC's *Today* show and the *New York Times*. Hogshead was recently inducted into the Speaker Hall of Fame, her industry's highest award for professional excellence.

HERE IT IS:

YOUR PRIVATE CODE TO LEARN YOUR OWN FASCINATION ADVANTAGE®

YOUR PRIVATE CODE IS WAITING UNDER HERE

BK1-2DHKQ9E

*This code is valid for one user only. Do not buy this book if the area above has been scratched off.

STEP 1: Go online to HOWTOFASCINATE.COM

STEP 2: Enter the access code hidden beneath the scratch-off above

HOWTOFASCINATE
DISCOVERED BY SALLY HOGSHEAD

THE 49 PERSONALITY ARCHETYPES

PRIMARY ADVANTAGE

	INNOVATION You change the game with creativity	**PASSION** You connect with emotion	**POWER** You lead with command
INNOVATION You change the game with creativity	**THE ANARCHY** Volatile • Startling Chaotic	**THE ROCKSTAR** Bold • Artistic Unorthodox	**THE MAVERICK LEADER** Pioneering • Irreverent Entrepreneurial
PASSION You connect with emotion	**THE CATALYST** Out-of-the-Box • Social Energizing	**THE DRAMA** Theatrical • Emotive Sensitive	**THE PEOPLE'S CHAMPION** Dynamic • Inclusive Engaging
POWER You lead with command	**THE CHANGE AGENT** Inventive • Untraditional Self-Propelled	**THE RINGLEADER** Motivating • Spirited Compelling	**THE AGGRESSOR** Dominant • Overbearing Dogmatic
PRESTIGE You earn respect with higher standards	**THE AVANT-GARDE** Original • Enterprising Forward-Thinking	**THE CONNOISSEUR** Insightful • Distinguished In-the-Know	**THE VICTOR** Respected • Competitive Results-Oriented
TRUST You build loyalty with consistency	**THE EVOLUTIONARY** Curious • Adaptable Open-Minded	**THE AUTHENTIC** Approachable • Dependable Trustworthy	**THE GRAVITAS** Dignified • Stable Hardworking
MYSTIQUE You communicate with substance	**THE SECRET WEAPON** Nimble • Unassuming Independent	**THE SUBTLE TOUCH** Tactful • Self-Sufficient Mindful	**THE VEILED STRENGTH** Realistic • Intentional To-the-Point
ALERT You prevent problems with care	**THE COMPOSER** Strategic • Fine-Tuned Judicious	**THE COORDINATOR** Constructive • Organized Practical	**THE ACE** Decisive • Tireless Forthright